Pen of Fire

PETER BRIDGES

THE KENT STATE UNIVERSITY PRESS
KENT & LONDON

Pen of Fire

JOHN MONCURE DANIEL

Frontis: Engraved portrait of John Moncure Daniel, *Democratic Review,* May 1852. Library of Congress.

Library of Congress Catalog Card Number 2001007195
ISBN 0-87338-736-8
Manufactured in the United States of America
06 05 04 03 02 5 4 3 2 1
Library of Congress Cataloging-in-Publication Data
Bridges, Peter.
Pen of fire : John Moncure Daniel / Peter Bridges, 2002
p. cm.
Includes bibliographical references and index.
ISBN 0-87338-736-8 (hardcover : alk. paper) ∞
1. Daniel, John Moncure, 1825–1865.
2. Newspaper editors—United States—Biography.
I. Title.
PN4874.D324 B75 2002
070.4'1'092—dc21
2001007195

The sonnet quoted from the Daniel Family Papers is reproduced by permission of The Huntington Library, San Marino, California. The sonnet by Basil Lanneau Gildersleeve from Ward S. Briggs Jr., *Soldier and Scholar: Basil Lanneau Gildersleeve and the Civil War* (Charlottesville: Univ. of Virginia Press, 1998) is reprinted with permission of the University of Virginia Press.

British Library Cataloging-in-Publication data are available.

This book is dedicated to the memory of my great-grandfather, John Alexander Bridges, who on May 8, 1861, being then a thirty-seven-year-old farmer, enlisted at Gloucester Court House as a private in Capt. Thomas B. Montague's company, 4th Regiment Virginia Heavy Artillery, and who, as the sergeant of Company A, 34th Virginia Infantry, was paroled on April 9, 1865, at Appomattox Court House.

Tu ne cede malis, sed contra audentior ito. . . .
—Virgil, *Aeneid*

My passions, from that hapless hour,
Usurp'd a tyranny which men
Have deem'd, since I have reach'd to power
My innate nature—be it so. . . .
—Poe, *Tamerlane*

Contents

Proem

It had been cold earlier that March but now was warmer. He could hear rain falling as he lay, very weak, propped up on his side on his bed. The doctor had come and stood by him. Over the mantle hung the miniature of the lovely woman who had befriended him—whom he had loved—so long ago in that faraway place where he had served America with honor, with distinction. He had good friends. And he had enemies. He had no fear. He had always written frankly, had upheld principle. He had taken on Jefferson Davis and his corrupt crew, and for good reason. The bullet wound in his leg, the work of that miserable minion of the president, never had quite healed. He could have killed the dastard, save for the battle wound he bore proudly in his right forearm, which forced him to fire with his left hand.

His friend John Mitchel had just come by this morning to tell him that the train from Petersburg brought amazing news. Lee had beat the Yankees back all along the line. The battle might finally be ours, said Mitchel. But could it be? He had told his friends, not many months since, that when this war was over he would use his wealth to rebuild the fine house in Stafford, up on the ridge that looked out toward the river, toward the sea. Not likely, now. No gold. No glory. It was the end.

Dr. Rawlings said, "John, I will prepare a toddy for you," and turned to the dresser to mix some brandy in a tumbler. The sick man stirred behind him. The doctor looked toward the bed and saw that he had turned onto his back and composed his hands on his chest. His eyes were closed; he must be praying. Rawlings turned back to stir the toddy and leave the man some time to pray. When the doctor stopped his stirring, he walked to the bedside and looked down. Daniel had died.

The next day was Friday, and the Reverend Dr. Moses Drury Hoge preached the funeral sermon of John Moncure Daniel at the Second Presbyterian Church in Richmond to his many friends and relatives, drawing on the text "For all flesh is as grass, and all the glory of man as the flower of grass." Then they carried him to Hollywood Cemetery and buried him by his beloved great-uncle, by another river that led down to the sea.

That Sunday, Lee sent word to Davis that the capital could not be held. The leaders left the city, and the grim generals burned the warehouses to keep the contents from Union hands. The fire spread. It spread downtown, burning down the *Examiner* and its press and fonts and paper and files and furniture. It burned down the desk of its proprietor, John Moncure Daniel, who had been the most influential editor in the Confederacy. And so just as there was no more John Daniel, there was no *Examiner* to tell the tale of Appomattox and the thin, tired soldiers who took the long roads home from defeat, back to their towns and farms.

But as April turned to May, the fruit trees bloomed and the mockingbirds began to sing in the warm night. And Celia, a woman who was still a slave in late March, when she was tied to a post and given twenty-five lashes because a white woman said she had stolen a piece of fringe at the Richmond market, could feel her back healing. And in Richmond, the new rains washed down the ashes.[1]

This is the story of a man born to a proud, once-prosperous family in Virginia, who by his own efforts became a much-admired journalist and then a leading diplomat; who returned to Virginia when the American republic was shattering to take the Southern side; who became the leading journalist in the Confederacy and also the fiercest critic of the Confederate administration; and who died in 1865 before reaching the age of forty, his full promise still unproven. If John Moncure Daniel was admired by many, he was hated by more, in the South as well as in the North. He was a brilliant and a fiery man, and he wanted the world to know he was a man of principles and beliefs—including the belief in state sovereignty and in African slavery.

I first found the name of John Moncure Daniel in the State Department's compendium of the chiefs of American diplomatic missions since 1776. I was then writing an article on George Perkins Marsh, the great conservationist and antislavery congressman Abraham Lincoln named minister to Italy. Daniel had been Marsh's predecessor as American minister at Turin and had headed the legation there for more than seven years, almost the full terms of two presidents. The State Department's listing showed that Daniel was a Virginian and that he left his post for good at the beginning of 1861, just as Southern states were seceding from the Union. I learned later that he had gone home to Richmond to resume control of his newspaper, the *Examiner*, but I was too busy then with Marsh and other subjects to dig further into the doings of John Moncure Daniel.

At a later date, I found myself in Rome, in the old archives of the Italian Foreign Ministry, studying the course of Italian–American relations. In the dusty old files there appeared again the name of John Moncure Daniel. He had arrived in Turin in October 1853 to take over the American legation. He was not quite twenty-eight and one of the youngest persons ever named to head an American diplomatic mission. (Since 1776, only eight others have been commissioned at such a young age.) Soon after his arrival in Turin, the papers there published a scandalous, libelous letter that he had written home about Piedmont and the Piedmontese. The foreign minister assumed, and clearly hoped, that Daniel would resign his post. He did not do so; he stayed for seven years more, and the Italian (and the American) record seems to show that Daniel became an accomplished and effective representative of his country and an accurate observer of the revolutionary Italian scene. He may have affected the history of Italy when he told Giuseppe Garibaldi that the United States would not protect an independent Nice, prompting Garibaldi to turn his attention to liberating the Italian South. Daniel's diplomatic record was indeed better, in at least some respects, than that of his colleague in London, James Buchanan, who later became president of the United States.

It appears that someone provided political support to Daniel in Washington when he was under fierce attack at home as well as in Turin. I understand how Daniel must have felt. In Italy in the next century, when I was working there in the U. S. Foreign Service, Soviet intelligence agencies enjoyed for years a surprising number of collaborators among Italian journalists,[2] and more than once the Italian press made unfounded charges against American diplomats. It is not a pleasant feeling to read lies about oneself, and a diplomat cannot respond as a private citizen can. True, Daniel's case was different. There was substance in what was said against him on that occasion in Turin, and on other occasions as well. But how much was substance and how much was the work of his enemies, who were numerous?

The more I learned about John Moncure Daniel, the more it became clear that he deserves to be remembered. Both before and after his diplomatic service, he weighed into American history, first as a bellicose journalist and a top spokesman for the radical Young America wing of the Democratic party, and later as the most influential editor in the Confederacy and the fiercest Southern critic of Jefferson Davis. Daniel was interesting—though not very likable.

In diplomacy, there is a not-uncommon malady that in the State Department is called "localitis." When one has served in a foreign country for some time and has gotten to know the place and the people, one may lose objectivity and start sending home reports that amount to apologias for the behavior of the foreign government and society. The malady can take extreme forms; one American ambassador to Italy became such an admirer of fascism that after leaving office he ghostwrote Mussolini's autobiography. Such diplomats are not rare; one can become too attached to—or repelled by—the object of one's labors. The record shows that Daniel had not succumbed to this malady in his seven years in Italy. He had, however, made friends; indeed, he became close to a lovely cousin of the emperor Napoleon III, so close that he may have dreamed of marrying her.

I do not think I lost my own objectivity in studying John Moncure Daniel. Some others have lost theirs. One twentieth-century historian, who certainly admired Jefferson Davis more than he deserved, decided that John Daniel could simply be dismissed from consideration since his newspaper "became downright scurrilous in its blasts at the President."[3] But again, even an objective study of Daniel is not likely to lead one to become fond of him. Daniel was a quarrelsome man who made many enemies and fought as many as nine duels in a rather short life. He might well have killed the brilliant, drunken Edgar Allan Poe, who once challenged him. Instead, though, he enlisted Poe for his paper and fairly described both Poe's poetic genius and faults and helped ensure for Poe a lasting reputation. Daniel's own faults are clearly visible. He was anti-Semitic as well as proslavery, and although he was not utterly anti-Northern, he despised what he identified as a particular kind of grasping Yankee—the kind who once had him arrested in New York on a charge of libel. In these prejudices, Daniel was not atypical of his times. He was also a kind eldest brother to five fatherless siblings and a helpful and thoughtful friend to a number of other Virginians. When he was still young and poor, he once walked twenty miles to pay some money he had collected for a friend and then, without funds, walked twenty miles home again. Douglas Southall Freeman called Daniel a strange blend of genius and misanthropy.[4] He was indeed a genius; but despite his hatreds, he was no misanthrope.

Daniel was an influential editor by his early twenties, and he soon made his *Examiner* the leading newspaper of the South.[5] In an age when editors were often seen as simply rude, hot-tempered duelists, Daniel (who did indeed fight duels) emphasized that journalism had become a key profession and urged the establishment of journalism as an academic discipline a full six decades before the first school of journalism was actually founded.

When Daniel was in his thirties, he thought he would be governor of Virginia within ten years.[6] He had seen the flaws in a number of top officials, beginning with Jefferson Davis and Abraham Lincoln, and he was not deceived in his own self-estimate. He had the potential to climb beyond a governorship, toward the very top of American society. He might have gone very far indeed, had he lived longer. As he told his friend George Bagby, he loved power. Bagby thought Daniel would surely have made a name for himself as a member of some president's cabinet—if he had lived.

The reader will perhaps find that John Moncure Daniel followed some causes uncritically, that his devotion could outdistance his reason. Certainly he was uncritical, even extreme, in his defense of slavery. Such uncritical devotion to a wrong cause, or to an outmoded usage or an obsolete phrase, was not uncommon in his day. It is not uncommon now.

Some have argued that Daniel's fierce criticisms of the way the Confederacy waged war and his frank reports of its problems in governance aided the enemy. At the same time, some argue that bad government deserves criticism and that Daniel's editorials rallied his readers and helped them keep on believing that the South might finally win. A more recent Richmond editor named Virginius Dabney concluded that all in all, despite Daniel's constant attacks on Jefferson Davis and his administration, he probably helped to maintain Southern morale when the South's fortunes were at their lowest. At least one Confederate soldier, who served in the trenches at Petersburg in the bitter final months of the war, always recalled Daniel's paper as the inspiration of Lee's army. Richmond always wanted to know what Daniel had to say; during the war the scarce copies of the *Examiner* brought premium prices. One rival editor once commented that no other newspaperman had such a talent for denunciation or ridicule as did Daniel, and that Daniel made everything he wrote about interesting.

We can perhaps regret that death cut down John Moncure Daniel early, for he might have done good things had he lived longer—when there was no more slavery system for him to help defend. But the same regrets can be said, and often on better ground, for the 600,000 men who died in a war that Daniel did not devise, but that he, along with many others, helped to bring on and continue. And although some historians, such as Lee Benson, claiming science on their side, have insisted that civil war was inevitable in America, this was not so, any more than the bloody conflicts of the Balkans in the 1990s were inevitable. One can argue inevitability with better reason in the case of the Balkans, where hatreds were and are far deeper and far older than those between the American North and South. Yet even in the Balkans, war was not inevitable but was largely the work of bad leaders like Franjo Tudjman of Croatia and Slobodan Milosevic of Serbia. In America, if influential men like John Moncure Daniel had believed and argued differently, there might have been no war. Was there ever any chance that John Moncure Daniel might take a different course? Horace Greeley once thought Daniel might do so. In any case, the man seems worth our study. But let the reader beware. There is not much encomium or romance here. Daniel's life was interesting and full of action, but it was not pretty.

One

Roots of a Virginian

The Virginia of John Daniel's youth has vanished, but we can try to reconstruct some of it, at least in our mind's eye. Today, travelers who leave Washington, D.C., to seek out John Daniel's old home in Stafford County take the great interstate highway toward Richmond and the South. After forty miles through suburban northern Virginia, they pass an exit sign for the Marine Corps base at Quantico. All that is visible on either side of the road is hardwood forest. Soon there is another sign, which marks the boundary of Stafford County. Three miles farther is a sign with the name of a small stream flowing under the highway: Aquia Creek. The woods continue, with only a glimpse of some new housing development and exits for places called Garrisonville, Aquia, and Stafford. Soon the traveler is even with Fredericksburg; Richmond is just fifty miles beyond. In twenty miles, in twenty minutes, the traveler has passed through Stafford County and seen little but oaks and tulip poplars, as well as other cars and eighteen-wheelers. There is, however, much that has been missed, and not just the dozens of housing subdivisions sprouting up in Stafford beyond the roadside oaks. If travelers take the side roads and look up the old books and records—those that survived the Civil War—they can still perceive the past, and perhaps better comprehend it. Certainly, to understand that proud man John Moncure Daniel, we must take a good look at his forebears and the landscape that they knew.

When Daniel was born in Stafford County in the autumn of 1825, this tidewater region already had a history of white settlement that went back two centuries. During the summer of 1608, the year after Jamestown had been founded, Capt. John Smith took fourteen men sailing up Chesapeake Bay to explore the new country. From the bay they went northwest into a broad river that the native people called "Patawomeck"—today's Potomac. Along this river's western shore, a hundred and fifty miles from Jamestown, in what is now Stafford County, John Smith and his men found an inlet where a tidal creek joined the river. Sailing into this inlet, they saw a wooded ridge between two tidal creeks. Somewhere nearby stood a chief's house. This was the center of the Potomac people, the northernmost tribe of the confederation over which the great Powhatan held sway. Farther north and west lived enemies of the Potomacs, the Manahoacs and Massawomecks and the giant Susquehannocks. In the first years, the colonists established friendly relations with the Potomacs, who had resisted inclusion in Powhatan's confederacy and hoped for help against their enemies upstream. Several Englishmen came to live among the Potomacs, and it is conceivable that the Potomac people who live in Stafford today owe some of their ancestry to liaisons of that early time.

Today, when we have established that a number of persons known as African Americans are descended from Thomas Jefferson's family, and when the question has been asked whether Pocahontas was half-English, we might ask whether John Moncure Daniel, who has been described as raven-haired, black-eyed, and "swarthy," may possibly have had a Potomac (or for that matter an African) forebear. Short of exhuming his remains for a DNA test, this can only remain speculation. There is no indication that Daniel himself thought his ancestry was anything but British. He did take a deep interest in old Virginia history; he knew the old vexed relationships between the Indians and the English. Powhatan's daughter Pocahontas, who had married a warrior named Kocoum, was living in the Potomacs' village in 1613 when she was kidnapped by Capt. Samuel Argall with the help of the Potomac chief, and taken to Jamestown where she married John Rolfe. When in 1622 the Algonquins, under Powhatan's successor Opechancanough, attacked the English, the Potomac people stood aside. But in the next several decades, disease and continuing strife with the ever more powerful colonists brought all the tribes to near-extinction. The Potomacs' lands were included in the area organized as Stafford County in 1664.[1]

Daniel's first ancestor in Stafford County was a colonist named Rawleigh Travers, who in 1662 received a patent for 3,650 acres. The land was an east-running peninsula, bounded on the north by little Accokeek Creek and on the south by broad Potomac Creek. Up on the ridge that runs along the peninsula was perhaps the place where once the Potomac chiefs' house stood. The ridge is covered today by a fine forest, and it rises more than 150 feet above water level, an unusual height for the Tidewater country. Even today, one finds pieces of Indian pottery and tools on the eastern point of the little peninsula, from which one looks out to where Potomac Creek joins Potomac River—the sea road to the rest of the Tidewater, and to the world.

We do not know where Rawleigh Travers was born but presume it was in England. His grandson told his own granddaughter many years later that Rawleigh Travers had been a nephew of the great Sir Walter Raleigh, but there is no proof.[2] Travers's first appearance in surviving Virginia records is in 1653, when he received a land grant on the Rappahannock River.[3] After receiving his patent for land a few miles to the north in Stafford, nine years later, he settled there. Travers had a grandson, also named Rawleigh Travers, who married a young woman named Hannah

Ball. Hannah's younger half-sister Mary married another colonist, named Augustine Washington, and in 1732 she gave birth to a son, whom his parents named George Washington. John Moncure Daniel, as he knew well, was therefore a distant, much younger cousin of the first American president.

Rawleigh and Hannah Ball Travers had a daughter whom they named Sarah, and Sarah later married a Captain Pierson, whose importance for this account is that he soon died. Sarah Travers Pierson then married, on July 15, 1736, in Stafford County, a thirty-year-old Virginian named Peter Daniel who had moved to Stafford from Northumberland County.[4] Like his father-in-law, Rawleigh Travers, young Daniel's ancestry is unclear but was no doubt English. Horace Hayden, a careful nineteenth-century Virginia genealogist, thought it possible that Peter Daniel the Virginian was of the same family as the Peter Daniel described in an English record as "a Captaine of Foote in the Army of his late Majestie K. Charles the first anno 1643."[5]

After marrying Sarah, Peter Daniel settled down on the Travers property. He became a prominent man in what was then a fairly prosperous county and came to serve as a vestryman of Aquia Church, one of the two Episcopal churches in the county, and he eventually became the president justice, the county's top judicial officer. The Virginians were becoming both ambitious and restive under British rule. After the French and Indian War ended in 1763, a number of Virginians, including George Washington, formed in Stafford the Mississippi Company to colonize some of the vast lands in the Mississippi Valley.[6] The company came to nothing. Then came the Stamp Act, widely seen in America as unfair taxation. The act led Peter Daniel and his son and fellow Stafford justice, Travers Daniel, to write Virginia's royal governor, Francis Fauquier, in October 1765 that "we would beg your honour to issue a new commission for our County in which we may be left out, as we will not in any case whatsoever . . . act as justice."[7]

The two Daniels were not remarkable in opposing the Stamp Act, nor was it remarkable that they, like most of their neighbors, supported the revolution that began a decade later. Travers Daniel, who was born in 1741 and died in 1824, was more remarkable in other ways. He was one of few Virginia landowners to maintain his own seagoing vessel, a black three-masted schooner that he named the *Crow* and used to trade directly with England. There was sufficient water near the foot of the family peninsula for the modest-sized *Crow* to anchor near shore. Today it may seem strange that Travers Daniel would send a schooner probably less than a hundred feet long across the Atlantic; but much of America's ocean trade was carried on then by just such vessels.[8]

Sometime in the late eighteenth century, up on the ridge between the two tidewater creeks, the Daniels built a fine wooden house on a brick foundation. It was only natural that it should be called Crow's Nest, and the site still has that name today, although the house burned to the ground during the Civil War.[9] Several hundred acres were separated from this property and named Selwood, and here John Moncure Daniel lived for a time as a boy.[10]

The extensive Daniel property depended on the labor of slaves. In 1787, Travers Daniel had sixteen slaves older than the age of sixteen, and six who were younger.[11] He may not have seen an alternative to slave labor, but it appears that he did not like slavery. His great-grandson, Moncure Daniel Conway, an abolitionist before the Civil War and later a biographer of Thomas Paine, wrote that Travers Daniel was "an ardent emancipationist." To demonstrate his views, said Conway, Daniel brought from England a set of window curtains for Crow's Nest that depicted Granville Sharp, cofounder of the Society for the Abolition of the Slave Trade, in the act of striking chains off slaves.[12]

In 1762, at the age of twenty-one, Travers Daniel married seventeen-year-old Frances Moncure. Her father, Rev. John Moncure, a native of Scotland, had served for twenty-six years as the rector of Overwharton Parish, which included both of Stafford's Anglican churches, Potomac and Aquia. The Moncures believed that their name came from the French *mon coeur* (my heart) and that the first Moncure in Scotland had been a Huguenot who fled France. Of Overwharton's two churches, Potomac Church is long gone. The first Aquia Church was a seventeenth-century frame building. After it burned down, the second church, a handsome brick building, was completed on the same site in 1757. The church was renovated after the Civil War and again in recent years. It stands today in Stafford, its sandstone quoins still marred by the graffiti cut by Union troopers in 1862 and 1863. John Moncure the rector is buried in the church and is well remembered in the parish.

The eighteenth-century Virginia of the Reverend Mr. Moncure was not known as a place of Puritans, and he himself was no dour Scot, if we may believe his descendant Moncure Daniel Conway writing a century and a half later, but "a merry fox-hunting gentleman, assiduous cultivator of literature, flowers, and of gay young people. He was a famous whist player."[13] There were, however, limits to his merriness. A sermon he preached in 1756, when the British were suffering serious reverses in the French and Indian War and settlers were fleeing east from the Valley of Virginia, describes "Our Friends and fellow Subjects murdered & massacred by cruel & barbarous Savages after an unheard of manner, & the Destruction drawing every day nearer & nearer to us."[14] The Reverend Mr. Moncure warned his congregation that their sins were responsible. But the causes lay not just in Overwharton Parish; there was National Guilt, and "a National Guilt necessarily requires National Punishment," as witness "that dreadful Judgment that befell the Land of Sodom and Gomorrah." One wonders what the congregation made of all that. In any case, Stafford County escaped the Destruction, at least for another century. Meanwhile the union of Moncures and Daniels was to produce three generations of men named John Moncure Daniel.

The first John Moncure Daniel, the grandson of this rector and the second child of Travers Daniel and Frances Moncure Daniel, was born at Crow's Nest in 1769. Nine other children followed. The most prominent was John Moncure Daniel's youngest brother, Peter Vivian Daniel, who was born fifteen years later at Crow's Nest and served on the United States Supreme Court from 1841 until his death in 1860.

As the eighteenth century neared its end, Stafford County was not as prosperous as it had been. The land was depleted, and the county's mineral deposits had not brought great prosperity although there were gold mines on the Rappahannock River, and on Accokeek Creek iron mines and a furnace where George Washington's father had begun to smelt iron in 1727.[15] There were also sandstone quarries along Aquia Creek, and Aquia stone was used to build the White House, the Capitol, and other government buildings in Washington. But Stafford people were beginning to move westward to more promising and fertile places. The county's population hit a high of 9,951 in 1800 and then began to decline.[16]

Several years after the American Revolution, the Daniels of Crow's Nest had sufficient wealth that they could send young John Moncure Daniel to study medicine in Scotland, the ancestral home of the Moncures. He graduated in 1791 from the medical school at the University of Glasgow.[17] In 1792, he returned to America and lived for some time in Stafford, becoming a justice of the county like his father and grandfather.[18] Later, he entered the U.S. Army's medical service and eventually became a senior army surgeon. After serving on the Canadian border in the War of 1812, Dr. Daniel returned to Crow's Nest. He died there in 1813, perhaps of malaria, at the age of forty-four.

The doctor had three wives. The first, Maria Nivin, was the daughter of a Spanish merchant of Cadiz who had a branch house at Glasgow, where John Daniel had met her. The couple married in London in 1792, and she died childless some months later after he took her to Virginia.[19]

The doctor's second wife, Margaret, was the daughter of Thomas and Margaret Stone of Maryland. Margaret had been born in Maryland in 1771 to an eminent family. Thomas Stone was the great-grandson of William Stone, a descendant of Lancashire squires who had been governor of Maryland when Oliver Cromwell ruled England. Margaret's father, Thomas, was one of the four Marylanders who signed the Declaration of Independence.[20] Altogether, Margaret bore seven children by the doctor, including two sons: the second John Moncure Daniel and his younger brother, Raleigh Travers Daniel. Raleigh Travers Daniel later headed the Whig party in Virginia, while his nephew, the third and last John Moncure Daniel was inveighing against Whigs—including his uncle—after he had become a leading Democratic editor. Raleigh Travers Daniel, like his uncle Peter, became a lawyer. While he would never reach the U.S. Supreme Court, as his uncle had done, for a time he acted as lieutenant governor of Virginia, and after the Civil War he served as the state's attorney general.

Prosperous times were almost over at Crow's Nest when the second John Moncure Daniel, born perhaps in 1800, was growing up. After his father died in 1813, his uncle Peter Vivian Daniel took young John into his own home in Richmond. Later it was decided that the young man should study medicine at the University of Maryland. After graduating in 1822, he returned to Stafford County to practice.[21]

There have been country doctors in Tidewater Virginia, in this century and before, who enjoyed a certain amount of prosperity. The second John Moncure Daniel was not one of these; he seems never to have had much money; the surviving Stafford County deed books show that he sold rather than bought land. In May 1824, two years after he had left the university, the young doctor married a young woman from Stafford County named Eliza Mitchell. May is a pretty month in Virginia. The fruit trees have bloomed, and the countryside is verdant. It is the mating season. In Virginia, in May, the male mockingbird may sing sometimes all night. The couple must have felt happy that spring, and hopeful about their future. The groom owned several hundred acres in Stafford, and the bride was the eldest child of James Mitchell, who had recently died in possession of two farms in Stafford that totaled eight hundred acres, plus a considerable fortune in slaves and other property.[22]

Within three years of their wedding, the couple sold a property in Maryland that John had inherited from his mother, as well as Eliza's interest in the two Stafford farms and a house in Fredericksburg. Their problems with money mounted. A decade later, in 1838, the doctor mortgaged all the property he possessed—fifteen hundred acres and seven slaves—to pay off debts of just over a thousand dollars.[23]

Eliza Mitchell Daniel bore six sons to the doctor before she died after sixteen years of marriage. The eldest was born in Stafford County on October 24, 1825, and was named John Moncure Daniel, like his father and his grandfather. Meanwhile, the doctor's younger brother, Raleigh, left Stafford County for Richmond to read law under their uncle, Peter Vivian Daniel, and he received his law license in 1826.[24]

The doctor and his wife and sons moved several times in the county. Their first home was at a place with the curious name of Lethe, near Fredericksburg, and their second was at Falmouth, a village just across the Rappahannock River from Fredericksburg. In 1839 Dr. Daniel moved his family to Selwood, which as noted was a part of the large Crow's Nest property that had been in the family since the seventeenth century. One assumes that the doctor, and perhaps his fourteen-year-old son John, were pleased and proud to move to their ancestral home; but the family soon moved from there, as the sell-off of their property continued, to their final home at Bells Hill, near Stafford Court House.[25]

This country doctor was a learned man, well read and a good Latinist. Although never wealthy, he had a large personal library.[26] He educated his eldest son, John, at home, introducing him to a wide range of authors and teaching him relatively good spelling—but, as one sees from his surviving letters, evidently less calligraphy. (It was not then usual in Virginia to educate a boy at home, but at least three famous Virginians of an earlier generation, Patrick Henry and George Mason and George Wythe, had been so schooled.) The doctor must have been a good teacher, for after young John was grown he continued to make frequent allusions to his father and his father's opinions and tastes and to the course of reading he had recommended to his son.

Years later, Supreme Court justice Peter Vivian Daniel wrote to his great-nephew John Moncure Daniel, at that time an American diplomat, that he had lately seen the doctor in a vivid dream. The justice went on at length:

> Poor John! his life affords a striking illustration of the fallacy of the brightest prospects and most cheering hopes which may attend the morning of existence, & of the gloom and disappointment which may overshadow even its meridian progress; for he had hardly advanced beyond that point in life's journey. With a mind of superior order, and highly cultivated and prepared both for usefulness and distinction; with manners the most attractive, calculated to grace the first circles in society, this man wore out existence in slavish drudgery and of [*sic*] restriction bordering on necessity, and died in poverty and almost literally in solitude. I had more than once proposed to him a removal to Richmond as a theatre more favorable for the display of his talents—where he had connections who would at once afford him employment to some extent and where he could not fail of being soon known and appreciated. But his apprehensions of the hazards of the measure, and fear of difficulties in supporting his family until success could be attained, prevented his accession to the change proposed. I was indeed warmly attached to this nephew, for besides his estimable qualities, he amongst my several wards was most remarkable for the deference, the complacency, and affection of deportment towards myself and my family.[27]

The doctor's younger brother, Raleigh, also became concerned about him. Raleigh had made a slow start in the law. In 1833, a good seven years after receiving his license, he wrote to John that he did not owe any money, but that he would be grateful if he could lend him $200 or $250.[28] At the beginning of 1837, however, Raleigh wrote John that he was getting on as least as well as he had expected. He had heard from their sister, Jean, that John was thinking about keeping a school. Did this mean that he would stop practicing medicine? Raleigh's advice to his older brother was similar to the advice from their uncle Peter: John should move to Richmond. In Richmond, keepers of schools got rich, and doctors not half so proficient as John made a good $3,000 to $4,000 a year, while the most popular—not necessarily the best—physicians earned far more.[29] But John never made the move, perhaps because, as his uncle surmised, he could not afford to do so even if ultimately it would mean more money. Several more years passed, and John was borrowing money from Raleigh, who by then had become prosperous.[30]

The hard-pressed country doctor must have made clear to his sons that there was no chance of them being sent to study at a college or university; they would have to make their own way in life. John, the eldest, was described by someone close to the family as "a very bright, handsome boy, giving promise to be of an unusual character."[31] He was an avid reader and by his early teens had gone through all the collections of books in the neighborhood to which he could gain access. He was said to have been particularly fond of the works of Addison, Steele, and Swift, and to have been studious rather than carefree.[32] Stafford was a green rural place with no real towns, not a bad place for a boy to grow up. One could enjoy hunting, fishing, boating, and swimming in the neighborhood, and no doubt the boy and his brothers did. When John was not quite seven, his uncle Raleigh bought for the doctor and his family "a Puppy of splendid Lineage and Promise" and taught him to hunt while waiting for a friend to take him from Richmond up to Stafford on the stagecoach.[33] John Daniel liked the water, and two decades later, as a young editor, he planned at least one summer trip to the seaside to fish and swim. But it does not seem likely that John, a fiery, intense adult, enjoyed a happy-go-lucky childhood. His cousin Moncure Daniel Conway wrote later that in adulthood John separated himself from society to a great extent because he had been "embittered by some circumstances of his early life."[35] We can only guess whether Conway was referring to the family's reduced economic circumstances or alluding to something darker.

In 1840, at the age of fifteen, John Moncure Daniel was sent to Richmond to attend school and to live with Justice Daniel and his family, as his father had done before him. It appears that John went to Richmond after, and conceivably as a result of, the death of his mother that year. Like her husband, Eliza Mitchell Daniel had been a cultured person who loved music and played the spinet. John's younger brother, James Mitchell Daniel, who was seven when their mother died, remembered her as a beautiful woman, all gentleness and lovingness, whose favorite airs were "The Last Rose of Summer" and "Bonnie Blue Bells of Scotland."[36] After she died, her husband's sister, Jean Daniel Crane, wrote the widower a letter of condolence that indicates Eliza had been a religious person, though the doctor and his sons had not yet found God.[37] She may have been off the mark; five years later, her brother, Raleigh, recalled that young John "used to visit us of Sundays when he came in to church."[38]

John Daniel's three years in the home of his great-uncle clearly affected him. A remarkable exchange of letters between the two years later reveals their mutual love and esteem. In his last will, John Daniel said with emphasis that his great-uncle had been his friend. Justice Peter Vivian Daniel was a friend of two presidents, Andrew Jackson and Martin Van Buren, and Van Buren appointed him to the U.S. Supreme Court in 1841 while his great-nephew was living with him in Richmond. The justice had married well; his first wife, whom he outlived by many years, was the daughter of Edmund Randolph, who had served as both attorney general and secretary of state under President George Washington. The justice was a man of importance in Richmond as well as in Washington, and in the 1820s and 1830s he had been a member of the so-called Richmond Junto, an informal group led by Thomas Ritchie of the *Richmond Enquirer* that did much to carry the state for the Jeffersonian party in national elections.

Peter Vivian Daniel had spent his childhood in the quiet and economically backward Virginia county of Stafford. His social philosophy had formed at a time when Virginia, and indeed the country as a whole, remained primarily agrarian. During his almost two decades on the Supreme Court he remained an anachronism in an age of social, political, and industrial change in America.[39] With industrial growth came a sharp increase in the number and importance of corporations; but Peter Daniel remained an enemy of corporations and refused to agree with the court majority that a corporation could bring suit as a person in federal courts.[40] His biographer, John Frank, called the justice "the last Jeffersonian to hold public office, . . . an intransigent, indefatigable, stubborn outpost of eighteenth century thought in the nineteenth century United States."[41]

The justice believed strongly in the sovereignty of the individual states and in gentlemanly conduct as practiced in Virginia—including dueling, which had been illegal in Virginia since 1810. In 1832, Peter Daniel came close to fighting a duel with Senator Stephen D. Miller of South Carolina, who was insulted by letters Daniel had written in the *Richmond Enquirer*.[42] More than two decades earlier, in 1808, a younger Peter Daniel, a war hawk, had engaged in a public debate in Stafford County with his friend and neighbor John Seddon over the advisability of America going to war with England. Seddon found Daniel's remarks personally insulting and challenged him to a duel. (In later years, the story was told that Seddon's sister urged him to send the challenge.[43]) Daniel was then just twenty-four years old, and Seddon twenty-seven. The unwritten dueling code gave the person challenged the right to choose weapons. Daniel chose pistols and then practiced assiduously, shooting from a distance of fifteen paces at his walking cane, which was stuck upright in the ground. When the day of the duel came, Seddon, Daniel, and their seconds crossed the Potomac to Maryland to evade Virginia's prohibition of dueling; and there young Daniel killed Seddon.[44]

Engraved portrait of Peter Vivian Daniel, justice of the U.S. Supreme Court and John Daniel's great-uncle. Library of Congress.

One may wonder how much young John Moncure Daniel knew about his family's history. There can be little doubt that he was proud of it. In 1941, W. J. Cash wrote that, although the Old South had created a kind of civilization based on the cavalier, the evidence was mounting that actual cavaliers or even near-cavaliers were rare among Southern settlers.[45] Cash also noted that, overall, Episcopalians were a relatively small minority in the South. However, in Tidewater Virginia, Episcopalians were not rare, and many had cavalier ancestors. The Daniels were Episcopalians, and in the Daniel ancestry there may well have been a cavalier (Capt. Peter Daniel of Charles II's army), as well as a Puritan (William Stone, Cromwell's governor in Maryland). John Moncure Daniel knew that his origins were distinguished.[46]

It is not surprising that young Daniel, growing up in this great-uncle's house, became a fierce proponent of state's rights and that he also became a duelist. In Richmond John Daniel began to make firsthand acquaintance with national politics. As a teenager, he met and listened to such men of national status as William Marcy, a longtime resident of Albany, New York, and secretary of state when John

Daniel first served at the Turin legation, and John Y. Mason, a Virginian who became U.S. secretary of the navy, attorney general, and eventually minister to France, in which post John Daniel revered him as his diplomatic mentor.[47] It appears that the justice also introduced the teenaged John Daniel to important people in Washington.[48]

In 1843, at the age of eighteen, Daniel left his great-uncle's house in Richmond and briefly returned home to Stafford County. His mother, Eliza Mitchell Daniel, had died several years earlier; she had been an invalid for her last year, with a constant fever and cough, conceivably from tuberculosis.[49] His father had remarried after his mother's death, and the doctor's new wife, Euphemia Tolson, brought property to the marriage—mainly a half-interest in her late father's twelve slaves, who were valued at $4,000—but this did little to change the doctor's financial prospects.[50] Young John went on to Fredericksburg to read law in the office of John Tayloe Lomax, a prominent jurist who had taught law at the University of Virginia and been an associate justice of the General Court of Virginia.[51] There was another student of law in Judge Lomax's office, young James Barbour from Culpeper County, who came to Lomax after a year each at Georgetown College and the University of Virginia. The two students became friends. Barbour, like John Daniel, later became prominent in the Democratic party, and on the eve of civil war William Seward tried to bring Barbour into Lincoln's cabinet to help keep the border states in the Union. But, like Daniel, Barbour opted for secession.[52]

Times were very tight for young Daniel as he pored over law books in Fredericksburg, as well as for his country doctor father. In January 1844, John returned home to tell his father that he was practicing self-denial but, nevertheless, needed $110 to meet expenses. The doctor could not provide the money and had to ask his brother, Raleigh, for a loan, assuring him that after he became county sheriff later in the year he would repay him. He added that young John was to go on from Judge Lomax's office to spend a year or two in the county clerk's office in Spotsylvania County, where he had been offered a good salary. He had no doubt that his son would soon be addressing juries.[53]

As a profession, law was not John Daniel's first choice. Young men who admire their fathers often want to follow in their footsteps. It appears that even after he had been in the Lomax law office for well over a year, and with a decent job in Spotsylvania presumably still awaiting him, the third John Moncure Daniel wanted to become a physician, like his father and his grandfather before him. His father knew how little money medicine brought in and was determined that John become a lawyer. The doctor asked his lawyer brother, Raleigh, to talk to John. Raleigh wrote back from Richmond in July 1845 that he questioned "how far in the choice of pursuits it is expedient to bias youths against their inclinations." Besides, he added, some doctors prospered, as he had told his brother earlier; the practice of one leading Richmond doctor was worth $7,000 to $9,000 a year. But he himself enjoyed the law; he would be happy to talk to John as the doctor wished. He added incidentally that he and his family had "escaped the scarlet fever, though it was very thick about us."[54]

The doctor and his wife were not so fortunate that year: they both died of scarlet fever within a week of each other at their Bells Hill home in Stafford County.[55] Young John Daniel gave up his legal studies in Fredericksburg and went back to Richmond. While it seems not unlikely that his father's death made it financially impossible for him to continue work toward a law license, his cousin Moncure Daniel Conway wrote years later that John gave up the law because of his continuing passion for literature. John's brother Frederick wrote that the law had never possessed any special attraction for John. After reading all the books he could find in Stafford, in Richmond John had gone through all of his great-uncle's large library, which included many works of belles lettres by major English and French writers.[56] He continued to be an omnivorous reader, and soon enough started to write, and through this began to find a focus for his life.

A Poor Young Man in Richmond

When John Moncure Daniel moved to Richmond in 1845, this city that was to provide the backdrop for over half of his fiery professional life was not large, but it was a prosperous and pleasant place—prosperous and pleasant, at least, for the half of the population that was not enslaved or poor. Within a decade it would become the wealthiest city of its size in America and perhaps in the world.[1] The site of the future city, at the falls of the James River, had been visited by Capt. John Smith just after the settlement of Jamestown in 1607, but a town was laid out only in 1737 on orders of the great landowner Col. William Byrd, and although it replaced Williamsburg as the state capital in 1779 Richmond was not chartered as a city until 1782, at which point it had a population of about two thousand. A year earlier, in January 1781, it had been occupied for twenty-four hours by a British force of 900 men commanded by the traitor Benedict Arnold.[2] Eight decades later, another army would find Richmond far more difficult to take.

The city that young Daniel moved to had numbered just over twenty thousand people, blacks and whites together, in the most recent census, that of 1840. Richmond was therefore a little smaller than the national capital which numbered 23,364 inhabitants, and it was far smaller than either the South's largest city, New Orleans, which had 102,193 people, or the largest city in the country, New York, which was soon to reach a population of a half-million.[3] Richmond occupied hills just above the James River; on one hill stood the white Capitol, designed by Thomas Jefferson on lines of the Maison Carrée, the old Roman temple at Nimes in southern France.

By 1845, when Richmond's total population had not quite reached 27,000, there was an impressive amount of industrial development. The city contained thirty-one plants manufacturing tobacco products, eight iron works and foundries headed by the large Tredegar Iron Works, five carriage factories, four flour mills, and three soap and candle works.[4] The James River and Kanawha Canal had opened up communication with the western part of the the state, although the canal had never reached over the Appalachians into the Ohio valley, its original goal. The canal had been expensive to build and soaked up capital that might have been better spent on railroads, but in any case the railroad era had now begun in Virginia as well as farther north. The Richmond, Fredericksburg, & Potomac Railroad, one of the first lines in America, had begun operation in 1836 on its first twenty miles of track. By 1842 it ran from Richmond north beyond Fredericksburg to Aquia Creek in Stafford County—passing just west of the old Daniel properties at Selwood and Crow's Nest—and from Aquia Creek steamboats took passengers up the Potomac River to Washington City. At the beginning of the century, stagecoaches had taken thirty-eight hours to reach Washington from Richmond; the steamboats which began running between Washington and Stafford County in 1815 had cut the Washington–Richmond travel time in half; the new water-rail route took just nine hours.[5] Virginia's political weight in Washington was lessening, but at least it was easier to travel there. With railroads, even New York City was not so far from Richmond, no more than ten hours beyond Washington by rail.

In Richmond, John Moncure Daniel found a proper, if not very remunerative, job for a student of literature. Sometime in 1845, at the age of nineteen, he became the librarian and acting clerk of the Patrick Henry Society, a club comprised mainly of younger men and that maintained a debating room in the large building of the Richmond Library Association on the northeast corner of Eleventh and Main Streets.[6] The position provided him one hundred dollars a year and "a large room with sofa bed and scant equipments."[7] It also gave him access to what was then Richmond's largest public collection of books, which in 1850 numbered perhaps 200,000 volumes.[8]

Daniel was a thin, intense, and handsome young man. He was of medium height and weighed no more than 120 pounds. He had a prominent nose and large mouth, dark brown eyes, and long raven-black hair. His longtime associate Judge Robert W. Hughes wrote years later that he possessed "strongly marked Jewish features, which, however, were antique and classical."[9] Daniel's cousin Moncure Daniel Conway wrote that Daniel's mother had some Spanish blood,[10] but there appears to be no evidence to support this claim. So far as known, John Moncure Daniel's ancestors were all English or Scottish. No portrait of any survives, but his mother is said to have had brown eyes, dark hair, and a "brunette complexion," whereas his father had fair skin and brown hair.[11] One might speculate whether Daniel, who became a strong supporter of white dominance and black slavery, was perhaps himself partly Native American or African, but there is no evidence of such heritage.

Daniel made a number of new friends while at the Patrick Henry Society. At least two of them—Robert W. Hughes and Thomas H. Wynne—remained his friends, although in later years he had serious differences with both. Hughes recalled four decades later that for a time Daniel, Wynne, and several others shared common religious views, perhaps Unitarian. Hughes thought that Daniel might even have considered, briefly, becoming a minister of "this singular evangel," and

Hughes still had at hand a sermon or lecture that Daniel had delivered to the little group, in which he flayed John Knox and John Calvin as fiercely as he later flayed political enemies in the press.[12]

Daniel's earliest known letter, dated June 29, 1845, was addressed to Virginia historian Charles Campbell soon after he went to work in Richmond. It is sprightly, if not flip, given the fact that he was just nineteen years old and was writing to a man twice his age:

> Dear Sir,
>
> As acting Clerk of the Patrick Henry Society, I write to inform you that the said Society has elected you an honorary member of their body, & ordered me to notify you thereof. I should have done so a week ago, but circumstances (i.e. negligence) prevented me. I hope you will excuse me.
>
> This letter claims an answer, and I am anxious to hear from you, in my personal as well as my official capacity. How wags the world with you? how is your health? when does your marraige [*sic*] take place? and more than all, how proceeds the "magnum opus[.]" I suppose that sometime this summer you will honour Richmond with a visit, & I shall hear all from your lips; but I am ambitious of receiving an epistle now, nevertheless
>
> Very truly yours
>
> Jno. M. Daniel.[13]

Thus began a correspondence between the two men, only part of which seems to have survived. A year later Daniel wrote Campbell that he had become very interested in the history of Virginia, and in his leisure hours during the summer he had been reading all the original material on this subject that he could find. Giving evidence of quickness to flatter and compliment, Daniel added that there was no work he was more eager to read than Campbell's forthcoming history of Virginia. Another author, Robert Howison, had just completed and sent to press the first volume of his own work on this subject; Daniel wished this had been Campbell's book instead.[14]

Campbell soon wrote back that he had seen an article that Daniel himself had written on Virginia history and was pleased it referred to his manuscript. Campbell had sent the manuscript off to Harper's, but he told Daniel that he had no assurance it would be published: "Writing would be far more attractive if one were in command of a publisher."[15] Campbell's history soon began to appear in serial form in the *Southern Literary Messenger*, but it was not published in book form until 1860.

Daniel was already well acquainted with the *Southern Literary Messenger*. The journal had been published since 1834, and Virginians could point to it with pride as evidence that good American literature did not come only out of the Northeast. In January 1847, the *Southern Literary Messenger* published an extended review by John Moncure Daniel of the first volume of Robert Howison's *History of Virginia*.[16] Daniel may not have been fond of Howison. For his part, Howison wrote later that Daniel was an omnivorous reader, "full of thought, bright in conversation, and so keen in wit and satire that I found him a very amusing companion,"[17] but that he agreed with Daniel on very few issues. Later, in 1851, Howison was so displeased by Daniel's review of another book that he attacked him fiercely in the Richmond press. In 1847, Daniel wrote a review of Howison's history that should not have entirely displeased the author, although at one point Daniel accused Howison of ignoring established facts of history. In the review, Daniel employed Howison to make strong points about Virginia's importance. Virginians, Daniel wrote, had never been "behind those of any other part of the globe in the matters of admiration for themselves, and interest in all that concerns them and theirs," but a lamentable lack of histories of the state made Howison's book especially welcome. Daniel then went on to emphasize his main point, the central importance of Virginia:

> Its settlement was the first experiment of England on this continent; and on its success depended their future efforts. . . . In the struggle which separated the politics of the old world from the new, Virginia was the chief actor; it began and ended here, and it was effected by her Generals and Statesmen. And last, and most important of all, it was the representative government of which Virginia has been possessed almost from the first, which moulded the form, stamped the character, and must guide the destinies of this country, so long as it holds a place among the nations. . . . [Virginia] has been the living heart of America, and has made the Union what it is.

This was heady stuff for readers in a state that had once headed the nation—after all, four of the first five presidents were Virginians—but was beginning to lose out politically and economically to states farther north. This change was perhaps most notable in the U.S. House of Representatives. In 1790, Virginia had been the most populous state and had nineteen members in the House, whereas the two next most populous states, New York and Pennsylvania, had ten and thirteen, respectively. In 1850, Virginia had only thirteen members, but New York had thirty-three, and Pennsylvania twenty-five.[18]

John Moncure Daniel's pro-Virginia review seems to indicate that, although he had previously interested himself in literature and history, at the age of twenty-one he had aims that were as much political as scholarly. One senses that he aimed to make himself a voice in Virginia, and an authoritative one. The question was how he might best do so.

In late 1846, months before Daniel reviewed Howison's book and after working at the Patrick Henry Society for about a year, Daniel had accepted a position as coeditor of a monthly magazine devoted to Southern agriculture, the *Southern Planter*. Years later, Frederick Daniel wrote that his brother's life had taken a new turn as the result of diaries or journals that John began to keep while employed at the Society. John Daniel's close friend Thomas Wynne, who had the journals in his keeping after Daniel's death—whether they survive today is not known—said in 1867 that what he was then holding began with the year 1844 and continued for as long as Daniel kept a journal; how long that was, he did not specify.[19] According to Frederick Daniel, his brother made of his journal "a register of meditations and criticisms upon miscellaneous topics, notably religious and literary."[20] Other relatives described it as recording "the most important facts and happenings of the time . . . a personal study of the men of the period and Daniel's criticisms of the government and head officials."[21] In any event he apparently shared the journal with a close friend, who urged him to begin writing articles for the Richmond newspapers and offered to help him place his articles. It has not been possible to identify these early newspaper articles,[22] but they began to attract readers' attention, as must have also been the case with his article on Howison's Virginia history, and they apparently resulted in the offer to coedit the *Southern Planter*.

The *Southern Planter* had been founded in 1841 by another Virginian, Charles T. Botts, who for six years worked as its editor and proprietor. Botts announced in the first issue that the magazine "will be devoted, exclusively, to the promotion of Agriculture, Horticulture, and the Household Arts."[23] He might have added that he did not aim his journal at masters of large cotton-growing plantations in the Deep South but, rather, at farmers—mainly in Virginia—who grew wheat and corn, kept orchards, and raised cattle, sheep, and hogs. The overall agricultural scene in antebellum Virginia was decidedly not the traditional stereotype of a tobacco-raising culture in serious decline on ruined land. Agriculture in Virginia was thriving, and, although tobacco remained a major crop, the prosperity was due in good part to the grain growers and animal raisers.[24] It was principally for these that Botts produced a journal full of short articles on such subjects as management of the horse, drought, rutabagas, madder, and the subsoil plough. Although his contributors and his correspondents were mainly Virginia farmers, he published letters and reprinted articles from people and journals in other states, including Northern ones. With its thirty-two-page issues, the *Southern Planter* appeared each month and cost just a dollar and a half a year, but Botts wrote in several issues that he was concerned that too many subscribers had fallen in arrears on payments. Perhaps it was because of financial problems that, after six years of publication, Botts announced in the December 1846 issue the journal's sale to Peter D. Bernard of Richmond.

In the 1840s, Richmond's publishing establishment was composed of relatively few people, all of whom, we may assume, knew each other fairly well. Peter Bernard was the son-in-law of T. W. White, who had earlier been the proprietor of the *Southern Literary Messenger*. After White's death in January 1843, a young poet named Edgar Allan Poe, who was later closely involved with John Daniel, thought of buying the *Southern Literary Messenger* with financing from friends.[25] As with other Poe schemes, nothing came of this; but the journal, which Poe had at one time edited, did print a revised version of his poem "The Raven" in March 1845 and offered him space for a monthly article, which he declined.[26]

John Daniel was no erratic poet—indeed, after Poe's death he would criticize that poet's lack of practicality—and he always understood the need to make money. Daniel worked quietly at the *Southern Planter* for a year, during which time Botts remained coeditor. In January 1848, Daniel became sole editor. He assured readers that he intended to keep the *Southern Planter* "a journal of practical agriculture, filled with *short* articles in plain words . . . a work for the intelligent farmer, not for the man of scientific research . . . and as we are anxious fully to inform ourselves of the wants of the planters of the South, we shall devote a considerable portion of our time during the present year to travelling among them."

Daniel remained editor of the *Southern Planter* for another year and a half, until June 1849. Years later A. N. Wilkinson would write that Daniel had made the agricultural journal both more political and more widely known around the South.[27] It may have become better known, especially if the editor traveled as much as he said he would, which is not clear. What is clear is that Daniel not only clearly understood the importance of "*short* articles in plain words," but he provided them for his readers. He had learned—whether from his father or his great-uncle or by himself—how to write cogently and succinctly in an age of stilted prose, and he set out his rule of writing in the *Southern Literary Messenger*: "A relation of events should always be clothed in the most simple, clear words which could be picked out. The interest and the current of connected ideas are lost among a profusion of adjectives and expletives."[28]

But if the *Southern Planter* was well written, it did not become noticeably political while John Daniel was its editor. Nor did it cotton to the cotton world. To the end of Daniel's tenure, it was filled with pieces on such nonpolitical subjects as the wheat harvest, marsh mud, fences, and weaning calves. His last issue also included an article lamenting that young Virginia property owners got liberal rather than agricultural educations in college, and that after returning home they left the management of their properties to overseers who, like them, knew too little about modern agriculture. In February 1849, the *Southern Planter* reprinted data showing how once-dominant Virginia was lagging economically: in manufacturing, it shared seventh place with little Rhode Island, and even in agriculture it was only fifth (although still first in tobacco growing). To be sure, there were political points to be made from this situation, but the editor of the *Southern Planter* did not dwell on them explicitly in that journal. Nor did the *Southern Planter* take a more anti-Northern turn under Daniel, who in later years made fierce anti-Yankee pronouncements; instead it admitted that there were lessons to be learned from the North. Daniel printed a letter from a correspondent at Goochland, Virginia, who wrote that "there may be Yankee tricks not so worthy of imitation; nevertheless, in all laudable business matters, if thrift be our object, we shall never err to take a Yankee model."[29] Later, though, the next publication edited by John Daniel would speak scathingly of the "vandal invasion of Virginia" by the Northern farmers who were settling there in the 1840s and 1850s, bringing in both modern farming methods and free labor.[30] Perhaps Daniel did not focus on the labor question while he was at the *Planter*, but the wheat and corn farmers like those who read the *Planter* found it made good business sense to employ seasonable free labor rather than maintaining a force of slaves all year long. This in part encouraged the manumission of slaves, and in Virginia the free black population increased in numbers. And all this encouraged the Northern abolitionists.[31]

Meanwhile, John Daniel, still in his early twenties, continued to seek the best place for his talents. There is no indication that he ever thought of buying an interest in the *Southern Planter*, but in 1847 he offered to buy the *Southern Literary Messenger* from its proprietor, Benjamin Minor, who was heading for California. Daniel's bid of $1,500 lost out to John Thompson's bid, but he was not sorry after learning that the journal had been losing subscribers at the rate of six hundred annually for the last three years.[32] It is doubtful that Daniel had $1,500 when he made the offer. It seems that he planned either to borrow the money from others or to give Minor a note for the sale price.

Charles Campbell agreed with his young friend Daniel that it was just as well he had not taken over the *Southern Literary Messenger*. The truth, said Campbell, was that literary periodicals had never flourished in the South; they probably never would. He added that there were, however, advantages to being an editor: editing was the only business in America where a man set up shop and then called upon all those qualified to assist him with their labors gratis.[33] Daniel, it seems, had already perceived this to be true. There were, of course, publications that were not literary or agricultural. It was becoming clear to John Moncure Daniel that the best path to pursue was editing not journals but newspapers.

Three

Daniel the Editor

While John Moncure Daniel was still new at the *Southern Planter* he took on additional responsibilities by going to work for a new Richmond newspaper with an old name, the *Examiner*. The first issue of the new paper appeared on November 4, 1847. There were both weekly and semiweekly editions, each composed of four large pages. The editor was Bennett T. De Witt, a Democrat who had lately founded the paper as joint proprietor with another Virginia Democrat, J. W. Wright. The original *Examiner* from which the new paper took its name had been founded in 1798 as an anti-Federalist paper, and in 1804 had become the *Richmond Enquirer*, published by Thomas Ritchie.

De Witt and Wright were experienced printers, and De Witt had founded the *Lynchburg Republican* in 1840. Dissatisfied with what they viewed as the Democratic machine politics of the *Richmond Enquirer* and seeing room for another Democratic organ in eastern Virginia, they had recently gone up and down the eastern part of the state soliciting subscriptions for a new *Examiner* and had returned to Richmond with a list of several thousand names. This was a large number for the time. John Daniel's later collaborator, Judge Robert W. Hughes, was wrong when he said two decades later that in 1846 the total daily circulation of Richmond papers was no more than one thousand; but it does not seem that any single paper sold more than several thousand copies.[1]

In 1845, the Richmond *Whig* had probably been first in circulation in the state, with 3,000 subscribers; by 1850 first place was held by the *Enquirer* with 4,000, while the *Examiner* was still behind but gaining. Of course, not all these readers were in Richmond; the *Enquirer* in particular circulated throughout Virginia and in other states. Newspapers were not rare commodities in antebellum Virginia. There was probably one paper for each two or three white families, and the proportion is more favorable if one takes into account the amount of white illiteracy, particularly in the western mountain counties.[2]

The proprietors of the new *Richmond Examiner* made their political position clear in the first issue. It was a position that the paper would continue to hold firmly: "THE ADVANCEMENT OF THE DEMOCRATIC CAUSE is paramount to all other objects we have in view. . . . [T]he EXAMINER will contend for the rights of the South, as guarantied [*sic*] by the Constitution. . . . It will consent to no *new* 'compromise' or 'restriction' of our rights. The slaveholding States already stand committed to too great a concession of their rights. They cannot, with safety or honor, surrender any *more* than they have done in the 'Missouri Compromise.'"[3]

Although De Witt and Wright both knew the printing trade and De Witt had talents as a writer, neither had a flair for editing. Hence, they turned to Daniel. It is not clear when he began to work for the *Examiner*. In April 7, 1848, a notice first appeared on the masthead that "Mr. John M. Daniel is associated with the editorial department of the Examiner." The proprietors quickly realized that in Daniel they "had found the proverbial round peg for the round hole... [They] had struck the mother lode."[4] Soon Daniel was the paper's chief editor.

The Richmond press scene in the 1840s was a volatile one. It had taken over a century after European settlement began in Virginia for periodical publishing to get its start. Indeed Governor William Berkeley had thanked God in 1671 that there were neither free schools nor printing in Virginia, "for learning has brought disobedience and heresy and sects into the world, and printing has divulged them and libels against the government."[5] The first Virginia newspaper, *The Virginia Gazette*, began publication in Williamsburg in 1736 and moved to Richmond in 1780, the year after the state government did so. A second paper began to appear in Richmond in 1786, and by 1800 there were four.

The Richmond periodical press soon became the scene of controversy. In 1800, James Thompson Callender, a Democrat who wrote for the newly founded *Examiner*, was tried in the U.S. Circuit Court in Richmond on the charge of having libeled the president of the United States; he had had the temerity to write that "Mr. Adams has only completed the scene of ignominy which Mr. Washington began." Samuel Chase, an associate justice of the U.S. Supreme Court, tried the case together with another judge. Under instructions from the court, the jury found Callender guilty and he went to jail, where he continued to contribute regular letters to the *Examiner*.[6]

As the decades passed, the main political contest both in Virginia and in the country as a whole became that between the Democratic and Whig parties. After a dozen years of Democratic administrations in Washington—those of Andrew Jackson and Martin Van Buren—the Whigs won the White House in 1840 with the election of William Henry Harrison and John Tyler who soon succeeded him, only to lose it to the Democrats in 1844 with the election of James K. Polk. Feelings ran high in Virginia and in the Virginia press, between Whigs who favored a stronger Federal system and Democrats whose banner was states' rights. While after 1844 the Democrats controlled not just the national government but the government of Virginia, Richmond remained a Whig stronghold.

At the beginning of 1846, some months after young John Daniel had moved to Richmond, there came a final clash in the city between John Hampden Pleasants, editor and proprietor of the *Whig* which he had founded in 1827, and Thomas Ritchie, Jr., who had replaced his father, longtime editor and proprietor of the *Enquirer*, at the head of that paper which was then still the Democrats' main paper in Virginia. For two decades Pleasants and the elder Ritchie had argued politics from their respective papers, "and their cacophonous duet had fostered a healthy spirit of controversy that helped preserve a competitive political system."[7] But Thomas Ritchie, Sr. had lately moved to Washington, to take over a new Democratic paper in the capital.

With his father gone from Richmond, the younger Ritchie took up the argument with Pleasants. Some years earlier, his brother William had challenged John Pleasants to a duel, but the challenge had been withdrawn. Now Thomas Ritchie, Jr. implied in his paper that Pleasants was an abolitionist and then flatly called him a coward. These proved literally to be fighting words. Pleasants sent word that he would meet Ritchie outside the city at dawn on February 25, 1846, armed with sidearms and attended by two friends. Ritchie complained that Pleasants was ignoring the code duello, which gave the challenged man the right to chose weapons, time, and place. But he went, and they met.

Ritchie, it was reported later by his friend and second William Scott, went onto the field carrying four dueling pistols in his belt, a six-barrel revolver in his coat pocket, and a sword under his coat.[8] Pleasants advanced on him with a pistol in each hand. Later it was said that Pleasants, concerned for his honor but not wanting to hurt Ritchie, had loaded his pistols with blanks; another story was that he had fired in the air. This may all be true; but after the firing began, Scott said, Pleasants came up to Ritchie and cut him about the face with a sword cane. Ritchie fired again, and his shots fatally wounded Pleasants. Ritchie was eventually tried for dueling but, as had happened before in such cases, he was acquitted.[9] John Hampden Pleasants would not be the last Virginia editor to meet bloody death in a duel; and it would not be many years more before another young Democratic editor, John Moncure Daniel, would fight his first duel. Meanwhile, with the two top Richmond editors gone, one to Washington and one to his grave, new space opened in Richmond for a talented newcomer.

Daniel came to the *Examiner* at a time when many Virginians agreed with the paper that their rights and their status were being eroded. Beyond the question of slavery as a legal and constitutional issue, Virginians were becomingly increasingly concerned about how quickly they, and the South overall, were losing out economically to the North during a time of robust expansion. Population was booming in Northern states and cities. In addition, the country was fast expanding westward. Texas joined the Union in 1845; Mexico declared war on the United

States in 1846; Richmond sent three companies of troops to join the soon victorious U.S. Army,[10] and the result of Mexican defeat was the addition to the Union of California and vast territories in the Southwest. Industry and technology too were booming. Still, even if the North was moving ahead of the South, Richmond was as noted earlier prosperous and full of industry; railroads were being built; and in July 1847 Richmond was linked with Washington and New York by the electric telegraph. It might still take a Richmond resident a day to come home from the national capital, but the news from there now arrived with lightning speed. At least some news did. The telegraph was expensive, and most news still came by mail (and by ship; the first attempt to lay a transatlantic telegraph cable would come only in 1857—and it failed).

There was also a movement, or better said two movements, of people out of Virginia. The West was opening up, and after gold was discovered in California many white Virginians joined the rush to the Golden State. All in all, Virginia may have lost as many as a million people to the westward movement.[11] It was not only whites who were leaving Virginia. With the continuing development of large plantations in the Deep South, many African Americans were sold out of the state.

The 1840s were for many if not most white Americans, certainly including Virginians, a time of exuberant nationalism. As David Potter wrote some years ago in *The Impending Crisis,* although Southerners as well as Northerners shared in the exuberance there was "a sinister dual quality in this nationalism, for at the same time when national forces, in the fullness of a very genuine vigor, were achieving an external triumph, the very triumph itself was subjecting their nationalism to internal stresses which, within thirteen years, would bring the nation to a supreme crisis."[12]

These stresses had largely to do with the changing balance between North and South, the constitutional question of states' rights, the question whether slavery could or should endure in America, and the question of how many of the new states of the Union should be open to slaveholding. Through the Missouri Compromise of 1820 that the *Examiner* had mentioned in its first issue, Maine became the twelfth free state and Missouri the twelfth slaveholding one, and slavery was barred north of latitude 36°30' in the territories of the Louisiana Purchase. The compromise satisfied neither the South nor the North (where, though there was no slavery, there was a color bar often embedded in legislation). Henry Clay defused a potential major conflict again in 1833 by securing approval for federal tariff reductions, after high tariffs pushed by the protectionist North had led South Carolina to declare the tariffs illegal through an Ordinance of Nullification—and President Andrew Jackson, a native Carolinian, had quietly begun preparations to invade South Carolina.

John Moncure Daniel had not yet been born in 1820, and he was a small boy in

1833. When he joined the *Examiner*, the stresses in the Union might be evident but no one imagined that the country was moving toward a great civil war—although a thinking person might wonder what ultimately would happen. South Carolina had already once considered leaving the Union, and "disunion" and "secession" remained part of the Southern political lexicon. Just recently, in August 1846, a Pennsylvania Congressman named David Wilmot had introduced a proviso to forbid slavery in any territory annexed to the United States as a result of the war with Mexico. The South had been outraged, and the Proviso did not pass.

Tendencies toward thinking on disunion were to some extent deflected, in the 1840s, by America's demonstrable progress and soaring patriotic spirits. The *Examiner* joined other papers in plumping for American expansion. For the *Examiner*, it was a question of the universal law of nature which said that all animate things must either increase or decay: "The Republic must either flourish or decline. . . . If we circumscribe its limits, it will overflow them; and the surplus of its wealth and population will go to neighboring countries to waste away entirely, or to build up other and rival nations."[13]

American nationalism led to the creation of a movement in the Democratic Party which helped John Moncure Daniel become known across the country. The movement was Young America. It owed its name to an enterprising journalist from South Carolina named Edwin DeLeon, who was born in 1818 and who as a young man went out toward, if not to, the advancing frontier, visiting Joseph Smith and his brethren in their new Mormon capital at Nauvoo in western Illinois.[14] DeLeon came back to South Carolina to publish, in 1845, *The Position and Duties of Young America* which argued that nations like people experienced infancy, manly vigor, and then decrepitude, and that America stood at the threshold of its "exulting manhood."[15]

The name and the basic idea of Young America had been suggested to DeLeon by Young Italy, founded in 1831 by the revolutionary Giuseppe Mazzini, who believed that every modern nation had a mission of its own. Mazzini had gone on in 1834 to announce a Young Europe, and in succeeding years the European continent would see Young Poland, Young Germany, Young France, and other similar movements, while others would spring up as far afield as Argentina and India. The mission for divided Italy was clearly national unity and independence, the mission Young America defined for the American nation was in good part national expansion.

Young America first became an important force through the work of the *Democratic Review*, founded in 1837 by a young Irish-American named John L. O'Sullivan[16] and his brother-in-law Samuel Langtree. O'Sullivan was a man of contradictions. He was a New Yorker who supported the doctrine of states' rights and would support the Confederacy in the Civil War. He was a reformer who wanted world peace, but he stood for American military intervention abroad in support of democratic movements, and he called for forceful acquisition of additional territory for the United States. It was O'Sullivan who coined that fateful term *manifest destiny.*[17]

In Richmond, young Daniel found these ideas to his liking. So did many other Southerners. If the Southern system based on slavery could not be extended into the North, there were great areas south of the country's sea and land borders where the United States, and especially the Southern states, might extend their influence and perhaps dominion. Northerners did not, in general, object to this idea. If the Monroe Doctrine warned European powers against intervention in Latin America, there was no promise of American nonintervention. Texas and the region west were won from Mexico, but there was speculation about acquiring all of Mexico, and every president from Jefferson on wanted to acquire Cuba. By the 1850s, many Northern Democrats hoped that Southern dreams of expanding slaveholding territories southward could lead the South to give way on the question of expanding slavery westward.[18]

John Moncure Daniel himself had not yet traveled abroad, when he was in his first years at the *Examiner.* But his readers were interested in foreign news, just as he was himself, and like other Richmond editors he gave the foreign scene good coverage in his paper. Eventually he went too far with what he took in from abroad—and he got caught at it.

Daniel's rivals at the *Whig* of course read carefully what the *Examiner* printed, as well as what journals elsewhere were saying. One can imagine these rivals rubbing their hands in glee when one day they found a little commentary in the *Examiner* beginning "None is less respected than a man who muddles away a large income nobody knows how." That sounded familiar. Sure enough, the *Times* of London had printed just a month earlier a commentary which was almost identical. The *Whig* printed the two commentaries side by side under the title "A most extraordinary coincidence!"[19] The *Examiner* commentary had not been signed, and we cannot be sure whether the writer was Daniel or another contributor. In any case there is no indication that Daniel ever again committed, or permitted, plagiarism.

Virginia writer John Esten Cooke, who published more than thirty works between 1854 and 1885, which are largely now forgotten, provides a striking portrait of young John Moncure Daniel in his stirring 1869 novel of the Civil War, *Mohun.* We do not know whether Cooke actually met Daniel, but the portrait is credible. Cooke wrote that on a visit to Richmond in 1849 or 1850, when he was nineteen or twenty years old, he went to "the Richmond library" to find some reference work for his father, and there he encountered the librarian, John Daniel, who was still living at the library and had begun working for the *Examiner.*

He was seated, half-reclining, in an arm-chair, surrounded by "exchanges," from which he clipped paragraphs, throwing the papers, as soon as he had done so, in a pile upon the floor. His black eyes, long black hair, brushed behind the ears, and thin, sallow cheeks, were not agreeable; but they made up a striking physiognomy. The black eyes glittered with a sullen fire; the thin lips were wreathed with a sardonic smile; and I was informed that the youth lived the life of a *solitaire*, voluntarily absenting himself from society, to give his days and nights to exhausting study.

He read every thing, it was said—history, poetry, political economy, and theology. Swift was said to be his literary divinity, and Rabelais was at his elbow always. . . .

Bitter, misanthropic, solitary; burning the midnight lamp, instead of moving among his fellows in the sunshine, he yet possessed hardy virtues and a high pride of gentleman. He hated the world at large, it was said, but loved his few friends with an ardor that shrank at nothing. . . .

His other virtues were self-denial, and a proud independence. . . . He would fight his own fight, make his own way; with the intellect heaven had sent him, carve out his own future, unassisted. The sallow youth, groaning under dyspepsia, with scarce a friend, and nothing but his brain, promised himself that he would one day rise from his low estate, and wield the thunderbolts of power, as one born to grasp and hurl them. . . .[20]

There is another, perhaps better, certainly more comprehensive portrait in the brief memoir entitled "John M. Daniel's Latch-Key," written after Daniel's death by his friend George W. Bagby. In a later book, Bagby wrote that there had been a half-dozen types of the old Virginia gentleman. He described each type, and there is little doubt that he had John Moncure Daniel in mind when he wrote of "a small, thin, sharp-featured, black-eyed, swarthy man; passionate, fiery indeed in temper; keen for any sort of discussion; profane, but swearing naturally and at times delightfully; hot, quick, bitter as death; magnanimous, but utterly implacable—a red Indian imprisoned in the fragile body of a consumptive old Roman."[21]

In a separate sketch in the same volume, Bagby described still another type, the pugnacious, hard-drinking, hard-gambling Virginia editor, neither gallant nor learned nor even very bright. But this was not Daniel, who was tenacious but not pugnacious; who drank little and did not gamble; and who was, indeed, gallant and learned and bright. He was, however, at least as good at making enemies as he was at making friends. Once he began work at the *Examiner*, the editor of the peaceable journal on farming leaped into the political arena against the Whigs and began to write biting pieces of ridicule and sarcasm that left him a number of lifelong enemies in Richmond and elsewhere in Virginia. [22] After a year, and the

Whig's last national victory in 1848, Daniel wrote that "Up to the close of the campaign, the Examiner has been almost entirely a political paper. It now ceases to be such. . . . [W]e shall hereafter publish a large quantity of miscellaneous intelligence."[23] If such were the editor's intentions, he did not carry them out. The *Examiner* had always printed a certain amount of "miscellaneous intelligence" and continued to do so; it did not become any less political in content after 1848.

What one sees reflected in the pages of the *Richmond Examiner* as its editor advanced into his mid-twenties is the sharpness and originality of commentary and analysis. For example, after former president James K. Polk died in June 1849 it was John Daniel who, perhaps first of all, pronounced Polk's administration the most successful and the most important yet seen by the republic.[24] This is hyperbole; yet recent historians have come to view Polk as extraordinarily successful in achieving his goals.

At the same time, Daniel became solidly proslavery and firmly prejudiced against black people. In this, he was far from original. He had not always been proslavery. When he was a boy, there had been considerable antislavery sentiment in Virginia. That great Virginian James Madison, who died when John Daniel was ten years old, had worked for years for emancipation—coupled, to be sure, with a colonization scheme that would remove blacks to Africa. At the end of 1831, when Daniel was a boy of six, the Virginia House of Delegates met in the wake of Nat Turner's rebellion and for a month debated the future of slavery. A delegate named Charles Faulkner argued that Virginia should abolish slavery and follow the Jeffersonian ideal of a republic based on yeoman farmers; the legislature in the end approved a resolution that condemned the institution of slavery but at the same time declared emancipation to be inexpedient. That did not resolve the question. Thomas Ritchie wrote in the Richmond *Enquirer* in January 1832 that slavery was at the heart's core "and has all along been consuming our vitals."[25] Shortly afterward, there appeared an essay by Professor Thomas Dew of the College of William and Mary, emphasizing that colonization could be no solution; the only alternatives were abolition, which most white Virginians could not countenance, or the continuance of the slavery system. Dew's essay became, as Daniel Boorstin said, the Bible of Virginia proslavery; it did much to bring Virginia opinion in line with the strong proslavery position of the lower South.[26] In subsequent years, the emancipationists grew far fewer as concerns mounted over Virginia's, and the South's, loss of power to the North. The Jeffersonian figure of the yeoman farmer took on antislavery overtones and was replaced in much Southern writing by a different ideal figure, that of the courtly planter on a large plantation.[27] While the readers whom Daniel wrote for at the *Southern Planter* tended to be of the former and not the latter sort, and while he was ever a Democrat, like his great-uncle on the Supreme Court, there would be little of the Jeffersonian in the editor's adult writings other than his expressed belief in states' rights.

The evidence of John Moncure Daniel's change of views on slavery comes mainly from his cousin Moncure Daniel Conway, who was strongly influenced by Daniel as a youth, but who as an adult took a strikingly different course from his cousin. Conway wrote in 1864 that John

> had evidently grappled with this terrible subject at an early date, and was startled by finding that he had come to the conclusion, with the American fathers, that "all men are created free and equal." His frank assertions of these, in that region, very paradoxical views, led some of his friends and relations to most earnest expostulations. But he was quite equal to them in the vigour of his opinions, even at that age, and not at all pained at being in a minority. Still I fear that, as he grew older, the desire for the commanding intellectual position which he felt himself amply competent to sustain, gave his mind a less independent attitude. . . . [T]he scientific advocates of the diversity of races found in him an eager convert, and he found in the new doctrines of race a justification of Slavery.[28]

One imagines that among his relations concerned about young John criticizing slavery must have been his great-uncle, the Supreme Court justice. Peter Vivian Daniel was to write, in his opinion paralleling that of Chief Justice Roger Taney in the Dred Scott case in 1856, that blacks had never been acknowledged as belonging to the family of nations, but only as "subjects of capture or purchase." Years earlier, in 1842, he had anticipated that case when he wrote in *Prigg v. Pennsylvania* that the great Missouri Compromise was wholly unconstitutional and void; that Congress had no power to restrict the introduction of slaves into new territories. Throughout his life the justice argued strongly for black slavery, and throughout his long service on the Supreme Court he fought inflexibly for what he thought was right, often in opposition to a majority of his colleagues.[29] Certainly much of this rubbed off on his great-nephew.

The main "scientific advocate" whose views, Moncure Conway later wrote, influenced John Daniel on race was Louis Agassiz, the Swiss scientist who came to the United States in 1846 and was named professor of zoology and geology at Harvard University the following year. In later years, Agassiz was sometimes called the greatest man of learning in America. Agassiz saw black people for the first time in America, and soon came to the conclusion that, as he wrote to his mother, "they are not of the same blood as we are."[30] Later, after he had twice been entertained by wealthy white planters in South Carolina, he decided definitely that blacks and whites sprang from different ancestors and were of different species, and he expounded this theory of polygenesis in articles in the Unitarian *Christian Examiner* in 1850 and 1851. Agassiz was not alone in these views. Voltaire and Hume had both suggested that blacks and whites came from different origins, as had Thomas Jefferson. By the time John Moncure Daniel came to manhood in Virginia, a number of reputable scientists and writers supported the theory of plural origins for humans,[31] including, at least for a time, Spencer Baird, the first assistant secretary of the Smithsonian Institution and later its secretary.[32]

Conway thought that Daniel's views about blacks were affected not only by Agassiz and other authorities but also by a scurrilous racist article that the much admired Scottish sage Thomas Carlyle published in December 1849 in London. In 1831, Carlyle had written that "The progress of man towards higher and nobler developments of whatever is highest and noblest in him, lies not only prophesied to Faith, but now written to the eye of Observation, so that he who runs may read."[33] Two years later, in 1833, slaves were emancipated throughout the British Empire. In succeeding years, West Indies plantation owners who grew sugar cane were hurt by the loss of cheap slave labor. Moreover, freed blacks understandably did not work quite so hard as they had done under the lash. Labor costs increased, and so did the price of sugar. Carlyle was incensed. In his 1849 article, he wrote not that humankind was progressing but that "where a Black man, by working about half-an-hour a-day (such is the calculation), can supply himself, by aid of sun and soil, with as much pumpkin as will suffice, he is likely to be a little stiff to raise into hard work. . . . [H]is own indolence is the enemy he must be delivered from. . . . Induce him, if you can, . . . but if your Nigger will not be induced? In that case, it is full certain, he must be compelled."[34]

After Agassiz and Carlyle had helped convert John Moncure Daniel to racist, proslavery views, Daniel for a time convinced his cousin Moncure Daniel Conway, who was seven years younger, of these views. Conway's father was a prosperous resident of Stafford County who owned a number of slaves and thought he treated them well. Later, to the elder Conway's surprise, they would all flee when the Civil War gave them the chance to do so.

Young Conway was sent north to study at Dickinson College in Pennsylvania, where Spencer Baird, soon to join the Smithsonian, was professor of natural history. From college, in October 1848, Moncure Conway wrote to John Moncure Daniel a letter forecasting a possible Democratic victory in Pennsylvania in the coming presidential election ("I have conversed with several of the most intelligent men in the town of Carlisle, and they seem to think that the State will give Cass and Butler a larger majority than ever."). Daniel published the letter from his "talented young friend" in the *Examiner*[35] and perhaps this, and his editor cousin's publication of other contributions of his, turned the young man's head. When

Conway graduated from college in 1849 and went home to Virginia, he had doubts about the institution of slavery. When Conway visited his older cousin, Daniel told him that he, too, had long pondered this issue and "had long been undergoing intellectual and spiritual struggles of which the world about him knew nothing."[36] Daniel had already accumulated an impressive personal library that contained works ranging from Spinoza to Carlyle to Emerson, which Conway found filled with John's marginal notes. Daniel talked to his younger cousin at length about race, emphasizing the findings of Louis Agassiz and stressing that slavery was not, as some said, contrary to the Bible. It was enough to convince Conway, who was just seventeen years old.

An allied question in Virginia was whether secession would ultimately be necessary if slavery was continued. Later that year, Conway attended a meeting of a Southern rights association in Fredericksburg. Although a slaveholder, his father thought slavery to be a doomed institution, and he was distressed that his son seemed to have given himself over both to slavery and possible secession. They quarreled, and in early 1850 Conway fled to Richmond and asked Daniel to help him find work. Daniel was willing to employ him but not to encourage rebellion against his father. Conway returned home. He was sent off to read law, the beginning of a long intellectual path that led him away from the law and into the struggle for the abolition of slavery.

In later years, Conway became known as the biographer of Tom Paine, who as early as 1775 had called for the abolition of slavery in America. Conway stressed that his cousin John Daniel, whom he remembered as a genius and who for a time had overwhelmed him, had been an Emersonian as well as a defender of slavery. Daniel's *Examiner* was the first Southern paper to give space to Emerson, Hawthorne, and other Northern writers and even to the abolitionist clergyman Theodore Parker. But in the end Agassiz and Carlyle had won out over Emerson and Parker in Daniel's mind, and the young editor had helped to create "a novel kind of radicalism—a negative counterpart of northern abolitionism."[37] The editor wanted his cousin to believe that he had reached his proslavery position after much reading and a long debate with himself. Still we cannot forget Conway's guess that at least in part, Daniel became a partisan of slavery not from independent thinking but because the support of slavery was the popular position—and certainly Daniel wanted to get ahead.

A dozen years after seeking employment with Daniel, Conway, by then a well-known Northern antislavery clergyman, paid a visit to President Abraham Lincoln, who in 1862 still was still insisting that he aimed to save the Union either with or without slavery. Conway asked Lincoln to deliver the nation from its one great evil. [38] No matter what proslavery arguments his cousin Daniel had used with him, Conway could never forget a scene from his childhood. A slaveowning neighbor of his father, who had killed one of his male slaves with impunity, later brought to Stafford Court House several female slaves, whom he charged with trying to poison him. After their acquittal,

> he took the women to a cart in which they had been brought to the courthouse; there he bound their ankles and wrists, and bound them to each other; then, after displaying six raw-hides—whips compared with which the cat-o'-nine-tails is merciful,—he tore down the dresses from their shoulders and backs, and ordering the driver, husband of one of the women, to drive homeward, began to beat and lacerate the backs of these women frightfully. The crowd stood witnessing all this with a mere curiosity, watching the cart as it went on its way with its tragical freight. . . . [T]he essence of the tragedy was, that any interference with the scoundrel would have been illegal. . . . [T]he ultimate effect of it all was to harden the people and demoralise the humane.[39]

We know more about Daniel's relationship with Moncure Conway than we do about his relations with his five younger, orphaned brothers. When their father and stepmother died in 1845, twenty-year-old John was old enough to fend for himself, but the others were sent to live with relatives. The fifth brother, named Peter Vivian Daniel after his great-uncle, died in 1853 at the age of seventeen, but the other brothers outlived their eldest sibling. Three died in Texas. One of them, James Mitchell Daniel, had been taken in by the boys' uncle, Raleigh Travers Daniel. In 1848, when fifteen years old, James Mitchell Daniel left his uncle's home in Richmond and went to work buying corn and fodder for a railroad contractor. Six months later, John Daniel found the youth a job as a rod man in the engineer corps of the Virginia and Tennessee Railroad for thirty dollars a month. This was the beginning of a long career in which James Mitchell Daniel surveyed the railroad line that became the Texas and Pacific; served as a Confederate artillery captain; spent several months in Europe in 1869 on behalf of former Union general, presidential candidate, and promoter John C. Frémont; returned to Richmond for several years in banking; went mining in Leadville during the Colorado silver boom of the 1880s; and bought a mine in Mexico that his sons operated and the family owned until the revolution of 1912. James Mitchell Daniel spent his final years in Paris, Texas, as one of the town's most honored and prosperous citizens; he died there in 1916 at age 82.[40]

We do not know if John Moncure Daniel tried to do anything during these years for his other younger brothers. George Cary Eggleston, a Virginian who moved north and tried to interpret the South to Northern readers, noted that although Virginia had abolished the law of primogeniture, in a Virginia family the eldest son almost always inherited the estate and took on himself his father's duties, including the education of younger children.[41] There was no way that John Daniel, without funds and just beginning a career, could take on such a burden. Helping one brother find a job was no doubt the most he could do. Later, he employed another brother for seven years in Italy and then concerned himself with what that brother might do next in life. Finally, in 1865, John Daniel remembered all his surviving brothers with bequests in his will.

Friends, Politics, and Duels

If young Moncure Conway had joined the staff of the *Richmond Examiner,* he would have found himself associated with several other energetic and interesting people besides his cousin John Moncure Daniel. We can name some but not all of them. The newspapers of nineteenth-century Richmond did not indicate who had written a particular editorial. Many noneditorial articles did not show more than a pseudonym, and sometimes it was difficult to tell where editorializing ended and other contributions began.

For a time, Bennett De Witt, the coproprietor, continued to provide material for the columns of the *Examiner* through his contacts in other parts of Virginia. At some early point, however, Daniel took charge of the paper's content, and he was soon joined on the editorial staff by Patrick Henry Aylett and Robert W. Hughes, who clearly worked on a part-time basis. From then until Daniel went abroad in 1853, the editorial writing rested in the hands of these three. Hughes recalled years later that "Mr. Daniel did the fierce writing, Mr. Aylett the humorous, and I the argumentative. I discussed; Aylett ridiculed; Daniel fulminated."[1]

Hughes and others who knew the workings of the *Examiner* all agreed that Daniel remained open to contributions from outside the regular staff. As Hughes noted, there were many people in Virginia who could truthfully say that they wrote for the *Richmond Examiner.* But if, as Hughes also said (and one may question this), Daniel was somewhat lazy about writing things of his own, he was tireless and meticulous as an editor, shaping and reshaping others' contributions to fit his own style and point of view.

Daniel's colleagues and friends Aylett and Hughes both came from well-known Virginia families. Like Daniel, Patrick Henry Aylett was born in 1825; he owed his given names to the fact that his grandmother was the youngest daughter of the famous Revolutionary patriot. Unlike Daniel, Aylett's family had not fallen on hard times. He was educated at Harvard, and in 1847 the death of his father left him the executor of a large estate.[2] For the first few years that he worked with John Daniel and Robert Hughes at the *Examiner,* Aylett was a bachelor, like Daniel; he did not marry until 1853. Aylett was a giant of a man, almost seven feet tall, and was said to have animal spirits and unfailing good temper[3]—a great contrast to his small and intense but not exactly exuberant friend.

Robert Hughes, four years older than Daniel and Aylett, was the grandson of an officer who fought in the Revolution and the son of a lawyer and plantation owner. He had been admitted to the Virginia bar in 1846 and had then gone to Richmond to practice law. In 1850, when he was combining the law with writing for the *Examiner*, Hughes married the adopted daughter of John B. Floyd, a leading Virginia Democrat, governor of Virginia since 1849 and the son of another Virginia governor. (Aylett, too, had a forebear who had served as governor: his great-grandfather Patrick Henry.) The relationship between John Daniel and Robert Hughes and John Floyd continued to develop and would prove profitable but also sometimes perplexing to Daniel as he strove upward and as Floyd became a national figure.

In addition to publishing work by Aylett and Hughes, Daniel began to accept contributions from a would-be painter in his late twenties who eventually decided to become a physician. This was Arthur Edward Peticolas, the grandson of a French army officer who had ended up as a teacher of music and painting in Richmond.[4] Neither the editor nor his collaborators could have imagined that within five years the actions of Arthur Peticolas and Robert Hughes would almost ruin Daniel's public life. At this point, Daniel was devoted to Peticolas. When Daniel and Peticolas were both still young and poor, Daniel once walked the twenty miles from Richmond to Petersburg to pay money he had collected for his artist friend. He then walked the twenty miles home again, although his health was probably less than robust.[5]

A long article entitled "THE EDITOR," which appeared in the *Examiner* on November 21, 1848, tells us that Daniel, who had just turned twenty-three, was confident he had found an excellent profession for himself. His was a new profession, but if somehow Gutenberg had lived in the time of Xenophon and Thucydides, said the writer, the Greeks would have passed on to the modern age the model of an editor that combined the learning of the academy, the invective of Demosthenes, and the humor of Aristophanes. (The editor of the *Examiner* was perhaps too modest to say that he himself embodied all these qualities.) As it was, Daniel continued, even though a modern editor was not appointed like a Roman censor or "called" like a modern clergyman, he filled a position that was reinforced by a kind of reverence and superstition as great as that which had given the church its power in its darkest days. This superstition was what Americans called liberty of the press, wrote Daniel, and it allowed an editor to say harsh things about a man although "he would knock you down if you said the same thing to him by word of mouth alone, on an open prairie." Even so, editors were not satisfied and wanted libel laws modified so that they could meddle with the private affairs of any citizen; but there was no true liberty where the personal rights of individuals were not respected. To set journalists on the right course, wrote Daniel, the first thing to do was recognize journalism as a distinct profession. There should be an endowed professorship of journalism in every college in the country. A body of accomplished men trained specially for newspaper work would give character, efficiency, and dignity to this profession which, Daniel suggested, had become far more important than that of the soldier.

Daniel was perhaps sixty years ahead of his time in calling for journalism as an academic discipline. It was not until 1908 that Walter Williams founded the world's first school of journalism, at the University of Missouri. Still, while there were no professors of journalism, there was already a new corps of American editors who, like John Moncure Daniel, were becoming leading voices. In the North, there were James Gordon Bennett, Horace Greeley, and Henry J. Raymond. In the Midwest, there were Edwin Cowles, Murat Halstead, and Joseph Medill. In the South, there were influential editors like the Ritchies of Richmond and the Rhetts of Charleston, as well as William G. Brownlow in Knoxville, John Forsyth Jr. in Mobile, and William T. Thompson in Savannah.

A good journalist needs to know all the powers at play in society, and Daniel did not neglect the power of organized religion in Virginia. Some Virginia clergymen disliked him, as he made clear in a long letter that he sent in July 1850 to a young clergyman who did like him and who had contributed a piece to the *Examiner.* Rev. Clement Read Vaughan, pastor of the First Presbyterian Church in Lynchburg, had offered to do a series of letters for the *Examiner* and had also taken Daniel to task for things that the paper published on the subject of religion. Daniel told Vaughan[6] that other clergymen had said even harsher things about him, even when they agreed with his paper's politics. The result, he said, was that when those who thought favorably of him as a writer and politician lent their voices to the cry of "blasphemer" and "infidel," his adversaries had reason to claim their charges as proven. Daniel wanted Vaughan to know that he believed in the absolute necessity of the religious element in human society and that he did not want to see its power diminished, but "I lay down the principle, that the slightest advance toward the introduction of that element into the machinery of political government should be resisted on the threshold with the most uncompromising resolution." We do not know whether Mr. Vaughan agreed. While there was no established church in America, in Virginia, as elsewhere, the leading Protestant pastors had a major influence on politics.

It is difficult to pin down Daniel's own religious views. His ancestor Rev. John Moncure had been an Anglican rector, but John Daniel clearly did not follow him into what had become the Episcopal Church. Perhaps we can best identify Daniel as a kind of Protestant. His friend Thomas Wynne wrote after Daniel's death that his beliefs had been of a standard sort. He followed closely developments in the Catholic Church, but not with sympathy, particularly when the population of Rome rose up against the papacy in 1848 and established the short-lived Roman Republic. Daniel's sentiments, like those of almost all non-Catholic Americans, were with the republic and not with Pius IX. At the same time, Daniel was more skeptical than many of his contemporaries about the extent of the Vatican's influence in America.

Daniel did not neglect the Jews. There was a Jewish community in Richmond, and one evening the editor attended the dedication of the new synagogue on Ninth Street. There was good music, he reported, and an excellent discourse by the rabbi. Daniel might have stopped with that comment, but he could not resist adding that the rabbi was "a gentleman with a German-Jew name, which we can neither pronounce nor write"—a slur not untypical of the time.[7]

There was relatively little religious content in the political contest between Democrats and Whigs in Richmond and beyond. The contest remained a fierce one from the time Daniel joined the *Examiner* until Franklin Pierce took back the White House from the last Whig president, Millard Fillmore, in the election of 1852. By 1847, Americans had begun to think that the president they elected in 1848 might well be a man with a military reputation, following in the tradition of Washington, Jackson, and Harrison. Gen. Winfield Scott led an army from Vera Cruz overland to capture Mexico City and end the war, but there was a court of inquiry into his conduct of the campaign, and it was Gen. Zachary Taylor on whom people fixed their attention, particularly after his victory at Buena Vista in February 1847. Taylor was a slaveowner who had a sizable plantation in Louisiana. He was also, people sensed, a man of Whig convictions, though he did not say so. People both North and South were taken by him. There was also an elder statesman who was a Whig and who was demonstrably better qualified to become the nation's chief executive, Henry Clay; but Clay was not a general.

Taylor was brave and steadfast but not a great general. At Buena Vista his victory was due in good part to talented subordinates and Mexican mistakes. Correspondence that he drafted personally was prolix and often unclear, yet that rising New York Democrat William Seward wrote his wife that Taylor wrote better than he fought. But the main point was that he was a victorious general. After Buena Vista, a Cincinnati editor urged Taylor as the Whig candidate for 1848, provided he agreed to Wilmot's idea of forbidding slavery in lands won from Mexico. Taylor wrote the editor that he would not enter the presidential race until the Mexican war was finally won—and that he would not state his political opinions—but that he approved in a general way what the paper had said.[8]

After Taylor's letter to the Cincinnati paper was published, Daniel and his colleagues mocked the presidential candidate for his clumsy attempts to disguise his ambition. They quoted the noncandidate's prolix and confusing compositions under titles like "DON ZACK'S NEW PRONUNCIAMENTO."[9] Clearly, said the paper, his published letters did not come from the same pen that had drafted the brilliant and tersely written reports from the field cited as evidence of Taylor's genius. On May 9, 1848, the *Richmond Examiner* reported the identity of the drafter: Maj. William Bliss, "a very polished and highly educated member of his staff." (Later in the year, Bliss married the general's daughter.)

In June 1848 a new Whig Club was organized in Richmond and was addressed by that well-known Richmond lawyer and state legislator Raleigh T. Daniel, John's uncle. The *Examiner* reported that Mr. Daniel had called calumniators and liars those members of the Democratic press who claimed that Henry Clay was not the man to be President.[10] Well, that seemed aimed more at the *Enquirer*, which did not care for Clay, than at the Democratic *Examiner*. In any case John Daniel did not directly attack his uncle in return. But several days later the *Examiner* commented that there was no Whig in the country who would not tell you that he preferred Henry Clay as a candidate to any other living man; yet Whig leaders had cast aside this well-qualified man in favor of Zachary Taylor, of whom nothing was known save that he was a successful general. They had done this because they realized "that if they elect a President at all, it must be by gulling and deceiving the people with military glory."[11]

Zachary Taylor won the nomination. The candidate for vice president would be Millard Fillmore, New York state comptroller and former chairman of the Ways and Means Committee in the U.S. House of Representatives. The *Examiner* dismissed Fillmore as a "notorious individual"[12] and subsequently published a digest of his voting record in the House to show that he was an abolitionist and an enemy of the (white) Southern people.[13] (A decade later diplomat John Daniel met Millard Fillmore in Turin and concluded that his earlier low opinion of the man was fully justified.)

In November 1848, Zachary Taylor and Millard Fillmore won the national election for the Whigs. As usual, the Whigs enjoyed a majority in the city of Richmond, but Virginia overall gave a slight majority to the Democratic candidate, Lewis Cass. Among Whigs in Richmond who had earlier indicated a preference for Henry Clay over Zachary Taylor was John Minor Botts, who represented the Richmond area in the U.S. House of Representatives and who later became a favorite target of the *Examiner*. Botts eventually gave his support to Taylor, but the paper suggested that Taylor's victory spelled the end of Botts's political life, and it offered an epitaph:

> Here lies John Minor Botts . . .
> Reader, if you be a Whig,

take warning from his fate;
And never, never forget that
adherence to principle
is treason to Whiggery.[14]

Whigs had gained control of the House of Representatives two years earlier; even the Illinois delegation had acquired one Whig member, a lawyer named Lincoln. From Richmond, the *Examiner* sent out a warning to its readers that Southern Whigs were already collaborating with Northern abolitionists. The paper supported a fiery resolution by John Floyd, then a member of Virginia's House of Delegates, that if the Congress passed any law abridging the rights of slaveholders and the South, Virginia should "resist such an act of aggression to the last extremity, and by every means which she can command."[15]

In March 1849, the presidential inauguration of Zachary Taylor took place in Washington, and the *Examiner* sent its representative to the ceremonies. On December 29, 1848, the paper had announced that J. W. Wright had given up his interest in the *Examiner* and that John M. Daniel and Bennett De Witt had become coproprietors. We cannot be sure that the paper's envoy to the presidential inauguration was John Moncure Daniel, but he would hardly have permitted anyone else to go instead, even De Witt.

The envoy took time to write his account; ten days passed before the paper carried a full and blistering report.[16] As usual, the new vice president was sworn in before the new president, and in his remarks Fillmore made an awful blunder. During the previous year, in 1848, democratic revolutions had been attempted in several European countries. The new vice president contrasted the tranquility of America with the condition of the various European nations "which were now the scenes of crime, confusion and bloodshed." There was a noticeable stir among the senior European diplomats present, and the envoy of the *Examiner* was surprised that they did not walk out. It was understood that the printed version of the vice president's remarks would soften what he had actually said.

The report described the ensuing speech by the president as

> full of namby pamby, and containing several contradictions. . . . Gen. Taylor reads badly. He was greatly confused, and stumbled through his short address. . . . He pronounces his words very differently from the way in which educated men accent them. His address has but a single merit. It is short. . . . The greater part was read to Chief Justice Taney alone—his back being entirely turned to the multitude, and his face and paper stuck down into the Judge's breast. When he had gotten nearly through, one of his friends . . . said something in a low voice. Then . . . the General turned around and continued

> reading with his face to the crowd. He did not raise his voice. No part of the speech was heard except by those within thirty paces of the speaker.[17]

That evening, the reporter attended the inaugural ball,[18] where everything went wrong. The scene became one of discord, hubbub, kicking, and starvation. Ladies were admitted to the supper room first, "and when the lords of creation came, they found Eve had ruined Paradise a second time." Nothing remained but the carcasses of turkeys and a few broken sweetmeats. Champagne, however, flowed like water, according to the reporter; and when a lady asked for water to wash her fingers, she was handed a bowl of champagne. Then came dancing, and although the cards handed to ladies stated positively that no set should dance until quadrilles were formed with side couples, "we had no effectual mode to join a single set with side couples." At that point, the eyes of the reporter lit on John Minor Botts and the lady he escorted. She was very ladylike, and "We never saw a finer specimen of *genus homo* than Mr. Botts—on this occasion. He was cleanly shaved, and perfectly well washed and brushed. . . . We felt proud of our Richmond Representative."

These and worse things the *Examiner* said about Botts—the next month the paper called him a demagogue whom the Whigs had picked up at the race course where he was losing a good deal of money[19]—could well have proven to be fighting words. For Botts was not cowardly. In 1842 he had tried to impeach President Tyler. In 1860 he was perhaps the only prominent Virginian to dare write a Northern friend that he hoped Lincoln would be elected president.[20] In 1862, a year after Virginia had seceded from the Union, he was still speaking out against secession, which gained him eight weeks' confinement in a Richmond jail. But when, after the war, Jefferson Davis was indicted for treason, Botts was one of those who bravely signed his bail bond.[21]

But if it was not with Congressman Botts that John Moncure Daniel fought his first duel, he fought it with someone probably in or near Richmond sometime in these years. As a duelist he had good company. This was an era in which gentlemen, and not just Virginia gentlemen, were very quick to perceive slights and demand satisfaction. The duel in which Aaron Burr killed Alexander Hamilton at Weehawken in 1804 remains the most famous of many such events around the country. Button Gwinnett of Georgia died of wounds received in a duel soon after he signed the Declaration of Independence. Andrew Jackson killed a man in a duel years before he became president. In 1826 Henry Clay, then secretary of state, challenged Senator John Randolph of Roanoke, and the two met just outside Washington. Neither was hurt. In 1838, eight members of Congress, including Henry A. Wise, later a governor of Virginia, were together involved in a duel as principals and seconds. Later, Wise would fight eight duels in less than two years.[22] During the 1830s and 1840s public support for dueling intensified in the South, which thought itself compelled to defend more than one peculiar institution.[23] It was in 1838 Charleston that the long recognized but unpublished rules of what was called the code duello first appeared in print in a volume called *The Code of Honor*. The author was no young hothead but the governor of the state.

John Daniel, knowing himself to be a Virginia gentleman, accepted dueling and its code. His cousin Moncure Conway said that Daniel fought as many as nine duels in his short life. This does not necessarily mean that he liked dueling. Nor did he write much on the subject. The long and thoughtful article on the role of the editor in America that appeared in the *Examiner* for November 21, 1848, and that must be Daniel's work—or must at least reflect his thinking—comments briefly and dispassionately that the possibility of receiving a challenge may place less restraint on an editor than it had done once, although "still in Vicksburg"—not Richmond, one notes—"an Editor and a Duellist seem to be synonymous." He might have added (but he did not) that if dueling had become mainly a Southern phenomenon, Northern editors had a long tradition of violent quarrels. In 1830, for example, Col. James Watson Webb of New York's *Courier and Enquirer* had caned the editor of the rival *Washington Telegraph* and had in turn been spat on and assaulted by William Leggett of the *Evening Post*. Webb also publicly beat up another rival who had worked for him, a man named James Gordon Bennett, whose *New York Herald* would soon become famous. The following year in New York, the famous poet and editor-in-chief of the *Evening Post*, William Cullen Bryant, attacked William L. Stone, editor of the *Commercial Advertiser*, beating him over the head with a whip.[24]

Whatever his philosophical view of dueling was, Daniel was quick to defend his honor. On February 23, 1849, the *Examiner* reported how he had faced down a journalist from a rival Richmond newspaper, the pro-Whig *Times and Compiler*. The journalist, William Carrington, had written that the Democratic *Enquirer* had been reduced to quoting "the scurrilous effusions of an unworthy ally in this city, so low in its ribaldry that it has long been treated with contempt, and regarded as beneath respectful notice, by the Whig press of the State." This was too much for Daniel. And since his fellow proprietor Bennett De Witt was out of town, he wrote to the *Times and Compiler* himself, taking Carrington's comments as a personal insult and demanding a retraction. Carrington replied that he thought he had written correctly about the "tone and temper" of the *Examiner* but that he did not intend any imputation in regard to the personal honor of its editors. Daniel decided that this explanation sufficed and published the exchange.

Another quarrel had already begun that would lead Daniel to duel with a more prominent Richmond journalist, Edward W. Johnston, at that time editor of the *Richmond Whig*, a duel that would gain national notice. The quarrel began with the *Greek Slave.* A New Orleans gentleman named James Robb had commissioned Hiram Powers, the great sculptor of neoclassical works who lived and worked in Italy, to sculpt for him a nude female figure in white marble. After completion, the *Greek Slave* was sent to America and exhibited for two years in the Northeast for the profit of the sculptor. The exhibitor then decided to show the statue in New Orleans before giving it to Robb. But when he sent it to New Orleans, the *Richmond Examiner* reported, "he was *Robbed* of his treasure. The proprietor ravished away the lady, and shut her up in his house. . . . The finale is that the beautiful bone of contention is lost to the public."[25]

It developed that Johnston of the *Whig* and Daniel of the *Examiner* differed as to the merits of the *Greek Slave* and over the question of a copy Powers made of it. These were hardly sufficient grounds for a duel. The previous editor of the *Whig*, Mr. John Hampden Pleasants, had challenged Thomas Ritchie of the *Enquirer*, and Ritchie had then killed Pleasants, over what was certainly a weightier issue: the charge of cowardice. As time went on, Daniel and Johnston apparently expressed their differences not just in print but also in person. The argument, coupled with the basic political differences between the two papers and their editors, sharpened into a quarrel.

What must have particularly irritated Daniel was that Johnston and his *Whig* most often ignored the *Examiner*, preferring to focus instead on the city's other Democratic paper, the older *Enquirer*. By August 1851, the quarrel had progressed to the point that Daniel decided to send a letter that must have come close to being an explicit challenge to a duel. Daniel's friend Arthur Peticolas delivered the letter. However, Johnston reported the letter and brought charges against Daniel and Peticolas before the hustings court of Richmond for breaking the law against dueling. The two men were indicted on August 16.[26] The *Examiner* reported, "All men of honor can regard this act of Johnston in but one light, viz: as the CAP STONE OF HIS COWARDICE." The paper quoted the *Petersburg Democrat* as claiming that it had long been apparent that the Whigs wanted to kill off the *Examiner;* but instead the rival paper's circulation had increased to almost four thousand and within a year could reach five or six thousand, much larger than any other Richmond paper.

Johnston printed this in the *Whig* and then went on the attack:

> Now, we are disposed to give ourselves exceedingly little trouble about the *Examiner*. While it was merely a raging slanderer, we thought the exposing of it a deed of grace. . . . We have in no manner, directly or indirectly, been the mover of any proceedings against Mr. John M. Daniel. This, the records of the court itself would have shown. . . . Were we disposed to be afraid, the very last sort of person whom we should select for the object of our terrors would be

> one of your heroes that keeps himself in constant "duelling practice," and always goes about with a "revolver" in his pocket. We carry no weapons for such; but are quite willing to trust to a few good stones or brickbats, such as the streets anywhere afford, as the only ammunition fit to be employed upon them.[27]

One assumes from the above that Daniel was boasting to others that he kept himself in good condition—and armed—for possible duels. Johnston's mocking and belittling words must have irritated him still more. The question was what he might do in return.

Johnston had come to Richmond from Roanoke, where he had opened and, for more than three years, operated, without much success, the Roanoke Female Seminary. He did not like to be reminded of that experience. Somewhere Daniel found an old prospectus for the seminary that specified "Dress. For Winter, Bottle-green Circassian or Merino, with Capes of the same. For those below 12 years, Pantalets like the dress," and Daniel drew a little picture of Johnston with the young ladies promenading in their bottle-green, escorted by the younger ladies in their pantalets.[28] That did it. This time, Johnston issued the challenge, and Daniel accepted. Virginia public opinion might condone dueling, but it was against commonwealth law. It was agreed that this duel would take place outside Virginia.

Afterward, Daniel sent his friend Henry A. Washington a detailed account of the event.[29] To avoid arrest, Daniel went up to the District of Columbia one Sunday in January and registered under an assumed name at a small hotel in Georgetown. Within an hour, his second, another friend named Powell, sent word to Johnston that Daniel was ready. Powell tried to schedule the encounter for Monday morning, but Johnston's second, a certain Rowan, insisted on Monday at 4:00 P.M. Daniel, Powell, and Daniel's surgeon, Alexander Garnett, arrived on time at the place but found no one.[30] The site was the traditional place for Washingtonians' duels, just over the District of Columbia line in Bladensburg, Maryland.[31] (Maryland had its own antidueling law, but it applied only to Marylanders.) Time passed. It had become too dark to fight when finally Johnston arrived with five or six hacks full of people. Johnston's people apologized for the confusion. Powell tried to reschedule for the following day, but Rowan insisted on the day after that, Wednesday, at 10:00 A.M. Daniel went to the meeting place on Wednesday morning, accompanied only by Powell and Garnett. Johnston and his seconds came and were soon joined by a crowd of people that included friends of Johnston and a number of Whig congressmen.

Daniel wrote Washington that, because his second did not know how to load Daniel's pistols, he had to load them himself; clearly he had practiced the process. While Daniel was on the field, Johnston sat in his carriage until called. "When he appeared however he was cool enough, though very much emaciated," wrote

Daniel. "As for myself, I never was calmer, never in better spirits, never so self-possessed in my life. . . . I give you my word as a gentleman, that I did not feel during that whole scene one single flutter in my heart—or one moments apprehension of any sort. . . . I do not believe that my pulse quickened a single beat at the moment I fired. Powell told me that I did not change the expression of my countenance—much less colour."

We can perceive some bravura in this account. Daniel continued that he could easily have killed Johnston but no longer felt any animosity toward him, and so he fired quickly to cause Johnston to fire quickly in return. Neither shot hit its mark, and Johnston's friends, including "Old Blair"—Francis P. Blair, adviser to several presidents—rushed up to the seconds. With that, the duel ended. Daniel told Henry Washington that this encounter rid him of all fears about dueling; his slight excitement had really been pleasurable.

The following day, the *New York Times* reported that the duel had come after a challenge issued several months earlier, that its cause had been entirely political, and that "Mr. DANIEL had an affair last year with a Mr. SCOTT, of Virginia, which ended in smoke." The affair with William C. Scott had taken place in April 1851 after the *Examiner* described Scott, a delegate to the Virginia legislature, as "the gentleman with a tongue as long as his cane." Scott, in turn, called Daniel "a living monument of imbecile malignity." Who challenged whom is not clear, but Daniel was arrested and released on $2,000 bail on the condition that he keep the peace. Scott's arrest was sought, but he could not be found. It was reported that the two had gone to North Carolina, where they would meet with rifles at twenty paces; they had, in fact, gone to Baltimore, where they addressed their differences without fighting.[32]

After the Johnston duel, Daniel and Peticolas were still under indictment for the first challenge. Where was this challenge that had been delivered in writing? Had Johnston perhaps torn it up, and did Daniel learn that he had done so? Or did Daniel perhaps suggest that he might retaliate and give to the court the challenge he had received from Johnston? In March, two months after the duel, the attorney for the Commonwealth of Virginia issued Johnston a subpoena to produce the challenge from Daniel. He apparently could not or would not, and the case was dropped the following December.[33]

However many duels Daniel actually fought, he avoided one with Edgar Allan Poe. Poe edited the *Southern Literary Messenger* in Richmond in the 1830s, and in 1843 he had tried to buy it with help from friends in the North.[34] In 1848, Poe was again in Richmond. Hearing that Daniel had made disparaging remarks about him and his close friendship with Sarah Whitman, Poe sent Daniel a challenge and, apparently primed with alcohol, went to the *Examiner* office to demand satisfaction. Poe walked into Daniel's office and found him sitting with two pistols on his desk. The editor asked the poet to sit down. Daniel said that he did not care to have the matter get to the police, that they could settle the dispute between them then and there. The newspaper premises were roomy enough, and the pistols were ready. Poe is reported to have suddenly grown sober. Perhaps, he said, the differences between them had been exaggerated. The two agreed that they should resolve their differences, friends waiting behind the door joined them, and the company repaired to a nearby tavern, and there Poe recited from his poetry.[35] One can hardly find Daniel much at fault here, as the poet's erratic, if not drunken, behavior is shown in another incident the same year, when a Richmond physician came on Edgar Poe pointing a pistol through the keyhole of a friend's apartment.[36]

Still another incident indicates that although Daniel could be litigious, he could also ignore clear provocations to fight. There is, for example, no reason to believe that he ever dueled with writer and historian Robert Howison, despite an insulting letter from Howison about Daniel published in the *Richmond Whig* on July 15, 1851. Four years earlier, in January 1847, Daniel had written a positive account of Howison's new history of Virginia for the *Southern Literary Messenger.* In 1851, Howison published a volume on criminal trials, and Daniel's *Examiner* gave it a brief review that Howison considered negative. Howison exploded:

> His defective education, and the humiliating employment in which he has been engaged for some years, have kept his mind closed to all sound learning and his ignorance . . . accompanied by overweening vanity, has led him into a variety of grotesque tricks and grimaces. . . . Like a monkey in a library, he has capered around the shelves of learning, pulling down a book here and there without the slightest knowledge of its contents. . . . A doubt is beginning seriously to prevail whether he belongs to the race of man. . . . Some have thought him a dog, but this supposition does great injustice to the dog species. . . . This creature at the Examiner office is probably an *Ourang Outang;* not unlike in person, and displaying the same ignorance and brutal ferocity, the same hatred of mankind, the same disposition to hide himself in recesses and accumulate foul missiles for attack. . . . In conclusion, let me say that I do not, and never will, wear *concealed weapons* among my fellow citizens. He who does so *must* be urged to it either by timidity or malice, and is therefore at heart, either a *coward* or an *assassin*. . . .

Men were killed in nineteenth-century Virginia for saying far less than that. One wonders whether Howison's own missiles looked so foul that Daniel laughed the whole thing off. To be sure, we do not have a complete record of Daniel's duels. We know only that neither he nor Howison killed each other and that Howison outlived Daniel by four decades.

A Poet, a Lady, and a Prominent Man

John Moncure Daniel kept the main matter of the *Richmond Examiner* firmly in mind—and that was not duels or dueling but politics. He backed Young America's program but was not distracted by the question of expanding America's borders southward. He focused on the prime political questions in both the South and North: how far slavery might be extended westward; and what changes, if any, might be made in the system regarding slavery in the country as a whole. The *Examiner* predicted in the late autumn of 1849 that the approaching Congress would decide whether slavery should cease to agitate the Union. But, added the editor, the North should realize that, although Southerners were attached to the Union, they were ready for dissolution. It was not just that the South had shown its attachment to the Union; the South, Daniel told his readers, had made sacrifices for it. The Boston Tea Party had been the work of Northern tea drinkers; people in the South did not drink tea. Nor had English troops been quartered on the population of the South. But the South had loyally joined in the Revolution. Later, Virginia alone had given up to the rest of the Union 262,000 square miles of the Old Northwest. The South had agreed to the Missouri Compromise and had tolerated high tariffs that protected Northern industry and hurt Southern trade. Most recently, the South had furnished three-quarters of the troops for the Mexican War. But there were limits.[1]

In 1850, Henry Clay brought about his last great compromise. On January 29 he presented in the Senate eight resolutions aimed at resolving the main grievances between North and South. California would be admitted to the Union as a free state. Territorial governments would be created in the rest of the region surrendered by Mexico, and Texas would gain federal compensation for surrendering its boundary claim against New Mexico. The slave trade, but not slavery, would be abolished within the District of Columbia, and Congress would be denied the power to regulate interstate slave trade. Two days later, the *Richmond Examiner* turned its editorial guns on Clay and his Compromise: "It is the capstone of treason on a life of fraud, self seeking and disguised abolition. To call those resolutions a compromise is the most wanton, base and monstrous insult to the Southern States which has yet been perpetrated on them. . . . The truth is, Mr. Clay surrendered one half of the South's rights in the Missouri Compromise, and now seeks to sacrifice the other half in a California Compromise."[2]

What should the South do? From Mississippi came the call for a Southern Convention to meet in Nashville in June and to be composed of delegates from all the Southern states. The *Examiner* believed it vital that Virginia send a delegation. Northerners thought they could work their will on the South, so united Southern action was required to oppose the Compromise. "It was our imagined insensibility to insult and wrong that invited their aggressions," asserted an editorial in the paper. "It was their settled belief in our imbecility and pusillanimous forbearance under every provocation, that prompted their injurious conduct."[3]

Many Virginians did not support the idea of a convention, which might imply eventual secession from the Union if Southern demands were not met. Indeed, in South Carolina, always at the forefront of secessionist sentiment, committees of safety and correspondence had been formed in imitation of the American Revolution. Meetings were held around the state of Virginia in the spring of 1850 to discuss the matter. The meeting in Richmond was addressed by Adrian Judson Crane, a local Whig leader, who made a tearful plea for opposition to the proposed convention. The *Examiner* called Crane a drunken lunatic, but by the end of April it was clear that the majority in Richmond, which the paper then scornfully called "this very dirty and insignificant village," opposed participation.[5] So did more than half of Virginia's counties. In the end the commonwealth was represented in the convention by a token delegation of three. The convention failed utterly to produce unified Southern opposition to the coming Compromise.

The final series of bills that made up the Compromise of 1850 was approved by Congress in September and signed by Millard Fillmore, who had assumed the presidency after Zachary Taylor died in July. California would be a free state, as Clay had initially proposed, but the new territorial governments of New Mexico and Utah would have power over "all rightful subjects of legislation," including slavery. Although the slave trade was abolished in the District of Columbia, the slaveholding community had reason to be pleased with the stringent new Fugitive Slave Law. For the *Richmond Examiner,* though, the Compromise was a great defeat for the South. "The South is prostrate and bound hand and foot. . . . The North has broken down the walls of the Southern City; and have yet to plunder it, to burn it, and to massacre its inhabitants. They have no more thought of leaving the work they have commenced, than the squirrel of quitting the nut whose bitter bark he has just cleared off."[6] Daniel lamented that the Compromise had been supported by a leading Democrat, Howell Cobb of Georgia, Speaker of the House of Representatives, who had allied himself with the enemy, the Whigs.

In late September 1850, John Daniel went to the lion's den, making a trip north

John Moncure Daniel in Richmond in the 1850s. Valentine Museum.

to Massachusetts, the heart of abolitionism. He reported to his readers that he visited Springfield, where a meeting of local residents at the town hall passed resolutions vowing to resist any attempt by U.S. marshals to capture fugitive slaves under the new law. In Boston, he went to hear a sermon by the celebrated abolitionist clergyman Theodore Parker. Daniel despised the abolitionist movement, and he found a particular sort of stingy, grasping Yankee despicable. However, there were a few New England intellectuals whose attainments he esteemed. One was Ralph Waldo Emerson, and another was Theodore Parker. The *Examiner* had earlier printed another sermon by Parker, who, Daniel told his readers, was outstanding in the English-speaking world for his scholarship and intellectual power. But this Sunday in Boston, said Daniel, Parker had denounced the Constitution and the laws of the United States with great bitterness and had complained that public opinion in Boston was "degraded"; in contrast to London, where slaveowners were scorned, a great slaveowner who visited Boston would be treated with perfect courtesy.[7] (One imagines Daniel sitting in a pew and thinking to himself, "What would Parker have to say to his congregation about the proper treatment for the proslavery editor in their midst?")

After Daniel returned to Richmond, he told his readers that the South no longer had the protection she needed for "her institution." However, he could not agree with those who saw secession as the only remedy. Conjuring up memories of rebel Nat Turner without mentioning his name, Daniel wrote that "Civil war would be secession's inseparable concomitant, which would light the fires of insurrection throughout the Southern confines, and bring murder and rapine to every Southern hearth. . . . It is a desperate resort, to be had only when every other remedy has failed, and association with the Yankee has become absolutely loathsome and insupportable."[8]

The problem, as Daniel saw it, was that the South needed to find some way to redress an imbalance in power; it seemed that the South kept losing out. One could perhaps discuss ways Southern states might tax Northern manufactures. Governor John Floyd was also proposing a new convention of slave states to ensure compliance with the Fugitive Slave Law, but the prospects were doubtful. Perhaps the only hope was that the United States would someday find itself in a major foreign war, which would restore the unity of interest and opinion—proslavery opinion, Daniel did not need to say—that had existed when the Union was formed. If nothing of that kind occurred, said the *Richmond Examiner*, the passage of time would bring separation.[9]

Through all his politicking and editing, Daniel also kept his eye on culture. The *Examiner* serialized Charles Dickens's new novel, *David Copperfield*, on its front page and was always full of reports on and criticism of new writing and art, with particular attention given to local genius Edgar Allan Poe.

The relationship between Poe and Daniel was both vexed and significant. The world probably owes a debt to Daniel for scaring Poe, as related earlier, out of a duel that might have terminated the poet's short life even earlier than it ended. Beyond that, Daniel did much to advance Poe's reputation although Daniel was criticized at the time, as he has been more recently, for his objective and hard-hitting criticism of a man whom he viewed as a unique genius but one with many flaws in both his character and his writing.

In the late summer of 1849, Poe, who had been in the North lecturing on "The Poetic Principle," returned to Richmond for another presentation. Daniel attended Poe's lecture on August 17 and told *Examiner* readers that he had been glad to hear Poe explode the idea that poetry must have a purpose. Poe had then recited a number of poems, but his recitation had been monotonous and disappointing. Poe, said Daniel, was a man of decided genius, but his reputation would rest on a very small number of works. Most of his prose compositions were "the children of want and dyspepsia," and only two of his poems, "The Raven" and "Dreamland," were not execrably bad. Furthermore, it was rumored that Poe's life resembled that of certain rowdies of the Elizabethan age; Poe was a Marlowe rather than a Shakespeare.[10]

The article distressed Poe. He wrote to his beloved mother-in-law, Maria Clemm, that his Richmond lecture had been a great success. He had never been received with so much enthusiasm. The papers had done nothing but praise him before and after the lecture, with one exception: the *Richmond Examiner.* Poe enclosed the offending article, noting that "It is written by Daniel—the man whom I challenged when I was here last year."[11]

The poet had no thought of challenging the editor again. He went to see Daniel. There is no record of what was said, but the conversation ended with Daniel offering Poe a desk and at least part-time employment at the *Examiner* reviewing books and writing other literary pieces. A number of Poe's poems were sent to the paper's composing room to be set in type and kept for future use.[12]

Poe soon left Richmond for Norfolk, returned to Richmond to repeat his lecture, and then left for the North, where, he told John Daniel, he would publish a new volume of his work.[13] Less than two weeks later Poe was dead in Baltimore. Poe's death distressed Daniel. He told his readers that it seemed only a few hours since the poet had left his office in Richmond, full of hope and in better health than he had enjoyed for years. Daniel still hoped that the news was not true.[14] He promised to return to the subject of Edgar Allan Poe, and did so, first in a long resumé of Poe's life and then in a long and thoughtful consideration of Poe's work.

Daniel wrote that he had reflected long and carefully on what to say about the poet. The man's life and character contained many blemishes, "yet it appears to every mind, hard and unfeeling in the extreme, to speak aught that is ill of the newly dead." Poe was an erudite man and the best conversationalist that Daniel had ever met. But Poe was overfond of talking and was known to sit down in front of a tavern next to any sort of dirty dunce and start expounding on his grand designs. The fact was, said Daniel, that thousands had seen Poe drunk in the streets of Richmond. As a critic, Poe was the best since Hazlitt, and his critical writing had made the reputation of the *Southern Literary Messenger.* As a poet, Poe left little that was good, but that little was "super-eminently good." Similarly, Daniel thought that much of his prose had little value; he could not paint men well because he did not understand them, and because he was not like other men. But he had written a few exceptional things like *The Narrative of Arthur Gordon Pym,* which readers had neglected.[15]

Daniel drew from his *Examiner* articles on Poe and wrote a long essay that appeared in the March 1850 issue of the *Southern Literary Messenger.* Daniel said that Poe's mother had written to him the day she learned of her son's passing to ask him to report on his death, to speak well of him. Daniel wrote, however, that he could not ignore Poe's blemishes if he were to give a full picture of "this most brilliant and original individual." Poe's taste for drink was not a question of pleasure or excitement but a disease; once the poison had passed Poe's lips, he would go to a bar and drink glass after glass until stupefied. But far beyond that, Daniel wrote, Poe's writing, although uneven, contained much that was pure gold. If people could not appreciate Poe, it was in good part because he had created a new kind of writing. James Russell Lowell thought Poe "aesthetically deficient" as a critic, but that was simply because Poe was incapable of appreciating Lowell and his set. Of all Poe's work, Daniel wrote, one poem in particular, "The Raven," was sublime, and "on its dusky wings he will sail securely over the gulf of oblivion to the eternal shore beyond." Daniel also repeated Poe's own fictions about his visits to Greece and Russia as a youth. In Europe, Charles Baudelaire picked up Daniel's portrait of the genius, outcast, and supposed adventurer, and in 1852 published in the *Revue des Deux Mondes* the first of his three articles which helped make Poe famous in France.[16]

Educated people in Richmond were good readers. The city had good bookstores, and the Richmond public library was making sizable additions to its collection, which, as noted, had numbered not more than 2,000 volumes when Daniel lived there.[17] Someone in the state legislature suggested a further step toward public enlightenment: opening to the public the collections of the Virginia State Library. That was a step too far, in the view of the editor of the *Examiner,* whose great-uncle had been responsible for the current regulations that restricted public access. It was certainly John Daniel himself who blasted the legislative proposal:

> Fashionable mamas will stroll into the Library with white-faced, slim-legged, fantastical city children. They will make it a prancing place and literary nursery for their disagreeable brats. Costly engravings, maps, and hot-pressed volumes will be smeared over with gingerbread and apples, and stuck together with candies. . . . Marriageable young ladies will make the State Library their hunting ground during the Legislature's sessions. The thousand and one literary idlers and trash readers will come there to pull down the books and yawn away their lazy hours. But all these will be a handful to the herds of Richmond lawyers, who will hereafter prowl about the Library.[18]

One might marvel at Daniel's readiness to alienate the many readers who were parents, or liked to browse through books—or were Richmond lawyers. But the editor no doubt calculated that if one did not put a specific name on those he mocked, readers would often be as ready to laugh—or at least to find truth in the depiction—as they would be to take offense. The following year, 1850, when the cornerstone was laid for the monument to be capped by Thomas Crawford's statue of George Washington, outside the Capitol in Richmond, the *Examiner* described the proceedings as "essential stupidity." It reported how local Masons had gone through their "mummery," several brass bands performed "with unexampled fury," and there had been a large turnout by the Sons of Temperance "remarkable for their red noses and faces."[19] Sales of the paper increased further.

At the beginning of 1853, the great British writer Henry Makepeace Thackeray visited Richmond during an American lecture tour. Details are sketchy, but it seems that Thackeray and his younger traveling companion, artist Eyre Crowe, met Daniel and perhaps spent time with him. Thackeray had been advised earlier to go easy on the question of slavery, and he did so in his American lectures. In any case, he wrote home, the blacks in Richmond were obviously happy and well off.[20] (His compatriot Charles Dickens, visiting Richmond a decade earlier, had seen things differently. For Dickens, Richmond was a place where, despite pretty villas and cheerful houses, the overall scene was set by the decay and gloom of slavery; he left "with a grateful heart that I was not doomed to live where slavery was."[21]) While in the North, Eyre Crowe had bought a copy of the shocking new novel *Uncle Tom's Cabin*; Thackeray declined to read it. One morning in Richmond, Crowe was sitting by himself "reading the ably conducted local newspaper of which our kind friend was the editor." It was not the editorials or articles on politics that attracted his eye as much as the columns containing the announcements of slave sales. Crowe decided this might be an interesting scene, and he went off to the slave market to make sketches. When the buyers and dealers caught sight of what he was doing, all business stopped. Crowe was told in no uncertain terms to stop drawing and leave.[22] After Thackeray returned to England, he wrote *The Virginians*, a novel set during the American Revolution, as a kind of tribute to the white ladies and gentlemen he had met during his Virginia visit.

Meanwhile, important events were occurring in the lives of some of Daniel's gentlemen friends: they were getting married. One of these was Henry Augustine Washington, to whom Daniel confided his account of the Johnston duel in 1852, and who was both a good friend and a distant cousin.[23] Some years earlier Henry Washington had been rumored as a candidate for Congress, but at the end of 1848 the Board of Visitors of the College of William and Mary in Williamsburg chose him to become the Professor of Political Economy and History. The College then had a total of six professors including its president.[24] One was Nathaniel Beverley Tucker, the Professor of Law, whose jurist father had been called the American Gladstone—while Professor Tucker was well known as the author of *Partisan Leader*, an 1836 novel describing a revolt by the Southern states. In July 1852, several months after Daniel's duel with Edward Johnston, Henry Washington married Cynthia Tucker, the daughter of this professor.[25] His cousin John Daniel wrote him a warm, indeed antic, letter of congratulations replete with quotations from a Catullus ode and other amatory poetry in Latin and with praise for "the very beautiful and elegant young person who was once pointed out to me in the Richmond Theatre as Judge Tuckers daughter."[26] Washington and his wife had two daughters, both of whom died in childhood, and after not quite six years of marriage he himself died, at age thirty-seven.

But what did John Moncure Daniel know of love and romance when he was in his twenties? Robert Hughes wrote years later that Daniel was neither a man hater nor a woman hater. He was attractive to women, and Hughes personally knew "ladies of exalted character . . . who hold him now in affectionate remembrance."[27] One was perhaps the lady Daniel took to Zachary Taylor's inaugural ball in 1849. Then or soon afterward, according to Moncure Conway's autobiography (which is not always accurate, though he was explicit about cousin John's lady), he became "attached" to a very lovely lady.[28] Conway identifies her as Eliza Barbour, daughter of noted orator and former congressman John Strode Barbour. Eliza was also the younger sister of James Barbour, Daniel's friend from the days when they read law together in Fredericksburg. It may be relevant to Daniel's pursuit of Eliza Barbour that in September 1848 the *Examiner* reported a political debate at Orange Court House in which the little-known, and not very prepossessing, James Barbour had trounced his older and experienced opponent. The article, obviously written by Daniel, continued, "Years ago, we recollect to have been thrown much in contact with this same Mr. James Barbour; and beneath shy and reserved manners, we found one of the most powerful and acute intellects which we had ever met."[29]

In the collections of the Huntington Library in California there are a number of letters exchanged between Daniel and his friends—and one sonnet, undated, in his handwriting (the only piece of his poetry extant):

Dear girl, it is a common wish, tho' vain,
That all thy days might glide in sunshine by,
And life no shadow know of misery:
Tis well the cup humanity must drain
Is dashed with bitter, tho' the lip would fain
Turn from the draught—for they are strong alone
To live and act; whose spirits oft have known
The stern and wholesome discipline of pain.
Therefore I say not, "may no greif [*sic*] be thine":
But whether joy or sorrow mark thy way,
O! be thy strength sufficient for thy day,
and cloudless sunlight gild that days decline
So shalt thou know, life's load at last laid down,
Who meekest bears the cross, is worthiest of the crown.

Was this perhaps written to Eliza Barbour? Conceivably, although it is certainly less than passionate—and perhaps tells us, incidentally, that Daniel did well not to seek a reputation as a poet. Yet this sonnet is certainly not lower in quality than many works of established poets of the period, including that prime object of Daniel criticism, Edgar Allan Poe.

Moncure Conway claimed that he always believed his cousin's suit for Eliza's hand would have succeeded had it not been for her brother, who was "frightened by the personalities and duels" of John Moncure Daniel.[30] If we are to believe Conway, James Barbour warned his sister not to become engaged to the combative and fiery young editor. Several years later, Eliza Barbour instead married Capt. George Thompson, who came from Culpeper County, as did her own family. She and the captain had six children, several of whom later became prominent. She died in 1887,[31] two years after Robert Hughes's mention of the unnamed ladies—or was it just one lady?—who still continued to hold in affectionate remembrance John Moncure Daniel, who had now been in his grave for more than two decades.

Certainly Daniel could be attractive and kind to women. If he had been a misanthrope, as some claimed, in his early years, he must have changed as he matured. Two years after the wedding of his friend Henry Washington, the wife of Thomas Wynne met a young lady from Williamsburg who still recalled "with no little pleasure" having met Daniel at the wedding.[32] A decade after Daniel's pursuit of Eliza Barbour, Mary Chesnut sat next to him at dinner one evening and found him "bright and clever beyond my wildest hopes."[33] In 1864, a young woman in Richmond named Constance Cary, who was beginning to write stories and poetry, ventured to submit a war poem to the awesome editor of the *Examiner.* Many decades later, she recalled: "I had met Mr. Daniel and considered him as unapproachable as the north pole, . . . but . . . the Jove-like editor not only gave me a place on the editorial page, but came to call afterward, and continued to be a kind friend. . . . Mr. Daniel, too, gave me sane and strong counsel."[34]

"Sane and strong counsel" meant that Daniel did not believe a Virginia gentleman had to be less objective about women writers than about men. In 1850, for example, the *Examiner* carried a long column on the death of Margaret Fuller, the pioneering woman correspondent of the *New York Tribune* who drowned off Long Island with her husband, the Marchese Ossoli. Fuller, said the *Examiner*, had been an uncommon woman. Although up to the end of her life she had expressed herself with awkwardness and difficulty on paper, in conversation she had poured out her thoughts with a brilliance that astonished all her listeners. (One wonders whether Daniel had perhaps met her on one of his visits to New York before she went to Europe.) Moreover, in the last minutes of her life, she had, Daniel said, exhibited a heroic nature, giving up her life preserver to a sailor so that he could reach shore and try to rescue others on board.[35]

If Daniel did not succeed in love as a young man, he at least rose fast in society. By the spring of 1849, when Daniel was twenty-three years old, he was already identified as a distinguished citizen of Virginia. The *National Intelligencer* reported in late April 1849, in a column that the *Richmond Examiner* was pleased to reprint on April 27, that the Virginia legislature had voted to present a sword to President

Zachary Taylor in honor of his courage and achievements in Mexico. The sword was presented to the president at the White House on April 24 by five men who constituted "the Committee of distinguished citizens of Virginia" and included both R. T. Daniel and J. M. Daniel. Such things do not happen by chance. As the *Examiner* noted, the committee had been named by the governor, who was John B. Floyd, the father-in-law of Daniel's friend Robert Hughes. We do not know how well Zachary Taylor was informed about newspapers outside Washington, but he may well have known that one committee member had aimed (and was continuing to aim) some pretty sharp arrows at him. Still he was no doubt pleased to receive the sword, and John Daniel was clearly pleased to be one of the presenters along with his uncle Raleigh.

Daniel could find further confirmation of his rise in Virginia society in the Virginia legislature's election of him as one of the three members of the Council of State. The was a hoary institution, created as the executive body of the new colony in 1621 and kept in existence by Virginia's 1776 state constitution. The constitution of 1830 had reduced it from eight members to three, and left it with little to do. Virginia legislators saw to it that the state's governor had few powers, and the responsibility of the Council of State was to make sure that he exercised these powers properly. Membership on the council, whose president was also the state's lieutenant governor, was nonetheless prestigious.[36] The president and lieutenant governor had been Peter Vivian Daniel, the editor's great-uncle, not many years earlier.

Robert Hughes later wrote that when John Moncure Daniel learned of his election to the Council of State he also learned that one of the people who had supported his election was a kinsman who, as a Whig, was often a target of the *Examiner*'s editorials. There can be little doubt that this supporter was his uncle, Raleigh Travers Daniel, who had also been a member of the council. John Daniel wrote to his uncle in embarrassment:

> My Dear Sir: You have heaped the living coals of fire on my head with an unsparing hand. I may say to you in reply, without inconsistency even in that which I have written frequently, though always in levity, that you have set me an example of good taste, courteous manners and kindly feeling, which I have followed, alas! too little.
>
> I would tell you this through my next issue, did I not think it most proper for me to say nothing about my election in my editorial capacity. I, therefore, take this means of assuring you that the contrast in our tone this morning is to me most mortifying.[37]

Daniel's election to the Council of State may have been backed by reform-minded members of the legislature for a cynical reason: to help ensure the abolition of the antiquated body by adding a new member who had many political enemies.[38] In 1851, the state adopted a constitution that for the first time provided for the popular election of both governor and lieutenant governor and abolished the Council of State. This development did not seem to matter much to John Moncure Daniel; indeed the *Examiner* welcomed the reforms. The important thing was that he had been marked as a man of importance.

Despite such prominence, however, Daniel was not becoming a man of wealth. Behind the masthead of the *Richmond Examiner* lay a history of financial problems. On November 27, 1852, Daniel wrote a frank and full account of this history to Robert M. T. Hunter, a leading Democrat and one of the two U.S. senators from Virginia. The *Examiner* had been set up in 1847 without a cent of money, and its original proprietors had been happy "to throw it in my hands" after six months, on condition that Daniel would assume the paper's debts. Daniel wrote that under his management the paper's circulation had mounted, and was continuing to do so. But he had started without funds, and the paper had not at first been profitable, in spite of good sales. (He did not mention advertising, but the *Examiner* contains considerably fewer ads for those years than do other Richmond newspapers, such as the *Whig*.) In 1850, Daniel had therefore been compelled to sell the paper back to Bennett De Witt. But Daniel had continued as editor, had gotten his affairs in better order, and in 1851 had repurchased the paper from De Witt and his new partners the Horsleys. Over the year that had passed since then, "the paper has been quite profitable; and I have at this time a subscription list larger by seven hundred than any other newspaper in the State of Va. I have also paid part of the debt incurred in the re-purchase, and now owe only twenty-five hundred dollars in the world. This I shall also be able in time to pay from the receipts, but while doing so I am cumbered, and the process is slow."[39] The account that Daniel gave the Senator accords with two agreements in Daniel's handwriting. By the first agreement, dated December 3, 1850, Daniel sells the paper to De Witt and derives from the sale no cash, but De Witt's agreement to take on the paper's debts in an amount not to exceed $6,500. By the second, dated October 18, 1851, Daniel repurchases the paper; he gives De Witt a note for $2,500, payable in six months, and authorizes him to raise $22,000 for the *Examiner* over the coming four years (half of which is to be paid to Daniel and half to be retained by De Witt) by collecting debts owing the paper and by selling new subscriptions.[40]

Daniel faced other difficulties of a financial nature that stemmed from an enterprising Yankee with the singular name of Shearjashub Spooner.[41] Born in Vermont in 1809, Spooner had become a successful dentist in New York—so successful that he had been able to retire from dentistry in his early thirties and devote himself to art. In 1842 he had bought in England a set of 100 plates illustrating Shakespeare's plays that had been commissioned half a century earlier by John

Boydell, an English engraver and printseller and Lord Mayor of London. The plates of Boydell's "Shakespeare Gallery" were made from paintings by famous artists, who included Joshua Reynolds and Benjamin West, but the etchings made from them did not sell as well as expected.[42]

After Boydell died in 1804, the plates were sold at auction and then resold; reportedly each time they were sold they were reworked. After they were sold to Spooner, as "old metal," he had them reworked again and announced that he would produce a new album of the Shakespeare Gallery, to be sold by subscription. But would not prints made from the reworked plates be much inferior to the originals? Yes, said a number of articles that appeared in British publications, including one in the April 1848 issue of the *Art Union Journal* that someone (conceivably John Daniel's quondam artist friend Arthur Edward Peticolas) noticed in Richmond.[43] The plates also had their defenders. Spooner told friends in America that the British articles had been planted by London dealers who were worried that Spooner's sales would hurt their own print trade. He got a number of prominent Americans including Washington Irving, Horace Greeley, William Cullen Bryant, and John James Audubon to sign statements recommending his version of the Shakespeare Gallery. In fact, Spooner said in his prospectus, his reworked plates were an improvement on the originals: "the lines are cut in deeper, which gives the prints a sharper and clearer appearance." (Perhaps as a dentist he did not care for shadings.) There were however not just English critics but some New Yorkers who did not share the judgment of Messrs. Irving, Greeley, Bryant, and Audubon. Such New Yorkers, said Spooner, were simply guilty of "black mail."[44]

By the beginning of 1851, an agent of Shearjashub Spooner had come south and was working in and around Richmond selling subscriptions for sets of the Boydell engravings for $100 a set. John Moncure Daniel leaped to the attack. He did not like Yankees as a type, and he was particularly outraged by this one with the rare name. On January 14, 1851, an editorial appeared in the *Examiner* claiming flatly that such engravings were almost worthless; the subscription offer amounted to a cheat, a swindle, an imposture. Daniel concluded the editorial by stating that "The public and the press of the Southern States cannot be too often warned of Yankee books, maps and engravings. If they take it as a social axiom that every proffer and offer which is made to them from the North is a trap for their fleeces, and that every man who crosses Mason and Dixon's line is a swindler and a rogue until he has given proof to the contrary; they will save themselves much mortification and vexation, and a considerable amount of hard-earned money."

It seems clear that Spooner's subscription drive in Virginia suffered as a result of Daniel's editorial. Spooner claimed later that the editorial cost him three hundred subscriptions, which meant $30,000, and that for six months his Southern agent could not even meet expenses.[45]

Five months after the editorial, in June 1851, Daniel traveled to New York City to look into the purchase of new type and a new press for the *Examiner*. On June 16 he was arrested on the basis of a warrant sworn by an attorney for Shearjashub Spooner in the city's court of common pleas. (A *capias*, or arrest order, was then a normal method in New York of beginning a civil suit against someone not resident in New York. There was, it seems, only one other state which ever employed this method with any frequency: Virginia.[46])

Spooner's affidavit told the court that the *Richmond Examiner* editorial had cost Spooner at least $10,000 in profits. It named John M. Daniel as the proprietor and editor of the paper, although not as the author of the editorial. How long John Daniel spent under arrest is not known. He found a New York lawyer, Henry Breckenridge, to represent him, and when Judge L. B. Woodruff of the court of common pleas set a bail bond of $2,000 Daniel raised the sum from friends in Virginia.

When the court held an initial hearing on June 24, 1851, Breckenridge asked that the suit be dismissed because John Daniel was not the proprietor and senior editor of the *Richmond Examiner*, as alleged in the suit, but only a junior editor on a salary. (The suit did not charge him as the author of the article and therefore legally responsible.) Daniel himself swore that he did not consider himself responsible for the debts and liabilities of the newspaper.

Unfortunately for Daniel, Spooner produced C. Glenn Peebles, who had been in Richmond to report for the *New York Post*. Peebles had met Daniel, and Peebles testified that Daniel had told him he was fully responsible for the *Examiner* editorials. Judge Woodruff thereupon refused to dismiss the case. Even if Daniel was not the proprietor, he had lent his name, influence, and ability to increase the paper's standing and circulation, and could therefore be held responsible if it published libelous matter. When Daniel returned to Richmond at the end of June, he faced the prospect of a trial to be held at an uncertain date on unfriendly territory and with unknown results.

The New York press did not take a friendly approach. Horace Greeley had earlier vouched for Spooner's plates, and his *New York Tribune* was very critical of Daniel, noting his attack on Yankee agents. (Greeley had some personal experience with libel cases: James Fenimore Cooper had sued him for libel a decade earlier; Greeley got off with a payment of just two hundred dollars.[47]) The *New York Express* asserted that Daniel needed a little education before he returned south; not all Yankees were rogues and swindlers. In the South, however, a number of papers saw in Spooner's suit a Northern plot to gag the Southern press and force it to take a submissive tone. The *Southside Democrat* of Petersburg, edited by Daniel's fellow Democrat Roger Pryor, wrote that "It has come to pass that, for his able advocacy of Southern rights, Mr. Daniel has incurred the hatred, and now feels the prosecuting sting, of abolition. Shall he not be sustained in his difficulties by the sympathy and approval of every generous Southern heart?"[48]

For his part, Daniel wrote that he was "hated by political opponents and Yankee swindlers" because he was an editor who "discharged his public duties with determination, with fearlessness, with power, and, more than all that, with *effect*." He could no doubt avoid trouble by trying to propitiate and conciliate, by becoming "a careful coward and a respectable hypocrite," but he would never do that. "We have too much pride, too much self-reliance, too firm a faith in the might of truth," wrote Daniel, "to pay such a price for security."[49]

Not all of the Richmond press sided with Daniel. This incident occurred in the summer of 1851, when the quarrel between Daniel and Edward Johnston of the *Whig* was moving them toward a duel. Johnston did not know, or professed not to know, that Daniel had sold his interest in the *Examiner* back to Bennett De Witt before the article on Spooner's Gallery had appeared. The *Whig* claimed that the *Examiner*, in order to escape monetary damages, "went into a New York court and swore to an affidavit of facts which every man in this community knew to be wilfully false."[50]

In September 1851, the case was transferred from New York City's court of common pleas to the U.S. Court for the Southern District of New York, perhaps because the defendant was not a resident of the state. Spooner's formal complaint was filed in the federal court only a year later, on September 2, 1852. Spooner had undertaken a second major project, to prepare two other major sets of engravings from France for subscription sales. These were known as the Musée Francais and the Musée Royal, and they had first been offered for sale a half-century earlier.[51] Spooner wanted the U.S. government to agree that they could be imported duty free; the government would not do so, and the project stalled. But if Spooner could not make money out of engravings, perhaps he could out of Daniel. Spooner's complaint asked for $50,000 in damages. Even if the eventual court decision should award a much smaller sum, it might still bankrupt John Daniel.

The editor, meanwhile, stayed hard at work. He was focused on the 1852 presidential election that could see a Democrat drive the Whigs from the White House. Daniel continued to militate for the Young American wing of the Democratic party. In 1851, Young America's main organ, the *Democratic Review*, had been acquired from John L. O'Sullivan by a fiery horse-breeder's son from Kentucky named George Nicholas Sanders. This gentleman had been a financial promoter, an agent of the Hudson's Bay Company, and a friend of European revolutionists, for whom he tried to engineer a sale of 40,000 muskets in the revolutionary year of 1848. Sanders's activism was reflected in the *Democratic Review*. Its May 1852 issue, noting that the subscription list had leaped to a record 30,000, focused on the upcoming Democratic national convention. The *Review* featured the views of John

Moncure Daniel in its leading article and carried a portrait of Daniel across from the title page. The article warned that the nomination of Lewis Cass, soon to turn seventy, as the party's candidate would be an "anachronism." The best candidate would be a younger man, around thirty-five, which was the minimum age set by the Constitution. (Senator Stephen Douglas, the *Review* did not need to mention, had just turned thirty-nine.) As Daniel had written in his *Examiner*, Young America was not against honorable old Democratic statesmen like Andrew Jackson and John C. Calhoun; it did oppose "the impotent, the imbecile, the corrupt, the worthless nonentities. . . . We can endure all Noodledom with entire composure with the assistance of friends like the brilliant editor of the Examiner."[52] Daniel, said George Sanders, had taken his place high on the roll of those who conducted the press in America. In Young America's fight, Sanders thought, such an ally was worth a thousand enemies.

At the beginning of June, the national convention of the Democratic party opened in Baltimore, the site of the five previous Democratic conventions. No state was to send more delegates to the 1852 convention than it had electoral votes. This meant fifteen delegates for Virginia. But Virginia sent 100 people, including John Moncure Daniel. In the end, only fifteen took their seats.[53] Perhaps we can assume that Daniel was one of those seated.

The notable candidates as the convention began were Lewis Cass, James Buchanan, William Marcy, and the young Illinois Senator and spokesman for Young America, Stephen Douglas. There were as well the favorite sons of various states—and a dark horse from New Hampshire, Franklin Pierce, who had served earlier in both the U.S. House of Representatives and the Senate and as a brigadier general in the Mexican War. Winning the nomination required the votes of two-thirds of the 288 delegates. In earlier Democratic conventions, the nomination had been decided fairly quickly, although in 1844 it had taken as many as nine ballots to decide on James K. Polk. Now, in 1852, things went differently. Over two days and thirty-three ballots, the contest was among the top four contenders, with each of the four in the lead at one point or another. Virginia cast its fifteen votes consistently for James Buchanan. No one was voting for Pierce. On June 5, Virginia abruptly changed its vote on the thirty-fourth ballot to support D. S. Dickinson of New York. Dickinson said that while the Virginians had done him a great honor, he hoped they would join him in supporting Lewis Cass.[54] There had been earlier reports that the Virginia delegates had been urging the nomination of their fellow Virginian Senator R. M. T. Hunter.[55] But on the thirty-fifth ballot, Virginia cast its votes for Franklin Pierce. It was the first time his name had appeared, and Virginia had been first to support him. On the forty-ninth ballot Pierce became the Democratic presidential candidate.

To Be an Envoy

About a year before the 1852 Baltimore convention, when John Daniel had not yet bought back the *Examiner* from Bennett De Witt, and when no one could predict a Democratic victory in 1852, Daniel wrote to some well-connected friend—probably James Barbour—that he wanted to look to the future. If, sometime in the future, there should be a Democratic administration, he would ask for help in getting "a chargé-ship in some European country, where I can make some money and see the world."[1]

It may seem strange today that a successful American editor thought he would be better off financially on an American diplomatic salary. A permanent chargé d'affaires, the rank then given to the chiefs of a number of less important American diplomatic missions, received a salary of $4,500 a year plus a one-time "outfit" equivalent to a year's salary for expenses and travel getting to the post, and on return home he received an "infit" of a quarter's salary. This would all have seemed a very large amount of money to the editor's father, the poor country doctor, and it must have been considerably more money than John Daniel was then earning in Richmond.

In November 1852 Franklin Pierce was elected president. The Whigs had won the White House for Zachary Taylor four years earlier, and this time they ran another Mexican War general, Winfield Scott, against Pierce. It was the final Whig disaster. Scott made a respectable showing in the popular vote, but Pierce carried all but four states and finished with 254 electoral votes to Scott's 42. As always, Richmond voted Whig, but by only a small majority, and Virginia overall voted solidly Democratic for Franklin Pierce. The *Examiner* had given fierce and effective support to the Democratic campaign.

John Moncure Daniel still wanted a diplomatic appointment, and for this he needed strong political support. Friends in Virginia could no doubt help, but Washington was where the appointments game was played. That was the sense of the letter Daniel wrote to Senator Robert M. T. Hunter on November 27, 1852. Hunter was in good standing with the incoming president, who in fact wanted him to join his new cabinet.[2] Daniel asked Hunter to support him for appointment as

Robert M. T. Hunter, U.S. senator from Virginia and, later, Confederate senator and secretary of state. National Archives.

a chargé d'affaires somewhere in Europe, just for a year. He laid out his financial situation in frank terms. The $4,500 salary coupled with the outfit and infit allowances would leave him, after a year, with several thousand dollars in hand. He continued:

> I could leave the paper in the hands of an able and ambitious editor who would willingly conduct it for the nett [*sic*] profits of the year, and I would be back at my post before times of serious political importance to any of us could return. The money would clear away embarrassments that have weighed on me for years, the office would give me position in the eyes of our little State world, and the sight of foreign countries would invigorate and revive my mind. In short this office would do me a great deal of good personally, and would render myself and my newspaper more efficient for my friends and my country.
>
> That you will exercise a powerful influence on the new administration, whether in the cabinet or out of it, appears to me very certain. At least you will be the most influential man in Virginia. If it shall be consistent with your dig-

> nity and sense of propriety to ask such a place for me, I should be much pleased to know it. . . .
>
> With the exception of one person, (an intimate associate—Mr. James Barbour) you are the first and only person to whom I have mentioned this subject. For I do not intend to become a beggar for office—not a public one at least . . .

Daniel had obviously thought matters through before writing to the senator. As the *Examiner* commented several months later, there would soon be "a dead calm" in politics in Virginia, with no elections to national or key state posts for two years after the May 1853 elections for the powerful state Board of Public Works.[3] Daniel was not, as he said to the senator, planning to miss out on any big political developments.

Daniel was also trying to be realistic by aiming at an appointment as a chargé d'affaires. He was only twenty-seven years old. Very seldom was anyone so young named to head a diplomatic post, although John Quincy Adams had been appointed American minister to the Netherlands when not quite twenty-seven. Daniel's Richmond friend Judge W. W. Crump had been still younger, just twenty-five, when appointed American chargé d'affaires in Chile in 1844. Chargé d'affaires was not the highest American diplomatic rank; it was not as high as minister. Unlike other major countries, the United States then had no ambassadors or embassies abroad on grounds that this would be too high a level of diplomatic representation for a republic that eschewed foreign entanglement. American diplomatic missions were legations, and the top ten legations were headed by American ministers who received a salary of $7,500, almost double the $4,500 received by the chargés d'affaires who oversaw the seventeen smaller American legations.

Daniel knew that he needed support from others beside Hunter. The senator had no doubt been flattered when the members of the Virginia delegation, which had included Daniel, made noises about nominating him as the Democratic presidential candidate at the Baltimore convention. However, as Daniel acknowledged to the senator, the two of them were only acquaintances, not friends or kinsmen.

Soon after his election, President Pierce completed his new cabinet. Jefferson Davis, who had served as an officer in Mexico, would become secretary of war. William Marcy, secretary of war in the administration of President Polk, was appointed secretary of state; two decades earlier, as a senator from New York, Marcy had made the famous statement "To the victor belong the spoils of the enemy." Decades would pass before the United States would create a career diplomatic corps. There was no question, as Franklin Pierce neared the moment of his inauguration in March 1853, but that he and his new secretary of state would continue the traditional diplomatic spoils system—a system that the United States, alone among developed countries, would continue into the twentieth and even the twenty-first century.

While still a youth, John Daniel had met Marcy in Richmond, at the table of his great-uncle Peter Vivian Daniel, associate justice of the U.S. Supreme Court. He had also made the acquaintance of Jefferson Davis, presumably either when Davis was a member of the House of Representatives before the Mexican War, or when he served as a senator afterward.[4] We can assume that Peter Daniel may have now approached Marcy—or Davis or perhaps even Franklin Pierce—on behalf of his great-nephew, just as he would do some years later with another new administration. It is even conceivable that Marcy and the Justice met in Richmond; we know that Marcy stopped briefly in Richmond in late February on his way back to Washington from the West Indies.[5] There is, however, no record of an approach by Peter Daniel on his great-nephew's behalf to Marcy or to others. What the record does contain is a total of nine letters written to Pierce on behalf of John Moncure Daniel in March 1853. The writers included several members of Congress, including two senators: Robert M. T. Hunter of Virginia and Stephen Douglas of Illinois, who had enjoyed John Daniel's support as Democratic politicians, and possibly in the Baltimore convention of 1852.[6] There was a letter from Virginia's governor, John B. Floyd, and one from John S. Barbour, father of James and Eliza, who had led the Virginia delegation at the convention. Most of the letters urged the appointment of John M. Daniel as chargé d'affaires in Belgium.[7] Why Daniel had Belgium as his aim is not clear, but the American legation at Brussels was a relatively unimportant post, perhaps not too big a plum to be awarded to a young man who had never held national office. Besides, the incumbent was a Whig from Delaware. Perhaps it was time for a worthy Southerner to take the job.

In May, a Southerner did get the job in Belgium, but it was not Daniel. The post in Brussels went to Alabaman J. J. Seibels. Other diplomatic posts were quickly being filled. A prominent and experienced Virginian, John Y. Mason, was soon named minister to France. Another Virginian, Richard Kidder Meade of Petersburg, was to become American chargé d'affaires at Turin, the capital of the Kingdom of Sardinia. John Daniel may not have known it, but while he relied on support from one of Virginia's two senators, Robert M. T. Hunter, the state's other senator, James G. Mason, had urged the candidacy of Richard Kidder Meade.[8] Meade was no upstart young editor, but a fifty-year-old Virginia Democrat and lawyer who had just finished his third term in the U.S. House of Representatives.

At the end of May, Meade called on the new president. Meade wanted something better than Turin; he wanted what he called a "full" mission, where he would be more than a chargé d'affaires. It had appeared earlier that he would be named minister to Chile, which would have been satisfactory. Meade told the president that he hoped Pierce would make him the U.S. commissioner to China. The president said that he would look into the matter and asked Meade not to say anything about their conversation. Meade unwisely ignored the request and promptly sent Hunter a full account of the conversation, asking the senator to support him. And on June 5 he wrote Secretary of State Marcy to decline formally the appointment to Turin.[9] Meade never did get the China job, nor was he given any other diplomatic post during the Pierce administration.[10]

Daniel worked quickly when he heard that the Turin post was open. James Barbour and others, including well-known Richmond jurist and former envoy William W. Crump, wrote to support Daniel, and Justice Daniel presumably weighed in as well. On July 23, 1853, the press reported that Daniel had been named chargé to Sardinia the previous day (though the *New York Times* incorrectly called him the editor of the *Richmond Enquirer* rather than the *Examiner*).[11] Daniel wrote to Marcy on July 29 to accept the appointment and offered to call on him the following week. He added apologetically that he was a little slow because he had been traveling and was in weak health.[12] Daniel had perhaps never enjoyed robust health, and now he suffered what he described several months later as having been a "dreadful attack."[13] Exactly what kind of attack this was we do not know, but apparently he had pneumonia. From this point onward there would be periodic indications that Daniel was not a well man. His mother had perhaps died of tuberculosis, and it seems not unlikely that he contracted it from her.

Daniel probably never knew how close he came to rejection by Franklin Pierce. In 1853 Howell Cobb was the governor of Georgia. He had not forgotten how Daniel's paper had attacked him as Speaker of the House of Representatives for allying himself with the Whigs in support of the Compromise of 1850. When Cobb heard that Daniel was to receive a diplomatic appointment from President Pierce, he wrote to his friend and fellow Democrat John Forney, Clerk of the House, asking him to protest to Pierce. Forney received Cobb's letter on July 29 and at once called on the president, who confirmed that he had made the appointment. "The President was amazed when I told him how you had been assailed by him," reported Forney, "and was evidently deeply mortified and chagrined. He said if he had known it things would have been very different."[14]

The newly appointed chargé d'affaires had followed closely and commented extensively on events in Italy and elsewhere in Europe during his five years as editor of the *Richmond Examiner*. He must have scurried now to learn what particulars he could about Turin, including the cost of living. He would at least not have to spend any of his outfit allowance on the sort of splendid uniforms that diplomats commonly wore at the foreign courts to which they were accredited, including the Court of Sardinia, which was as insistent on protocol as any other royal court in Europe. William Marcy had just issued a circular to the chiefs of

Department of State, Washington, D.C., ca. 1860. Historical Society of Washington, D.C.

American diplomatic missions instructing them that in carrying out their official duties they were to wear no uniform but just the plain dress of an American citizen. This June 1 circular was given to Daniel as part of his set of instructions from the Department of State. Just several months later this instruction would, indirectly, almost lead to the end of Daniel's mission.

Daniel received his appointment while the Senate was in recess. He would sail to Europe on the strength of the recess appointment, hoping for quick confirmation when the Senate met in the fall of 1853. He wrote Senator Hunter that he did not expect any senator to oppose his confirmation, "but it is possible as I have many enemies," so he hoped that Hunter would be present when his appointment was voted.[15]

Daniel sold the *Examiner* to his friend and colleague Robert W. Hughes for $5,000 in cash. He told Senator Hunter that he could have sold it to others for still more but that he was unwilling to see the *Examiner* in the hands of anyone who was not closely aligned with his and his friends' views. Daniel placed a farewell note in the paper to inform his readers that he had sold it to one of its ablest contributors but was reserving the right to repurchase it at a future time, which he intended to do. Meanwhile, though, he had no control over the journal and no rights or responsibilities connected with it.

The new diplomat left Richmond in mid-August for several days in Washington, during which time he intended to call on Secretary of State Marcy. In 1853, the

Department of State was housed in the Northeast Executive Building, a medium-size, two-story brick structure near the White House on Pennsylvania Avenue. The building had a portico with six white pillars. Inside, several dozen employees were organized into seven bureaus, including a diplomatic bureau that managed correspondence with American legations abroad, like that at Turin, and a bureau for archives, laws, and commissions. This latter bureau had prepared for Daniel a letter of instructions that enclosed several important documents:

1. A new U.S. special passport
2. A letter of credence to present to the foreign minister of the Kingdom of Sardinia, confirming that Daniel was the new American chargé d'affaires in that kingdom
3. A letter of credit on Baring Brothers, the bankers of the United States in London, authorizing and instructing them to pay Daniel's drafts for his salary as they came due, said salary to be $4,500 per annum commencing August 14, in addition to which he was to receive one year's salary for an outfit and a quarter's salary, the infit, when he finally returned to the United States; he would also be allowed up to $500 per annum for "the contingent expenses of the mission"
4. A copy of the standard "Personal Instructions to the Diplomatic Agents of the United States," to which were attached several circulars, including a new one dated June 1 concerning the proper dress for such agents. This circular required American diplomats to wear plain suits rather than uniforms, even on formal occasions, and it would cause considerable stir in European capitals, including Turin. European states were monarchies, and diplomats wore uniforms at court—including American diplomats. Even Andrew Jackson's democratic-minded administration had specified that American ministers should wear a black coat with a gold star on either side of the collar, a three-cornered hat with black cockade and gold eagle, and a sword with white scabbard. And these instructions had remained in effect until Marcy's new circular.

The way to Turin lay through New York City. Daniel was no stranger to the North. Indeed, he had probably seen more of the North than most influential Northerners had seen of the South. He had been in Manhattan a number of times and had traveled all the way through New York State to Niagara.[16] He had paid at least one visit to New England and had heard abolitionist Theodore Parker preach from his Boston pulpit (while Parker himself had never visited the South, and never would although he once wrote to a South Carolinian that he wanted to "see a *Slave* country").[17]

On August 16, Daniel left Washington on a train headed for New York, where he spent three days in that great and diverse metropolis before sailing for Europe.[18] A teenager from Missouri named Samuel Clemens was working there for a Manhattan printer, earning four dollars a week and reading all he could in the free library down the street. Across the river in Brooklyn a man named Walter Whitman, who had failed as an editor, was dabbling in real estate and putting together a book of poems. A Gramercy Park resident, Cyrus Field, was looking for new things to do; soon he would hear about undersea cables. The energetic editor Horace Greeley, who had come to the city as a poor boy from New Hampshire, had already become famous with his *New York Tribune*, which was running frequent commentaries on the European scene contributed by an emigré in London named Karl Marx. There was a large Irish population in the city, and two months later they would give a huge welcome to the Irish patriot John Mitchel, whom the British had sentenced to fourteen years' transportation but who had just escaped from captivity in Tasmania and was making his way to America. Mitchel, whom the Irish looked to as president of their future republic, would a decade later become a close friend and collaborator of John Moncure Daniel.

Greeley's *Tribune* printed some rather kind words about Daniel on the occasion of his departure. It seems likely that Greeley recalled Daniel's positive critique of Margaret Fuller, with whom Greeley had had a curiously close relationship before Fuller went to Rome. If, as seems possible, Daniel had met Fuller in New York, perhaps he had met Greeley too. Perhaps there was a kind of envy involved on Greeley's part, given Daniel's new appointment and Greeley's never-satisfied lust for high public office.[19]

Daniel, said the *New York Tribune*, was far more clever than Richard Meade, who had turned down the Turin post. Both Meade and Daniel were proslavery, but the *Tribune* had some hope that Daniel would outgrow this absurdity, if indeed he really believed in it. Daniel had brains, and it was a sad waste of talent to send him to such an insignificant post as Turin. But then his health and strength had been impaired by his work, and the *Tribune* was glad he would have a chance to "lay off" in Italy. Turin was a pleasant city, but there would be little work for Daniel there, so he would probably spend the autumn in Florence, Rome, and Venice; the winter in Naples; the spring in Milan or Nice; and the summer on rambles among the glaciers of Switzerland or on the breezy mountains of glorious Savoy. After three or four years' sojourn in Italy, Daniel would, the *Tribune* predicted, return to the United States invigorated and ready to edit a more genial, liberal, and progressive journal than Virginia had yet known. But for now, admitted Greeley's paper, the *Examiner* was the ablest and "spiciest" paper in the South.[20]

The *New York Times*, however, did not see the need to compliment Daniel. Without specifically naming him, two days before his departure the paper reprinted from the *Philadelphia Ledger* some points for new American diplomatic agents heading abroad. Among other things, "Let no gentleman from the South, who may have the honor of representing us abroad, endeavor to convince foreign *diplomates* and persons of influence in Europe, that slavery is a necessary concomitant of a high degree of civilization, and, therefore, a benefit to mankind. . . . [E]very American Minister abroad represents the free States as well as the Slave States."[21]

It was fair advice. Whether or not Daniel read it, it does not appear that he ever ignored the fact that he was representing his country as a whole. But neither does it appear that he changed his views on slavery and on race, as Greeley's paper hoped he might. One wonders, in fact, why the *Tribune* was so hopeful about Daniel. Only a few months earlier, it had put a question to the *Richmond Examiner:* if the *Examiner* insisted that "Negroes are not men, what would it say about the people of various shades who could be seen in Richmond, . . . many of them currently reported the sons or half-brothers of heads of the 'first families?'. . . Mr. Jefferson is reputed to have left progeny of this sort." Daniel, holding to the theory of polygenesis, replied with a comment that at least some of his readers must have seen as a piece of ignorance. It was, he said, a well-known physiological law that a hybrid race did not exist anywhere. Mules were sterile; dogs could not breed with wolves; and even among dogs alone no mongrel type had been perpetuated. A mulatto race of humans was therefore an impossibility; after two or three generations such people would produce either no children or only short-lived ones, and so the line would disappear.[22] Whether Frederick Douglass, the black leader of the North, ever saw this article is not known. But he thought he knew enough of Daniel's views to write in his Rochester newspaper on August 5 that while Daniel was far cleverer than his late rival for the job, Richard Meade, "they are just alike in regarding the support and extension of Human slavery as the great end of all government."[23]

Daniel booked first-class passage on the paddlewheel steamer *Arctic,* of the Collins Line, for departure on August 20, 1853, from New York to Liverpool. The *Arctic* was one of the biggest, fastest, and most luxurious vessels in the North Atlantic service. We can imagine Daniel enjoying his ten late-summer days on the ocean, recuperating from the pneumonia that had laid him low the previous month.[24] He was beginning the greatest adventure of his life, to live in an unknown capital under the high Alps. Turin was not Europe's greatest city, but it was a considerably larger place than Richmond, and he would be the senior representative of the American republic in a kingdom of five million people. Best of all, perhaps, Turin was well situated. The kingdom's major port, Genoa, gave access to all the Mediterranean. As the *New York Tribune* had noted, if Daniel got bored in Turin, there were other places to visit.

Pierce and Marcy had by now made most of the new administration's appointments to posts abroad. Several of those appointed, including George Sanders, came from the ranks of Young America. Sanders had done a flip-flop after Franklin Pierce was nominated. His *Democratic Review* forgot about the need for a young president, saying Pierce would be only forty-nine when inaugurated. The problem now was "the whole nest of Old Fogies, who hold diplomatic station." Among the worst of the outgoing administration's diplomats, in Sanders's view, was Lewis Cass Jr., son of the recent presidential candidate and American representative to the Papal States in Rome. When the Roman Republic was declared, the younger Cass had reportedly turned his diplomatic back on Giuseppe Mazzini, who thought (wrongly) that the appointments of Young Americans like Sanders to posts abroad had been made in order to reward efforts that he and his republican comrades had made on Pierce's behalf during the American presidential campaign. If Cass had only given the Roman Republic official recognition, said the *Review*, the French might not have sent in troops to reclaim Rome for the papacy.[25]

One problem for George Sanders was that in backing Douglas in 1852, he had been so fierce in his attacks on other Democratic leaders that Douglas was embarrassed and asked Sanders to back off. Another problem was that Sanders had an enemy in William Marcy and had urged that Marcy not be made secretary of state.[26] Not surprisingly, Marcy, once appointed, opposed any reward for Sanders. In the end Sanders got his appointment, but not as chief of a diplomatic mission; he was named consul in London, where the new American minister would be the former secretary of state, James Buchanan. Sanders was in good company; Nathaniel Hawthorne, who had written Pierce's campaign biography, was made consul in Liverpool. But some other Young Americans came out better than George Sanders in getting jobs with prestige: John Daniel was appointed to the legation at Turin; Edwin DeLeon was made diplomatic agent and consul general in Egypt; August Belmont went as chargé d'affaires to the Netherlands; John L. O'Sullivan became minister to Portugal; and Pierre Soulé, the French-born senator from Louisiana, was named minister to Spain. Sanders, however, knew that he could do much more in London than just pocket fees for issuing passports and consular invoices. He would meet the leading revolutionaries, many of them now in London, and offer his help. He could help to revolutionize all Europe.[27]

Seven

Garlic and Scandal at Turin

When at the end of August 1853 John Moncure Daniel stepped onto the quay in Liverpool, he was the first of his family to visit the land of his ancestors since his grandfather had gone to study at Glasgow, six decades earlier. The historian in him must have given some thought to family history, but there is no reason to believe that he spent any time in England seeking his family roots. He did not care for these latter-day English; they were not his ancestors. They were people who took the cotton of the American South and then criticized it for holding slaves while they made war on the Chinese to force them to take opium and held India in subjection.[1]

The new diplomat passed through London on his way to France. Whether he called on the newly arrived American minister in London, James Buchanan, we do not know. In Paris, he met with his older compatriot, the new American minister to France, John Y. Mason. Daniel may have been in Paris for quite some time; he took more than a month to get from Liverpool to Turin. A good part of the delay in reaching his new post, Daniel later wrote apologetically to Secretary of State Marcy, was because "I was compelled to wait in France for some members of my family."[2] (Daniel later hired his brother, Frederick, as his private secretary.)

In Paris, Daniel and Mason found that they had a good deal to discuss, including Marcy's new circular on dress. This would undoubtedly cause difficulties for American representatives across Europe, because diplomats of all European countries wore uniforms to official functions. Mason and Daniel agreed to stay in close touch on this and other matters. Finances were also an issue for both men, although Mason's salary as a minister was $7,500, much larger than Daniel's annual pay of $4,500. Mason came from grander circumstances than the young editor. He owned large properties in Virginia and Mississippi, had twice been a cabinet member, and had apparently hoped earlier in 1853 that President Pierce might name him to head the Supreme Court after reports appeared that Chief Justice Roger Taney was seriously ill.[3] During the next several years, Daniel saved all he could, while Mason spent large sums entertaining Emperor Napoleon III and his entourage. Mason's health deteriorated, and he apparently suffered a stroke soon after Daniel's visit.[4] He recovered, but as the diplomatic years progressed, he went through all his property; when he died in Paris in 1859, he left his widow and son burdened with large debts.[5] Mason in his spending and his debts resembled his Virginian predecessor in Paris, Thomas Jefferson, who had spent more than his annual salary to rent and furnish a "Parisian Monticello" on the Champs d'Elysées.[6]

Daniel also met with August Belmont, who was proceeding to The Hague to take up his new post as American chargé d'affaires.[7] Belmont was nine years older than Daniel and came from a much different background. He had been born in Europe, was Jewish, had represented the Rothschilds' interests in America, and had served as Austrian consul in New York. But Belmont and Daniel were both Democrats, and they found themselves on friendly terms.

From Paris, Daniel proceeded south and east to the Kingdom of Sardinia. In 1853 there was no railroad across the Alps from France into Savoy and Piedmont. It was the beginning of October and snow had not yet fallen, so instead of going around by sea from Marseilles to Genoa Daniel took the more direct stagecoach route over the Mont Cenis Pass, 6,500 feet above sea level. The scenery was grand, but the road was rough. Daniel did not feel well when he reached Turin on October 5, 1853. Once there, he moved into the Hotel d'Europe and quickly sent a note to the Sardinian minister of foreign affairs to inform him of his arrival and to request an appointment to present his credentials.[8]

Turin was the most beautiful city Daniel had ever seen. The Savoy family, which had ruled the western Alps as their dukedom for eight hundred years, had made Turin its main seat in 1562. The state was declared a kingdom in 1720, after they had added the island of Sardinia to their domains in Piedmont and Savoy, and over the next century and a half, Turin had become a handsome and impressive capital city. There were fine royal palaces in the city, one of which incorporated a Roman tower (the city had been the *colonia* of Augusta Taurinorum in the time of Augustus Caesar), and three other palaces just outside the city. Turin also had a great pentagonal citadel, a number of elegant churches, impressive buildings for ministries, and a range of residences and commercial buildings. It was not Paris or Berlin, but it was growing; the population would reach 200,000 within the decade. Turin enjoyed an impressive location. The great Alps rose, twenty-five miles away, to heights of more than 10,000 feet above this city along the River Po.

Daniel's legation had its office in an old building at Contrada Rocca 122.[9] His predecessor, William Kinney, an editor from Newark, New Jersey, had left Turin soon after learning of Daniel's appointment. Kinney was a Whig and an anti-slavery man; one of his papers was the weekly *Sentinel of Freedom*. (Three years earlier, another New Jersey paper, the *Daily Mercury*, had recommended the whipping post and the penitentiary for the editor of the *Examiner*, and Daniel had responded that "an oak tree and a grape vine noose is ready for all such wretched spawn of Abolition as himself."[10]) The secretary of legation under Kinney, and the only other American employee at the post, was a man named William Magoun, who was waiting for Daniel when he arrived. Magoun continued to work at the legation for the next eight or nine months, after which time John Daniel's younger brother, Frederick, replaced him.[11] In addition to the legation at Turin, there were three American consulates in the Kingdom of Sardinia: at Nice, Genoa, and La Spezia. The nearest to Turin, and the busiest, was the consulate in the bustling port of Genoa.

It turned out that William Kinney had, as chargé d'affaires at Turin, enjoyed a close relationship with Count Cavour, the Sardinian prime minister, and had often impressed on Cavour and other leading residents of the capital the virtues of America's liberal institutions. One could only wonder what he had told them about the American South.[12] Kinney, it seemed, had not gone home to America but had moved just a couple of hundred miles south to Florence. He was a friend of the Brownings, and he had thoughts of writing a history of the Medici family.

Not just Kinney but a majority of previous American representatives in the Kingdom of Sardinia had been Northerners. Charles Edward Lester, who had been the consul at Genoa for five years and had just published a two-volume work called *My Consulship*, was a great-grandson of the New England minister Jonathan Edwards, and had been known for his antislavery writings before he went to Genoa.[13] It is not clear how much Daniel knew about Lester's work as consul in Genoa, but his reputation was bad. Lester had involved himself personally in a contract to deliver four hundred tons of American tobacco to the Sardinian government and had made an extended trip to the United States apparently in connection with the contract. While he was away for more than a year, complaints poured in to the American chargé d'affaires in Turin, Robert Wickliffe, about the consul's shady fiscal affairs, including charges that Lester had appropriated for his own use the wages of sick American seamen in the Genoa hospital. It appears that the four hundred tons of tobacco was never delivered.[14]

Daniel found that Italy was not an expensive country. Young John De Forest, who would later write a notable novel of the Civil War, was traveling in Italy and elsewhere in Europe at this time and living the life of a dilettante on $1,200 a year. The occasional correspondent of the *New York Times* who called himself "Dick Tinto" reported that Florence was undoubtedly the cheapest city in the world. A young man with an annual income of $400 could live a very decent life there after he learned local ways. Restaurant meals cost little, clothing was cheap, two furnished rooms could be had for sixty dollars a year, and a servant could be hired for one dollar a month.[15] Turin was more expensive, and the American chargé d'affaires there obviously had to spend more than a fancy-free young American in

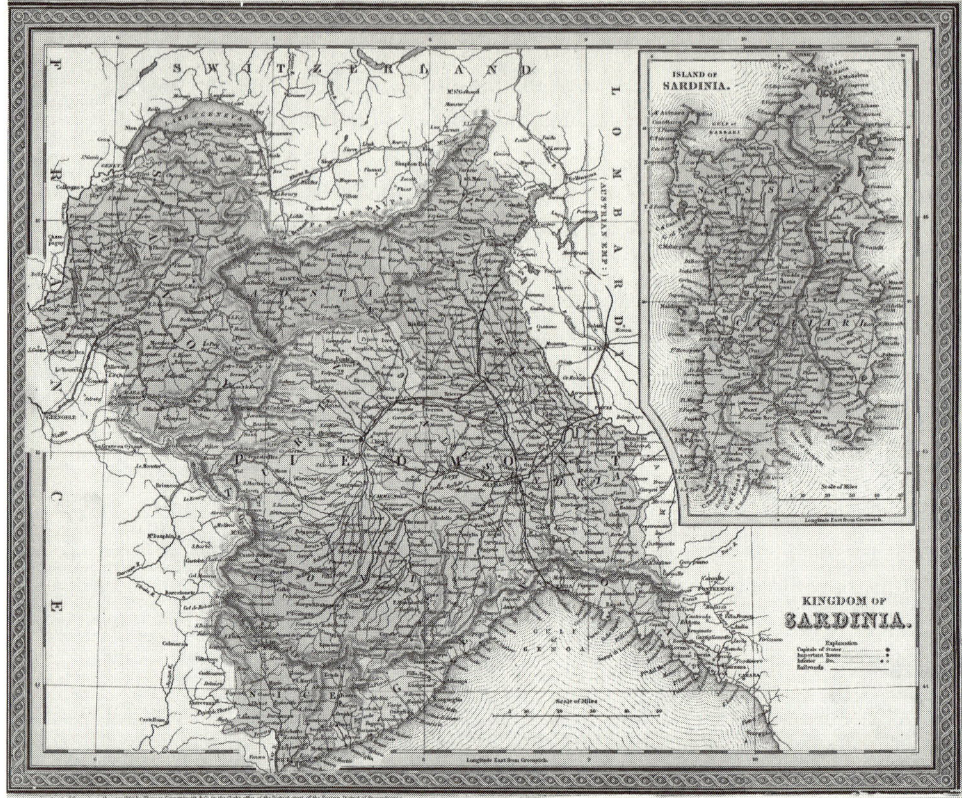

The Kingdom of Sardinia in 1850.

Florence—for proper lodgings, office expenses, his brother's pay, and entertainment—but John Daniel's annual income of $4,500 left him certain that he would be able to return to Virginia with a good amount of savings.

The Italy in which Daniel lived and worked was a place of divisions. There had been no united Italy since ancient times. In 1853 there were over a half-dozen political entities on the Italian peninsula. The Kingdom of Sardinia controlled prosperous Piedmont and Savoy, plus the much poorer island of Sardinia. Between Sardinia and the Piedmontese mainland lay the island of Corsica, once a possession of Genoa and later briefly independent, but after the mid-1700s part of France. East of Piedmont were Lombardy and the Veneto, constituent though unwilling parts of the Austrian empire. To the south and east were the Grand Duchy of Tuscany, the Duchies of Parma and of Modena, and the Papal States. The Papal lands stretched south from Rome to a border roughly halfway to Naples. Beyond that border, the rest of the Italian "boot," plus Sicily, made up the Kingdom of Two Sicilies, which was ruled by the Bourbon monarchs at Naples.

Italian dreamers of the nineteenth century talked about national unity and a democratic system, but several attempts in those directions had been repressed, most recently in the case of the Roman Republic of 1848–49. If the *Risorgimento* was a fact it was not yet a success. Europe's great revolutionary year of 1848 had left one major legacy in Italy: the *statuto*, or constitution, that the House of Savoy had been forced to accept for their Kingdom of Sardinia. The statuto had created a parliamentary system and ended arbitrary rule, but the kingdom was certainly not democratic. Yet many Italians pinned their hopes on this kingdom.

American dreamers also spoke of a better future for Italy. There was no sort of Italian-American lobby, but Italians had a good name in America. They had begun coming to the New World, and indeed to Virginia, very early—and not just as explorers. The first Italian immigrant, a man named Albiano Lupo, had arrived in Jamestown from England as early as 1610. The Taliaferro family, later prominent in the Tidewater, left Genoa for England in 1632 and arrived in Virginia by 1637. In the next century, a number of Italians from Virginia and other colonies fought for American independence. Thomas Jefferson's Virginia friend and neighbor Filippo Mazzei, a native of Tuscany, had gone back to Europe during the Revolution as Virginia's representative on the Continent. But despite the long history of contacts across the sea, in the mid-1800s the number of Italians in America remained small. When Giuseppe Garibaldi found a place of exile on Staten Island after the fall of the Roman Republic in 1849, the Italian population of New York City numbered at most several hundred. The 1850 census showed a total of only 3,645 Italians among the American population of foreign origin.[16]

There was also movement in the other direction. Educated Americans were visiting Italy in numbers. Jefferson had, in a sense, led the way, coming down to Piedmont from Paris in 1786–87, hoping to obtain for rice farmers in the American South seeds of the better-grade Piedmont rice. The Kingdom of Sardinia forbade export, but Jefferson filled his pockets with enough to send home to friends. While in Turin he also acquired a plan of the city that four years later he sent, together with plans of other European cities, to Maj. Pierre L'Enfant, who was working on the plan for America's new capital.[17]

By the 1850s American writers were coming to Italy for extended stays, following the example of James Fenimore Cooper, who lived from 1828 to 1830 in Florence, Naples, Rome, and Venice. Sculptors Thomas Crawford, Horace Greenough, Hiram Powers, and William Wetmore Story made their homes in Italy, as well, shipping such works as Powers's *Greek Slave* and Crawford's figure of George Washington back home to America. Among American painters in Italy was John Gadsby Chapman, a Virginian whose somewhat Italianized son Conrad Wise Chapman, also a painter, later returned to America to join the Confederate army, becoming its most important war artist.[18]

These American expatriates and visitors sent home the message that sunny Italy badly needed changes and reforms. It was not only Americans that carried the message. Giuseppe Garibaldi was only one of a number of Italian political activists and revolutionaries who made their way to the New World. Another of these revolutionaries, Eleuterio Felice Foresti, had been imprisoned by the Austrians in the grim fortress of Spielberg, immortalized earlier by Silvio Pellico in his 1832 book *My Prisons*. Foresti made his way to America in 1836, and in 1842 he became professor of Italian language and literature at the University of the City of New York.[19] He was named American consul at Genoa in 1853, an appointment that would present John Daniel his first diplomatic problem.

After the Roman Republic was put down in 1849 and Pius IX regained political control of Rome and the surrounding territory, American opinion, including the editorials of the *Richmond Examiner,* was decidedly negative on the once-liberal but now reactionary pontiff. The Vatican tried to mend matters by sending an envoy, Monseignor Gaetano Bedini, on an extended visit to the United States in 1853, but press and public reaction turned still more negative.[20] Most Americans—and not just Young Americans—wanted to see democracy in Italy, and many saw the papacy as a threatening force for America as well as for Europe.

There was also a heightened interest in America among those Italians who stayed home. Among the American works being translated and published in Italy was *Uncle Tom's Cabin*, which was published in the Turin and Milan in 1852, the same year it appeared in the United States. By 1854 there had been nine Italian editions. (And, as Daniel learned later and angrily reported, the book even inspired an Italian ballet.)

Given the political division of Italy, the legation in Turin was not the only American diplomatic post on the peninsula. The United States had diplomatic relations with the Holy See, and the American chargé d'affaires in Rome was Lewis Cass Jr., who had been there since 1849 and was to remain there for some years to come. There was also an American legation at Naples, capital of the Kingdom of Two Sicilies, headed by a new chargé d'affaires who reached Naples about the same time Daniel arrived in Turin. This new chargé was Robert Dale Owen, former Democratic congressman and son of Robert Owen, who had founded the utopian socialist community of New Harmony in southern Indiana.

America's relationship with the Kingdom of Sardinia was of some importance. The United States had maintained a naval squadron in the Mediterranean since the wars with the Barbary pirate states of North Africa earlier in the century. Since 1848, the squadron had been based at La Spezia, which, together with Genoa and Nice, was one of the chief ports of the kingdom. Trade was increasing fast between the United States and the Kingdom of Sardinia. One of the principal

American exports was tobacco, much of it grown in Virginia, and another was Southern cotton. Between 1850 and 1860, American exports to the Italian states tripled, and much of this trade went through Genoa. The kingdom was building railroads rapidly, as was America, and was steadily building up its army, as the United States was not. American locomotive and weapons manufacturers saw good possibilities for sales to Sardinia.

America's official representation in the Kingdom of Sardinia had begun on the consular rather than diplomatic level when an American consulate opened at Genoa in 1798. The kingdom reciprocated, but only after years had passed. A royal decree finally issued in 1815 called for a consulate general at Philadelphia and consular posts in eleven other American cities. The first of these opened in 1817 in Savannah. Diplomatic relations between the two countries came two decades later—and American tobacco played a role. In 1837, President Martin Van Buren sent a Vermonter named Nathaniel Niles as a special agent to the Austrian empire with the task of clearing away Austrian obstacles to free import of American tobacco. While in Vienna, Niles met the Sardinian minister to Austria, Count Vittorio Bertone, and reported home that Bertone agreed with him that United States–Sardinian diplomatic relations would prove advantageous to both countries. In his own report to Turin, Bertone suggested that the existing consular relationship was sufficient. Fortunately, Foreign Minister Clemente Solaro did not agree with Bertone, and he won King Carlo Alberto's agreement to begin diplomatic relations with America.[21]

In 1838, Niles was sent to Turin, where he successfully negotiated a treaty of commerce and navigation that opened the way for diplomatic relations.[22] The kingdom then acted quickly, naming a Piedmontese nobleman and experienced diplomat, Count Augusto Avogadro di Collobiano, as its first chargé d'affaires in the United States. The instructions he received from his foreign ministry made clear that Turin, like Washington, thought the main result of the new relationship should be increased trade. Besides, said the ministry, distances were being shortened by modern means of communication (presumably steamships), and relationships of all sorts were multiplying between the Old and the New Worlds. Incidentally, said the ministry, many individuals in America were supporting rebellion in Canada, which raised questions about whether officials in Washington were playing some role behind the scenes. Collobiano was instructed to do his best to ascertain whether the American government had any sort of hidden agenda in regard to the Kingdom of Sardinia. He failed to find any.[23]

Nathaniel Niles wanted to be America's first envoy resident at Turin, but that honor fell instead to an obscure young gentleman from Pennsylvania named Hezekiah Gold Rogers, who arrived in Turin in September 1840 and was quickly seen to be seriously unbalanced. The British legation's doctor found him in such bad shape that he relieved him of his pistols. The Sardinian foreign minister wrote to the American consul at Genoa about Rogers; the consul was away, so the American chargé d'affaires was put under the care of the chief nurse of Turin's insane asylum. Soon afterward, Rogers left the kingdom, only to return six months later. Meanwhile, the ministry had learned that the new American consul at Genoa, a Mr. John Bailey, was a notorious bankrupt. Collobiano was instructed to make clear, in confidence, to the American authorities that the Sardinian government believed that it was wrong to leave a madman and a bankrupt as America's chief representatives in the kingdom. They should be replaced.[24] Eventually they were. (There was good reason for concern that a bankrupt consul might harm American interests as well as Sardinian. Until 1856, American consuls in Europe did not receive salaries and were expected to earn a living from fees they charged foreigners and fellow citizens for their services.[25] A bankrupt consul might well be tempted to overcharge and gouge the public.) Rogers was finally succeeded by a Georgian named Ambrose Baber, and his mission also ended badly. Baber was replaced in late 1843, after he had become involved in a long and senseless dispute with the Sardinian authorities over his use of horses from the Royal Post to make an urgent business trip.[26]

Even now, Nathaniel Niles did not get the job he hoped for in Turin. It was only at the beginning of 1848, ten years after he had negotiated the treaty in Turin, that he was finally named chargé d'affaires. The next year, Taylor the Whig replaced Polk the Democrat in the White House. The Sardinian foreign ministry instructed its chargé d'affaires in Washington to make clear to appropriate Americans, in the most discreet way, that Nathaniel Niles was highly esteemed in Turin, and the Sardinian authorities could not imagine that anyone better could be found to replace him.[27] This accomplished nothing, and Niles was replaced by a Whig, Kinney. The foreign minister sent Niles a very warm letter on his departure, hoping that this might help secure Niles's reinstatement.[28] But Niles never returned to Turin.

John Moncure Daniel was the sixth American chargé d'affaires in Turin. In 1853, the American representative in Turin was not as important as those of Britain, France, Austria, or Russia. These representatives were all ministers; a chargé d'affaires ranked lower. The relationship with America was simply not as important as that with Europe's main powers. As Daniel reached Turin, the Kingdom of Sardinia was sending its own new chargé d'affaires to Washington, Andrea Taliacarne. The foreign ministry's instructions to Taliacarne made clear that "for now we have no political question or affair in train with the United States government." (The instructions added that Taliacarne should continue the established practice of using French for correspondence with the ministry on political matters and Italian for commercial and other matters.[29])

Daniel's first official step was to call on the Sardinian foreign minister, a former general named Giuseppe Dabormida. The minister made clear that he was unhappy the United States government had recently named Felice Foresti as consul at Genoa and then requested Sardinian authorities to issue Foresti an exequatur, the permit that a host government gives a foreign consul. Foresti, said the minister, had for many years been a chief agent in political intrigues throughout Italy. The kingdom was overflowing with political refugees from other parts of Italy. If Dabormida permitted Foresti to come to Genoa as an American official, he had no doubt that Foresti would soon become involved in revolutionary plots; he would, in effect, be the chargé d'affaires in Italy of the revolutionary Mazzini, and the kingdom would find itself embroiled in conflict with every other government on the Italian peninsula.

Dabormida had therefore instructed his chargé in Washington to protest Foresti's appointment to Secretary of State Marcy. Dabormida told Daniel that Marcy had replied that if the United States government had been aware of the situation, it would not have appointed Foresti; the United States would therefore not insist on him being granted an exequatur. Daniel said that he had no instructions on the matter—a situation in which he would often find himself as long as he served at Turin—but that if the United States had requested an exequatur, it certainly had done so on the basis that Foresti should confine himself strictly to the duties of his consular office.[30]

This exchange did not end the matter. Marcy was furious when he read Daniel's report about his meeting with Dabormida. Marcy wrote back to Daniel that the Sardinian chargé d'affaires in Washington had limited knowledge of English. The chargé had not understood what Marcy had told him, that the U. S. government would look into the matter and that *if* there were good grounds for Turin's objections the president *might* change his mind about the appointment. Marcy had then seen Foresti himself, and Foresti had assured Marcy that there was no reason for the Sardinian authorities to object to his appointment. That was good enough for William Marcy, who enclosed Foresti's commission and instructed Daniel to request, again, an exequatur. [31] Dabormida would not budge, and in the end the State Department sent a South Carolinian named Herbemont to fill the post instead. Five years later, Felice Foresti did come to Genoa, which reveals much about the political changes in the Italian peninsula during the years that John Daniel spent in Turin.

Diplomatic practice calls for a newly arrived diplomat to make calls on officials of the host government and on counterparts in other diplomatic missions. Daniel made the rounds assiduously. He was delighted to find one familiar face among the members of the Turin diplomatic corps, British minister James Hudson, whom he had known in Washington, when Hudson was secretary of the British legation there. Daniel's new diplomatic colleagues, as well as the members of Turin society, were naturally curious to meet the newly arrived American, who was known to have some reputation as an editor and was, moreover, young and unmarried.

The new diplomat already understood that a legation could, in its way, be as good a pulpit as could an editor's desk. The readers of diplomatic dispatches from Turin were far fewer than the readers of the *Richmond Examiner,* but they were the makers and executors of American foreign policy. Daniel began to provide the State Department with both reports of notable events in the kingdom and with analyses of trends taking place there. One point to which he returned several times over the coming year was that Sardinia, needing help from larger nations as it faced Austrian dominions to the east, had little freedom of movement. "Its statesmen from the necessity of things are in a great measure puppets, whose wires are in the hands of England and France," he wrote in 1854.[32] He also reported growth in the kingdom—in the economy and, more notably, in the army: whereas the American army was minuscule—with only about 10,000 men to defend a huge country with a population that numbered 23 million, according to the census of 1850—the Kingdom of Sardinia was relatively small and had a population of perhaps five million, but its army nearly numbered over 50,000.

Daniel soon found that his absence from the United States did not leave him free from attacks by critics and enemies at home. His colleagues in London and Paris, Buchanan and Mason, had decided to amend Secretary Marcy's requirement for plain dress after Buchanan warned Marcy that he would obey the department's instruction "unless I should clearly discover that the success of my mission will be impaired by pursuing this course."[33] In the end, Mason decided to wear a kind of semi-uniform to official affairs; and Buchanan wore tights and a sword, which officials at the Court of St. James decided was sufficient.

Not so with John Daniel in Turin. He decided that his diplomatic uniform would be a plain dark suit, as Marcy had clearly instructed. Daniel wore that suit both for his initial audience with the king and, later, for the court's New Year ball, where every other diplomat and official came in full and glittering uniform with decorations. Daniel wrote to Secretary Marcy that he received a polite intimation from the prefect of the Royal Palace that if he hereafter would attend court balls in some sort of uniform, it would be seen as an act of great civility. Daniel did not want to appear uncivil; he simply would not attend any more balls. After all, he wrote Marcy, "I am accredited to the Foreign Office—not to the Court—and have no desire to masquerade for the satisfaction of titled non-entities." [34]

All in all, Daniel was not happy. He was not well, and he was homesick. His good friend Thomas Wynne sent frequent letters that kept him informed in detail

Piazza Castello, Turin, in the mid–nineteenth century. Library of Congress.

about events in Richmond and throughout Virginia. Wynne wrote that people in Richmond kept asking him to send Daniel their best regards and that his wife and little daughter sent him their best love. In addition, Wynne reported that Virginia had enjoyed a particularly fine Indian summer that autumn.[35] Daniel also heard from his friend Arthur Peticolas, who had recently written to ask what Daniel was doing about Marcy's strictures on uniforms. Daniel wrote back, marking his letter "strictly private and confidential" and proceeding to bare his feelings to Peticolas, emphasizing that none of what he wrote should reach the papers.[36]

Daniel wrote that Turin was the most beautiful city he had ever seen. He reported that he was working hard on his spoken French. He had unfortunately still not recovered fully from his "dreadful attack" of the previous July, and soon after reaching Turin he had come down with some sort of chronic irritation (most likely tuberculosis). The air could be bad at Turin, especially for someone with weak lungs; the city was covered in a thick fog in winter and summer.[37] Fortunately, he had met an able Piedmontese physician, Giacinto Pacchiotti, who had cured the irritation by prescribing a daily hot bath and "a decoction of tamarinds and poppies, a tumblerful every three hours." One wonders how long Daniel continued to take the decoction, and whether it may have produced some addiction to opium; there is no indication that it did.

Daniel admitted to Peticolas that he was as homesick as any little girl might be during her first quarter at boarding school. For years before coming to Turin, he had been haunted by intolerable longings for Europe. Since he had come to Europe, he had been living a life of nonsensical travel and idleness that was much less pleasant than a life of work and study in America. When he finally did return home, he said, he would be cured of the urge to travel.

Daniel wanted Peticolas to understand what Turin was like. The people were simply not as good as Americans. The women were uglier, and the men had fewer ideas. Daniel told about studying not only French but also what was falsely styled the "great world" and "polite society." He had dined with dukes and jabbered bad grammar to countesses. Counts who stank of garlic—as did the whole country—had sponged on him for seats in his box at the opera. He received visits from diplomats who had "titles as long as a flagstaff, and heads as empty as their hearts." All in all, he found the whole concern more trashy than he had ever imagined. Europe had fine paintings, opera, and ballet, he admitted, but its people, governments, and society were more contemptible than one could conceive. Still, he had to deal with these people, "for that is the only way of seeing the elephant of European life. So I dance the dance of fools, like the rest of them, and return their visits sedulously." Daniel also assured Peticolas that he was following Marcy's instructions and was not going to wear any court dress and that he had made his position clear to the Sardinian authorities.

Daniel was not the first American diplomat to write about the deficiencies of Europe. Thomas Jefferson, when minister to France in 1785–89, wrote letters to friends and colleagues in America, as well as notes to American travelers in Europe, in which he described France, and all of Europe, as a sinkhole of avarice, ignorance, and poverty. Europe's monuments were worth seeing; but, he warned travelers, they distracted attention from the deep corruption of European society. Jefferson did not say such things in public, of course; he told the French that they were his brethren in spirit and France was his adopted home.[38] (Nor was Daniel the first foreigner to observe garlic on the breath of even well-born Italians. Percy Bysshe Shelley had written that in Italy even "countesses smell so of garlic that an ordinary Englishman cannot approach them."[39])

Two or three weeks later, in a conversation with Robert Hughes, who had taken over the *Richmond Examiner*, Peticolas mentioned that he had recently heard from John Daniel and that Daniel was adhering strictly to Marcy's instructions about diplomatic dress. Hughes asked to see what Daniel had written so that he could deny authoritatively a recent charge by Horace Greeley's *Tribune* that Daniel had appeared at court in Turin wearing a uniform of unusual splendor. Peticolas agreed to let Hughes see Daniel's letter. Hughes then told Peticolas that he was constantly being asked for news about Daniel, not only by the former editor's friends but also by subscribers. He suggested that it would gratify them to read extracts from Daniel's letter. Peticolas may have hesitated, but he agreed, and he gave the letter to Hughes. In a hurry, the editor printed the whole letter, omitting only the part about Daniel's health and his request that the letter not be published. Hughes later wrote apologetically that his aim had been to please and amuse Daniel's many friends and readers.[40]

Hughes had not thought about the possibility that Shearjashub Spooner, in New York, might seize on the printed letter. (Spooner, whose libel trial with Daniel was still pending, had an agent in Richmond who kept close watch over the contents of the *Examiner.*) Nor did Hughes foresee that when Spooner saw the letter he would see that it got reprinted in the New York press, in the *Herald* and the *Tribune* and in the Italian-language *L'Eco d'Italia.* It was not long before Daniel's brutally frank comments on people in Piedmont reached the Continent. Apparently, the first European paper to reprint the letter was *Galignani's Messenger,* which was printed in Paris in English and was widely distributed throughout Europe; one American sojourner in Italy called it "the instructor and consoler of wandering Anglo-Saxons throughout the Continent." (One might call it an 1850s version of today's *International Herald Tribune.*)[41]

At the beginning of February 1854, John Moncure Daniel, who had been in Turin for four months, had no inkling of what was afoot with his letter to Arthur Peticolas. He had, however, seen in the *Tribune* and other newspapers the false report of his appearance at court in uniform. Meanwhile, Daniel had received a kind letter dated December 15, 1853, from Secretary of State Marcy, who wrote that he really did not have time to send private letters to friends abroad but that he hoped to be favored by such letters from them, including John Daniel.[42] Marcy went on to say that there been a rumor in Washington that the new American chargé d'affaires was somewhat remiss in making calls on other members of the Turin diplomatic corps. He added politely that he was not attempting to direct Daniel's course in this regard, or to censure it.

Daniel was pleased with the warmth of Marcy's letter and replied in a letter of February 1.[43] He wanted the secretary to know that as soon as he had been received at the foreign ministry, he had called on the head of every other diplomatic mission and had received return calls from each of them within a few days. James Hudson the British minister was a personal friend from Washington, and he had taken Hudson's advice on all points of etiquette about which he himself had been doubtful. He did not think he had made a single false step. Daniel added that he had seen the report in the papers that he had appeared in uniform and that it was absolutely false. A uniform had never been part of his wardrobe. He acknowledged that he had been a polemical writer in America and that it was not surprising that people who disliked him should start petty falsehoods like these. He wrote that he hoped that if any further such reports should reach the secretary of state, he would pay them no heed until Daniel had had the chance to rebut them. And although he did not say so to Marcy, Daniel may have had in mind not only the *Tribune*'s criticisms but its earlier advice that he do some travel around Europe. He took the opportunity to ask Marcy for permission to travel outside Turin to neighboring cities for a few days at a time. He added that William Magoun, who had been the secretary of legation for seven years, was still in the job and could handle routine matters; and, if anything came up requiring his personal attention, Daniel could return to Turin in a few hours. (Marcy "cheerfully accorded" his permission in a dispatch sent to Turin on February 27.)[44]

Daniel went about his business unaware of the trouble that was brewing. He went to Rome for the Carnival in February, to experience the festival and savor the milder climate of the Eternal City. We cannot know what preoccupations he may have had; but presumably he was concerned about the Senate's approval of his appointment as chargé d'affaires. On January 31, 1854, President Pierce submitted Daniel's nomination to the Senate. The Senate then referred it to the Foreign Relations Committee, which gave it to Senator Stephen Douglas for the required report. Not surprisingly, Douglas reported favorably, and the Senate confirmed John Moncure Daniel as chargé d'affaires at Turin on February 8, 1854.[45]

Then came the bombshell. On February 16, 1854, the text of Daniel's letter to Arthur Peticolas appeared in *Galignani's Messenger;* within several days it was reprinted in the Turin press. The horrified secretary of the Turin legation, William Magoun, wrote to Daniel in Rome that a letter of his to a friend, which contained much criticism of Piedmont and the Piedmontese, had been published in the press and was raising a storm in Turin. Rumor had it that various men in Turin intended to challenge Daniel to duels when he returned.

The American envoy hurried back to Turin as fast as he could, probably taking a steamboat from Civitavecchia near Rome up the coast to Genoa and then the train to Turin; there was still no rail line between Genoa and Rome. Daniel found on his return that the storm continued to rage but that the rumors were wrong: he had received no challenge to a duel.[46] Still, he wrote to a fellow Virginian, Daniel Lee, who was serving as American consul at Basel, that he might be challenged and hoped, in that case, that Lee would come down to Turin and act as his second.[47] (Piedmont was no less a place for duels than was Virginia. A famous story from the previous century was that of General St. Amour, who when he first became colonel of a Piedmontese regiment was challenged by his captains because he was a peasant's son and they thought him unworthy. He killed the first four of the twelve and then announced "There are now but eight left." The remaining eight thought fit to let the matter drop.[48])

Perhaps the only encouraging correspondence that awaited Daniel when he returned to Turin was the six-page letter that his counterpart in the Netherlands, August Belmont, had written him on February 5.[49] Belmont, too, had seen the report in the *New York Tribune* that Daniel had appeared at the Sardinian court in uniform despite Marcy's instructions, and Belmont had received a letter from Daniel assuring him that the report was false. Daniel had asked Belmont whether he thought he should give in to court officials' requests that he wear a uniform in the future, or whether he should simply stay away from formal functions. Belmont responded that he thought Daniel should do neither. After all, American diplomats in plain suits were wearing the same dress they wore in the presence of the head of their own government, so they could hardly be accused of disrespect. No one criticized Turkish envoys, who wore "outlandish garb," including a turban or fez that they did not doff in the presence of ladies. Belmont did think, however, that it would be useful for the U.S. Congress to reinforce Marcy's circular by passing a bill that restricted the wearing of uniforms to members of the army and navy. Belmont told Daniel that he had written Senators Slidell and Mason to urge this action, and suggested that Daniel write to his own good friends in the Senate, Douglas and Hunter.

But John Daniel had other worries just then. Some of the "long-titled" and "empty-headed" diplomats whom Daniel had described to Peticolas were members of the Whist Club of Turin, the city's most prestigious men's club. Daniel had joined the club; after sending his morose letter to Peticolas, he had found the club a convivial place and spent considerable amounts of time there before going to Rome. After returning, he received a polite letter from the Count de St. Marsan, president of the club, enclosing the text of Daniel's published letter and saying that, since the publication had caused "an unpleasant impression" among members, the governing board would be happy to receive whatever explanations Daniel might wish to make.[50]

Daniel was disturbed to see that the count had written his letter a full eight days earlier, and that it had been forwarded to the address where he had stayed in Rome. He hastened to reply, somewhat apologetically. He explained that soon after reaching Turin, while still feeling indisposed from his long journey, he had written a letter to an intimate friend in America to furnish him with his initial impressions of Europe. He intended this letter only for the eyes of the friend, and he had used the "unguarded phrases" of actual conversation. Daniel continued:

> By what means the seal of confidence was broken, and the fragments of such a letter placed in the newspapers, I do not know. But I am free to say that I have seen them there with great mortification and regret. . . . [I]t is with pain that I

> perceive myself placed in the attitude of rendering an ingracious return for courtesies received among a people whom a more intimate acquaintance has caused me to respect. . . . I hold myself bound to render redress to all who conceive themselves (if such there be) personally aggrieved by that publication. The politeness of your address to me and the motive of your inquiry have rendered a civil reply and a certain degree of unreserve necessary on my part; but as the letter referred to was written before I had any acquaintance with the Club . . . I conceive that it is in no manner concerned therewith. . . .

Daniel ended by expressing the hope that this letter would not receive publicity; there had already been enough of that.[51]

For a week, John Daniel held himself ready to receive a challenge to a duel. But no challenge came. Instead, a second polite letter came from Count de St. Marsan saying that the club's governing board had been fully satisfied with Daniel's letter. It might have been best to publish the letter, it continued, but they would bow to his wishes.[52]

This may have resolved Daniel's problem with the Whist Club, but he still faced serious problems with the government to which he was accredited, as well as with his own. The day after St. Marsan sent his second letter to Daniel, Foreign Minister Dabormida wrote to Andrea Taliacarne, his chargé in Washington, that, although he at first thought the published letter spurious, it was clearly authentic. Dabormida had not seen Daniel since he had left the kingdom on a trip some time earlier. Perhaps Daniel was lying low because he had submitted his resignation and awaited a reply from Washington. The letter had placed the American in a difficult position vis-à-vis his diplomatic colleagues and Turin society, and Daniel's resignation seemed the only honorable way out. Supposing that the resignation would be accepted, Dabormida asked Taliacarne to make it known to appropriate people in Washington that the Sardinian government hoped the next American envoy would be a person capable of maintaining good relations with his host country.[53]

However, Daniel had not resigned his post. Nor had he realized what a stir his letter to Peticolas had caused in Washington. The foreign diplomatic corps there had discussed the report fully, and several of its members had raised the matter with Secretary Marcy and his subordinates. It appears that the State Department defended its representative. The Sardinian chargé d'affaires reported to Turin that Assistant Secretary of State A. Dudley Mann had pointed out to him that the letter contained no criticism of the Sardinian government.[54] Still, no matter what U.S. officials told foreigners, the letter was of sufficient concern that President Pierce and his cabinet discussed it at least once. Marcy was pleased and perhaps relieved when he received a letter from Daniel dated April 4 assuring the secretary of state that the matter had been put to rest in Turin. Daniel enclosed the texts of the letters that he had exchanged with the Count de St. Marsan. Nothing more had appeared about him in the Turin press, and he was now enjoying normal relationships with his diplomatic colleagues and with Sardinian officials.

Daniel told the secretary of state that his first impulse had been to resign and that he had written an official dispatch tendering his resignation. After thinking things over, though, he had decided that resigning would only make matters worse for himself and more disagreeable for his friends: "If I were to come home now, I should be the gibe of my adversaries and my power as a public man in Virginia would be forever destroyed. But if I stay around till this miserable business is blown over and forgotten, it may do me no eventual injury. This is however, the point on which I am anxious to have your advice. I am of course ready and desirous to conform my steps to what is due to my country and to propriety."[55]

Marcy did not call for Daniel's resignation. On April 30, he wrote with approval: "The course you took in relation the unpleasant affair was manly and prudent and the termination fortunate. A rumour reached this country through some foreign journal that you had tendered your resignation. . . . I rejoice that you abandoned the notion of resigning." Marcy added that he would take the liberty of sharing Daniel's letter with the president and the other members of the cabinet. After the letter to Peticolas had been published in America, it had been discussed in the cabinet.

> They all felt as I did the embarrassment of the position in which you would be placed when the unfortunate publication should be known at Turin; but none of us concluded that it involved the necessity or the propriety of your resignation.
>
> It cannot be denied that the occurrence was one to be regretted by your friends, but not of a character to keep possession of the public mind. Indeed it is here even now a forgotten event, and if ever recalled to mind it is done by those whose motives are unfriendly to you or yr. friends.
>
> Its most serious effects were to be looked for in your social relations at Turin.—I rejoice that you have so well counteracted them in that quarter.[56]

Marcy said nothing about Daniel's great-uncle, the associate justice of the Supreme Court. However, the Sardinian chargé d'affaires wrote home to his ministry that he thought it likely Peter Vivian Daniel had weighed in on behalf of his great-nephew.[57]

Although Daniel never did send off the letter of resignation, he must have come very close to doing so, to the point that he told the Sardinian foreign minister he was resigning. Early in June, Foreign Minister Dabormida wrote to his chargé d'affaires in Washington, Andrea Taliacarne, that he was surprised by Taliacarne's report that Assistant Secretary of State Mann had told him that Daniel had not resigned—since Daniel had told Dabormida that he had done so. Presumably, Daniel had said the same thing to Hudson, the British minister, since in March Hudson had reported to the Foreign Office in London that Daniel had resigned in the wake of his letter to Peticolas, with its "typically American tone."[58]

Daniel may have wondered whether his Yankee enemy Shearjashub Spooner had anything to do with the fact that a number of papers that reprinted his letter to Peticolas after it first appeared in the *Richmond Examiner*. Thomas Wynne wrote Daniel in March that Spooner had clearly been involved, and he had heard that an Italian, a German, and a Frenchman in Richmond had each "forwarded a translation to their respective countries for your benefit."[59] Wynne's next letter commented that Horace Greeley's *New York Tribune* had at least given Daniel credit for not having written the letter for publication. Unfortunately, Wynne added, a lot of people in Virginia thought that Daniel had, in fact, written it for that purpose.[60]

A long time passed before editors in America forgot Daniel's garlic letter. In May 1854, the editor of *Harper's* devoted more than two full pages of the "Editor's Easy Chair" to Daniel and his letter and hit home as perhaps no earlier commentator had done, saying that the fact that "he should be willing to remain in an atmosphere strongly impregnated with garlic . . . and undergo all the other martyrdoms of his position is only to be explained upon one hypothesis, namely, that the emolument awarded by a grateful country recognizing his self-sacrifice, is more considerable than the annual revenues of his paper."[61]

Sometime early in 1854, John Moncure Daniel received welcome news that he was no longer simply chargé d'affaires; he had been promoted to the rank of minister resident. This still did not put him on the level of Buchanan in London and Mason in Paris, each of whom bore the full title of envoy extraordinary and minister plenipotentiary. Nor would he earn any more as minister resident than as chargé d'affaires. And the change did not really reflect Washington's judgment on either Daniel personally or on the obviously good state of American relations with Sardinia. The State Department was simply following up on congressional action of March 3, 1853, that permitted chargés d'affaires to be raised to the rank of minister resident. [62] In any case, the promotion was pleasing to an envoy's ego.

While there had been such a flurry in Turin (and Washington) over a private letter, in London the American minister, James Buchanan, had lately attended a dinner at the house of the American consul, former Young America leader George Sanders, that could have threatened America's official relations with every government in Europe, including that of the Kingdom of Sardinia. In late February 1854, Consul Sanders and his wife had invited to dinner a group of men who led Europe in planning and fomenting revolution. The guests included the Italians

Giuseppe Garibaldi, Giuseppe Mazzini, and Felice Orsini (whom the French were to execute four years later, after he tried to assassinate Napoleon III); Alexandre Ledru-Rollin, who in 1849 had tried to impeach then-President Louis Napoleon; Arnold Ruge, the German Hegelian and one-time friend of Karl Marx; Lajos Kossuth, who had led Hungary's revolt against the Austrian empire; and, not least, the great Russian thinker Aleksandr Herzen. (Karl Marx was not present, and it is not known whether he was invited.) Apparently only one Englishman attended, not a revolutionary but a liberal member of Parliament. At one point during the dinner, Minister Buchanan turned to Sanders's wife, Anna Reid,[63] and asked if she was not concerned that all the combustible materials in the room would explode and blow them all up. Indeed, there was a danger of a political explosion if the report reached European governments that the American consul's house in London had become a meeting place for revolutionaries.

The dinner accomplished nothing. Herzen, never forgetting that the kind of republics that their American host wanted was for whites only, remembered it in his memoirs as "the *red* dinner, given by the defender of *black* slavery."[64] After dinner, Minister Buchanan went home, and George Sanders offered the others some old Kentucky whisky. Only Herzen, used to vodka, could get it down. Herzen recalled that this raised him very high in Sanders's eyes:

> "Yes, yes," he said: "it's only in America and Russia that people know how to drink."
>
> "Well," I thought, "there is an even more flattering affinity; it's only in America and Russia that they know how to flog serfs to death."[65]

Buchanan hastened to inform Secretary Marcy about the dinner, saying that it would have been indiscreet for him to invite the group to his own residence but that it would have been wrong for him to refuse the invitation of a friend "simply because these men who have suffered in the cause of liberty were to be present."[66]

Deliberately or not, Buchanan missed the point: a government can legitimately be criticized, indeed attacked, if it gives encouragement to persons seeking the violent overthrow of a government with which it maintains relations. And this fact is not modified by the other government being nonrepresentative or even tyrannical. In 1854, the United States government would have wished to see democracy installed on the European Continent, but not at the cost of a rupture of relations with existing governments. Those governments, moreover, perceived (and with some reason) that there were threats to their stability not just from revolutionaries of their own nation but from others. Three years earlier, for example, when the Hungarian revolution had been put down and Lajos Kossuth and his comrades had been invited to travel to America on the USS *Mississippi*, the Sardinian foreign minister had requested Daniel's predecessor, William Kinney, to tell the commander of the *Mississippi* that if the ship called at a Sardinian port, none of the Hungarian leaders should be permitted on shore.[67] *Mississippi* did call, to take on coal, at La Spezia, the site of the depot for the U.S. Mediterranean squadron. The ship was soon surrounded by boats carrying admirers and musical bands. The Sardinian government became increasingly worried, and finally *Mississippi* broke off its uncompleted coaling and sailed west.[68]

There was no rupture of American relations with Europe after George Sanders's London dinner in 1854. But Buchanan and Sanders did not deserve credit for this—far from it. When Mason, the minister in Paris, heard about the dinner he is reported to have been "greatly disgusted" and concerned about what effect it might have on his relationships with the French government.[69] The French were in fact angry and even refused to permit the American minister to Spain, Pierre Soulé, to travel through France when returning to Madrid.

But there would be no more such dinners at the consul's home; George Sanders had little time left as consul in London. In the mid-1800s, unlike today, American consuls required confirmation by the Senate. There were many Senators, Whigs and also Democrats, who disliked that Young American, and on February 14, 1854, the Senate rejected Sanders's appointment to London by a large vote.[70] That did not end his interest in European revolution. Sanders stayed on in London for some months, and in October 1854 the former consul issued a long "Address to the People of France," calling on them to revolt against Napoleon III and reestablish a republic.[71] (Years later, in 1870, after serving as an audacious Confederate agent in Canada and Europe, Sanders would go to Paris and see, finally, a new French Republic founded.)

Although Daniel did not say anything to Secretary of State Marcy in his account of the so-called garlic letter, he had benefited from the help of at least two people in Turin in getting through his troubles. One of these, he wrote to his friend W. W. Crump, was his friend from Washington, James Hudson, the British minister. Hudson, he said, had stood by him from the first and gone out of his way to demonstrate his support (the British legation was the most influential foreign mission in Turin).[72] Daniel cannot have known that Hudson had reported to the Foreign Office in London that he believed Daniel had in fact resigned. Nor can Daniel have known that, despite Marcy's letter assuring him that the administration never thought he should resign, Daniel's fellow Virginian, Roger Pryor the Petersburg editor, had told the Sardinian chargé d'affaires in Washington that he was slated to replace Daniel in Turin.[73]

Daniel's other help had come from a noble lady, one of the countesses to whom, as he had mentioned in his letter to Arthur Peticolas, he had been jabbering in his imperfect French. Her name was Marie de Solms, and she was a grand-niece of the Emperor Napoleon I and thus a cousin of Louis Napoleon, who had become Emperor Napoleon III. Marie de Solms was the daughter of Laetitia Bonaparte, the daughter of Napoleon I's brother, Lucien. Laetitia had married Sir Thomas Wyse, a member of the British Parliament. In 1831, when she had been separated from her husband for three years, Laetitia gave birth in Northamptonshire, England, to a daughter, whom she named Marie. The father was said to be her paramour, an Irish captain named Hodgson.[74]

Laetitia raised young Marie in France, gave her an excellent education, and adopted the name of Bonaparte for herself and her daughter. At seventeen, Marie married a rich gentleman from Strasbourg named Frédéric de Solms, who soon left her to go to America. Marie remained with her mother, who kept a brilliant salon in Paris that was frequented by Victor Hugo, Eugene Sue, Alexandre Dumas *fils,* and other writers. Marie was beautiful and cultivated, and she became the star of the salon—which became a seat of opposition to her cousin, Louis Napoleon.

In the early 1850s, Marie had an affair with Count Alexis de Pommereu that produced a son in 1852. In February 1853, the French Ministry of Police ordered her expulsion from the new empire. She was accused of having illegally taken the name of Bonaparte and of stirring up "scandalous disorders." There may have been more to the story. Although Marie did not care for the imperial regime, it appears that the emperor cared for her and paid a number of private visits to his beautiful young cousin. Reportedly, the jealous Empress Eugenie learned of these visits and told her husband that Marie was maintaining a salon of subversives. It was then that she was expelled from France.[75]

Marie went traveling, and in August 1853, as John Moncure Daniel was making his way across the Atlantic to the Kingdom of Sardinia, she went to live at Aix-les-Bains on the shore of the Lac du Bourget, in Savoy, in the Kingdom of Sardinia. There her friend Pommereu built her a chalet with a little theater where she could put on plays. She soon had a new literary salon in her Aix chalet. She went often to Turin, where she established another salon at the Hotel Feder.[76] Either in Turin or at Aix, she met the new American chargé d'affaires soon after his arrival in the kingdom. Marie de Solms was lovely, with a head of raven-black hair, as black as John Daniel's own.[77] Much later, in 1859, Daniel wrote to John Floyd, U.S. Secretary of War: "Six years ago, when, as you know, I was in great trouble here, she took my part in the very highest circle of society; and since then I have found the most agreeable social intercourse since leaving Va. among the French people who gather at her house."[78]

We know few details of their relationship, although they saw each other often and her portrait in miniature was hanging on his wall in Richmond when he died. We would like to know more of Daniel's meetings with the people who frequented her salon at Aix. One of them, Eugene Sue, the author of *Wandering Jew,* was as little liked by the regime of Napoleon III as was Marie de Solms. When in 1855 Napoleon pressed Sardinian authorities to exile Sue from their kingdom, the author asked Daniel whether his election in 1848 to "une académie littéraire dans l'Etat de New York" gave him some right to American citizenship. The American minister gave a negative reply and apparently did not bother to report the matter to Washington.[79]

The time would come in Turin when Marie de Solms would ask John Daniel to do a great service for her and her friends, who included the King of Sardinia. This service, like Daniel's letter to Arthur Peticolas, would for a time threaten to do grave damage to his career.

An Interesting Kingdom

In mid-May 1854, the anniversary of the Sardinian national constitution was celebrated. It was a major national holiday, and for the first time since the publication of his notorious letter, John Moncure Daniel made a number of appearances in public, taking part together with the king and his ministers and the rest of the diplomatic corps in a series of ceremonies that included a great open-air Mass. Foreign Minister Dabormida had by now reconciled himself to the fact that the American representative, lately promoted to minister resident, was not, after all, going to leave. Daniel's presence on the constitution holiday caused no particular stir, although he remained faithful to Secretary Marcy's circular and wore the plain dark suit of an American citizen. Still, he wrote in strict confidence to his friend W. W. Crump in Richmond, he did not think his unfortunate letter would ever be totally forgotten in Turin. Daniel begged Judge Crump not to say anything, but he intended to try to trade places with a colleague, either Robert Dale Owen at Naples or August Belmont at The Hague. Both, he said, were agreeable to a trade, assuming the State Department concurred.[1] There is no indication that he ever asked Washington; he perhaps came to realize that the chances of working such a scheme were minimal.

Daniel had in no way forgotten the damage that Peticolas and Hughes had done to him. Since publishing Daniel's letter to Peticolas, the new proprietor of the *Richmond Examiner* had apparently taken it on himself to defend Daniel from subsequent attacks by the Northern press. At the beginning of April 1854, Daniel wrote to Crump:

> Will you do me a favour?—It is, that you ask that man Hughes for the sake of decency, to let my name alone and keep it out of his infernal paper. Not content with spoiling my career by stealing my letters and violating every law of honour in the publication of them, I see that he continues to talk flabby nonsense about every vile report that the press of New York sets afloat about me. . . . I had as leif [*sic*] have the fingers of the hangman busy about my neck as see his clumsy thumbs tampering with my name. . . . I always knew him to be soft of brain, and

> to be destitute of all high-level delicacy in his sentiments, and he is just the last man in the world to whom I would entrust my case. . . .
>
> If there ever was a man who received base treatment from both friends and enemies it is myself. . . . You are one of the few persons to whom I can look with confidence now.[2]

Eventually, both Peticolas and Hughes made their peace with Daniel, who meanwhile worked his way into the affairs of the Kingdom of Sardinia. As he had suspected, the work was not terribly taxing. In all of 1854 he sent only eighteen official dispatches to the Department of State, plus several letters to Secretary Marcy. Aside from legation business, he did his best to keep up with events in Virginia and elsewhere in America. His devoted friend Thomas Wynne sent him the Richmond newspapers, and he seems to have received the *New York Tribune*, and perhaps other New York papers, on a regular basis. There are indications that he maintained regular correspondence with friends and acquaintances, but few of these documents have been found other than Daniel's letters to Judge Crump, which focused on his next crisis: his trial for libel in New York.

Shearjashub Spooner's suit against Daniel had not originally made the news in Turin. However, in early June 1854, with the garlic letter mess hardly settled, the press in Turin reprinted a report from the New York Italian-language paper *L'Eco d'Italia* that the chargé d'affaires of the United States in the Kingdom of Sardinia had been ordered by a New York court to pay a fine of eight thousand piastres for calumnies uttered in the newspaper of which he was editor. According to the report, the editor had not been permitted to leave for Turin until he paid the fine. The report caused a new sensation in Turin society, and the foreign minister instructed his representative in Washington to ascertain the facts.[3]

The facts were that the two thousand dollars (or eight thousand piastres) Daniel had paid was not a fine but bail, and a trial was yet to come. In preparation for that trial, Congressman Thomas H. Bayly of Virginia, acting as U.S. commissioner, a common practice in such cases, took depositions in Virginia in April 1854 from Bennett De Witt, the previous owner of the *Richmond Examiner*, and Robert Hughes, to whom Daniel had sold the paper before departing for Europe. De Witt stated that at the time of the *Examiner* article attacking Spooner and his Boydell engravings, he employed John M. Daniel on salary, and Daniel had "no power to insert anything in the columns of the paper contrary to my wishes." Hughes said in his deposition that he had been John M. Daniel's attorney for two months prior to the alleged libel, and that Daniel's position had been that of "associate editor with Mr. De Witt," but that Daniel had no financial interest in the paper at that time.[4]

The case was set for trial in New York on May 15, 1854, before Judge Samuel R. Betts, whom President John Quincy Adams had appointed a federal judge in 1826 and who now, at the age of seventy-eight, was perhaps the outstanding American expert on equity. Daniel's attorney, Henry Breckenridge, was suddenly called to Niagara Falls when his mother fell sick, but Breckenridge's partner failed to notify Judge Betts about Breckenridge's absence or to appear in court himself on the day of the trial. Daniel, in Turin, was unaware that his interests were not being defended. What he did know was that Judge Crump, on whom he depended to oversee Breckenridge's conduct of his defense—and to keep him informed—was a poor correspondent. (Later, it was learned that one or more of Crump's letters to Daniel had gone astray.) Clearly Crump was neglecting Daniel's interests. Thomas Wynne wrote to Daniel on April 30 that he had tried again and again to see Crump about the forthcoming trial, but Crump had not responded. At best, letters from Richmond to Turin took over two weeks to arrive. But Crump wrote few letters to keep Daniel abreast of the Spooner case, despite continuing appeals from John Daniel. Daniel wrote later to Crump: "[Y]ou have allowed me to languish like an impaled Turk, spitted through the gizzard by Shearjashub, when a word from you could have releived [*sic*] my pains. Do you suppose it is a pleasant thing for a man of honour to be put away on a shelf 5000 miles from the scene of action where his character for integrity—for common honesty—is at stake, while his friends seem too entirely indifferent to take the slightest notice of his appeals?"[5]

To complicate matters, still another scandal seemed to be looming for John Daniel. A young gentleman named G. A. Meyer had recently called on him, identifying himself as a naturalized American of Hungarian birth and a member of the New York bar. Meyer said that he had decided to take some time off from his law practice. He planned a visit of several months in Turin, and it would help him find his way in Turin society if Daniel could give him the nominal title of "attaché" of the legation. Daniel foolishly agreed to do so. Then, in late June 1854, Daniel left Turin for a few days in the neighboring mountains. His sojourn was cut short by a letter from William Magoun, still working at the legation, who told him that Meyer had persuaded young Frederick Daniel to accompany him to a Turin bank. There, Meyer had used his credentials to draw on the legation's account in London for fifty pounds sterling. He then vanished from Turin. Daniel returned to Turin and repaid the Turin bank for the draft, which Barings had refused in London (and which was equivalent to several weeks' salary for Daniel), and then hastened to inform the State Department as well as Judge Crump.[6] This time, a potential Daniel scandal stayed out of the papers.

Back in New York, Judge Betts entered a default judgment of eight thousand dollars against John M. Daniel when no one appeared to defend him. This was far less than the fifty thousand dollars Shearjashub Spooner had sought but much more than Daniel had in the world.

Lawyer Breckenridge wrote Daniel that he should not be alarmed: the judgment would be set aside and the trial rescheduled.[7] Fortunately for Daniel, Breckenridge was right; he arranged to have the judgment set aside after payment of court costs. The case was retried before a jury in New York between October 17 and 20, 1854. In his charge to the jury, Judge Betts (who perhaps kept in mind the possibility that the case might ultimately be reviewed by the Supreme Court, on which the defendant's great-uncle was still sitting) noted that there was hardly any evidence to show that the defendant was the author of the article in question. He went on, however, to destroy much of the defense's argument, emphasizing that it was not only a question of who had been the responsible editor of the *Richmond Examiner* when the article appeared. In the judge's view, "every writer in the newspapers of the day should be held to a rigorous responsibility for the free use of his coarse and vigorous epithets." The judge concluded that, although the jury should not punish the defendant for what he had written against the Northern people as a whole or against Spooner as a Northern individual, "You will award Mr. Spooner damages in accordance with the injury he has received."[8]

The jury awarded Spooner damages of $3,250. This sum was lower than Judge Betts's earlier judgment but still a very large amount for Daniel. His former associates De Witt and Hughes took up a collection for him in Virginia, but apparently raised little money. Virginians liked to read what Daniel wrote, but one might say that they declined to put their money where his mouth was. Daniel agreed that his friend Thomas Wynne, who had become superintendent of the Richmond gas works, could offer Daniel's personal library of about two thousand books for sale to raise the money. Daniel thought the sale might bring twelve to fifteen hundred dollars, which, together with the two thousand dollars paid earlier for his bond, would satisfy the judgment. However, the library sale brought just over six hundred dollars, far less than Daniel had hoped. Then, however, Shearjashub Spooner, who apparently feared the outcome of a possible appeal, offered to settle for a thousand dollars less, or $2,250. Early in 1855, Judge Crump succeeded in reaching a settlement for only $2,000. In addition, John Daniel agreed to pay Henry Breckenridge several hundred dollars in legal fees. Although costly, the case had not left him bankrupt.

As journalist Sexson Humphreys commented, the case had important effects on both principals. Shearjashub Spooner, distraught over the low judgment and his failure to obtain duty-free entry for his separate French collections, began to suffer from a nervous disorder that ended his life less than five years later. John Daniel, his personal financial plan set askew, must have realized that he would need to stay abroad longer if he expected to go home, as had been his plan, with some capital. When he finally returned to Richmond and journalism, six years after the Spooner case ended, his attitude toward the North showed the effects of what a Yankee had done to him. At the time the trial ended, however, Daniel seems to have had no thought of a long tour of duty in Piedmont. Writing to Judge Crump in January 1855, he insisted that he would be home soon.[9]

The Spooner trial distracted Daniel, but it did not apparently affect his legation work. The American minister found that the sizable amount of trade between the United States and the Kingdom of Sardinia created recurring problems that involved American shipping. Although consuls were expected to deal with such problems locally, sometimes they escalated to the diplomatic level. In late 1854, for example, the American ship *George Green*, H. C. Redman master, arrived in Genoa from New Orleans laden with cotton and tobacco. Daniel later reported to the State Department that Captain Redman had to spend his first days in port dealing with "a mutinous crew of negroes."[10] Whether any were slaves is not clear, but there was no slavery in Sardinia (or elsewhere in Western Europe) and the kingdom had lately enacted a law that granted freedom to any slaves who entered its territory.[11] Preoccupied with the crew, Redman neglected to give the customs authorities the required list of his stores and provisions. Worse, the weight of the tobacco unloaded from the ship was understated. That was serious. As Daniel reported at another time, tobacco was more dangerous than gunpowder to an American ship in a Sardinian port. Even the slightest irregularity could subject a ship to serious fines. If the authorities found that a considerable amount of tobacco had been smuggled in, the entire ship could be confiscated, as had happened to the American vessel *Louisa* at Genoa in 1849.[12] In the case of the *George Green,* Sardinian officials levied a hefty fine, equivalent to almost four thousand dollars. Consul Herbemont reported this to the American legation in Turin, and Daniel got it reduced to 210 francs, or forty dollars. Daniel told the State Department that he was reporting this to Washington because in some cases the facts might be misrepresented, even by the Sardinian legation in Washington. (But perhaps Daniel's reporting from Turin was occasionally self-serving: he would not want Washington to think he was underemployed.)

For some months in 1854 Daniel also found himself occupied occasionally with the question of the principality of Monaco, an enclave along what was then the coast of the Kingdom of Sardinia. Monaco had belonged to the princely Grimaldi family for eight hundred years but became part of Napoleonic Europe. After Waterloo, the Treaty of Vienna in 1815 put it under the protection of Sardinia. It went still further under Sardinia's protection after the revolutionary year of 1848, when, as Daniel noted to the State Department, the Monegasque people had driven out the Grimaldis.

In 1854, a rumor persisted in Europe that the United States wanted to buy Monaco for use as a station to host its Mediterranean naval squadron. Two vessels from the squadron had called at Villafranca, the port nearest Monaco. The local people had given the ships an exuberant welcome, seeing them as proof that the

Americans were coming to stay. In addition, an American journalist visiting the American legation in Paris had seen in the waiting room a man who styled himself Prince of Monaco and who told the journalist that negotiations were proceeding in Paris for the sale of Monaco to the United States. Little did the journalist know that that the man was insane. Daniel wrote the State Department that the rumor was carried to America and "again crossed the Atlantic to disturb the digestion of European politicians. It has been frequently pointed to in the press, as a proof of the grasping disposition of the United States towards a general system of European annexation."[13]

Soon the Sardinian foreign ministry called in the American minister to ask about American views on Monaco. Daniel replied flatly that the rumors were a canard, adding—equally flatly—that American naval vessels had a treaty right to call at Sardinian ports and that their business was not a subject for inquiry. Eventually, the Grimaldis returned to Monaco, and the principality regained its full sovereignty. (A century later, the U.S. Navy established a home port for a cruiser at Villafranca, by then the French port of Villefranche. It does not appear that this raised any questions about possible American annexation.)

The main question for the Kingdom of Sardinia was that of Italian unification. Could the Italian people ever find themselves united in a single state—a constitutional, if not democratic, one—rather than remaining divided into various duchies and kingdoms and the Papal States, with many northern Italians under the heel of Austria? Above all, it was Austrian rule just east in Lombardy that preoccupied the leaders of Sardinia. In 1848 and 1849, before John Daniel had ever dreamed of serving his country at Turin, Sardinia had attempted a trial of strength against the Austrian empire, which Daniel later called "that composite giant."[14] After liberating Milan, Sardinia had suffered defeats at Custozza and at Novara, then given up all it had won in Lombardy.

In 1855, Sardinia fully felt the need for the support of England and France if it was ever to make headway against Austria. Sardinia therefore joined those two powers in their alliance against Russia and sent 15,000 troops, more than a quarter of its army, to the Crimea under its best general, Alberto La Marmora. Daniel, hearing the rumor that Sardinia might send the troops, initially reported to Washington that he disbelieved it.[15] His next dispatch rectified his mistake, and he commented correctly that if the Crimean War ended quickly, without sizable losses for the Sardinian expeditionary corps, Sardinia's new alliance with France and England would be a great coup for the kingdom. Otherwise, Sardinia would pay dearly for the privilege of recognition as a European power.[16]

Since 1852, the prime minister of Sardinia had been a Piedmontese nobleman, Count Camillo Benso di Cavour. The foreign ministry remained in the hands of General Dabormida, but it was Cavour who made foreign policy. Like Daniel,

Camillo Cavour, prime minister of the Kingdom of Sardinia. Library of Congress.

Camillo Cavour had been a journalist and editor. In 1848, when revolutions had broken out elsewhere in Italy, Cavour had played a leading role in getting the monarchy to accept a constitution (though not a very liberal one) in order to avoid revolution in the Kingdom of Sardinia. It is not clear when Daniel met Prime Minister Cavour, but it was not long after Daniel reached Turin. Later, Daniel came to admire the shrewdness of Cavour and then to take pleasure when Cavour was briefly thrown out of office, but later still he would suffer Cavour's wrath. When Cavour eventually left office, it was the doing of the king, Vittorio Emanuele II. This king was a strong-willed man, and he used frank, barracks language. When he visited England in 1855, he told Queen Victoria and other eminent people that he would like to execute the revolutionary Mazzini, shoot Sardinia's priests en masse, and exterminate the Austrians.[17] He eventually became fond of the frank young American envoy who did not wear customary court uniform.

The more Daniel learned about the Kingdom of Sardinia, the more interested he became. The Sardinian army was not only much larger than the American, but it was well trained and well equipped. On a continent still composed of authoritarian, often tyrannical, kingdoms and empires, Sardinia had a constitution, and, Daniel thought, a decent one at that. It even had a free press, although, as Daniel wrote to his friend Crump, the authorities did not tolerate criticism in the press of other, more powerful European states. Recently, a group of editors had been sent to jail for reprinting sneers from English papers about the chastity of Queen Isabella of Spain.[18]

Nor, Daniel found, was much public commentary on the Catholic church permitted, although the government of Sardinia was not pro-clerical and had decided to close down most of the religious houses and monasteries in the kingdom. Daniel found it amazing that, although the Papal States and the papacy were in a weak and rotten condition, shrewd Presbyterian pastors back in America prated about the Catholic threat. Such talk was nonsense, wrote Daniel: "They have been trying for more than eight years to build a rail-road on the Tiber banks, and have not been yet able to get the route surveyed. These are the people who are to turn the world upside down some day."[19]

Sometime after April 1854, Daniel began to make occasional trips to Paris. He enjoyed the chance to consult his more senior counterpart and fellow Virginian, Minister John Y. Mason. He also began to consult Paris doctors. There is no indication that he was dissatisfied with Dr. Picchiotti in Turin, but Paris appears to have had the specialists he thought he needed. One of these was an American physician named Rawlings, who years later was at Daniel's side when he died. Daniel did not want his chief in Washington to think he was neglecting official business. He wrote Secretary of State Marcy in late May that the season for political business ended in Piedmont with the onset of hot summer. The king and court then left for the mountains and watering places, and the foreign diplomats took leaves of absence. Daniel added that he would be grateful if Marcy would grant him a short leave of absence, apparently in order to return to America. It seems that Marcy was unwilling to do so; after all, Daniel had been at his post less than a year. But the secretary of state had already agreed that Daniel might make short trips to neighboring cities as the press of his duties permitted, and Daniel seems to have seen this agreement as sufficient authority for trips he made over the coming months and years to Paris, other points in the Kingdom of Sardinia, and beyond.

In July 1854, Daniel received a visitor in Turin whose statements raised questions about James Buchanan's conduct of America's business in London. The visitor told him that his name was Albinola. He bore letters that identified him, Daniel subsequently wrote to Buchanan, as "a political emissary of the so-called republican party of Europe." The letters asked John Daniel to give Albinola the protection of the American legation in Turin and to arrange his passport. Albinola then produced a passport issued by the American legation in London, and signed by

James Buchanan, that identified the passport holder as a bearer of official dispatches. However, places on the passport for the bearer's name and destination were blank. Albinola asked Daniel to write in an assumed name and make the passport good for all of Italy. Daniel refused. He questioned the mysterious visitor at length, and the man finally admitted that he was not an American citizen and said that he had never set foot in the United States. Indeed, he apparently spoke no English. Daniel wrote Buchanan that this visitor then "said he received the letters and the passport while at Geneva from an American gentleman who was, if he is not now, in London." (Might this have been George Sanders?)

Albinola was certainly in a risky position in Turin, and he finally threw himself on John Daniel's mercy. If, he told Daniel, the American minister just gave him an ordinary emigrant's passport (which would not identify him as an American citizen), he would promise to go directly to America. Daniel issued him such a passport after satisfying himself that wherever the man came from, he was not a citizen of the Kingdom of Sardinia. Daniel made the passport good only for one month, and only for passage by sea from Genoa to England and then to America.

Daniel wrote to Buchanan that Albinola's was not the first such case: "Numbers of these numskulls [*sic*] come to me under the belief that I am an active partizan [*sic*] of their crack-brained theories and willing to prostitute my office into a bureau for their contemptible intrigues and conspiracies—which never have produced any result, and never will." Daniel was, in a sense, right to scorn the Italian revolutionaries. It was not through their efforts that Italy would be unified, and after reunification Italy would still have to wait nearly another century for democracy; but there were many dedicated and noble-hearted people among them.[20]

Daniel also wrote, very politely, as one might well write to a man who undoubtedly still dreamed of the presidency, that he suspected Buchanan had been imposed on, tactfully suggesting that if Buchanan had signed the blank passport with knowledge of how Albinola planned to use it, he no doubt had wise and sufficient reasons to do so. Daniel wrote that he thought it more likely that Buchanan had been induced to sign it by some false statement. Daniel also reported the case to the secretary of state, who asked Buchanan for an accounting. In response, Buchanan sent Marcy a somewhat temporizing reply in October 1854: "[I]t is scarcely possible for any person more faithfully or more rigidly to have carried out his instructions in relation to the granting of passports than myself; this, too, in the face of strong efforts to induce me to make exceptions under special circumstances."[21] Buchanan added that he was sorry Marcy had not communicated to him the name of the person who carried a passport he had purportedly signed. One wonders whether he wanted to pass the name to George Sanders.

The matter was apparently dropped, although Buchanan eventually admitted to Marcy that, allegedly because of the press of business, he was "compelled" to sign blank passports.[22] There were more important concerns for Mr. Buchanan and Mr. Marcy. There were rumors that Marcy might resign as secretary of state and replace Buchanan in London. Might Buchanan then again become secretary of state? Buchanan wrote Marcy that he was ready to resign and that he would retire; he did not want to be secretary of state.[23] But Marcy stayed where he was, and so did Buchanan.

Daniel continued to be troubled by press rumors and by the effects of his strict adherence to Marcy's circular on dress. In late October, the *New-York Daily Times* commented that the conduct of three American officials abroad, Pierre Soulé at Madrid, John Daniel at Turin, and ex-consul George Sanders at London, had "pointed many an editorial shaft with peculiar venom."[24] The shafts were still being fired. On December 15, 1854, Daniel wrote in a private letter to Marcy that he had seen in an American newspaper a story, originally in the *New York Herald*, claiming that the American minister at Turin had been expelled from a club of gentlemen. As Marcy knew, this was false, and Daniel hoped that Marcy would get the pro-administration *Washington Union* to say so, unless the secretary of state thought it best simply to let such things run their course.[25]

Daniel's letter continued. Recently, Luigi Mossi, Sardinia's former chargé d'affaires in Washington who was now secretary general of the Sardinian foreign ministry, had asked him to come by. The question that Mossi wanted to discuss was proper dress. Daniel, who did not think Mossi was well disposed toward Americans, was astounded to hear that the ministry had asked all of Sardinia's diplomatic posts abroad to report what kind of apparel American ministers wore on formal occasions in other capitals. Daniel reported to Marcy:

> I learned how Mr. Buchanan wore his tights and sword, how Mr. Jackson dressed in his militia uniform,[26] &c &c &c. The end of it was, that many American Ministers wore court dress, and it was therefore mildly suggested that I might wear one too! It was true that none had been required of me last year; but as so many others had done so, it was expected that I would array myself in purple and fine linen in time for the festivities which would commence anew on the 1st of the coming January.
>
> I replied that the want of a court dress did not interfere with the fullest discharge of my official duties, as it was not required when I went to see either the Foreign Minister or the King himself; and although I might be personally willing to conform my dress to the taste of the King's courtiers, yet as my own Government had expressed a wish on the subject, I could not hesitate as to which of the two I should regard. But, I continued, there was a way to avoid all unpleasantness in the matter, and that was for me to *stay away* from the as-

semblages in question altogether, and as the cause would not now be attributed to disrespect on my part, that was the course I should adopt.

Daniel concluded by telling Marcy that he hoped never to have to report to him again on this particular subject.

The American minister to the Kingdom of Sardinia played at most the role of distant spectator in that flurry of American diplomatic activity in late 1854 that produced the Ostend Manifesto. The idea was that several American ministers from European capitals—Pierre Soulé, Madrid; James Buchanan, London; and John Mason, Paris—should meet privately to discuss what the United States ought to do about Cuba and then give Washington the benefit of their wisdom. In October the three met at Ostend, Belgium, and subsequently at Aachen, Prussia, and agreed on a document stating that the United States should try to buy Cuba from Spain, for a fair price. That was nothing new; American presidents since Thomas Jefferson had wanted Cuba for the United States, and both Soulé and his predecessor at Madrid had been authorized to negotiate the purchase of Cuba for $100 million or more. What was new was the statement, agreed on by the three American diplomats at Ostend, that if Spain should refuse to sell Cuba (as it had consistently done), and if the United States should decide that Spain's continued possession of it threatened America's security, the United States "shall be justified in wresting it from Spain."[27]

What had been agreed on at Ostend soon began to leak to the press. It caused a sensation in Europe, above all in Spain, and in the end the United States came no closer to acquiring Cuba, either by purchase or by force. Marcy was distressed by the publicity, and so it seemed was President Pierce. The three ministers were to have met quietly, but when Pierre Soulé and James Buchanan came to Paris, a number of other American ministers also found themselves in there, including John O'Sullivan from Lisbon, August Belmont from The Hague, Lewis Cass from Rome, and John Daniel from Turin. Belmont had hoped to get into the Ostend talks, but the presence of O'Sullivan, Cass, and Daniel seems to have been coincidental. O'Sullivan was simply passing through Paris; Cass had come up on private business; and Daniel is said to have come to Paris to escape the cholera epidemic that had broken out in Turin,[28] but perhaps he had also come to see his doctors. In addition to the Europe-based diplomats, Assistant Secretary of State A. Dudley Mann was present and made himself audible and visible in London and in Paris. Even before the Ostend document hit the press, Secretary Marcy wrote to Minister Mason in Paris, "We are all suffering—we here, and you abroad—by the indiscretion and misconduct of certain persons who have been sent abroad. . . . The assemblage of so many American Diplomats in Paris at this time is a *malheureux accident*. I cannot but suspect that the *unfortunate notoriety* given to the proposed conference has added to their number."[29]

He was right. European public opinion—at least insofar as public opinion was reflected in the press—was decidedly negative in regard to the foreign policy of the Pierce administration. A long *New-York Daily Times* article, datelined Paris,[30] reported that

> there is, as you know, a Congress of our American Representatives in Europe, in session in this city. At the head of them is M. SOULE, who, it is said, used his efforts, while in Spain, to overturn the throne of the Queen to whom he was accredited. Mr. BUCHANAN, said by thousands of documents sent over Europe to be a political sympathizer with SANDERS, is to be here. Mr. DANIELS [*sic*], of Turin—whose letters have secured him an immortality of ridicule—Mr. SICKLES, whose character, public and private, is as well known in Paris as it is in New-York; the Jew, BELMONT, who talks English with an accent; Roman CASS and Lisbon O'SULLIVAN, *et id genus omne*, are here or are to be here. It is said they are plotting about Cuba.

Donn Piatt, the secretary to Minister Mason at the Paris legation, would write years later that the Ostend affair had been an absurdity but had proven decidedly useful to one participant. James Buchanan had angled for the presidency in 1852 but had lacked the support he needed from Southerners and from the leaders of Young America. The next time around, he could point to the Ostend Manifesto as a move he had made that accorded fully with their views.[31]

In late 1855, Daniel learned that a certain Gaspare Belcredi had been arrested by Sardinian authorities on the border between the Kingdom of Sardinia and Austrian-held Lombardy. The authorities suspected him of planning to stir up trouble for the Austrians in Lombardy. Although the Sardinian government had its own dreams for Lombardy, it did not countenance activities by revolutionaries at a time when it wanted to keep relations with Austria normal. Belcredi produced an American passport issued to him in Paris by the secretary of the U.S. legation, Donn Piatt. Passports were usually signed by the minister; however, this one seemed to be in order. From what the Sardinian authorities told him, Daniel suspected that Belcredi was not an American citizen and wrote to Piatt for confirmation. Daniel wrote that he did not like such people "who go to the United States not to live, but simply to get some hook on the protection of a generous people, and who then come straight back to what they still call '*their* country' and which 'they too much love,' to involve the United States in disputes about their lousy carcasses."[32]

Belcredi asked Daniel to arrange permission for him to remain in Piedmont, but Daniel refused. The Sardinian government, which had identified Belcredi as one of Mazzini's chief revolutionary agents, planned to deport him to France. Belcredi tried to call John Daniel's bluff, threatening to report him to Washington for neglecting his responsibilities toward American citizens. Daniel thereupon reported the matter himself to the State Department.[33] Meanwhile, Donn Piatt wrote back to Daniel, admitting that "Belcredi (may he be hung) was I suppose a citizen of my creation."[34]

Piatt added that he had just resigned his post at the Paris legation, after two years there. His letter was sent from Le Havre, and he was apparently on his way out of the country. Subsequently John Mason wrote Daniel that Piatt had not even said good-bye; his letter of resignation had been delivered after he had left town. Piatt's creditors were complaining that he had left large debts; and every day, some new evidence came to light of how he had degraded his official position.[35] Separately, St. George Peachey, a Virginia physician who had been living in Paris, wrote Daniel that "the Americans who made use of the mailbag for transporting silks, laces, pictures and bronzes mourn his loss loudly. . . . Perhaps a more villainous life was never led than that of Donn's in Paris."[36] (Peachey, who was conceivably one of the Paris doctors Daniel had consulted about his health, also wrote that he hoped Daniel would recommend him for a position at the penitentiary in Richmond.)

But some of the fault in the Piatt case was that of Minister Mason, for failing to provide proper supervision of his mission. The state of affairs in the Paris legation had become visible even from Washington, and the secretary of state wrote Mason several times about it, noting as an example that once a newspaper had been sent by the legation to the State Department through the mail wrapped in an official dispatch.[37] The problem stemmed basically from Mason's weak health in the aftermath of the strokes he had suffered. As Donn Piatt had written to John Daniel earlier in the year, Mason had come to rely heavily—too heavily, it seems—on Piatt to run his legation.[38] In contrast, the indications are that Daniel supervised the legation at Turin carefully and efficiently. The letterbooks of the Turin legation show that when Daniel's accounts were audited by the Treasury in Washington, there were few discrepancies. Practically his only lapse of judgment came in giving young Meyer a letter of accreditation as attaché, and Daniel paid out of his own pocket for that mistake.

Daniel was initially suspicious of Italians who came to him claiming to be naturalized American citizens, but he stood up for them if they could prove their citizenship. In 1855, he took up the case of Giacomo Zanoni, a naturalized American who had returned to Piedmont on a visit and was called into service in the Sardinian army. Daniel consulted his counterpart in Paris, Mason, who had once been U.S. attorney general. Mason admitted that he had no experience with such cases, but nevertheless recommended that Daniel send a note to the Sardinian foreign ministry claiming Zanoni's exemption from military service. Mason's argument was that a "sojourner" was not liable to conscription laws, and that the right of naturalization necessarily included the right of expatriation.[39]

Daniel thereupon sent a note to the ministry—which did not agree with the argument. Nor did the State Department after Daniel reported the case to Washington. There were, in fact, many precedents, said the Department, and "The general principle is that the naturalization of a foreigner does not exempt him from the effect of contracts entered into or penalties incurred in his native country prior to his naturalization."[40] That settled the matter for Daniel, and he reluctantly dropped the case. In succeeding decades, more than one of his successors would take up similar cases, especially during the First World War and large-scale Italian mobilization.

In 1856, a somewhat similar case came up, but it did not involve citizenship. Two Sardinian military musicians deserted and sought refuge on a ship of the U.S. Mediterranean squadron. Daniel told the commodore of the squadron that the United States had no treaty of extradition with Sardinia, and there was no need to hand back the men to the Sardinian authorities. This time the State Department agreed.[41]

In 1855, John Moncure Daniel still planned to return soon to Virginia. However, he was curious about the effect on him of the act of March 1, 1855, regarding American diplomatic ranks and salaries. Henceforth, the act provided, there would be a gradation in the salaries of American ministers abroad, from $17,500 for the minister at London down to $7,500 for ministers in charge of smaller legations. As for ministers resident like Daniel, they would apparently cease to exist as such after July 1, 1855; the act stated that the president should raise them all to the rank of envoy extraordinary and minister plenipotentiary, the title held by those who headed the biggest posts.

The act seemed to mean that Daniel, whose salary was $4,500, would receive a raise to $7,500. However, President Franklin Pierce and Attorney General Caleb Cushing[42] protested that Congress did not have the power to prescribe the power, rank, or number of public ministers; the ministers resident would remain just that. Eventually the matter was resolved to the satisfaction of the administration by an August 18, 1856, act that provided that smaller missions could still be headed by ministers resident or even chargés d'affaires.[43] Meanwhile, though, in October 1855, Daniel wrote a private letter to Secretary of State Marcy in which he said that the question of rank was not unimportant but the main thing was pay.[44]

Daniel told the secretary of state frankly that it had always been his intention to be back in Virginia by the end of March 1856, in time for the meetings preliminary to the national convention of the Democratic party and elections in the autumn. After hearing about the new act on ranks and salaries, he and his diplomatic peers in Europe had expected a raise in salary. However, when the long-expected envelopes arrived from the State Department, wrote Daniel, "[W]e found in place of new letters of credit the ingenious Opinion of the learned Attorney General, for which, I fear, few of us were properly thankful to Providence. He clipped the wing of vain imagination—rendering it optional with the President to convert his Residents into Plenipotentiaries, and making the increase of salary dependent on that conversion."

Daniel made it clear that he still planned to resign his commission during the coming year. But was it possible that the president would make the promotions and Congress then authorize back pay at the higher rate from July 1, 1855, onward? In that case, he could return to Virginia next spring somewhat better off financially than when he had left. It was not just a question of a salary increase. The new law had done away with outfits and infits, but he had received his outfit allowance when he came to Turin, and he very much hoped that on his return he would be paid the "infit," the expenses for his return (which amounted to three months' salary) that he had been entitled to when commissioned.

No answer was forthcoming. In December 1855, Lewis Cass Jr. wrote to Daniel from Rome, asking him to add his signature to a joint petition to Secretary Marcy on the salary question that Cass and Robert Dale Owen, in Naples, had already signed. Daniel declined because he had already written Marcy.[45] However, he badly wanted the extra money. He wrote Judge Crump in January 1856 that he had been "strictly economical" in Turin, and that if the government did him justice, "I shall have in all five thousand dollars in hand to commence the world again." Crump asked what Daniel planned to do. For now, Daniel responded, he thought of associating himself with the *Washington Union*, but perhaps he would take back the *Richmond Examiner*, if it was still in existence, when he returned. Except for an occasional worthwhile editorial, it seemed to have turned into "just an old village hack."[46]

Crump also wondered whether John Daniel planned to write a book about his European experiences. Daniel's answer was No, although since his arrival in Turin he had collected an immense number of curious letters, papers, and notes that he had carefully arranged and copied. If he chose to weave these things into a volume, Daniel thought they might make "a most extraordinary affair," which would sell by the hundred thousand, produce a most prodigious uproar, and make him rich; he could not fail to make less than fifty thousand dollars from it. But he was not going to write that sort of book. Instead, after he came home he would write his autobiography and leave it to be published after his death. During the next four years he also intended to write a history of the United States from the close of the War of 1812 to the end of the Pierce administration. The public wanted such a book, he believed, and it should gain him money and fame. Daniel also assured Crump that he would return to the world of journalism during the political campaign of 1856.[47]

Meanwhile, Daniel kept his focus on the work of his legation. He had not forgotten that the Personal Instructions to Diplomatic Agents received with his commission recommended that envoys report to Washington about political, historical, and statistical information not available in the United States. At the beginning of 1856, Daniel had been at Turin over two years. During that time, he had written a number of less than comprehensive reports on significant events and on conditions in the Kingdom of Sardinia. On January 1, 1856, he sent three dispatches which, in succinct form, provided a good overall picture of that kingdom.[48]

The Savoys had ruled their state for 800 years, and unceasing care and energy had been and were still required to maintain the little country, which was surrounded by powerful and lawless neighbors. Until recently, it had been an absolute monarchy, but now, Daniel wrote, there was a constitution and government was in the hands of the people, though it was guided by an oligarchy. The rule of this oligarchy had been beneficial, as witness the boom in railroad construction. In 1855, the kingdom had 548 kilometers of rail lines, and 296 kilometers more were under construction.

The Catholic Church still held more power in the Kingdom of Sardinia than in any other part of Europe except the Papal States, reported Daniel. There was a priest for every 214 inhabitants, compared to one in 600 in Belgium and one in 610 in Austria. Church revenues were half those in France, although the population of France was eight times that of this kingdom. However, the Sardinian government had closed ecclesiastical courts, the Church was prohibited from acquiring property without government permission, and the number of bishops was being reduced by not filling vacant sees. Daniel reported that the government planned to continue such actions until the Church was reduced to the status it had in Belgium and France: that of "a dependent and salaried agent of the Civil Power."

As for the kingdom's relations with America, Daniel reported that in 1852 the United States stood in sixth place among Sardinia's trade partners; in 1853, it was fourth; and now, in 1856, the kingdom probably had more trade with the United States than with any other country except England and France, whose support was key to Sardinia's position in Europe.

Daniel told Washington that this interesting kingdom had a population that probably numbered about 5.5 million persons, 60 percent of whom lived in Piedmont. It also had a well-trained regular army that numbered 50,000 men. In comparison, Daniel noted, the last figures he had seen for the American army showed a strength in June 1853 of only 10,329 men. Daniel added that the artillery was the best he had ever seen (there is no reason to believe that John Moncure Daniel had ever seen much artillery) and that the Sardinian navy was "far from contemptible," and had a number of modern steam vessels.

A month after sending these reports, Daniel commented to Washington that the kingdom seemed to have gained little other than additional debt by sending a large army corps to the Crimea, where its troops had been decimated by disease and the sword.[49] Daniel was right in regard to the financial and human costs. However, Cavour was proving to be a capable manager of his country's debt, and the Crimean experience was a step toward a critically useful alliance against Austria formed three years later with France, while England looked on benevolently. By then Daniel had become a still more incisive observer of the Italian, and European, scene.

Americans in a Changing Italy

Visitors from America were fairly frequent at the Turin legation. One of the more notable, and more useful to John Daniel, was James Gordon Bennett, founder and proprietor of the *New York Herald.* Bennett's paper was no great friend of the *Richmond Examiner,* although Bennett in general supported the Democrats in the mid-1850s. However, Daniel was not a Southern Democratic editor at that time; he was the American minister in Turin, and he and Bennett had a friendly meeting there at the beginning of 1856. Bennett, thirty years older than Daniel, seems to have taken a liking to the young envoy. Afterward, Bennett went from NUrin down to Florence, and when he read during his sojourn there a disrespectful allusion to Daniel in the *Herald*, he sent orders home, as he informed Daniel, "to prevent any such ill-natured remarks in future towards one whom I esteem so highly." Daniel sent back his thanks, adding that he had to admit he was not insensitive to criticisms of him in the American press, which were all the more disagreeable while he remained in a position where he could not defend himself.[1]

Another prominent visitor to Turin was former president Millard Fillmore, who had left the United States in March 1855 to spend a year traveling in Europe and around the Mediterranean. In France, Fillmore provided some personal financial assistance for the release of Horace Greeley of the *New York Tribune*, a political enemy, who had also gone to Europe, only to be imprisoned for debt.[2] Fillmore went to Turin and the American minister saw a great deal of him during his visit, although Daniel greatly disliked him. His own political views were sharply at odds with those of Fillmore, a Whig who was later nominated for president by the American Party—the Know-Nothings—while on this trip through Europe. Daniel wrote to Judge Crump in Richmond that he found Fillmore an utterly self-centered man who "talks commonplace and truisms." Fillmore, said Daniel, was traveling in Europe for the purpose of being introduced to kings and, if possible, dining with them. (Fillmore had been presented to Queen Victoria, who supposedly thought him the handsomest man she had ever seen, and subsequently to Napoleon III in Paris.) The former president was an utter Anglophile, wrote Daniel the near-Anglophobe, and would be content to see all legations closed except that in London. "I cannot call him a humbug," wrote Daniel, "because a humbug is a man who has an idea greater than himself and pretends to act it out in life, without being what he tries to seem. But Fillmore has no idea larger than himself."[3]

The most irritating American visitor during Daniel's years at Turin was probably Lucy Ward, wife of a gentleman from New York City. She rang the minister's door bell at 2:00A.M. one night in January 1855. She was distressed. She explained to Daniel that, while her husband remained at work in New York, she had taken their seventeen-year-old daughter, Genevieve, on a tour of Europe to complete the young lady's education. Alas, said Ward, on their travels through Italy they had met a young Russian nobleman, Capt. Constantine Grebel. Young Genevieve had soon become infatuated with Grebel, and he had gotten her to leave her mother and go traveling with him, telling the girl that they would be married in Turin—or maybe in Moscow. Ward wanted to have her daughter rejoin her, after which the mother intended to take her away to France. However, the daughter was with Grebel and, to make matters worse, the mother lacked funds to pay her bill at the Hotel Feder in Turin, and the proprietor had seized her luggage.

Daniel leaped to the lady's aid. He told Signor Feder that he would be good for the hotel bill if Ward did not pay within a month. He asked Secretary General Mossi at the foreign ministry whether the authorities could have Genevieve, who was a minor, returned to the care of her mother and then provide a policeman to escort them as far as the French border. Mossi for once was forthcoming, and agreed to do so. In addition, the authorities called in Grebel, who agreed to stay away from the two American ladies. Lucy and Genevieve Ward left Turin under escort, but that was far from the end of the matter.

J. B. Wilbor, the American consul in Nice (then a part of the Kingdom of Sardinia), soon reported to Daniel that the Wards had not gone to France but were staying on in Nice and that Captain Grebel was with them. He also said that after Lucy Ward had gone to Count La Marmora, the general intendant of the province, with some complaint, had investigated and obtained from Grebel convincing proof that not only Genevieve but Lucy Ward as well had been carrying on affairs with him. Meanwhile, Lucy Ward told Daniel that she had other debts besides the one to the Turin hotel and asked him to take care of those, too. Daniel knew what to do: he withdrew his guarantee to Hotel Feder. It turned out that the lady did have funds. She paid the bill, then wrote Daniel a furious letter saying that "under no circumstances will I ever address myself to a Minister so little attentive to the interests of his compatriots."[4]

Daniel never saw the two female Wards again, but over a year later he was still receiving correspondence about them from other posts. In April 1856, Robert Dale Owen, in Naples, wrote that his Russian counterpart had approached him about the case, and that he had heard from the American minister in St. Petersburg that

Grebel had married the young lady. Owen asked what John Daniel thought. He no doubt laughed, and answered briefly: "*Non so io*. . . . Perhaps, perhaps not. *Che so io?*" Fortunately, there were not many Lucy Wards. However, there was still the presumably cuckolded Mr. Ward, who showed up in Turin one day at the end of 1856. Daniel was not pleased to learn that Owen had shared with Ward the frank letters Daniel had written to him. Since Owen had done so, Daniel reviewed for Ward all that he knew, including the fact that love letters from his wife to the young Russian had been shown to the Sardinian authorities. Forgeries, said poor Mr. Ward, and then he departed.[5]

Although Daniel had told the secretary of state that he wanted to be back in Virginia by the end of March 1856, he had subsequently written to Crump in January that he would not leave Turin before the end of April. Just before then, Daniel received another letter from Robert Dale Owen in Naples. Owen had just heard from August Belmont in The Hague and Henry Bedinger in Copenhagen, both ministers resident like Owen and Daniel, that they had received statements of account from the fifth auditor of the Treasury "in which their salaries *are credited at the rate of $7,500 from 1st July last*."[6] However, when Bedinger had written to Barings in London to ascertain whether he could begin to draw his salary at the higher rate, they had said no. Still, it sounded as though things were in train to give Daniel and the others a huge raise from their present salary of $4,500. Some of the richer, titled diplomats in Turin might have been surprised to know how concerned these Americans were over a matter of three thousand dollars a year. However, it was a sizable amount, as much as a professional man might expect to make in a year in most parts of America. Even cabinet members in Washington received annual salaries of only eight thousand dollars.

In the spring of 1856, Daniel put aside for the moment such questions as pay, or offering his resignation, and went on a long leave outside Turin without informing the State Department. (He did still have Marcy's agreement that he might visit neighboring cities when his duties permitted.) Whether he had a companion on this trip is unclear. On May 16, Daniel was back in Turin and sent a note of congratulations to Count Cavour, who, while remaining prime minister, had taken on the job of foreign minister. Daniel explained his tardiness, writing that he had returned to Turin the previous evening, "after an absence prolonged by involuntary and unexpected causes to the extent of some weeks."[7] One might imagine that he had fallen sick; that he had perhaps gone to consult the Paris doctors. That was not the case, this time, as he wrote to his friend Thomas Wynne in Richmond. Daniel told Wynne that he had gone on a pleasant tour through the south of France. He had visited Nimes, where he saw the Maison Carrée, Jefferson's model for the state capitol in Richmond, and Arles, where he had watched a bullfight in the old stadium. Arles had the most beautiful women in France, he wrote, and passing down the main street was like strolling through a gallery of antique statues.[8]

When the Crimean War ended in 1856, Daniel reported that it had left Sardinia as England's satellite in Europe. If there was to be a liberal revolution someday in Europe, he wrote, it would have to begin with revolution in France. But the French seemed content with their "able despot" Napoleon III.[9] At this point neither Daniel nor, it seems, other observers could foresee what would occur three years later: no liberal revolution, no Sardinia under the thumb of England, but a French-Sardinian alliance whose successful invasion of Austrian-held Lombardy would begin the process that soon made Turin the capital of a reunited Italy. Cavour was already working in that direction. He needed to convince the French, who did not want Sardinia to become a powerful neighbor on their southeastern border, that his territorial aims were relatively modest. But, Cavour told his king, his secret objective was "to extend the boundaries of the royal domain and ensure its predominance over the rest of Italy."[10] Cavour would have to work cleverly and hard if he was to obtain such results; Sardinia was still small enough that it might be ignored by larger powers. On April 15, 1856, in the wake of the Crimean War, France and England signed a secret treaty with Austria to guarantee the status quo in Europe without informing Cavour.[11]

Another result of the war was the Declaration of Paris, also dated April 15, 1856, which was designed to regulate aspects of future wars at sea. All powers, including the United States, were called on to adhere to it. The declaration stated that a wartime blockade must be effective if it was to be binding on other states; a belligerent country could not simply announce a blockade of enemy ports but must send a blockading force sufficient to ensure compliance. The United States could agree to that in 1856, but, subsequently, it would cause some difficulty for the Union during the Civil War. What was more important, and unacceptable, to the United States was that part of the declaration which proclaimed an end to privateering. During its most recent naval war, the War of 1812, the United States had commissioned privateers. In 1856, the U.S. Navy had several squadrons stationed abroad, among them the Mediterranean squadron that, with its stores depot at La Spezia, was effectively based in the Kingdom of Sardinia. However, the U.S. Navy was not large, and Washington was concerned that putting an end to privateering would mean, as Secretary Marcy wrote the French minister in Washington that "[T]he dominion over the seas will be surrendered to those Powers which adopt the policy and have the means of keeping up large navies."[12]

Not many years later, Union shipping suffered serious losses to Confederate raiders like the CSS *Alabama*. The *Alabama*, which today still holds the North American record for destroying enemy shipping, was regularly commissioned by the Confederacy and no privateer. Still, the Union would have benefited from a complete ban on privateering. It is therefore amusing to see John Moncure Daniel, the American minister, going to Count Cavour on instructions from Washington to ask for support against such a ban.[13] Cavour temporized, but finally told Daniel in February 1857 that Sardinia, "a weak power," would support the United States if the text of the Paris Declaration was ever opened for renegotiation. However, Sardinia had signed the declaration, and Cavour made clear to Daniel that he could do nothing.[14] Daniel had another talk with Cavour in March. (Daniel may not have known that his influential friend James Hudson, the British minister, apparently had instructions to oppose the American position.) Cavour did not tell Daniel definitely what his government would do about American privateers in case of war. Given the Kingdom's adherence to the Declaration of Paris, he told Daniel, it would probably not let such privateers use its ports as bases for operations, but American privateers could always seek refuge if necessary.[15]

There can be no doubt that Count Cavour took a positive attitude toward the American naval presence, and generally toward the United States. He had at least two good reasons to do so. For one thing, the Americans might somehow prove useful, and were unlikely to be inimical, in some future crisis. Later, in 1859, when war with Austria loomed and England's attitude was not clear, Cavour was heard to suggest, not very realistically, that the United States might even threaten war with England to force it to intervene on the continent.[16] Second, and more practically, the Sardinian authorities were finding it useful to convey undesirable political activists to America on vessels of the Sardinian navy. The mayor of New York City protested when a group of exiles was landed there, but federal authorities did not prevent the landing, and the next group was put ashore in Boston. American opinion was divided on the subject of political exiles from Italy. Some papers called them shiftless adventurers, but in 1851 the American minister to the Holy See, Lewis Cass Jr., had paid three thousand dollars of his own money for passage to California for thirteen well-born young Romans imprisoned for supporting the short-lived Roman Republic. Daniel himself did not much care for such exiles and thought the Sardinian authorities should be told to stop using the United States as a kind of Botany Bay.[17]

Despite the positive Sardinian attitude toward the American naval squadron, there were two occasions when the squadron's depot at La Spezia was threatened with the need to move elsewhere. In 1852, before Daniel arrived, the Sardinian government had decided it needed the facilities for its own ships, but then it had changed its mind. In 1857, the authorities actually did take over the depot buildings, but Cavour assured Daniel that his government wanted the American squadron to stay and would let the Americans use all of Panigaglia Bay, an excellent anchorage. There were two ruined convents there that could be rebuilt as warehouses. In the end, the municipal authorities of La Spezia, eager to see the Americans stay in their city, provided other buildings, and the depot remained at La Spezia.[18]

Daniel had written to Thomas Wynne in mid-1856 that, for the moment, Europe was relatively quiet; European eyes were focused on America and its coming elections. Wynne responded that, although the main contenders for the presidency were Millard Fillmore and James Buchanan, he suspected neither would win and that the election would be thrown into the House of Representatives, resulting in the election of an abolitionist president[19]—a terrible prospect for the South, but Daniel had given up the idea of returning home for the 1856 political season. He could still hope for a pay raise if he remained in Turin. Perhaps he also realized that after three years abroad he was simply not a figure in Virginia politics, although he could hope to become one again.

At the end of September 1856, good news reached the American legation in Turin. The minister would indeed get his raise in pay from $4,500 to $7,500 per annum, and it would be retroactive to the previous July 1.[20] There could be no question of him submitting his resignation just then; it would presumably be required of him soon enough by the new president who would take office in March 1857.

Late in November 1856, Daniel learned that James Buchanan, who had left the London legation in March, would be the next president of the United States. Daniel wrote to the State Department to indicate obliquely that he was pleased. Those who ruled Europe, he reported, had earnestly hoped for the election of John Charles Frémont, the candidate of the new Republican party. "The supremacy of an experienced statesman like Mr. Buchanan . . . is distasteful to these men for the sure and simple reason that they wish to see us crippled in our foreign relations and disjointed by discord at home."[21]

Buchanan told the American nation in his inaugural address that all the practical problems in America had been resolved. Could that be so? In any case, Daniel saw his days in Turin ending soon. He wrote to John Y. Mason, who hoped to stay on in Paris, that he believed the new minister at Turin would be William Ritchie, and his strong wife. Daniel had heard long since that the lady wanted to go abroad, and Buchanan owed something to the veteran editor who had always been "a pillar in his church." As for himself, John Daniel said he looked forward to resuming an active life; idleness was purgatory anywhere, but idleness in exile was simply hell.[22]

How idle or underemployed Daniel had really been at Turin is difficult to say. If he foresaw the loss of his post, it was perhaps natural for him to say that it mattered little. Separately, he wrote to Thomas Wynne that at times he was quite busy at legation work. He had also written several private essays for Wynne, but he thought they had turned out flat and did not want to send them. One described a trip he had made to Lombardy and Venice. Another described a tour up to the St. Bernard Pass, where he had spent a night "among the monks and big dogs, dead horses, &c., &c." A third described an execution he had witnessed behind the citadel of Turin. These were interesting scenes, but "[N]othing could induce me to spend another term in this accursed country. The banks of the Po are wearisome when I recollect the shores of the River James."

Perhaps Daniel sincerely believed what he wrote. However, the shores of the James would become considerably dimmer in his mind before he went home, for he was to spend four more years on the banks of the Po. Meanwhile, the devoted Wynne continued his more or less monthly letters to Daniel about events at home. One wonders whether some of what Wynne wrote really sharpened Daniel's interest in Richmond. Much of it amounted to what Wynne admitted was "tempests in teapots," the broils of Richmond city politics and city scandals. Robert Hughes asked Wynne to tell Daniel that he was tired of running the *Examiner* and that he wished Daniel would come back and take it over.[23] The American minister to the Kingdom of Sardinia did not leap at the opportunity.

Figure Four and the Minister

John Moncure Daniel learned at the beginning of 1857 that his great-uncle had recently suffered a great loss. A decade earlier, Peter Vivian Daniel had lost his first wife, Lucy, after a marriage of thirty-seven years. In 1853, when he was sixty-nine years old, he took a second wife, a young woman named Elizabeth Harris, who was the daughter of a Philadelphia physician. In January 1857, she died, reportedly when her dress caught fire. John Daniel wrote immediately to his great-uncle to express his condolences and to say how much respect and affection he had always felt for him.[1] There is no reason to believe that John Daniel had an ulterior motive in writing, but the relationship revived by his letter of condolence was later to prove extremely useful to the American minister at Turin.

James Buchanan took office as president on March 4, 1857. He had always stood for rotation in office. John Daniel wrote to John Mason in Paris that "there will be the greatest run for office on the new Administration that has ever been heard of since Adam was expelled from his comfortable berth and fat fish beside the slow-flowing Euphrates."[2] Daniel tried to reassure the worried Mason about his chances of staying at the Paris legation. After all, he noted, Mason and Buchanan had served together as members of Polk's cabinet; Buchanan had stayed with Mason when he came down to canvass Virginia in 1852; and Mason had been Buchanan's steady and able supporter. (But what had Buchanan in London really thought of his colleague across the Channel who, aside from everything else, had suffered at least two strokes in the last four years?)

Mason had reason for concern about keeping his post. Buchanan made clear that he did indeed plan to replace officers who had served all or most of the four years of Franklin Pierce's administration. This, the outgoing secretary of state wrote wryly in his diary, was being called the "boys' trap" or "figure four."[3] Marcy himself was famous for his statement years earlier that trumpeted the spoils system, but in 1857 he complained in his diary that "Pierce men are hunted down like wild beasts."[4] There were some exceptions; Southern officeholders were claiming exemption from the four-year rule, and it appeared that Buchanan was agreeing to their requests.

Although a Southerner, Daniel assumed that he would probably be replaced. He gave new thought to where he might go after Turin. From a letter he wrote to Judge Crump several weeks before Buchanan's inauguration, it appears that he had less interest in buying back the *Examiner* than in acquiring some other paper. He hoped to have around $11,000 after receiving his retroactive salary increase. That sum would not buy the *Richmond Enquirer*, whose proprietor overvalued it, but Daniel hoped that Crump would nevertheless sound out William Ritchie on what he would take for it, assuming Ritchie was given a post abroad. Daniel wanted Crump to understand that "[A] pecuniary independence has become a sine-qua-non in all my views of life. Now that I have got before the wind, I am completely indisposed to undertake any course that will set me to beating against it." He was therefore not going to hurry home, since he was saving at the rate of three to four thousand dollars a year. He would wait to submit his resignation until the new secretary of state formally notified him that he had entered office and would plan to stay on in Turin until his successor arrived, which he guessed might be in May or June 1857.[5]

Soon after Daniel sent his letter to Judge Crump, he heard surprising news from his faithful Richmond correspondent, Thomas Wynne. On February 8, Robert Hughes of the *Examiner* had called on Wynne to say that Hughes's father-in-law, John B. Floyd, was to become a member of the new president's cabinet. Hughes had reason to know that, although almost all American ministers abroad would be replaced, neither Mason in Paris nor Daniel in Turin would be disturbed. Daniel could either stay in Turin or take an equivalent position elsewhere in Europe. Hughes suggested that Daniel send his thoughts on this subject to someone like Judge Crump, who could communicate them to Governor Floyd.

Daniel saw no need to use intermediaries. On March 3, 1857, he wrote to Floyd that he would consider himself extraordinarily fortunate, on two counts, if he could stay in Europe. First, if he could continue to receive the salary of his present position for several years more, he could become almost financially independent. Second, although his first appointment had not been entirely happy, if he received a second proof of consideration from his government, all blemishes on his record could be erased. He would be pleased to remain in Turin, which was considered one of the most desirable of the minor missions, but because he had been there four years, and for "other reasons," there was no other mission of similar rank that he would not prefer to have instead of Turin.[6]

The same day, Daniel wrote to his great-uncle. He told him about the letter he had received from Wynne and the one he was sending Floyd. He knew that his great-uncle's relations with Buchanan were good; perhaps he could ascertain Buchanan's intentions in regard to his great-nephew; perhaps he could see Floyd. "I know too well what is due to you, to ask that you should solicit office for your nephew. All that I desire is to receive some intimation through you as to the step I should take and the treatment that I may expect to receive. As the head of my family, it has seemed to me that you might advise me of the truth without indelicacy."[7]

At the end of March, Daniel received a circular from the Department of State announcing that Lewis Cass had become the secretary of state. Daniel responded in a polite dispatch that expressed his pleasure at the news, but he did not offer his resignation.[8] During his long career, Cass had spent six years in diplomacy, as an able minister to France, and he would naturally take particular interest in how John Y. Mason was running the Paris legation, as well as in the flow of dispatches from neighboring Turin.[9]

Outside the American legation at Turin, other interesting things were happening in March 1857. Emperor Franz Josef of Austria paid a visit to Milan, and the Sardinian press published biting comments about it. Cavour had reined in the press before, when it criticized foreign personages, but this time he did not. The Austrians broke off diplomatic relations with the Kingdom of Sardinia. Daniel reported to Washington that the event had no serious significance. The apparent peace between Sardinia and Austria since Sardinia's defeat in 1849 was really a continuous long war on the diplomatic level. For now, Daniel saw little likelihood that the situation would escalate into a military conflict.[10]

He was right—for the time being. But there was more to the affair than Daniel could know. As a sign of goodwill, Vittorio Emanuele II had intended to send a special envoy to Milan for the emperor's visit, but he changed his mind after the Austrian police arrested and expelled a Sardinian senator who was visiting friends in Lombardy. Thereafter, the Austrian government sent an angry note to Turin demanding explanations for a number of Sardinian actions. Cavour made a cold and dignified reply, and it was then that Austria withdrew its envoy from Turin, and Sardinia followed suit in Vienna.[11] Later, Austria turned more conciliatory. Diplomatic relations resumed with Sardinia, and the young and attractive Archduke Maximilian was sent as viceroy to Milan to calm the restive Lombards. But it was too late. The Lombards wanted an end to Austrian rule. War was to come in just two years.

Sometime late in April 1857, John Moncure Daniel received a letter from his great uncle dated April 6. The justice had gone to see Floyd, who had received John's letter and told Peter Daniel that he would use whatever influence he had for the accomplishment of John's wishes; he would speak to President Buchanan. At this point, Justice Daniel decided that he himself would go see the president, although he had never seen Buchanan's predecessor, Franklin Pierce, unless invited by him.

> Departing from my habit, I called this morning on the President. . . . I said to him . . . that I had never asked of the Federal Government [any] favor for

> myself, or for kith or kin of mine, . . . that I considered myself nevertheless warranted in submitting to him a plain enquiry. . . . I then mentioned your position, and stated that whilst you were willing to retain that position, yet that as a man indued [*sic*] with a just cause of selfrespect, you were unwilling to be viewed as importuning the Government for its retention. . . .
>
> The President replied that he was aware of no dissatisfaction or objection as to yourself whatever; and in the event that change should become inevitable, it would not be made before the expiration of the full term for which the appointment had been given, and then only in such a mode as would be neither abrupt nor unkind;—by which I understood him to mean, that the change if made, would be upon a resignation (as to mode) and not upon a recall. The President farther [*sic*] remarked, that he was much urged upon the subject of diplomatic appointments from Virginia. . . . That Mason and [Henry] Bedinger [minister to Denmark] were each extremely anxious to be retained, and that to each of them the emoluments of the place was [*sic*] perhaps essentially important.—I mentioned to him the wish which Floyd had expressed with reference to yourself, and he said that he would converse with the Secretary of War about the matter. . . . From the interview with the President, I went immediately to the Secretary of War, and narrated to him the conversation. . . .
>
> Floyd said he intended to write you soon—that if I were writing you now, "tell him that I mean to commit myself upon his appointment, as the only thing I shall insist upon being done for me—as I have no favor to ask for myself."[12]

The urgency Buchanan mentioned about appointments from Virginia seemed to arise mainly because of Richard Meade, the man offered Daniel's job four years earlier who had turned it down because of the salary. The justice concluded by saying that he himself was broken down in health. If John remained abroad long they would probably never see each other again.

John Daniel was grateful to his great-uncle, and a little apologetic that he had asked him for help when he was not in good health. He wanted his great-uncle to know that neither the pleasures of Europe nor a capacity for happy idleness made him want to stay abroad; he was simply saving four thousand dollars a year and there was no enterprise in Virginia that would permit him to do that. News had reached Turin of the Supreme Court's decision in the Dred Scott case, but he had not yet seen Peter Daniel's own opinion. From what John Daniel could see, the court's decision, coupled with the new Kansas-Nebraska Act, amounted to unusually good news for the country. The decision and the new act together "seem to settle our great dispute so far as Constitutional Law and Congressional Precedent can settle it. All that the North can do now, must be done out of doors and in defiance of the national system. . . . [T]his decision so fully bears out the opinion which I heard you express many years ago . . . that the Missouri Compromise was without constitutional warrant and therefore utterly void, and that the Supreme Court would so decide whenever it should be brought up there."[13]

Unfortunately, Daniel continued, all the noise made by "Yankee traitors" found an eager echo in the English press. Although the English hated all countries, they hated America most, and all that Europeans knew about America came through the English press. When he had been in Genoa several days earlier, Daniel reported, he had spent an evening at the Carlo Felice Opera House. Before the opera, a ballet entitled *Bianchi e Negri* had been presented. The scene opened in the splendid salon of a planter's villa in the American South, where thirty pretty women who "personated our wives and daughters" danced with thirty splendid gentlemen, the planters. Then the scene changed to the slave quarters, and the ballet ended with the white ladies dancing with black slaves. Daniel was disgusted and described the ballet at some length in his letter.

Several days after writing to his great-uncle, Daniel repeated his account of the ballet in a letter to Thomas Wynne, adding an account he had heard from two Americans who had recently visited famous American sculptor Hiram Powers, who lived and worked in Florence. During the Pierce administration, it appeared, Powers had been engaged by the administration to make a statue of an idealized America for the princely price of $25,000. Powers had then separately contracted with a Mr. Genin, a New York hat store owner, to make an exact copy of the statue for only $10,000 for Genin's store. When President Pierce heard about this, he had properly refused to pay. Powers had thereupon festooned the pedestal of the statue with chains, to represent slavery, and hoped to sell it to some buyer in England. This incident, wrote Daniel, corresponded with fifty other things he had heard about Hiram Powers, a man "avaricious and malignant in the extreme," who would never return to America and used his American identity only to help him demand extravagant prices in America.[14]

Peter Daniel wrote back that he had been so impressed by John's account of "the Ballette" that he had ventured to read it aloud to President Buchanan, Secretary of War Floyd, and Secretary of the Treasury Howell Cobb. The three had expressed "a strong disgust at & contempt for the contrivers of such scenes," and Cobb had thought the account should be published but Justice Daniel had said no.[15] (Cobb had apparently forgiven Daniel for his editorial attacks, now years ago.)

The justice enclosed with his letter a full published account of the Dred Scott decision. He added that the conduct of his fellow justices John McLean and Benjamin Curtis had been censurable in the highest degree. Instead of trying to prevent or to allay public excitement over the decision, "as was their sacred duty," they had played the role of incendiaries, handing over their own opinions to the

Yankee papers and, no doubt, to British agents, before delivering them from the bench. As a result, they had created false impressions before the full reasoning of the court could be made known. The good news was that Virginia had a strong Democratic majority. The nation in general required a unified South determined "to roll back the tide of northern aggression and to prove that the men of the South are fixed and resolved, & ready to accomplish this or perish in the effort for its attainment."

How this might be done, the justice did not say. As to Buchanan appointments, Peter Daniel reported that Richard Kidder Meade was no longer interested in going to Turin but wanted the mission at Rio de Janeiro. (He got it; Meade was named minister to Brazil in late July.) He also reported a rumor that William Ritchie would sell out to Robert Hughes, that the *Richmond Enquirer* and *Richmond Examiner* would merge, and that Ritchie would become minister to Sardinia. Floyd, however, had reiterated his support for John Daniel and did not think Buchanan would replace him with Ritchie.

The justice also had rare news about two of John's brothers. Peter Daniel's son was president of the Richmond & Petersburg Railroad Company and had gotten Walter a job on the line that paid eight hundred or a thousand dollars a year. [James] Mitchell was working as a civil engineer in Texas, making an annual salary of two thousand or twenty-five hundred dollars.

The correspondence between great-uncle and great-nephew continued. Late in June 1857, John Daniel noted that he had kept the right to repurchase the *Examiner,* so theoretically he could come home and prevent the merger of Richmond's two main Democratic papers. He revealed that Ritchie had proposed to him almost ten months earlier that they trade positions, with Daniel taking over the *Enquirer* and Ritchie becoming minister to Sardinia. But again, Daniel felt that Ritchie and his family overvalued the paper, which in any case was not making money. "Besides," wrote Daniel, "the commission of a Minister and eight thousand a year are not things that any sensible man without fortune can throw away as if they were old shoes."[16]

In June 1857, the French police sent word to the Sardinian authorities in Turin that an insurrection was about to break out in Genoa. Their information was correct; an armed rising occurred at the end of June, but it was not massive and the authorities, forewarned, put it down. Daniel reported the incident to superiors in Washington with the comment that it would probably turn out to be just another of those "insane conspiracies" that always existed somewhere on the Italian peninsula.[17] However, Daniel considered the matter worth looking into, and several weeks later he sent a second dispatch. It appeared that there had been attempts at uprisings not only at Genoa but at Livorno and Pisa in the Grand Duchy of Tuscany and in the Kingdom of Two Sicilies. These were the fruits of a plan by Mazzini and his colleagues in London to attempt a series of revolutions in France, Sardinia, Tuscany, and the Two Sicilies, with the aim of establishing a European republic. The French had learned about the plot and sent warnings to Turin, Vienna, and Naples. Apparently, Mazzini had learned that the plans had been compromised and tried to call off the uprisings, but the conspirators on the spot had not heeded the warnings and had gone ahead. John Daniel commented that the conspirators seemed to think only a spark was needed to produce a conflagration. It was true that Italy was badly governed, and that those Italians who gave any thought to political subjects wanted major changes; but he thought the Italians were far from the point of exasperation.[18]

There was more to the story than Daniel had learned. Cavour was furious at the outbreak and concerned that the French might think he was involved with the conspirators. Mazzini had spent several months at Genoa the previous year, untroubled by the police. The fact was that Cavour, the wily premier, could see potential benefit from revolutions, provided they were not directed against *his* king's dominions. However, as Mack Smith has noted, Napoleon III needed Cavour's help as much as Cavour needed the French. A popular war—one with Austria—could strengthen the position of the emperor's dynasty more firmly in France and also strengthen France's position in Europe. So the scheming continued.

On a different scale and with different agendas, Daniel and his Virginia friends and allies were as much involved in schemes and plots as were the Europeans. Secretary of War Floyd wrote to Daniel on June 1, 1857, to assure him that he had urged Daniel's retention in office several times and that he would, if necessary, tell the president that this was the only personal request he would make of him. (This last may have sounded to John Daniel as a little weak; Floyd had indicated more definitely to Peter Daniel that he would tell the president that John Daniel's case would be his only such request.) Floyd added that a major struggle loomed between two Virginia politicians, Robert Hunter and Henry Wise, who had been friendly a few years earlier but were now at daggers drawn as each dreamed of being elected president in 1860. Floyd mentioned in closing that he was writing to Daniel from his office at a moment of tumult in Washington. There was a demagogic new political party in America, the Know Nothings, and a mob of Know Nothing supporters had resorted to violence over municipal elections in Washington. Several members of the mob had just been killed and wounded by Marines, Floyd hastened to add, who were under the Secretary of the Navy, and not by his own army men.[19]

Daniel may have received in the same mail a letter that Thomas Wynne wrote him on May 31, 1857, the day before Floyd wrote, enclosing a letter from Robert Hughes. Hughes wrote that Daniel was sure to retain his diplomatic post and that Floyd would try to arrange his transfer to the Naples legation but was not sanguine about any success. In any case, Daniel's commission was understood to be good for four years from the date of his 1854 Senate confirmation as minister resident, so there was plenty of time to work things out.[20] Hughes wrote directly to Daniel, confirming that he had agreed with Ritchie to merge the *Examiner* and the *Enquirer* and that Hughes would become editor of this new Democratic paper. Hughes said that his business expenses, including $3,000 for a new steam press, had been heavy, and that the circulation of the *Examiner* remained at its level when Daniel had left Richmond four years earlier. During these four years, Hughes wrote, he had made less than three hundred dollars from the paper.[21]

Daniel was angry. He replied that "persons capable of advising me" had agreed that his contract with Hughes, which allowed Daniel to repurchase the paper, obligated Hughes to maintain its separate existence. He did not want to stop the merger but suggested that Hughes postpone it until it became clear that Buchanan would retain Daniel in office for the remainder of his administration. Daniel could not understand how Hughes had made only three hundred dollars. As editor, he himself had drawn $1,500 to $1,800 a year while at the *Examiner* and had left with large amounts owed to the paper and capable of collection.

The plot became thicker when Daniel received a "private & confidential" letter in July from William Lloyd, who worked under Hughes at the *Examiner.* Lloyd apologized for writing at the last moment; but after Daniel's letter to Peticolas had appeared in the *Examiner* (three and a half years earlier), he did not think Daniel wanted to hear from anyone at the paper. Lloyd told Daniel that the underlying purpose of the proposed merger was to promote the political interests of both John Floyd and Henry Wise, each a former Democratic governor of Virginia.[22]

According to Lloyd, the *Enquirer* had never been friendly to Floyd since his election as governor in opposition to the regular Democratic nominee, whereas the *Examiner,* which had opposed Wise during Daniel's time as editor, had stepped up its opposition under Robert Hughes. Lloyd claimed that Wise had recently gotten Floyd out of his way to the U.S. Senate by getting Floyd a seat in Buchanan's cabinet. Wise's chances of taking Robert Hunter's Senate seat were good and would be better if the two Democratic papers merged. Lloyd understood that Hughes would become editor of the paper and that Ritchie would go abroad.

Lloyd wrote that Hughes had told him that Ritchie had his eye on Daniel's job; Lloyd thought that he would get it. Lloyd knew that Floyd had said he would make it a personal matter to have Daniel retained, but Lloyd did not believe him. Even Buchanan's own cabinet members did not know what the president intended to do. What Lloyd knew was that the Virginians he was talking about feared John Daniel's power in Virginia and wanted to disarm him by amalgamating the two newspapers before his return and installing Robert Hughes, who would wield power through the newspaper in behalf of both John Floyd and Henry Wise.

William Lloyd continued that it was not too late to save the situation. Lloyd said he himself did not want the merger, which would tie the *Examiner*, which was still in good shape, to the *Enquirer*, which was on its last legs. Lloyd claimed he could stop the merger, because he had until November (he wrote in July) the contractual right to buy one-third of the *Examiner*. In closing, Lloyd expressed willingness to be guided by Daniel's wishes. Daniel replied that he would let Lloyd know his wishes before November. He told Lloyd that if he repurchased half of the paper and Lloyd a third, Hughes would be left with only a sixth. With Daniel's capital, he and Lloyd could put out a good paper.[23]

Clearly someone was not telling the truth. Judge Crump wrote Daniel in mid-July 1857 that he had been in Washington and seen Secretary Floyd, who had "declared he would strain every nerve to retain you in place."[24] Crump also enclosed a letter from Hughes, saying that he, too, had seen Floyd, and that "John Daniel is the safest man in the diplomatic corps and can kick up his heels accordingly." Was that really true?

If there was one man whom Daniel could trust, it was his great-uncle, and he wrote the justice to fill him in on all he had heard from America.[25] What made things even more disturbing was that John Daniel, having gotten through the previous winter's fogs and smoke in Turin, was sick in the middle of the summer. In July, his Turin doctor sent him to Paris, as Daniel wrote John Floyd, "to present myself before a famous prince of the medical science and get his opinion on this body of mine, which always gets worse and never better."[26] Perhaps a measure of his ill health was the fact that he told Floyd about his visit, although news of his health might be used by those—conceivably even Floyd—who did not want Daniel to remain in Turin.

However, Daniel's main reason for mentioning the trip to Paris was to tell the secretary of war that, while there, he had learned from Minister Mason that the French government intended to confer the cross of the Legion of Honor on Lt. Matthew Maury. Maury was the distinguished naval officer from Virginia whose work on hydrography had led to an international conference at Brussels in 1853 that greatly benefited navigation and meteorology. Daniel urged Floyd to advise Maury not to accept the foreign bauble. It would be humiliating if Maury placed himself on a footing with "certain persons who paint, who pretend to be American citizens but who live in these countries because they hate all that is American, who have also obtained the same glorious prize." (One recalls Daniel's earlier expressed scorn for Hiram Powers: the American minister to Sardinia did not care much for expatriate artists.)

Before Peter Vivian Daniel received his great-nephew's most recent letter, he spent a private evening with the secretary of war toward the end of July 1857. Floyd told the justice that he was confident John Daniel would be retained. Floyd then went on to say that the Buchanan administration was very dissatisfied with other American diplomatic representation abroad, and "that it was regarded as scarcely competent to maintain the rights and interests of the nation in the event of a crisis, and not calculated to inspire much respect at the Courts of Europe."[27] Floyd then cited specific cases. John Y. Mason at Paris, whatever his earlier qualifications, had become "impotent from disease." George Dallas, whom President Pierce had sent to London as minister after Buchanan left, was looked upon as better fitted for a fete than for deep talk and action. Yet London and Paris were the capitals of the most powerful governments in the world, and therefore the places where America most needed able representatives. Going on, Floyd said that the ministers at St. Petersburg [Thomas Seymour], Vienna [Henry Jackson], and Berlin [Peter Vroom] were quite mediocre. The minister at Madrid was "*Caesar Augustus* Dodge (what a fall!)," and Dodge had not favored his government with a single word since either his appointment or the beginning of the Buchanan administration—Floyd could not remember which.[28]

There was an opportunity in this situation, Floyd suggested to the justice, for John Moncure Daniel. The justice wrote to his great-nephew that

> Under these circumstances, it is the opinion of Secretary Floyd that a Dispatch from you, such as he says you are more capable than anyone he knows of writing, unfolding, so far as you have power to apprehend them, the policy of England & France and that of Spain as influenced in her particular views by the designs of the two former powers, and pointing either to the modes of operation or to the effects of their measures upon the interests of the United States, would be very acceptable to the administration. He thinks such a document would be useful to the Government, who, from the inefficiency of our diplomatic agents abroad, are left to conjecture merely on matters involving the welfare of the nation, and would be beneficial to yourself, as exhibiting you in advantageous contrast with others whose position is in truth little else than a mere formality.

John Daniel took some time to think over this interesting and flattering proposal. Probably two weeks passed after he received his great-uncle's letter before he wrote directly to Secretary of War Floyd. Daniel said that he could see the usefulness of such a report as Floyd had suggested and that he was pleased Floyd thought him capable of writing it. A diplomat in even an out-of-the-way capital could write general things about Europe, and if he was as able as Henry Wheaton had been at Copenhagen some years earlier, his reports would be read and well regarded in the cabinet.[29] However, detailed information about particular subjects could only be had in the country or countries concerned; Europe was not like America, where everything was reported in the press. If he attempted such a report as Floyd suggested, people would call it a newspaper editorial rather than an official paper. As for Sardinia, it was his duty to know the country, and when he thought that its affairs might interest the United States government, he reported precise and certain facts coupled with his own analysis.

Daniel continued that there was perhaps something in this corner of creation to attract the attention of the distinguished secretary of war. He had just attempted a comparison of the armed forces of the United States with those of the Kingdom of Sardinia. Repeating what he had reported to the State Department earlier, Daniel told Floyd that in 1853 the United States Army had numbered 10,329 officers and men. In 1857, Sardinia had an army five times larger: 50,039 enlisted men and 4,448 officers. Yet the total Sardinian expense for its military, including fortifications, military schools, and so forth, was only 41 million francs each year. Furthermore, Daniel considered Sardinian weaponry was as good as American. In contrast, the much smaller American force cost almost ten million dollars annually, or around 36 million francs. The reason American armed forces cost so much was pay: a Sardinian major general received only about $1,400 a year, while his American counterpart received, with rations, $4,512. Daniel concluded with the observation that the scene was different in diplomacy. To put an American frigate to sea cost more than what the United States spent annually on its whole diplomatic apparatus, whereas the diplomatic expense of Sardinia each year covered the cost of many frigates.

After Daniel saw the Paris specialist, his health apparently improved. He had, however, been sick enough to give more thought than ever before to "the uncertain tenure of life," and, although not quite thirty-two years old, he had written a will.[30] To help with his recuperation, Daniel's Turin doctor recommended that he take the waters at some resort. Daniel went to the little town of Leukerbad, or Loeche-les-Bains, some miles southwest of the Jungfrau in the Swiss Alps, for several weeks in the late summer of 1857. There he met and befriended an older Englishman named Plowden, who had spent decades in India. Daniel understood Plowden to say that he had been a "director" of the East India Company.[31] (This was perhaps George Plowden, who had been the Company's commissioner at Nagpur.) Eighteen fifty-seven was the year of the the bloody insurrection in India, the Great Mutiny, and India was a main subject of their conversation. Plowden and Daniel spent many days together at Leukerbad, and the Englishman readily told the American of his long years in India. Listening to this account, Daniel decided that Plowden and the other British administrators of India, although relatively few in number, had wielded a power surpassed only by that of Chinese emperors or Russian tsars. Despite the power Plowden had held, Daniel wrote to his great-uncle after returning to Turin, "[H]e was a simple man, and gave me during some weeks with the utmost naiveté details of what he had seen and heard during his long career—details of a policy that would have shocked the moral sense of Richelieu, and of a social system which resembled only the perpetual sack of a stormed city."[32]

The possible effect of this encounter on John Moncure Daniel is worth considering. There is no reason to believe that Daniel's views about slavery in America or African Americans changed during the four years he had been in Europe, despite the hope that Horace Greeley's *New York Tribune* had expressed in 1853. Daniel remained a Virginian. He had become a senior American representative in Europe, and he owed this position to his standing and accomplishments in Virginia. If he remained in Europe, it would be because of help from Virginians like his great-uncle and John B. Floyd. If he ever had doubts about slavery during his Turin years, no trace of any such doubts has survived. Daniel knew that if he wanted to continue advancing in society, he must remain a Virginian and a defender of Virginia—including its slavery.

Yet perhaps he needed some reinforcement of his beliefs. That ballet in Genoa, which threw the idea of black-white equality in his face, helped serve that purpose. In 1857, everything he heard about India confirmed his view that the British ruled India in a way far more cruel and unjust than the social system of the American South. The British, Daniel thought, fully deserved the cruelties visited on their own people in India. He insisted to his great-uncle that "the Indians are only making a slight requital for the atrocities practiced on themselves and their women by the off-scourings of England . . . . Did you ever see the House of Commons' Blue-Book called the 'Report on Torture'? If you have not, you are not aware that the habitual means of collecting the taxation of the East India Government in all the rural districts, is by torturing the miserable ryot, or his wife."

Two wrongs do not make a right, but it was quite true that many Englishmen in India in the mid-1800s treated Indians abominably, viewing even upper-class Indians as "beastly niggers," thrashing their servants and dispossessing many landowners. This situation had worsened from earlier decades, when British officers mixed freely with Indians and learned to speak their languages fluently.[33] Conditions in Virginia, Daniel wanted to believe—and did believe—were better than that.

Decades ago, an American scholar accused John Moncure Daniel of doing nothing at Turin to promote cultural and commercial relations between Sardinia and the United States.[34] This accusation is perhaps true in regard to culture, although Daniel carried out with dispatch occasional instructions he received about exchanges of scientific data. The fact was that American culture needed no official help in Italy. American artists and writers went there without official urging, and so did American books, like *Uncle Tom's Cabin,* which had gone through several printings in Italian within a year of its appearance in America in 1852, and had provided the inspiration for that ballet in Genoa.

But Daniel was assiduous about trade, although sometimes he got tired of defending American ship captains—most of them, it seemed, Northerners—whose tobacco cargoes tended to be undervalued on the forms they submitted to Sardinian customs. Daniel decided, he wrote to the consul in Genoa in late 1856, after he had gotten a fine for tobacco smuggling against Capt. Lewis Webb reduced from 40,000 to 600 francs, that

> It is the last case of the sort in which I intend to interfere. I find that there is no end to them. It is time that these Yankee captains were taught to order their ships and crews according to the laws. Unless then, some case should occur in which great injustice is done to the shipowner and where the damages are exaggerated to a great point, I shall not touch the matter. It is the business of the Consul to manage those matters. . . . It is not becoming or useful to the United States that its representative should be a solicitant at the doors of a Government which is a satellite of our enemies; and these paltry concessions are used by its Agent at Washington as a means of extorting others of a much more serious character.[35]

Daniel correctly realized that seeking concessions from the Sardinian authorities left them free to seek a quid pro quo in Washington, though whether he knew of concrete cases is not clear. The Sardinian authorities would not have been amused to hear themselves described as satellites, nor would his French and British colleagues have liked to hear their countries referred to as America's enemies. However, the letter did not leak.

In late 1857, the State Department sent instructions to American missions to provide help to Samuel F. B. Morse, and Daniel quickly complied. Morse was the first to develop the electric telegraph. Not long after the first line that used his system went into operation between Baltimore and Washington, in 1844, the system was adopted by European governments. However, they had never paid Morse, and American legations were asked to help him press his claims. Daniel did all he could, but he warned officials in Washington that he doubted much money could be gotten out of the stingy Sardinians, who were committed to a vast program of internal improvements. The most expensive of these was an eight-kilometer rail tunnel under the Mt. Cenis Pass that would link France to Piedmont. The Sardinian king had recently struck the first hammer blow on the tunnel; the project would take years to complete.

In succeeding months, Daniel had several meetings with Sardinian officials on behalf of Morse and kept in direct touch with Morse, who was in Paris. The French minister of interior suggested to Morse that the best solution would be a general agreement among European governments to compensate Morse, and Morse agreed. On January 1, 1858, Daniel wrote to Morse that the foreign ministry had just informed him that "the Sardinian Government will cheerfully meet in its due proportion the terms which may be agreed upon by the other powers in your behalf."[36] However, in spite of John Daniel's best efforts, Morse still needed to wait a long time to get his money.

In late 1857, serious and worrisome political developments occurred in both the Kingdom of Sardinia and the United States. Parliamentary elections in Sardinia produced a relative victory for right-wing forces which Daniel described to Washington as "a thunder-clap for the Cavour Ministry."[37] Cavour, with the full support of his king, had continued to whittle away the power of the Church, and clerics had come out in strength against him. One bishop appeared at the polls with 260 priests in procession behind him.[38] There was also voter discontent over the high taxes Cavour was collecting to pay for the large army and his program of internal improvements. The elections had tripled the parliamentary strength of the conservative, pro-Church faction. Although Cavour still had a majority, Daniel thought there would probably be new elections in less than six months. Among other results, Cavour, weakened politically, became more vulnerable to pressure from France. Napoleon III pressed Cavour to dismiss his minister of the interior, a liberal named Urbano Rattazzi. Rattazzi agreed to resign, to help save Sardinia's alliance with France as well as to lessen domestic attacks on the government.That was not the end of Rattazzi. He was to serve more than once as prime minister, first of Sardinia and then of the new Kingdom of Italy; and in 1863, two years after Daniel had returned to America, Rattazzi married the American's young friend, Marie de Solms.

In America, it was becoming clear that James Buchanan was not a masterful president. John Daniel put it to his great-uncle that Buchanan was a manager, not a ruler; he was not born to command, and he lacked strength.[39] For his part, Peter Daniel thought that Buchanan had made a particularly unfortunate choice in making Robert J. Walker governor of Kansas. In the justice's view, Walker had "always been an adventurer and a speculator in public as in private matters; guided I believe by the predominant motive to push his own fortunes no matter at whose cost."[40] The justice thought Walker was aiming at a Senate seat; he had already had a cabinet seat, as secretary of the Treasury during the Polk administration. In any case, his policy aim was to make Kansas a Democratic state if it could not become (and it seemed doubtful that it could become) a slave state. Soon enough the proslavery constitution for the proposed new state would be defeated, Walker would resign, and the Democratic party would be badly split between North and South. The strife in bloody Kansas foretold a greater struggle.

As summer turned to autumn in 1857, John Daniel still owed a response to William Lloyd about his proposal for a joint purchase of the *Richmond Examiner*. In recent months, Robert Hughes had tried to force the paper's merger with the *Richmond Enquirer*, first telling Lloyd that the new paper would be awarded $100,000 in printing contracts by the Buchanan administration, and then simply announcing the merger despite Lloyd's continued opposition. Lloyd had thereupon told Hughes he would sue him for damages if the papers merged, and Hughes had backed off. On the surface, Lloyd wrote Daniel, he was on friendly terms with Hughes and, as publisher, had agreed that Hughes's editorial salary should be paid in advance. Although Hughes had told Daniel that he had not realized even three hundred dollars from the paper, it was not so. Lloyd wanted Daniel to know that in Lloyd's first year as publisher, Hughes had been paid a salary of $1,730; in 1857 he was receiving $2,400.[41]

In early October, Lloyd notified Robert Hughes that he wanted to exercise his option to buy a one-third interest in the paper. The transaction was completed the following month.[42] Reporting this to Daniel, Lloyd added that in recent travels around Virginia he had often been asked about John M. Daniel and when he planned to return home. If Daniel came back home and took over the *Examiner*, Lloyd knew it could achieve the greatest circulation any paper had ever had in Virginia.

It must have been comforting to Daniel, as the first months of 1858 passed, to know that Lloyd's move had kept the *Examiner* alive. There was more afoot than petty city quarrels; there was political work to be done, and not just in Richmond but beyond. Justice Daniel sent his great-nephew a long and depressing account of the Buchanan administration in April 1858. The cabinet members were disappointing; the attorney general, Jeremiah Black, was the ablest of them, but even he seemed more in his element as an officer of a court than as a statesman. Secretary of State Cass was "no longer equal to himself," and even at his best Cass had always been a temporizer and indecisive. The justice did not think that Secretary of War Floyd had proven himself as able or efficient as his great-nephew had expected. As for President Buchanan, his "want of decision and [of] political integrity and consistency" had made the difficulties over Kansas still worse. Buchanan's weakness and vacillation had left him, said Peter Daniel, even more dependent on the South. Yet the Yankees correctly perceived that the South no longer possessed the courage or integrity to stand up for its rights; they saw that the South had long since surrendered "the equality guarantied [*sic*] to us in the Constitution." Outside the administration, Senator Stephen A. Douglas had discovered that abolitionist sentiment had increased so much in his home region as to endanger not only his hopes for the presidency but his chances of remaining in the Senate; he had ruined himself by becoming the dupe of that intriguer William Seward.[43] (Douglas had split with the administration after President Buchanan committed himself to supporting the proslavery Kansas state constitution that had been voted by an assembly in the town of Lecompton.) What John Daniel made of all this is not clear, but the news was not encouraging. Aside from everything else, the Democratic party was split.

Some weeks later, John Daniel learned just how far John Floyd was willing to go to help him stay abroad. Early in June, William Crump wrote to Daniel that on June 1 he had received a letter from Robert Hughes in Washington presumably at Floyd's dictation. The letter contained the following sentence: "The President told Gov. Floyd yesterday that he found it impossible, in the face of the pressure upon him, to allow our foreign ministers appointed by the last administration to remain abroad longer than the 1st of September next, & that Judge Mason & Daniel would have to resign their positions by that date."[44] There was no indication that Floyd insisted on Daniel's retention, as he had promised he would do. Crump wondered if Daniel still had the same energy, self-denial, ambition, and singleness of purpose that he remembered. If Daniel did, and if he wanted to go home and edit a political paper, then the *Examiner* in his hands again would make a sensation.

Now, indeed, it was time for Daniel to go home to Virginia. As the hot summer of 1858 deepened in Piedmont, Daniel learned the reason for the sudden and unexpected demand for his resignation. President Buchanan had promised the legation at Turin to Warren Winslow, a Congressman and former governor of North Carolina.[45] Judge Crump wrote Daniel that Robert Hughes had mentioned that Daniel's right to repurchase one half of the *Examiner* would expire on August 9.[46] It was time to act. On July 10, 1858, Daniel sent William Lloyd his power of attorney and asked him to tell Hughes that he wished to repurchase one-half of the *Examiner* for the sum of $2,500. Lloyd was to publish the paper until Daniel's return to Richmond, "which cannot be farther off than the 1st of October."[47] The repurchase was completed on August 9, just before John Daniel's right expired,[48] and John Daniel and William Lloyd together owned five-sixths of the newspaper.

At the beginning of August, after almost five years as the American representative to the Kingdom of Sardinia, Daniel sent two consecutive dispatches to Secretary of State Cass. The first was not about himself but dealt with Felice Foresti, the Columbia College professor and former Italian revolutionary whom the Sardinian government had refused to accept in 1853 as American consul at Genoa. The United States government had again named him to the same post. This time Foresti was accepted, a measure of how politics had changed at Turin over the last five years. With the king and Prime Minister Cavour looking at a possible war to liberate northern Italy from Austrian rule—and dreaming of other changes in still-divided Italy—the revolutionaries and monarchy were no longer at such odds as before. Mazzini had been permitted to return to Genoa, and his former follower Foresti was welcomed as American consul there. In fact, Daniel told Washington,

Cavour had more than once urged Daniel to recommend Foresti's appointment, which Daniel had not thought prudent, and the Sardinian government had actually become eager to see him in Genoa.[49]

(Parenthetically, Daniel had just recently been confronted by a still more vexing problem regarding American consulates in the Kingdom of Sardinia. For several years there had been unverified reports of persons impersonating American consular officers in the kingdom. In the spring of 1858, Daniel was surprised to discover that the new official register of the Sardinian government listed seven fictitious American consular posts in the kingdom—almost all of them on the island of Sardinia—in addition to the three legitimate American posts at Genoa, Nice, and La Spezia. Daniel acted quickly to have the Sardinian authorities notify the public and local officials that these "consuls" had no official status.[50])

The second dispatch had a different tenor. In compliance with Buchanan's wishes, Daniel wrote to Secretary Cass: "Having reason to believe that the President desires to make further changes in the diplomatic corps now representing the United States in Europe and desiring to prevent all embarrassment relative to the office which I have the honour to fill, I beg leave to tender my resignation of the same."

Daniel then went off to Aix-les-Bains, presumably to visit his young friend Marie de Solms. He may have stayed there for some weeks. He was still there in early September, when former President Franklin Pierce wrote him at Aix from Geneva, hoping that they might meet.[51]

Back in Turin in mid-September, Daniel reported to Washington that he had received the dispatch from the State Department informing him that the president had accepted his resignation. However, Buchanan asked that Daniel remain at his post until the arrival of his successor, who had not yet been appointed. In his report, Daniel also included the latest, surprising news regarding Felice Foresti: he had died in Genoa three days earlier.[52] Foresti's adopted country did full honors to him, and he was escorted to his final rest in Genoa by an honor guard of officers and men from the frigate USS *Wabash*, led by the commodore of the Mediterranean squadron.[53]

Soon enough a new consul, William L. Patterson, was appointed to Genoa. But no new American minister was appointed to Turin. Daniel must have wondered what was going on in Washington. Eventually, Peter Daniel wrote to his great-nephew that Buchanan had reportedly changed his mind about sending Warren Winslow to Turin. The cabinet had discussed the matter, and Justice Daniel was told that, although Secretary of War Floyd had originally not stood up for the retention of John Daniel, this time "[Y]our continuation was pressed by the Secretary of War and was acquiesced in, with the probability of its remaining until the close of the President's term."[54]

So it was that John Daniel, who thought he would be back in Richmond by October 1858, would apparently be able to remain at his post at least until the beginning of 1861—and conceivably longer if the Democrats held onto the White House in the November 1860 elections. His financial affairs were certainly looking up. We do not know what funds he had in Turin late in 1858, but the comptroller of the Treasury informed him in January 1859 that the audit for his accounts through the previous March showed a balance due to him of almost eleven thousand dollars.[55] Both politically and financially, he could feel reassured, even if his physical health remained worrisome. Moreover, interesting things were continuing to happen in Italy.

A Ball, a War, and Home Again

If the summer of 1858 seemed momentous to John Daniel in personal terms, it was far more momentous for Italy, and indeed for Europe. In July, after the Sardinian parliament adjourned for the summer, Count Cavour went off to Switzerland on vacation. From there he went secretly into France, and on July 24 he joined Napoleon III at Plombieres, where, as A. J. Whyte said, the two archconspirators planned the future of Italy.[1] It was agreed that late in the following spring an army of 300,000 men, two-thirds French and one-third Sardinian, would invade Austrian Lombardy. Victory would rid northern Italy of Austrian rule, and the Savoys' Kingdom of Sardinia would become a considerably enlarged Kingdom of Upper Italy, stretching from the western Alps to the Adriatic. There would also be a new Kingdom of Central Italy, to be offered to the Duchess of Parma. The Papal States would remain, as would the Kingdom of Two Sicilies at Naples. These four Italian states would form a loose confederation, with the Pope as overall president.

Napoleon III wanted a price for going to war with Austria, and Cavour agreed to pay it. The price was the cession to France of Savoy, ancient homeland of the Sardinian royal family, and of Nice. The bargain would be sealed with the marriage of Prince Napoleon, the emperor's profligate cousin, who was in his mid-thirties, to Princess Clotilde, the fifteen-year-old daughter of King Vittorio Emanuele II. Having come to terms with the emperor, Cavour sent a frank report home to his king and then went over the border to Baden to sound out Prussian and Russian envoys on the general question. The attitude of England was also critical. However, not least of Cavour's problems was the attitude of his own king. Vittorio Emanuele did not like the idea of putting young Clotilde in the hands of a philanderer who had, moreover, it was said, shown cowardice in the Crimean war, winning him the derisive nickname of Plon-Plon.

It was impossible for France and Sardinia to keep their plans secret. By the autumn of 1858, rumors were heard in Turin that the two countries planned war against Austria. Daniel refrained from reporting or commenting on these rumors until early January 1859, when he sent a dispatch to the State Department stating that, although until recently the rumors had seemed unfounded, the best-informed circles now generally accredited them. Several pieces of evidence backed them. First, Vittorio Emanuele had gone to review his troops and commented to one regiment that there would be work for them the following spring. Then had come the "famous allocution" that Napoleon III addressed to the Austrian ambassador at the New Year's reception in Paris. The emperor commented that he regretted his relations with Austria were not as good as he might wish, and this had been taken to indicate that he planned war. The day before Daniel sent off his dispatch, the king had told the Sardinian parliament that "the present condition is not devoid of peril, for, while we respect treaties, we are not insensible to the cry of pain which so large a portion of Italy raises toward us."[2]

The Austrians, Daniel reported, were reacting by sending into Lombardy additional forces, which would soon total 200,000 men. The Lombard population was restive, and well-informed persons believed there would be an immediate uprising if people were not held in check by the expectation of a war to liberate them from the Austrians. Still, the minister concluded, "I do not and cannot yet believe Europe is to be plunged in hostilities without reasonable cause; and despite of all that has been said and done expect no important results from the present uproar." He quickly changed his opinion. In fact, the next day Daniel wrote to Secretary of War Floyd that "Sardinia promises to be a more fertile place of residence than it has been, as it is certainly going to war with Austria. I was long incredulous about the predicted earthquake, because I could not believe that in our age Europe was to be plunged into hostilities merely because France and Piedmont have enormous armies unemployed, but so it is. If they commence this business, God knows where they will end. . . . Perhaps it may reproduce that Italy which has disappeared from the political stage for twelve hundred years."[3]

At the end of January 1859, Prince Napoleon arrived in Turin for his betrothal to Princess Clotilde. Daniel reported to Washington that after Cavour had arranged the match at Plombieres the previous summer, it had been kept in such secrecy that as recently as two weeks before the members of the king's own family did not know about the planned marriage. In any event, it put an end to any doubts about Napoleon III's intention to support Sardinia against Austria. The Sardinian army was concentrating all its troops in Piedmont early, but a pretext for war still needed to be found.[4]

What Daniel did not report was the court ball held on the occasion of the royal betrothal—and the uproar that he and his good friend Marie de Solms caused. Like Clotilde's bridegroom, Marie was the cousin of Napoleon III, but a cousin whom the emperor disliked and had expelled from France. She was, however, close to King Vittorio Emanuele II. As Daniel wrote to Secretary Floyd six months later:

> Last winter the time came when she and her friends—the king among them—thought I could render her a great service; and, though I was then aware of the fact that the most powerful man in the world [Napoleon III] frowned on her might do me an evil turn, and though it cost much to a shy man to undertake an affair so delicate, yet, after enjoying her hospitality and kindness for so many years, I could not turn my back and I would not shrink into excuses, as I might have done. I met the occasion straight and plumb: and despite the great danger I have run, when I look back I cannot regret it for I think it was the point in my life when I gave the best proof of manliness.[5]

The great service requested of Daniel was to take de Solms to the court ball, to which the French had arranged that she not be invited. There can be no question that Marie de Solms liked to cause trouble—someone had nicknamed her "Princess Brouhaha"—and, in particular, to needle her imperial cousin.[6] When still in Napoleon III's good graces, she had refused to accept the title of princess or to attend his marriage. In February 1853, she had refused to cancel a ball she was giving in Paris, although it coincided with an official ball at the Tuileries.[7]

The entry of the American minister with Marie de Solms on his arm caused an uproar at the royal ball in Turin. The French emperor was outraged. The Sardinian King, whatever he may have said to the emperor, was pleased to see the discomfort of a Bonaparte who had claimed the king's young daughter for his disreputable cousin. The king did not forget what John Daniel did. The following July, Daniel told the State Department, when he called on Vittorio Emanuele II to deliver a formal letter of congratulations from President Buchanan on the marriage of the princess, the king "made me special assurances of personal regard and good-will, and, at parting, shook me warmly by the hand, expressing a desire to see me oftener. He is about to leave Turin for a Royal Progress through Lombardy and advised me to visit the country at the same time."[8] This was a Royal Progress through a Lombardy that had just been joined to his kingdom, for in these last six months a war against Austria had been waged and won. There had, however, been a number of critical moments and critical developments. And Daniel had throughout this period sent a continuing series of acute reports and analyses to Washington that had won him high praise from the secretary of state.

Before praise, though, there were some doubts in Washington about Daniel's conduct. Count Cavour had done his best to ruin Daniel's reputation at home after Daniel's appearance at the ball with Marie de Solms on his arm. Clearly without consulting the king, Cavour instructed the Sardinian minister in Washington, Giuseppe Bertinatti, to make it known that the chief American representative in Turin had been guilty of the ultimate rudeness: taking a courtesan to a royal ball. Bertinatti was effective, and at the highest level. He had never quite mastered the English language, but "dear old Bertinatti," as one Washington lady later remembered him, was well known and liked in Washington society, especially after his marriage to Mrs. Bass, a wealthy widow from Mississippi.[9]

Peter Daniel wrote his great-nephew that sometime in March he had seen Secretary of War Floyd, who "said that he was glad to see me . . . and then went on to say, as nearly as I can recollect: 'We are in great trouble about your nephew'—adding, that complaints of him from Sardinia had reached this Government alleging an indignity offered by him either by introducing or attending at the Court to which he was accredited a female of bad fame—a Courtezan, who had been the mistress perhaps of Louis Napoleon. . . . [H]e said that he had asserted both to the President and Secretary of State his confidence of its falsehood, nay of the *impossibility* of its truth."[10]

Cavour's chief reason for his calumnies was that Daniel's act had enraged the chief ally of Sardinia at a time when everything depended on Napoleon III carrying through with his agreement to help Sardinia take Lombardy. In addition, as Daniel wrote Floyd by way of clarification, "He may have found his impulse in certain private griefs which he is said to have received from the lady herself. . . . It is a private attack of such a nature that either I must ignore it or seek a reparation which would be out of place."[11] Daniel added that Bertinatti was a man of low origin who had professed great friendship for Daniel while in Turin and to whom Daniel had given letters of introduction when he had set off for America. As Daniel's letter indicates, he must have considered sending Cavour a challenge to a duel. However, for the American minister to challenge the prime minister of his host government would, indeed, have been out of place. Like his "garlic letter" more than five years earlier, the memory of his appearance with the lady at the ball began to fade in America and Sardinia. However, the incident was not the sort of thing that Daniel would ever forget. In July 1859, after the war with Austria ended and Cavour resigned as prime minister, Daniel was perhaps less than frank in saying, "I have no longer resentment to gratify, now that my assailant is reduced to ramble about the mountains in a state of mind which his worst enemies might pity."[12]

It is probably impossible at this distance in time to understand clearly the nexus of relationships that involved Marie de Solms. She was a woman of some importance in the life of John Moncure Daniel, but one wonders how much he may have mattered to her. Certainly she could entrance men. As noted earlier, Napoleon III seems to have been taken, for a time, by his beautiful young cousin. Some years later, at the time of her marriage to Urbano Rattazzi, there were rumors not only that Camillo Cavour had fallen for her but that the king himself had been in love with her and had wanted to marry her. When she married Rattazzi, Vittorio Emanuele II sent her a brooch of enormous value as a wedding present.[13]

In those fateful early months of 1859 in Turin, preparations for war with Austria were far advanced by March. Daniel reported to the State Department that general opinion considered the French emperor willing to set Europe in flames. (There was no guarantee that a French/Sardinian attack on Austria would not turn into a general European war.) However, French public opinion was said to be strongly against a war, and there were indications that Napoleon III was backing away from his agreement with Sardinia. Daniel emphasized that the situation not only in the Kingdom of Sardinia but throughout Italy was very different. Italians throughout the peninsula backed the Sardinian government, and all over Italy insurrectionary plans had been set aside in the hope that Sardinia would start a war to accomplish the aims of the Risorgimento. Daniel reported hearing that over six thousand young men had recently come from Lombardy to Piedmont to join the Sardinian army. If there was no war, Cavour's liberal government would fall and the old aristocratic party, which had governed until 1848, would return to power; there was no third force. Such a right-wing government would take away freedom of speech and press, reinstate the priests in their old position of importance, put down the army, and perhaps even abolish parliament. This would in turn lead to a popular insurrection, which would be suppressed with much bloodshed. All hopes of liberating Italy would be dashed. Such prospects, Daniel reported, could not be contemplated by those now in power in Turin, and so if France backed out, Sardinia would attack Austria single-handed while calling on the people of Lombardy to rise up against the Austrians. However, if that happened, Daniel believed that the kingdom would certainly be defeated, Austrian troops would occupy Piedmont, and the war might spread.[14]

In mid-April 1859, Cavour returned from a visit to Paris, and it appeared that the French would carry through with their commitment. Daniel reported that war seemed every day more imminent. Sardinia had a force of 75,000 men on the Genoa–Novara rail line that in twelve hours could be made ready to invade Lombardy. Daniel did not know what France's exact war plans were, but 20,000 men stood ready to embark at Marseilles, and 30,000 more on the Savoy frontier could reach Turin in two days. In contrast, Austria had 200,000 troops in Lombardy and 50,000 more on the way. Even if it assigned 100,000 men to subdue the Lombard population, Austria could still begin the war with three army corps of 50,000 men each.

On the political level, Daniel reported, Cavour had managed the affair ably. Russia had proposed an international congress to settle the Italian question. Wrote Daniel: "Neither Piedmont nor France desire at heart a Congress, yet [Cavour] has succeeded in making it appear that all the difficulties come from Austria. He now wishes to force Austria to commence the actual hostilities, and I am of opinion that he will be equally fortunate on that point also."[15] On April 21, Daniel reported that Italians were enthusiastic for war, and not just in Piedmont. Two steamers from Tuscany had recently arrived at Genoa with twelve hundred volunteers, and every day Daniel could see hundreds of young men filing up the street from the railroad station. He had been told on good authority that twenty thousand of these volunteers had already been enrolled.[16]

Daniel had guessed right about Cavour's ability to make Austria appear to be the aggressor. Hudson, the British minister, told Sardinian authorities that the British had learned Austria was sending an ultimatum to Turin to cease military preparations within three days. On a Saturday morning, Cavour convoked parliament and told members about the expected ultimatum. Sardinia, he said, would not comply. Parliament quickly passed a law giving the king and prime minister the authority to rule by decree. At 5:00 P.M. on that same day, an Austrian military officer arrived at the Sardinian foreign ministry and delivered the ultimatum, saying brusquely that he would wait three days in Turin for a reply. Daniel reported the outcome on Monday to Washington: "Negotiations appear at an end, and it is certain that Austria has been damaged by them. That France and Sardinia have been and are always[17] bent on war cannot be doubted; but they have managed Austria as the Matador provokes the bull with his red rag. . . . It is Austria that seems the aggressor and all the appearance of moderation and deference for other nations seems to be with her adversaries."[18]

Sardinia refused the ultimatum, the French army began to move into Piedmont en route to Lombardy, and the war was on. Daniel reported that many people thought France would not only take Lombardy but overthrow Austria. He disagreed. When France conquered Austria and dominated Europe a half-century earlier, France had been ruled by the greatest military leader since Julius Caesar, Napoleon I. Napoleon III did not have the capabilities of Napoleon I. Moreover, for the last twenty years Austria had been expanding, reforming, and modernizing its army. Daniel was not sure whether France and Sardinia would prove victorious, but he had learned that if they prevailed, both Lombardy and the Veneto would be added to the Savoy kingdom and the rest of Italy would comprise three states. Furthermore, Daniel understood that the Russians were involved, in the person of Grand Duke Constantine, who had been commuting between Paris and Turin and then gone off to Sicily where, Daniel thought, the Russians might have wanted to establish the major naval depot in the Mediterranean they had been seeking.[19] (The previous November, a small Russian battle fleet had taken up station at the base Cavour had leased to them at Villafranca—the same port where, as mentioned earlier, a call by a ship of the U.S. Mediterranean squadron had fueled speculation about U.S. aims on nearby Monaco. Cavour dreamed of a Russian alliance and had tried to further the idea by suggesting, in vain, to the king that he give up his mistresses and marry a Russian princess. In the end Cavour obtained from the tsar no more than a promise of benevolent neutrality in the event of war with Austria.[20])

It was not only Sardinia which had stepped up activity to a furious pace; so had John Moncure Daniel. He could no longer complain of being bored in a backwater of Europe. Turin had become the center of the Western world's attention, and he was America's man in Turin. Two years earlier he had turned down a suggestion by the secretary of war that he do some reporting on the overall European scene; but in 1859 he was essentially filling that role through his reports on France and Sardinia's war with Austria. Furthermore, whatever his colleagues in other capitals may have thought, his reporting was welcomed in Washington. Daniel could not go into Lombardy and see the fighting, but at one point early in May he was on Mt. Cenis Pass and reported watching the French army pour into Piedmont: "thirty thousand pushing on over that pass, white with snow, but in the highest spirits."[21] There was increased ferment elsewhere in Italy. In Tuscany, Grand Duke Leopold fled, and the Sardinian government sent in a commissioner to take over the government. Veteran freedom fighter Giuseppe Garibaldi formed a corps of volunteers in Piedmont, which marched into northern Lombardy. Daniel reported that their chief "has done wonders with them. . . . Men of the greatest fortune, birth and education in all Italy serve in the ranks as common soldiers. . . . Garibaldi has boldly marched into Lombardy on the northern line so as to take away from the Austrians the command of the lakes Como and Maggiore and to enable the province of Milan to rebel. In this hardy movement he has been perfectly successful."[22]

On June 8, Daniel reported that Napoleon III had won a great battle at Magenta, that Vittorio Emanuele II had entered Milan in triumph, and that "the rest is only a matter of time. Austrian domination in Italy is doomed."[23]

A number of Americans asked Daniel to make arrangements for them to follow the Sardinian army in the field. He at first refused, because Sardinian authorities had made it clear they would not permit foreigners, or indeed any noncombatants, to join their military forces. However, Daniel made an exception after Lt. George Carr, from the U.S. Army's 9th Regiment, arrived with a letter of recommendation from Secretary of War Floyd.[24] Daniel went to see Cavour, who provided for the lieutenant not only a safe conduct but letters to Sardinian commanders that asked them to afford Carr all possible facilities for observation. Cavour, who believed that there might be an American card in the Italian game, told Daniel that he would do the same for any other American officer who came with similar recommendations. Soon Carr was sending Daniel useful reports from the front.

At the end of June, the Austrians lost another major battle, at Solferino. And then in early July came news that Napoleon III and the Austrian emperor had agreed to an armistice without consulting Cavour or Vittorio Emanuele. Daniel reported to the State Department that the news hit Turin like a bombshell: "The king of Sardinia . . . was not taken in account. Indeed I can assure you that this news was known here in Turin to Cavour by dispatch from the Sardinian Minister at Paris before it was dreamed of in the camp of Vittorio Emanuele. The sensation was prodigious and not at all pleasant."[25] Other, less pleasant news soon followed. The French and Austrian emperors had agreed that Austria would cede Lombardy—not to Sardinia but to Napoleon III, who would then give it to Vittorio Emanuele. However, they had also agreed that Austria would retain Venice and northeastern Italy and that the remaining states of Italy—the duchies of Tuscany, Modena and Parma; the Papal states; the Kingdom of Two Sicilies—would keep their independence. Daniel reported, "This lame and important conclusion to a career of unexampled success has . . . caused a terrible disappointment to the Italian people, and the word *tradimento* is on every lip. . . . Italy makes enormous gains in this arrangement. . . . But they expected so much more, and they had such good reasons for expecting more, that the half-loaf which they receive seems to them the rations of starvation. . . . When Napoleon III left Paris he declared to all mankind that Italy should be free to the Adriatic."[26]

Two months earlier, the French emperor had been cheered wildly when he arrived in Piedmont to make war on Austria. However, when he went to Turin in July, "had he been a Polar bear, he might yet have been chilled by the reception."[27] At the depot, Daniel watched Cavour and his ministers take off their hats when the emperor arrived, but stand in their places without approaching him. In contrast, two months earlier, at Genoa, Napoleon had thrown himself into the arms of "Mon cher Cavour!" Cannon on the citadel were fired for the emperor's arrival, but at the rate of one a minute, which sounded more like a funeral than a welcome. Daniel recalled that during the war many people in Turin had hung portraits of Napoleon III in their windows; but in July they replaced them with pictures of Felice Orsini, who had tried to assassinate him. Furthermore, the Turin press, held under tight rein during the fighting, expressed itself unhindered in July, "and the free violence of their expressions about the late demi-god very far excels anything we are accustomed to see in partizan newspapers of the United States, even during a Presidential canvass." Cavour and all his ministers then resigned. He was artful and unscrupulous, wrote Daniel, and he fancied that he was managing Napoleon, but the emperor proved still more artful and unscrupulous.

If Daniel wondered how his reporting and analysis was received in Washington, he soon learned. A dispatch from the State Department assured him his recent reports had been read with much interest.[28] Other, warmer, commendations followed as Daniel continued to report on the startling developments throughout the Italian peninsula. Years later, according to Robert Hughes, old Lewis Cass recalled John Daniel's dispatches as "the ablest and most instructive" he received as secretary of state.[29] It bears noting that Daniel's reporting from Italy was always considered frank and objective, even after he had lived and worked there for some years. In contrast, his British colleague Sir James Hudson (Hudson had been knighted in 1855) became a wholehearted and certainly no longer objective supporter of the Italian cause. When Hudson was called to London in April 1859 his greatest fear was that he would not be permitted to return to Turin. Lord Malmesbury wrote at the Foreign Office that "he is more Italian than the Italians themselves, and he lives almost entirely with the ultras of that cause." Nevertheless Hudson was sent back to Turin, and remained there as minister until 1863, when he retired—in Italy.[30]

Decades later, an American scholar would write that John Daniel had been greatly impressed by the Italian nationalist movement and would thereafter, on his return to America, begin preaching the idea of a Southern nationalism.[31] Certainly Daniel was impressed, and indeed stirred, by what he observed in Italy from 1858 until his mission there ended; and, as we shall see, after South Carolina seceded from the Union he became a major force for the secession of Virginia, and then a major spokesman for the independent South. But it is far from clear that he found much of a lesson or inspiration for the American South in Italian events. And the growth of Southern nationalism did not begin with John Moncure Daniel.

By the autumn of 1859, not only Tuscany but also the duchies of Modena and Parma and the northernmost Papal States had sought annexation to the Kingdom of Sardinia. Napoleon III was not pleased; this was not what he had agreed to with Austria, and he did not want to see an overly strong Savoy kingdom. Nevertheless, these Italian states moved toward full absorption into the kingdom. The next question was what would happen to papal rule in central Italy and to the Bourbon kingdom in the south.

Although Daniel remained preoccupied with events in Italy in 1859, his friends in Virginia kept him apprised of events at home. Some of the news from Virginia must have seemed relatively minor. Thomas Wynne wrote to Daniel that his old friend and colleague Patrick Henry Aylett had fought a duel with O. Jennings Wise. The underlying cause was politics. Aylett, writing for the *Examiner,* was a supporter of Senator Hunter, whereas Wise, at the *Enquirer,* supported his father Governor Henry Wise. Aylett did not want a duel, but Wise provoked him, essentially calling him a coward and thief. Aylett and Wise met in North Carolina to avoid the Virginia police. Neither was hurt in the duel, but the quarrel remained unresolved.[32] What Daniel's friends in Virginia wanted from him were details of the war raging in Italy, which might conceivably spread further in Europe and even involve America.

Daniel's beloved great-uncle had written to him in December 1858 that he would be sorry if John stayed much longer abroad, because it meant that they would not meet again, given the justice's deteriorating health. The justice therefore sent his great-nephew "the farewell expression of solicitude by one who sincerely and anxiously wishes that nothing may occur in your life which may embitter or disturb the reflections of after times. . . . [T]he hope that the opinions, the morals, the habits, or the toleration of a society grown old in corruption and profligacy, may have no power to involve you in any predicament which as an American gentleman, (and I would like to add as a Christian,) you could not recall with approbation and even with pride."[33]

Although Peter Vivian Daniel believed he was nearing his end, he wrote a long letter to John that December. It concluded with rare news of John's younger brother Travers, who had gone west and held a government office in Washington Territory. There could, however, be little question that, as the months went by, the justice's health worsened. In mid-December 1859, Thomas Wynne wrote John Daniel that, because of his health, the justice had left Washington and moved into his son's house in Richmond.[34] Perhaps the great-nephew thought a pin-prick might help. Daniel wrote Peter Vivian Daniel on January 1, 1860, to wish him a happy New Year, adding that although the justice frequently alluded to his bad health, "I have believed you to be slightly hypocondriac [*sic*], and . . . have confidently anticipated for you many and many years good and honorable."[35] However, John added, he had recently lost one of his most revered friends, Judge Mason, whom he had first met at his great-uncle's table and who, as minister at Paris, had frequently offered his younger colleague in Turin useful advice and kind sympathy. Mason had died in Paris in October 1859; he had not been replaced as minister, but, Daniel noted, he had gone through all his money. After Mason's death, Daniel had made another visit to Paris, that December of 1859, perhaps to consult his doctors again, and he returned to Turin at the end of the year.[36]

As John Daniel continued his letter, that New Year's Day of 1860, he had many reasons to be depressed aside from his great-uncle's poor health. When he had been active in politics in America, he wrote, he never believed there was any real danger to the Union; he thought that in time of crisis the good sense of his countrymen would work to avert catastrophe. Recently, though, Thomas Wynne had written that unless something superhuman occurred, the Union could not last much longer.[37] Daniel agreed.

> We are involved in a current which seems irresistible and which is surely and rapidly hurrying us on to an abyss. If the faction of the North is indeed determined to do what they have ever threatened, it is certain that the Union must be riven. . . . Who can contemplate the physical condition of the United States at this moment without tears? What an ignoble fate awaits us! We have built up a great, prosperous, free, glorious country, which would soon over-shadow

all the earth, . . . and it is now to be assassinated by such base and feeble hands as those of Greel[e]y, Parker and Garrison. . . .

Affairs in Europe are not less troubled. It is my belief that there will be a renewal of the war in Italy this spring. . . .

The letter went on to tell Peter Daniel that the main reason John had not written for so long was that he was troubled by serious problems in his private life and that he had hesitated to disturb his great-uncle with them. And there, with a curlicue and no signature, ends the copy of John Daniel's letter in letterbook from the Turin legation. The original clearly did not end there, but what he wrote his great-uncle was apparently too sensitive to be copied. Were these personal problems to do with his own poor health? Did they involve a lady? We do not know. By the time Daniel's letter reached his great-uncle, the justice's condition had worsened further. Early in April, he replied to his great-nephew. Presumably the response offered John Daniel offered some advice about John's personal problems, but the text was not copied into the legation letterbook. After reading his great-uncle's letter, Daniel wrote Thomas Wynne: "I fear I shall loose [*sic*] him, the truest, most manful friend that I ever had."[38] Indeed, this was the last letter that Peter Vivian Daniel wrote to his great-nephew. The old, twice-widowed Jeffersonian died in Richmond at the end of May 1860. Had he expressed some hope, in his last letter, for the continuance of the Union? John Daniel himself professed, in a letter to Judge Crump at the end of April, to be less than completely pessimistic: "Even should a black republican be elevated to the Presidency, I am not one of those who think it is the knell of the Union, or that we should immediately set about its destruction. We must wait for a practical illustration of their theories. I hope and believe however that we will never have to make such calculations."[39]

That same month of May, down in Florence, another American died, aged not quite fifty, from tuberculosis: Theodore Parker, the minister and abolitionist, whose views were so different from those of Peter and John Daniel. John Daniel had respected the man's intellect, though not his politics, and had even gone to hear a sermon in Parker's Boston church ten years earlier. Parker had lost most of his family to tuberculosis; he had written to Charles Sumner even before reaching Florence that "Consumption is a Tiger who has eaten up my Mother, one Brother, and seven sisters—besides two neices [*sic*]; that ugly beast has now put his claws into my side, and his nose into my bosom, and threatens to cut me up also."[40] The same tiger was also attacking John Daniel, if so far less violently.

Peter Vivian Daniel's death was the occasion for the first letter in many years to John Moncure Daniel from his younger brother Travers, who had come back to the East from Washington Territory shortly before their great-uncle's death. Travers wrote that he was setting out for Texas to see their brother Mitchell and to make a fresh start.[41] Travers had made a busy life for himself at Port Townsend on Puget Sound as a judge, member of the territorial legislature, and editor. Before going west a decade earlier, he had become engaged to a young lady from Baltimore. The engagement continued, but a continent separated them, and eventually Travers wrote the lady that despite his several occupations he despaired of making enough money to care for her as his wife. She wrote back that her father would help them financially, whereupon Travers resigned his positions in the territory and went east to marry her and then, he thought, move to Texas to go into cattle-raising. A week before the wedding, the girl told him she could not marry him; Thomas Wynne (who wrote all this to John Moncure Daniel[42]) thought her brother wanted her to marry someone else. So poor Travers set off for Texas alone, without a bride.

Meanwhile, the Italian situation turned more critical as 1860 began. John Daniel continued to give Italian matters his careful attention. In January, Count Cavour returned to power. In the new government he was not only prime minister but foreign minister and interior minister as well. Daniel reported that other members of Cavour's new cabinet were insignificant men who were in fact nothing but his secretaries. Cavour's return, said Daniel, indicated that his ally Napoleon III was again encouraging the ambitions of Piedmont. The American envoy, who had no liking for Cavour, described him as being not a statesman but an adroit, clever, and bold politician. He had begun his career on the far Right but moved Left and was now with the party of all of Young Italy. Cavour, said Daniel, was always careful never to lag behind popular sentiment.[43]

On January 31, 1860, Daniel reported that the kingdom's annexation of the duchies of Tuscany, Modena, and Parma was practically completed. He believed that England, France, and Sardinia intended to settle the Italian question during 1860, beginning, if necessary, a new war with Austria to force it to cede Venice and northeastern Italy to the Kingdom of Sardinia. It seemed that Sardinia, too, would lose some territory; word was circulating "on high authority" that Cavour wanted to give Savoy as a peace offering to France.[44] (In fact, as described earlier, Cavour and Napoleon III had secretly agreed in 1858 that Savoy and Nice should go to France.) This loss of territory would, it seemed, not raise much of a stir in the Kingdom of Sardinia, since two-thirds of the parliamentary deputies from Savoy favored French annexation and the Italian public realized that if Venice was a natural member of Italy, so Savoy was equally part of France, "geographically, by language, by character and by race."[45]

In February 1860, Daniel reported to Washington that the Sardinian government was calling up troops, and his Italian friends all thought there would be a new war with Austria.[46] Among those called up was Daniel's own thirty-year-old valet de chambre, Pascal Charvier, for whom Daniel unsuccessfully sought exemption from military service.[47]

In March, Daniel reported that Napoleon III was talking peace. While Sardinia had called up 50,000 men, the emperor had announced a reduction of 150,000 in the French army. But it appeared that Sardinia had gone too far toward war to turn back.[48]

As the pace of Italian events and Daniel's reporting accelerated, he wrote a personal dispatch to Secretary of State Cass, saying that while he should perhaps apologize for occupying the secretary's attention so often with Italian events, these were the focus of attention in Europe. Furthermore, the United States might have a real interest in the outcome of events in Italy, which could someday become one of the most important maritime powers of Europe.[49] Cass thought that Daniel had no need to apologize. Within a month, Daniel received two dispatches from the State Department assuring him that his timely and valuable reporting was being read with much interest and satisfaction.[50] Daniel was delighted at these commendations. He wrote Cass that for years he had felt that events at a minor legation in a small country could not possibly interest his government, and that he had therefore refrained from sending more reports than absolutely required. His situation had been disheartening; however, "The kind attention which you have given to my observations during the past year and the words of encouragement which you have twice addressed to me have changed and rendered much happier my life here, because they have placed in it an object and aim worth of all my efforts."[51]

The American press was filled with news from Italy, but Daniel's confidential reporting to the State Department, based on better sources than those of most journalists, rounded out the picture of Italian events for Secretary of State Cass and the Buchanan administration. Lewis Cass had long taken a personal interest in Italy and had traveled throughout the Italian peninsula during his service as minister to France.[52] In August 1850, when Giuseppe Garibaldi had found refuge in Staten Island after French troops had put an end to the short-lived Roman Republic, then-Senator Cass had written Garibaldi a warm letter of welcome and praise: "You raised the standard of liberty upon the Capitoline Hill, and history will do justice to your noble efforts to maintain it there. . . . You yielded to an overwhelming force: to another descent of the Gaul upon Italy. . . . The battle of freedom may be lost once and again but it will yet be won."[53]

Early in 1860, Daniel reported to the State Department that not all Italians were satisfied with the prospect of France annexing Nice and Savoy, even if this were to be accomplished after a plebiscite in those areas. Giuseppe Garibaldi, born in Nice and in 1860 a member of Sardinia's parliament as well as a famous general, was enraged by the reports. He sent one of his officers to ask the king if Nice was really going to France. Yes, said Vittorio Emanuele II, and not only Nice but Savoy as well. And if he could reconcile himself to losing the ancient cradle of the Savoy family, Garibaldi could reconcile himself to losing his own place of birth.[54]

This did not mollify Giuseppe Garibaldi. He spoke out bitterly in parliament against the "sale" of Nice to France. Daniel looked on as thousands of people waited outside the building to cheer Garibaldi afterward. Soon after, Garibaldi called on Daniel. The American minister subsequently reported to Washington that the general

> desired to know whether the United States would give protection or assistance to Nice in case it should separate both from France and Sardinia and establish a free form of government for itself? I told him at once that the United States would interfere in no manner with such a matter; and that though I believed it to be the policy of our republic to recognize all governments that succeeded in establishing themselves and that could be regarded as responsible organizations, yet I doubted whether they would hold any intercourse, even of the most temporary character, with a mere province in rebellion against powers so much more powerful than itself as to render its immediate subjection almost a certainty. He said that he had anticipated the reply I made to his inquiry, but, in the present moment, he thought it right to leave no chance for assistance untried.[55]

The American minister had done the right thing. If he had shown any sympathy for the idea of an independent Nice, or even if he had temporized by offering to put the question to Washington (a question that could not have been answered in less than a month, since there was not yet a transatlantic telegraph), it is conceivable that Garibaldi might have thought American aid was possible, and might have tried to raise up the Niçois to oppose annexation. Any revolt would have been crushed, and one imagines that Garibaldi would not have concentrated his efforts on the South as he did. Plebiscites were held in Savoy and Nice on April 15, 1860, and, under heavy pressure from the authorities, an overwhelming majority voted for annexation to France.

On May 5, Garibaldi sailed out of the Gulf of Genoa with a thousand or so volunteers and a few cannons to invade Bourbon Sicily. The Sardinian authorities were aware of preparations for the expedition (Garibaldi had conceived the idea at least a year earlier) and did not stop them. Daniel reported to Washington that Garibaldi's expedition was the most startling and significant event in Italy so far that year. He told the State Department flatly that if Garibaldi landed in Sicily, he had no doubt at all that he would succeed—an astounding and daring prediction, since the Kingdom of Two Sicilies had a large professional army and no one could be sure whether the local populace would help the little force of invaders from the north.[56] In fact, in a conversation with Garibaldi shortly before the general launched his expedition, Daniel had noted that even the warmest advocates of revolution in the Kingdom of Two Sicilies admitted that in a free election, the people of

Naples would vote to retain the present dynasty. Garibaldi "reluctantly assented but added with much simple faith, that 'Liberty itself must sometimes be forced on the people for their future good.'"[57]

Daniel turned out to be right in predicting Garibaldi's success. With determination and amazing luck, he and his Thousand landed at Marsala on May 11 and marched across Sicily from west to east. Within two weeks, Garibaldi had taken Palermo and declared himself dictator of Sicily in the name of Vittorio Emanuele. Soon after he crossed the Strait of Messina to the southern Italian mainland—disobeying an order from the king, who was concerned about displeasing Napoleon III—and marched north to take Naples and end the Bourbons' reign. At the beginning of July, John Daniel reported that "the revolution of Southern Italy pursues an uninterrupted course to its goal, which will be the formation of a great Italian kingdom."[58]

There was, Daniel added, an important point in this for the United States. No matter how badly the Bourbon regime had ruled, and however indubitable the right of a people to revolt, the invasion of a legitimate kingdom amounted to a violation of international law. Moreover, it had been supported by the Kingdom of Sardinia, though not openly. Yet people and press in Sardinia and its allies England and France never ceased to rail against the United States for any move toward acquisition of new territory. The contrast, wrote Daniel, made clear the insincerity and hypocrisy of European criticisms of America.

Daniel learned with some delay—the American Consul at Genoa perhaps deliberately neglected to inform him—that four of the vessels involved in Garibaldi's expedition were American. Three of these, he reported to Washington, had been bought in Genoa by William de Rohan, "stated to be an American citizen," and transferred in a deed executed at the American consulate.[59] (William de Rohan was indeed an American citizen. His original name was Dahlgren, and he was the brother of John Dahlgren, inventor of the Dahlgren gun and Union admiral during the Civil War, and the uncle of Ulric Dahlgren, the young Union colonel killed in a daring raid on Richmond in 1864. There were also several American citizens who did distinguished service as volunteers in Garibaldi's army, including Alfred Benthuysen of New Orleans, the nephew of U.S. senator Jefferson Davis.)

In September 1860, just after Garibaldi entered Naples and completed the conquest of the Kingdom of Two Sicilies, Sardinian troops invaded the Papal States in central Italy. By the end of September, papal rule had been reduced to Rome and its immediate hinterland. As a result, Vittorio Emanuele and his government in Turin controlled all of Italy except for the Pope's ministate and the reduced Austrian holdings in the northeast. Daniel reported to Washington on mid-October that "Judging by present appearances, the Italian Millennium is at hand."[60] Cavour told the parliament in Turin that Rome would eventually become the capital of a new Italy of 25 million people. (Cavour prophesied correctly, but it would be another decade before this happened.)

These changes in Italy echoed in Washington. In April 1860, even before Garibaldi invaded Sicily, the U.S. House of Representatives adopted a resolution introduced by Anson Burlingame, Republican of Massachusetts, which instructed the House Committee on Foreign Affairs to consider the question of raising the legation and minister at Turin to the top level, equivalent to posts like London, Paris, and St. Petersburg. Subsequently, in June, both House and Senate approved a bill to raise the rank of the American representative at Turin from minister resident to envoy extraordinary and plenipotentiary, with a salary of $12,000 per annum. (Daniel was continuing to receive $7,500 as Minister Resident.) The president signed the bill into law on June 16, 1860.[61]

Unfortunately for Daniel, the new law did nothing for him. His enemies, and political opponents of the Buchanan administration, insisted that America needed someone new for the higher-level job in Turin. They had not seen Daniel's reports to the State Department, but they did dredge up his old garlic letter and reports of his "shocking" behavior in taking Marie de Solms to the court ball. The *Cincinnati Daily Gazette* said that if the Sardinians had kicked Daniel out in view of his vulgar and brutal manners, they would have done no more than justice to him and themselves.[62] The *New York Times* believed that "[T]he best thing we can now do is to wipe out the memory of Mr. DANIELS [*sic*], and his epistolary efforts, as rapidly as possible, by sending to the new Italian Court an Envoy at once of more exalted official rank, and of more creditable personal character."[63] President Buchanan was dissuaded from promoting Daniel despite the authority he had to do so, and Daniel remained minister resident, without further promotion or raise in salary, to the end of his years in Italy. Daniel was naturally bitter. He wrote a friend, "The interpretation given here to this fact is that the President does not wish to remove me, but does not regard me as a person worthy to be a Minister Plenipotentiary of the United States."[64]

Even without a raise, Daniel continued to save money. The comptroller of the treasury informed him that, as of the quarter that ended June 30, 1860, he was due $14,944.15—almost two years' salary.[65] We do not know just how Daniel lived in Turin, but his ability to save money may have depended primarily on low local prices and careful management, not on miserly ways. He was, of course, called upon to reciprocate for hospitality he received. At some point, he later told his friend George Bagby, he hired a (presumably impoverished) Italian count as his *chef de cuisine*. As is clear from his later years in Richmond, Daniel liked to live well, and in Turin he could afford to do so.

Meanwhile, in 1860 the fate of the *Richmond Examiner* remained unresolved. William Lloyd had arranged for Daniel to buy back half of the paper from Robert

Hughes, but in September 1859 Lloyd had offered to buy Daniel's half for three thousand dollars, or more if the paper's modern steam press turned out to be Daniel's property. This question had remained in contention between Daniel and Hughes. Daniel wrote to Lloyd that he was willing to sell his share. Lloyd wanted to make the purchase by giving Daniel a bond payable in five years; Daniel answered that it must be payable on demand.[66] In March 1860, Lloyd agreed and sent for Daniel's approval the corresponding deed, bond, and bond of indemnity. However, Lloyd himself had not signed, and in April Daniel wrote back that he declined to sign "blanks."[67] The situation of the paper was not satisfactory, and his great-uncle was still alive but fast declining; on April 25 the minister asked the State Department to grant him a leave of absence for sixty days so he could return home for the first time in seven years.

Did Daniel really expect superiors in Washington to let him leave his post for two months, and at such a critical time? Secretary of War Floyd wrote to Daniel on May 25 that the cabinet had discussed his request for leave,

> and, upon consideration of the complications here quite as much as in Italy, the President thought it best to decline it. I did not interpose any objection to this decision, although I am sincerely anxious to see you, for many reasons. You can form no idea of the condition of parties here. All allegiance & organization are completely annihilated, and the country is given over to one wild hunt for place & plunder. . . . Presidential candidacy has become a mania. . . . Pretty nearly every member of Congress is an aspirant, & now that "Abe Lincoln" is nominated by the Black Republicans, the contagion has spread among the masses as the cholera does in an infected city. Virginia, always foremost in any race of [for?] honor & distinction, comes forward with her legions for the combat—she rejoices in furnishing candidates in great abundance for each & every party & parts of parties—Hunter, Wise, Faulkner, Caskie, Lewis Harvey & Dewitt, for the regular Democrats—Botts for the Black Republicans—and since the Know Nothings have set the example of diving into Herculaneum for a candidate [Millard Fillmore] from amongst the mighty dead to lead them to another death, the process of resurrection has been going on, and Rives, Sandy Stuart, Summers, Ballard Preston, Wm. S. Archer & Watkins Leigh, have broken their cerements, and advance in solemn minuet towards the White House.
>
> You and most certainly your office would be made the object of violent contention by some of the hungry men . . . the very moment you set foot upon the shore, and for this reason . . . I have thought it best for you to remain at your post as yet. . . .
>
> I spoke to Hunter to call [in the Senate] for your dispatches, that you might appear before the country. He promised to do so. . . .[68]

Floyd added that Secretary of State Cass, who had sent Daniel a brief, official denial of his request for leave, had asked Floyd to send this private letter to explain in detail the reasons for the decision.

Daniel appreciated the information, but he did not like the idea of having his dispatches to the State Department made public. He quickly wrote back to Floyd.

> Every word would be instantly translated into the newspapers here, and every phrase which does not indicate full approval of everything done in Italy and admiration of the Italians would expose me to violent abuse. The Italians are tetchy, vain and extreme in everything. Their passions are naturally much engaged in what is going on here. All who are not for them, they consider as against them. Now in writing to my Government I have written neither as their friend nor their enemy but simply as a spectator. . . . [I] stated what I had to say simply and *with great freedom*. . . . [N]o Minister can . . . write to his Government with any confidence if everything is to be printed in the newspapers. . . .
>
> You may think it quite unnecessary for me to lecture in this way. . . . But I have one of those unlucky pens that can never touch paper without hurting somebody somewhere. Others write reams without disturbing the equanimity of any living thing, but I never could learn the art. . . .[69]

The minister with the sharp pen added some frank comments about the new Republican candidate for president: "The nomination of Lincoln by the Republicans is worse than I expected of them—a buffoon for 25 cents a night—an itinerant lecturer: why not a traveling dentist? And this may be our next President. They are to elect on his name of Uncle Abe; next time they will have a free negro and call him Uncle Tom."

But while the Republicans had agreed on a presidential candidate from the prairies, the Democratic party was coming apart. As Daniel saw it, the Democrats had been disintegrating ever since electing James K. Polk to the White House in 1844. The Whigs owed their victory in 1848 largely to the irregularities of Southern Democrats, and the next two Democratic presidents, Pierce and Buchanan, owed their elections more to the weakness of their opponents than to Democratic unity. In 1857, Senator Stephen Douglas had split with the Buchanan administration over the question of slavery in Kansas. Although this development had won him the support of Northern Democrats, he had lost the support of most Southern Democrats even though all thinking persons—South and North—believed that no other Democrat stood any chance of winning the 1860 presidential election.[70]

By November 1860, the unification of Italy under the Savoy dynasty was almost complete. Daniel reported to the State Department on November 13 that "Sardinia is borne forward on the fullest tide of success. Every new development in Italy turns to its advantage. The king Victor Emmanuel is enthroned at Naples. . . . Garibaldi has been quietly bored [*sic*] off to his islet of Caprera to live there with his goats and cow until wanted for the Venetian revolution yet to come. . . . I have been long satisfied that the movement of Italy is no temporary disturbance created by statesmen and soldiers, but one of those great tides in the affairs of nations which change the physical configuration of the world, over which individuals have little control."[71]

A week later, on November 20, Daniel decided to raise the question of what the unification of Italy meant for his own responsibilities. Joseph R. Chandler, who since 1858 had been American minister to the Kingdom of Two Sicilies, had just notified Daniel that since the government to which he was accredited no longer existed, he had closed his diplomatic mission. Daniel believed that he should begin to act as American minister in areas annexed to the Kingdom of Sardinia. However, doing so would amount to recognition by the United States of the validity of the annexations. Therefore, Daniel wrote the secretary of state, he would be glad to receive advice or indication as to the extent of his powers in "the new arrangement of Italian territory."[72]

There was no answer; there was no need for an answer. Within a day or so of sending his dispatch of November 20, Daniel must have received the news that Abraham Lincoln had been elected president of the United States. Lincoln had gained only a plurality of popular votes, but he received a majority of the electoral votes. The Democrats had split and fielded rival candidates, Stephen Douglas and John Breckenridge, and a new Constitutional party had acted as spoiler. Lincoln's victory meant that Democratic officeholders would soon be replaced by Republicans. Furthermore, Daniel probably saw Lincoln's election as the prelude to dissolution of the American Union. Now, indeed, it was time to go home.

On December 4, 1860, Daniel wrote a private letter to Secretary of State Cass, to say that in a short time he would conclude his mission in Italy and return to his native state.[73] He urged that the United States government hire someone to take charge at Turin until his successor arrived. Daniel suggested as a temporary replacement his brother Frederick, who had served at Turin all these years without a government salary. On December 11, 1860, Daniel asked the State Department for a leave of absence beginning on January 10, 1861, to return to America. He noted that he had never been granted leave to return home while in the public service of the United States—well over seven years—and he added, responsibly, that his absence would not damage American interests; the affairs of Italy had been settled for some time to come, and nothing of interest to the United States government was likely to transpire over the coming winter.[74]

On December 20, 1860, as Daniel's request for a leave of absence made its way to Washington, South Carolina seceded from the Union. He must have heard the news sometime during the first week of January 1861. Frederick Daniel, still acting as his brother's secretary, recalled that when John heard the news he said, "It has got to come to this at last, and the sooner the better."[75] About the same time, John Daniel learned from the Department of State that Jeremiah Black, the former attorney general, had replaced Lewis Cass as secretary of state on December 17, 1860, and that his own request for a leave of absence had been granted. Black wrote Daniel that "your conduct of the affairs of the Legation has been entirely acceptable to the President and to this Department."[76]

Daniel did not tarry at Turin. His final dispatch to Secretary Black was dated February 5, 1861. He accepted the leave of absence to run from January 10 until March 2: "On that date, in view of the retirement of the distinguished gentlemen who compose the present Administration, I shall cause my letter of recall to be delivered at Turin. . . . Permit me to add that while the actual Chief Magistrate of this nation and the great officers of the law who surround him have always received my entire sympathy and profound respect, their approval of my official conduct, most kindly communicated by yourself, will be a source of justifiable pride to me for the rest of my life."[77]

Daniel's farewells with officials and friends, includeing Prime Minister Cavour and Marie de Solms, must have been brief. Several months earlier he had perhaps dreamed of remaining in Turin longer as American minister plenipotentiary to a great new Italian kingdom—if a Democratic candidate and not Abraham Lincoln had somehow won the presidency. He would have been able to continue his friendship with the princess. Perhaps he had even dreamed of marrying her. Years later, Moncure Daniel Conway wrote that his cousin had indeed loved the lady.[78] Or had it been rather a case of infatuation, with the young American simply "a charmed visitor at her salon"?[79] But aside from the lady, over these years in Italy Daniel had become, he had reason to believe, America's best diplomat.

No matter. The Italian dreams of John Daniel were gone. He had been not quite twenty-eight years old when he arrived in Italy. In 1861, he was thirty-five, a sophisticated and decidedly more prosperous man, if not happier and perhaps not healthier. It was apparently some form of tuberculosis that continued to plague him. The Paris doctors whom he had seen over the years had in fact diagnosed him as tubercular. As Frederick Daniel later said, his brother "had been apprised of his tendency to consumption." But John Daniel refused to believe them, or at least said that he refused to believe them.[80]

Daniel was not the only American officer to leave the Mediterranean for the new Confederacy. There were various resignations from the U.S. Mediterranean squadron based at La Spezia, culminating in the departure of Capt. Duncan N. Ingraham, commanding officer of the squadron's flagship.[81]

Within a few days of hearing that South Carolina had seceded, Daniel was on his way to America, leaving his brother Frederick temporarily in charge of the legation. (It is possible that he had already left Turin before the date of his February 5 dispatch.) He must have gone north through Paris to London, where presumably he received the monies due to him on account at Barings. At Liverpool, he boarded a ship to cross the wintry Atlantic to New York.

Daniel returned to America with deep concerns but well supplied with funds—thirty thousand dollars, it was said later. How he could have accumulated so much money (a full four years' salary as minister) is not clear. There is no reason to believe that he made any of it improperly. At least half that amount was due to him in salary. Perhaps he made the other half by selling off items he had collected over his long tour of duty in Turin. Frederick Daniel said that his brother had been an industrious collector of "antique coins, books, &c.," and had been regarded as a connoisseur by the antiquarians in all the principal Italian cities.[82] His friend Thomas Wynne, perhaps knowing of John's activities, had sometimes pestered Daniel to send him small coins and antiques. (Wynne, incidentally, had no inkling that his close friend Daniel was returning to America, at least so soon. In mid-January 1861 he instructed a friend how to send newspapers to "Hon John M Daniel, Minister Resident US Turin."[83])

John Moncure Daniel returned to America with the satisfaction of having done the American republic excellent service and with the equivalent of several years' income. But the republic he had served was fast tearing apart, and blood and carnage soon followed. He saw the horror coming. It was a horror that Daniel, like many others, would seek to guise as glory.

Twelve

The Need to Secede

Landing in New York in February 1861 after the crossing from Liverpool, John Moncure Daniel proceeded to Washington and took a room at Brown's Hotel, registering simply as "Mr. Daniel, Liverpool." After so many years abroad, he needed to talk with a lot of people and catch up on a lot of things before he went on to Richmond. Brown's was just the place. It was located on Pennsylvania Avenue several blocks east of the White House and the State and Treasury Departments. It was not as elegant a place as Willard's Hotel just down the avenue—Abraham Lincoln was soon to put up at Willard's, before his inauguration on March 4, and for now it was full of people seeking posts in the new administration—but for years Brown's had been a meeting place for distinguished people, particularly for Southern members of Congress and other Southern politicians.[1] (There is some irony in this; Jesse Brown had been one of Washington's first black businessmen.)

In early 1861 the federal city was full of oratory, plans, plots, and uncertainty. On March 26, the correspondent of the *Times* of London wrote of the "chaos of opinions" he encountered in Washington.[2] On January 5, fourteen U.S. senators from Southern states, including Jefferson Davis, Floyd's predecessor as secretary of war, had met in Washington to discuss independence for the South. Initially, it was proposed that John Daniel's old acquaintance, Senator R. M. T. Hunter of Virginia, should become president of the new Confederacy and Davis its secretary of war. However, Hunter turned down the idea of heading the Confederacy; he did not want war over the federal forts along the Southern coasts, a sore point from the beginning of secession.[3]

In January, five states—Alabama, Florida, Georgia, Louisiana, and Mississippi—followed the example of South Carolina and seceded from the Union. Texas seceded on the first of February. Most of the senators and representatives from these states had already made their farewells from the Congress of the United States. Several Southern states, including Virginia, had not decided to leave the Union—yet. The first states that had seceded sent delegates to a congress at Montgomery, Alabama, which convened at the beginning of February. That body promptly adopted a provisional constitution for the new Confederate States of America, and on February 9 elected Jefferson Davis of Mississippi the provisional president. Disunion was a fact.

John Moncure Daniel had one last official duty to perform in Washington: a farewell visit to the Department of State, to which he had reported for almost eight years. His mission to Italy had formally ended on January 28, when President Buchanan had signed the warrant for his recall.[4] One day in February Daniel paid a call on the new secretary of state, Jeremiah Black, a Northerner who had taken office only two months earlier, after the resignation of Lewis Cass. Black had been the U.S. attorney general and a successful lawyer in Pennsylvania. Daniel's great-uncle had considered him the ablest member of Buchanan's cabinet. Three years after their 1861 meeting, John Daniel recalled that he had expressed Southern sentiments to the new secretary of state. The two had talked about the troubles that were approaching, and Daniel had alluded to the matter of slavery. According to Daniel, Black had replied: "Sir, slavery is but an accident in this quarrel. Slavery is only the John Doe and Richard Roe case, in which this mooted question is to be decided—whether your states shall continue their sovereignty and self-government, or the Northern majorities shall govern you and all of you as they please and according to their own separate interest. If they had not the point of slavery convenient, they would try it on other points just the same."

Daniel recalled that Black also approved of the Southern determination to resist as the only course by which Southerners could hope to continue as free citizens. Daniel wrote in 1864 that Black's sentiments did not prevent him from declaring two months later that the United States was about to make a gigantic effort to wipe slavery from its escutcheon, and that for this reason alone the sword was drawn.[5]

John Daniel's later account of what Jeremiah Black had told him in February 1861 does not square with what we know of Secretary Black's beliefs. There is no doubt that Black strongly disliked the abolitionists, whom he saw as fanatics who might well go on from attacks on slavery to attacks on the Christian religion and the institution of marriage. But for Black that did not justify secession, and as attorney general in November 1860 he had expressed the opinion that the United States had the right to prevent secession. He thought such action would amount to repelling aggression by individuals against the Union, and he viewed this as a totally different thing from the aggressive war that some Northerners wanted. In the first Cabinet discussion on secession, Black had similarly urged coercion against individuals resisting federal authority.[6] And just several weeks before he saw John Daniel, he had written to a fellow Pennsylvanian that "when war is made against us a moderate self-defence is righteous and proper."[7] One can therefore conjecture that in Daniel's meeting with Black, when Daniel pushed, as he said he had done, the question of slavery, Black may have responded that he disliked abolitionists but that slavery was not the main question—and that Daniel, who may well have been at a high pitch emotionally, came away from what may have been a fairly brief conversation with the erroneous feeling that Black found secession justified. The question is not unimportant. It is not clear that Daniel believed Virginia should secede from the Union, when he arrived back in America; but by the time he went on from Washington to Richmond he was certainly in favor of secession. Conceivably what he heard, or wanted to think he heard, from the secretary of state helped form his opinion.

There is no indication that Daniel saw in Washington his Italian counterpart, Minister Bertinatti. There was no love lost between the two, and unlike many members of the Washington diplomatic corps, Bertinatti's sentiments were already firmly pro-Union. In mid-January he had written to Foreign Minister Cavour in Turin that while it might be difficult to understand in Europe why the American president had not carried out his constitutional duties and put down the incipient rebellion, one should realize that Buchanan's cabinet had until now contained three separatists. These, he added, should and would have been charged with high treason in Italy, but in America they had been allowed to depart in peace. Cavour, in turn, confirmed to Bertinatti that the Italian government had decided to support the North, "for the cause that they support is not only the cause of constitutional legality but of humanity."[8]

John Daniel spent two or three weeks in Washington in urgent discussions with political friends and acquaintances. No complete record of whom he saw survives. Aside from seeing the secretary of state, we know that he met with his fellow Virginians James Seddon, a representative of the South to the soon-to-fail Peace Commission, and Muscoe R. H. Garnett, who had served two terms in the House of Representatives and was calling for Virginia to secede.[9]

Daniel's patron, John B. Floyd, had resigned as secretary of war at the end of December and returned to Virginia. It was rumored that Floyd was guilty of peculation. A number of Indian Trust Fund bonds had been stolen by a clerk, and it was said that Floyd, who was related to the clerk, had profited from the theft. (Evidence available today indicates that Floyd may have been careless but was not dishonest.) One evening in Washington when Daniel was in company with others, a member of the group said that John Floyd was no better than a thief. Daniel leaped from his chair with a white face and trembling lips, saying this was an accursed slander. He tried to calm himself but could not; his agitation continued, and the party soon dispersed. Clearly his personality had not been tempered by his years in Europe. Just as he harbored, it seems, for years the bacillus that would one day kill him, so it seems he had for long had a kind of mental fever, a rage that only rarely broke out in the open, but that continued to tell on his work and fiery writing. There is at least one other instance of this rage taking him over. One night in Richmond, sometime after Daniel had resumed control of his paper, he heard that a certain article in a rival paper had been written by a former employee of the *Examiner*, and for twenty minutes Daniel strode up and down the room exclaiming again and again "I'll put a ball through him!" But he did not do so. Indeed, though he was known as a dueling editor, there is no reason to believe that he ever put a ball through anyone.

During his stay in Washington, Daniel also met his old acquaintance, Robert William Hughes, who had lately been editing the *Washington Union*. Daniel could not put his full trust in Hughes in view of their past differences over the *Examiner*. Nor could he forget that Hughes had almost ruined his career by publishing Daniel's "garlic letter." Seven years earlier, Daniel had written to his friend, Judge Crump: "I had as leif [*sic*] have the fingers of the hangman busy about my neck as see his [Hughes's] clumsy thumbs tampering with my name. . . . I always knew him to be soft of brain, and to be destitute of all high-minded delicacy."[10] Hughes, who had previously left his editorship, had come back to Washington on behalf of his father-in-law, John Floyd, to ascertain what was happening on the Indian bonds scandal.[11] Daniel was quick to defend the actions of the recent secretary of war, and he no doubt found it useful to have firsthand news of Floyd, with whom he had been in touch only by letter in recent years. Moreover, Daniel had decided that he needed Hughes to help him resume editorship of the *Examiner*.

If we can believe what Hughes wrote years later, it was Daniel who sought out Hughes in Washington and who told him one day that fateful February that the South had committed a blunder and that he was glad he had no part in "making" secession.[12] Now, though, the die had been cast. Daniel believed that the South could not afford to be divided, and so Virginia and the remaining Southern states must also secede. Disunion need not last; if it acted in unanimity, the South could bring about a reconstruction of the republic, even by the act of seceding. Sitting far away in Turin, Daniel told Hughes, he had seen no choice but to come home and cast his lot with the South. Hughes's account is consistent with Frederick Daniel's statement that as soon as his brother learned in Turin that South Carolina had seceded, he decided to return home "to take part in the fortunes of Virginia."[13] However, sharing the fortunes of Virginia did not necessarily mean working for its secession, as Daniel soon did.

It seems likely that the position of John B. Floyd was a factor in bringing Daniel to a firm stand for secession, if he had not already made up his mind when he reached Washington. Floyd as a member of Buchanan's cabinet had continued to oppose secession well into December 1860, and he had lately published a letter in a Richmond paper stating this position. But Buchanan had apparently then decided that because of the unproven allegations of Floyd's complicity in the bonds theft, Floyd should no longer remain in the cabinet. According to what Jeremiah Black later wrote (but never published), Buchanan—in what might be called cowardly

George W. Bagby, author of "John M. Daniel's Latch-Key," in 1877. Cook Collection, Valentine Museum.

fashion—did not directly inform John Floyd of his decision, but asked some relation of Floyd to tell him. This, according to Black, immediately converted Floyd from an outspoken opponent of secession to a strong and open advocate. Nor did it help that he was also under suspicion for having lately engineered the shipment of extra arms to Southern garrisons. There was another account of what had happened in the Cabinet: that Floyd had written a memorandum which he read at the December 27 Cabinet meeting, insisting that federal troops must be withdrawn from Charleston harbor, but that Buchanan had not agreed and Floyd had then resigned. Whatever the reasons, Floyd resigned as secretary of war on December 29 and returned to his Virginia home, but as related then sent Robert Hughes back to Washington, where Hughes met Daniel.[14]

During Daniel's stay in Washington, he was called on by a Virginian whom he had not met before, George William Bagby, who for some months had been editing the *Southern Literary Messenger* in Richmond. The *Messenger* had just come out for secession in its January issue. Bagby was to become an occasional contributor to the *Examiner,* and after the war he published a favorable and fascinating account of the paper's editor.

Daniel had been clean shaven when he went to Italy. The man George Bagby met at Brown's Hotel, who was elegantly but simply dressed, had a heavy black mustache and a closely trimmed beard that covered his thin cheeks. His small and well-shaped head was surmounted by masses of black hair; his face was dark and refined, his nose slightly aquiline. Daniel spoke with a curious hesitation or tripping, almost a stammer. Bagby at first thought this an affectation, but the tripping had disappeared by the time he encountered Daniel again, a few months later, in Richmond. Bagby concluded then that the tripping must have resulted from Daniel's long years abroad, during which time he had apparently become used to speaking French or Italian instead of English.[15]

By late February 1861, after eight years away, Daniel was back in Richmond and back at the helm of the *Examiner*. The trip south from Washington, on the steamer that left the city every evening for Aquia Creek, was not inspiring if a passenger remained in the low, close, smoky cabin full of men drinking and arguing about what might happen to America. One can imagine John Daniel going on deck to gaze westward over the Potomac River at the dim shore of Virginia and George Washington's old house on the hill. In 1861, Washington's republic was shattering.

The years in Italy had been long and interesting, but it must have felt good to Daniel to reach Aquia Creek and disembark in his home county. As Turin was a fine city, so was Richmond, he must have thought when his train steamed into the depot at Seventh and Broad Streets, just two blocks from the noble Capitol. The city had continued to grow in prosperity and population. The census of 1860 reported that Richmond contained about 38,000 people, over 30 percent of them slaves and not quite 7 percent free blacks. Some free black people earned good wages, but they suffered from a series of legal restrictions. For example, no gathering of five or more black persons was permitted except for church services. Nat Turner's rebellion three decades earlier had not been forgotten.

Thomas Cooper DeLeon, arriving in the city a few months after Daniel, recalled later the beauty of Capitol Square, with its winding walks and rare old trees, and the wide open streets that reached out from it on all sides. One could climb to the Capitol roof and see the rolling countryside, cut by the sluggish silver of the James River, for a radius of twenty miles. Just outside the city lay the green treetops of Chimborazo Heights, soon to become the site of a huge war hospital, and Belle Isle, where thousands of Union prisoners would be quartered. To the west, one saw the taller monuments in Hollywood Cemetery, surrounded on three sides by the river that flowed down from the western highlands. The scene was not all parklike. As noted earlier, Richmond possessed a considerable amount of industry, and not far from the city center, down by the river, were the slate roofs of the Tredegar Iron Works, puffing endless black smoke against the sunshine. Here already, heavy guns and shell and shot were being produced at full speed for Virginia's forces.[16] In 1861, Tredegar Iron Works was the only arsenal in the South; three years later there would be ten others as well.[17]

On February 25, Daniel and William Lloyd concluded an agreement in Richmond "to associate themselves as joint and equal owners of the Examiner newspaper."[18] Lloyd would be the manager, Daniel the editor. Daniel owed a personal debt to Lloyd for having protected his interests against others (including Robert Hughes) while he was in Italy. Nevertheless, the partnership did not work. Daniel complained that Lloyd stayed out of sight and that they could not agree on details of management. Perhaps there was also a clash of personalities. After three months, Daniel gave Lloyd written notice on June 1 that the partnership was dissolved. In late September, Daniel arranged to buy Lloyd's interest—over Lloyd's protest—and henceforth Daniel became the sole proprietor of the *Richmond Examiner*.[19] He remained so until the end of his life.

One of the *Examiner*'s first editorials after Daniel returned to Richmond marked the inauguration on March 4, 1861, of Abraham Lincoln. The paper sadly remarked that the inauguration represented the end of a line of presidents who had brought the American republic, within a single human's lifetime, from insignificance to grandeur. Those high personages were now to be replaced by "those despicable tyrants whose dismal roll commences on the peristyle of the Capitol under the light of the sun now shining."[20]

Nevertheless, Daniel was certainly sad to see the Union dissolving. His paper had written freely and perhaps even glibly about the prospect of disunion during the years before he went to Italy. But he had served the Union there with great distinction for over seven years. The experience had in no sense made him more of a rebel. However, the Union that he knew and wanted to preserve was a Union with Southern slavery. Although Horace Greeley had suggested in 1853 that a tour in Italy would modify Daniel's views on slavery, this had not happened.

In March 1861, many in the North and South shared John Daniel's regret that the country was coming apart. Many in North and South also found James Buchanan largely to blame. Daniel had seen firsthand some of the faults in Buchanan's management of the legation in London. Later, Daniel had learned from a first-hand observer, his great-uncle, the associate justice, how flawed Buchanan's presidency had been. On Inauguration Day 1861, Daniel wrote scathingly about James Buchanan, who had looked and spoken like his predecessors and *endeavored* to act and think as they had done, but had not filled their measure. It was impossible to deny, the *Examiner* said, that Buchanan had left chaos where he had found order, and ruin where he had found prosperity; and much of the looming disaster might be fairly charged to Buchanan's faults of character and policy.

Buchanan, Daniel added, at least possessed decorum and dignity. His successor was a "King of Shreds and Patches," a combination of Western county lawyer and Yankee barkeeper, and no one could read without shame Lincoln's statements on his way to Washington, which Daniel described as condensed lumps of imbecility, buffoonery, and vulgar malignity. (Malignity is hard to find in what the president-elect said on his way east, but at a number of stops Lincoln had spoken poorly, saying that no one was hurt and that nothing was going wrong. In Cleveland, Lincoln insisted that "this crisis is artificial. It has no foundation in fact.... Let it alone, and it will go down of itself."[21]) The editorial continued that Lincoln had brought with him to Washington something worse than rag-tag rowdyism and brutality, something worse than a family headed by "Bob, Prince of Rails, and that successor to Miss Lane, in diamond eardrops and with ivory fan to wave over the faces of the diplomatic corps in the East-room."[22] The worst of Lincoln, said the *Examiner*, was that he was bringing in arbitrary power and that he was intent on destroying every federative feature of the Constitution in order to create one great antislavery community.

At this point, in March 1861, Jefferson Davis had already been sworn in as president of the Confederacy. A number of American newspapers—including many in the South—were continuing to forecast a relatively peaceful division of the country, although Southerners were warning proudly that they were prepared to fight. Daniel was more forthright: he predicted on March 4 that before another year had passed, Abraham Lincoln would have deluged in blood the shattered Union. Daniel wrote that when he had come back to Washington after years abroad, one dawn he had heard in the capital a bugle call, a roll of drums, and a tramp of armed guards that almost made him think he was in Austrian-occupied Venice or Russian-occupied Warsaw. What, wrote Daniel, could come of all this but civil war and public ruin? He perhaps exaggerated the nature of the scene in Washington; it may have been martial, but it was hardly authoritarian. Thirty companies of volunteers were hurriedly being organized to add to what had been a total force of no more than four hundred Marines in the capital.[23] But Daniel's vision of a coming bloodbath was more acute than that of other editors.

Before Daniel had returned to Richmond, the general assembly of Virginia had ordered the election of a state convention to decide the state's future course. The 152 members began their session in Richmond on February 13, 1861, by which date a new Confederacy had formed. The great majority of convention members were Whigs and Unionists. Some of these, and particularly those from the western and northern parts of the state, saw Southern independence causing economic disaster for Virginia. The northeast bought Virginia's wheat, tobacco, and livestock; salt and coal from the state's western counties went to the Ohio and upper Mississippi valley.[24] Still, there were many Virginia Unionists who would not support maintenance of the Union at any cost. Many wanted to preserve the Union only if it provided new and better guarantees of Southern rights, including the right to hold slaves.[25] Daniel quickly went to work on this majority. Seven states had already seceded, and the battle cry of the *Examiner* became *En dat octavum Virginia* (Lo, Virginia provides the eighth). In South Carolina, that fierce voice of seccession, the *Charleston Mercury,* expressed its pleasure that Daniel had come home and was writing scathing articles against the "submissionists." Clearly, said the *Mercury*, the day of Virginia's redemption was at hand; Virginia was Southern, and it would go with the South.[26]

When Daniel resumed the editorship of the *Examiner,* the paper had already taken a position in favor of Virginia's secession under its most recent editor, William Old Jr.[27] Daniel stepped up the force of the paper's rhetoric and argument. In earlier years, the *Examiner* had made good use of mockery and ridicule, which Daniel once called a formidable weapon, and it did so again. After a series of attacks on the "submissionists," on March 19, 1861, the paper printed a long piece entitled "Gli Animali Parlanti," which it described as "the EXAMINER's translation of Casti." (Giambattista Casti's 1802 poem characterized European nations as animals to contrast European monarchism with the new republican spirit of France; it had been translated into English as "The Court and Parliament of Beasts.") The "translation" began with the election of the new king of the birds and beasts of North America, "an ugly and ferocious old Orang-Outang from the wilds of Illinois, who was known by the name of Old ABE." After the new king ordered an invasion of the Southern states in order to subdue them and free their slaves, the Boar of Rockbridge, governor of the beasts of the Old Dominion (Virginia's governor, John Letcher), "notorious for the amount of swill that he could consume," called for the wisest and most learned of Virginia's beasts to meet and decide what to do. Leading members of the convention were described as foxes, jackals, terrapins, hyenas, and so forth. The animals voted to submit humbly and cheerfully to the authority of the Orang-Outang. They also resolved "that we will resist with all our might and to the last extremity any attempt at the coercion of our Southern brethren, but that we do not consider the enforcement of the laws to be coercion; and if our Southern brethren resist the enforcement of the Federal laws, coercion then becomes simply resistance to rebellion, and must be acquiesced in by all good citizens."

Most if not all of the "animals" were easily identified by readers. One of the convention delegates from Richmond was Marmaduke Johnson, a Whig, successful lawyer, and popular orator who would be recalled in some quarters, in later decades, as "the idol of the people."[28] Johnson was clearly the dark, sleek, fat pony who was "much affected with the Botts" (John Minor Botts, the Whig congressman

Daniel had loved to ridicule a decade earlier) and who "neighed submission . . . to every proposition for secession he would give a most unqualified neigh."

There had never been such a rush for an issue of the *Richmond Examiner* as this satire occasioned. In part, the demand arose from distinguished citizens lampooned in the piece who were intent on buying and destroying all the copies they could.[29] Several weeks later, Marmaduke Johnson caught sight of John Daniel walking down Franklin Street in downtown Richmond. There are differing versions of what ensued. Johnson, much larger than the slightly built editor, either assaulted Daniel with a cane or slammed him against a wall and threatened him with a knife, saying he would cut off his ears.[30] A duel might well have resulted if the elderly mayor of Richmond, Joseph Mayo, had not put both under a $3,000 peace bond.[31] Marmaduke Johnson may well have thought that the "Italian" satire was the personal composition of Editor Daniel, just back from Italy, but it was apparently the work of Daniel's part-time contributor, Edward Lorraine, superintendent of the James River and Kanawha Canal Company.[32] Daniel had no doubt sharpened the piece before its publication.

The animal satire and other *Examiner* articles that urged secession did not have an immediate effect. On April 4, 1861, the Virginia convention voted 88–45 against secession. However, Daniel continued to push as hard as he could. George W. Bagby, writing in the same month as editor of the *Southern Literary Messenger*, said admiringly that if Daniel had entered the fight for secession six months or a year earlier, Virginia would have already become a member of the Confederacy: "His pen combines the qualities of the scimitar of Saladin and the battle-axe of Coeur de Leon [*sic*], and he is wielding it like a very Orlando."[33]

Daniel was helped in his push for secession by events both South and North. John Tyler, the last Virginian in the White House, had been presiding over a futile peace conference in Washington. Tyler returned home to Richmond, took a seat in the state convention, and called for Virginia to secede. It appeared that the immediate casus belli would be Fort Sumter in Charleston, which was being held by a small Union garrison. Would the North attempt to reinforce it, or would the South attack it?

Abraham Lincoln made a final, personal effort to dissuade the Virginians from leaving the Union, sending a messenger to Richmond to ask that, as a matter of urgency, one of the prominent Unionists in the Virginia convention come see him in Washington. John B. Baldwin was such a man, and he went to see President Lincoln on April 5. Lincoln is said to have told Baldwin that if the Virginia convention would adjourn without passing an ordinance of secession, he would order the evacuation of Fort Sumter. Baldwin later denied that Lincoln had made such a proposition, but John Minor Botts later wrote that he, too, had seen Lincoln, on

April 7, and that Lincoln had told him of his offer to Baldwin, which, he told Botts, Baldwin had declined. Botts then offered to carry Lincoln's message to the Richmond convention, but Lincoln told him it was too late; a Union squadron had sailed for Charleston.[34]

In Charleston, Gen. P. G. T. Beauregard's troops began on April 12 to bombard Fort Sumter, still held by Union troops. It surrendered the following afternoon, Saturday, April 13. The news reached Richmond later that day, and approving crowds poured into the streets. An impromptu parade took place, led by Smith's Armory Band. Guns were pulled out of the armory and a 100-gun salute was fired. Governor Letcher came out on the porch of his mansion and said he could see no occasion for the demonstration, since Virginia was still part of the Union. The crowd hissed, and there were suggestions that the guns should have been turned on the governor.[35]

If any hope remained in Southern minds that the South could leave the Union peacefully, it was quashed when, on April 15, 1861, Lincoln issued a proclamation calling for a force of 75,000 men to suppress the "combinations" opposing U.S. laws in the states that had seceded. Virginia was requested to provide three regiments as its share. Governor John Letcher responded to the U.S. secretary of war, Simon Cameron, that the United States government intended to subjugate the Southern states and was inaugurating civil war; Virginia would resist. The Virginia state convention resumed its session, and on April 17, 1861, by a vote of 88 to 55, repealed Virginia's ordinance of 1788 that had ratified the U.S. Constitution.[36] A week later, the Confederacy's new vice president, Alexander Stephens, went to Richmond, and Virginia approved the agreement that six Virginia commissioners had earlier entered into at Montgomery, Alabama, for a "temporary union" with the Confederate States. Years later, Robert W. Hughes wrote that John Daniel, more than anyone else, had been the author of Virginia's secession.

Much more needed to be done, and quickly. It seemed vital to Daniel that the capital of the new Confederacy be moved from Montgomery to Richmond and that President Jefferson Davis move quickly to Richmond and assume supreme power.

> We need a Dictator. Let lawyers talk when the world has time to hear them. Now let the sword do its work. Usurpations of power by the chief for the preservation of the people from robbers and murderers will be reckoned as genius and patriotism by all sensible men now and by every historian that will judge the deed hereafter.
>
> If President Davis is the man for the times, and if the Southern Confederacy is worthy of existence, both will come at once to the front. . . .

> Especially should President Davis give Virginia the advantage of his presence. It would be worth an army of fifty thousand men. . . .[37]

On April 26, the Confederate Congress decided, over Jefferson Davis's veto, that Richmond should become the Confederacy's capital. Government employees and hangers-on began to flood into the city, and Davis himself arrived there on May 29. Over the next four years, the war would in good part be fought over the ground between the two capitals, Richmond and Washington. That ground was Virginia, including Daniel's Stafford County. A different, perhaps wiser Southern strategy, might have left the capital at Montgomery and paid more attention to defending the Southern heartland. That this was not done owes something to John Moncure Daniel.

Daniel and Davis were acquainted before Davis entered Pierce's cabinet in 1853, and Davis had certainly gained further impressions of Daniel when he was secretary of war and Daniel was America's envoy in Turin. Daniel wrote to Davis in late February 1861, saying that although he feared that "eight years of absence from the country might have obliterated my name and person from your memory," he wanted to recommend for a Confederate army commission the young Lieutenant Carr, whom he had met in Italy two years earlier.[38]

Davis undoubtedly remembered Daniel, if perhaps mainly for the affair of the garlic letter, which had been discussed at least once in Pierce's cabinet. Davis no doubt felt flattered by what the *Examiner* was currently writing, and he was hearing good things about its proprietor. Former U.S. senator James M. Mason wrote Davis in April 1861 that he agreed with a suggestion from fellow Virginian James Seddon, whom John Daniel had recently seen in Washington, that advertisements and notices by Confederate agencies in Virginia, which appeared only in the *Enquirer*, should be split between that paper and the *Examiner*. Mason wrote that "the 'Examiner' is now in the hands of *Daniel*, late minister at Sardinia, & is conducted with great ability—besides its efficient & telling shot at the Unionists of the state has attached us all strongly to it's [*sic*] fortunes—I't's [*sic*] circulation, I understand, since the new Editorship, far exceeds any paper in the State—I suggest of course no direct interference by you in such matters—but it may be brought to the notice of those controlling the subject."[39]

It appears that Davis listened and acted. On July 21, 1861, Daniel was elected public printer of the Confederacy. He declined the post two days later, but in late 1861 and in 1862, after the Confederate capital had moved to Richmond, the *Examiner* received a modest amount of government advertising.[40] Why Daniel turned down the post of public printer is unclear, but he may have done it to avoid corruption. Daniel indicated a year later that the arrangement would have required him to share profits with some unnamed third person, and that he would not agree to do so but that the person selected as printer in his stead—whom he did not name but who was William F. Ritchie, lately but not then editor of the rival *Enquirer*—had agreed readily to the arrangement.[41]

By the middle of 1861, Daniel must have relegated to the back of his mind most memories of his long years in Italy. His brother Frederick left Turin not long after he did. Romaine Dillon, who had been appointed chargé d'affaires *ad interim* by the outgoing Buchanan administration, reached Turin on April 12, 1861 and took over the legation. Daniel might well have grimaced, had he known that Dillon was soon being besieged by applications from officers and men of Giuseppe Garibaldi's army of Italian liberation, eager to join the Union army in America. Dillon was at length obliged to publish a notice in Turin's official gazette, stating that he had no authority to take enlistments.[42]

On June 14, 1861, the first American minister to the new Kingdom of Italy—no longer just the Kingdom of Sardinia to which John Moncure Daniel had been accredited—arrived in Turin. He was George Perkins Marsh, former minister to the Turkish Empire, former member of Congress from Vermont, and well-known writer, lecturer, and abolitionist. Marsh presented his credentials on June 23 to Victor Emmanuel II, lately so friendly with Daniel, and began energetic and successful efforts to keep the Italians pro-Union. Soon, indeed, Giuseppe Garibaldi himself would graciously offer to become Union commander-in-chief. When he was subsequently offered a commission as a major general, Garibaldi—who considered himself the equal of sovereigns and prime ministers—declined, to Marsh's relief.[43]

Despite Daniel's initial praise for Jefferson Davis, tension began to mount between the two of them soon after the Confederate president arrived in Richmond. Davis biographer Hudson Strode claims that a rift developed within six weeks of Davis's arrival, and that it started because Davis refused to accept as confidants John Moncure Daniel and his new *Examiner* colleague, Edward A. Pollard.[44] Certainly, the rift also grew over Daniel's admiration for Joseph E. Johnston, a general whom Davis found the most difficult to deal with in his entire army. As the rift deepened, the reasons for it multiplied.

Meanwhile, Daniel gathered a notable staff at the *Examiner* after resuming charge. Edward Pollard was the son of a distinguished Virginia family; he had roamed west to California and then to Asia after his expulsion from the law school at the College of William and Mary; he became the paper's associate editor.[45] His brother, Henry Rives Pollard, also joined the staff. Robert Hughes, despite his past differences with Daniel, worked with him well at the paper. Daniel's friend Patrick Henry Aylett continued to contribute, and among other notable wartime contributors was Basil Lanneau Gildersleeve, a professor of Greek at the University of Virginia who later enlisted as an army private.

A serious difference soon developed between the *Examiner* and the Davis administration over the proper shape and size for the Confederate army. The U.S. Army had grown under Secretary of War Jefferson Davis, but it numbered only 16,000 officers and men in December 1860. Most of them stayed with the North after secession. Both South and North faced the problem of making generals out of majors and colonels—and civilians—and of greatly increasing the numbers in the ranks. Jefferson Davis initially believed that a sufficiently large army could be formed from existing militia units and volunteers. Daniel, however, had recently come from seven years in a relatively small European kingdom that, as he had more than once reported to Washington, deployed an army five times the size of the American army of the 1850s. Furthermore, this Sardinian army depended largely on involuntary conscription to fill its ranks. Davis had fought in the Mexican War and had headed the War Department, but one suspects that Daniel thought he knew more than Davis about how modern war should be waged. Daniel invited Louis T. Wigfall, a Confederate senator from Texas, to meet with him several times, and he described to Wigfall the possible elements of a Confederate conscription system.[46]

The first public suggestion for a conscription law was made by Daniel's *Richmond Examiner,* which argued for conscription on several bases, noting that it was only in England and America that such a system did not exist. Conscription was, the *Examiner* asserted, the only system that was just to all the classes of the (white) population. Many men then in the Confederate army had volunteered for only twelve months, and their enlistments would expire by the summer of 1862. The *Examiner* thought that conscription was the best way to replace them, and it would provide a badly needed "iron rule" of enforced enlistment and regular discipline. With conscription, the paper posited, the Confederacy could field a force of 500,000 men without doing any damage to its internal economy.[47]

The idea of conscription was fiercely opposed by the Davis administration and by other papers that charged the *Examiner* with denigrating Southern patriotism and with revealing a weakness that gave aid and comfort to the enemy.[48] Daniel eventually won over the opposition. Europe might seem far away to him, but he kept recalling for readers how little Sardinia had, through conscription, maintained an army five times larger than that of the United States, and at an overall lower cost. If Napoleon III in France faced a situation like that of the South, wrote Daniel, France would quickly have every able-bodied man under arms. Wigfall's conscription bill was eventually enacted by the Confederate Congress and signed by Jefferson Davis on April 16, 1862, thus creating the first military conscription system in North America. Only a year later did the North follow suit; Lincoln signed the Union's conscription act on March 3, 1863. (Anticonscription riots soon followed in the North, most notably in New York City.)

Louis Wigfall, described as a man of scarred face and fierce aspect, one who drank heartily and had rare gifts of oratory, eventually became the leader of the congressional party against Davis.[49] Even as Daniel's own press attacks intensified and multiplied, Wigfall exceeded Daniel in his hatred of the president, eventually suggesting (in private) that Jefferson Davis was insane.[50] Wigfall and Daniel seem to have remained on good terms; there is a brief mention by the senator's daughter that Daniel dined at their house in November 1862.[51] Wigfall was not Davis's only enemy in the Confederate Congress. The opposition included such men as Henry Foote, who had gotten into a fistfight with Davis in 1847 when both were U.S. senators from Mississippi; Robert Toombs of Georgia, who initially served in the Davis administration as secretary of state; and even Vice President Alexander Stephens, another Georgian who, as the war continued, began to spend most of his time in his home state.

War raged in earnest long before conscription was finally approved in the Confederacy in 1862. Richmond first realized it might be in jeopardy from Union action on a sunny Sunday in April 1861, when the rumor spread in the city that the Union vessel *Pawnee* was steaming up the James River to shell the city. The *Pawnee* never arrived, but a point had been made; people in the city did not forget "Pawnee Sunday." A month later, Union troops crossed the Potomac River and occupied the city of Alexandria. Now the North stood on Virginia soil, and Richmond lay only a hundred miles south.

On May 29, 1861, the war first came to Daniel's birthplace, Stafford County, when Union vessels shelled a Confederate battery at the Aquia Creek railroad terminus.[52] Two weeks later, on June 10, came the baptism of blood, a fairly sizable engagement at Bethel Church in the Tidewater: a Union column of four thousand men was repulsed by a Confederate force half its size, and thirty Union men were killed. But in the next encounter, at Rich Mountain in western Virginia, the Confederate troops were badly beaten. The Southern public of that time has been described as essentially mercurial in its changes of mood and morale.[53] While the victory at Bethel was, as the *Examiner* said two days later, the first event of the war that gave comfort to the heart of the South, the subsequent defeat at Rich Mountain caused near-universal gloom. (An enthused correspondent of the *Southern Literary Messenger* called Bethel "the grandest victory the world has ever seen."[54]) But nothing important had yet been decided on the battlefield, although a number of skirmishes continued. It is never easy to predict how long a war may last. In 1861 perhaps no one, North or South, thought that this war might last as long as four years. Southerners were flocking to enlist in the army, but in the expectation that the struggle would certainly be short, if fierce. Thomas DeLeon recalled how even the meanest private panted to have his share in the triumphant work while there was yet a chance.[55]

As the summer of 1861 approached, Daniel struck a tone in his paper that had been heard before in the South and would often be heard again. The men of the South, he claimed, were more skillful than Northerners in the use of arms, and their natural courage had been fostered by the Southern educational system. Yankees, who had not been taught to shoot and ride in childhood, were afraid of guns and horses; indeed, cowardice was inculcated in them from birth. In July, Daniel leaped beyond that claim to insist that slavery did not enervate national character but strengthened and improved it. Northern society, he wrote, had been debased by universal liberty and equality, and Northerners lacked self-respect because they found no one lower or meaner than themselves, whereas in the South the presence of "an inferior race" inspired every white citizen with pride. Daniel was taking a tone of near-absurd gallantry, indeed jingoism, that might have been ridiculed in peacetime. But this was, or was becoming, war.[56]

The *Examiner* and its editor also tried to set forth in the summer of 1861 a larger rationale for war than just the defense of slavery. It was not, the *Examiner* said in August, a civil war. It was a war of two different countries, a war not of opinion but of patriotism. The North was inspired by the universal Yankee hatred of the South; the South was inspired by principle. One doubts many readers disagreed with these sentiments.

General Beauregard, who had taken Fort Sumter, had lately come to northern Virginia and was now in command of the Army of the Potomac, a force of 22,000 men. Gen. Joseph E. Johnston was at Winchester, in command of a smaller Army of the Shenandoah, numbering more than 8,000. On the Northern side, Brig. Gen. Irvin McDowell led a new army of 35,000 men, which in mid-July pushed west across northern Virginia toward Beauregard's forces at Manassas Junction. On July 21, the opposing armies met in force north of Manassas near the stream called Bull Run. None of the senior officers on either side had experience in leading large units in war. McDowell, the Union leader, was a professional soldier who had served as a staff officer in the Mexican War, but he had been a major only as recently as two months earlier. Beauregard and Johnston, too, were professionals; but, though more senior in prewar rank than McDowell had been, they had no experience in war except as mid-grade officers years earlier in Mexico. None of the other Union or Confederate officers was more experienced; and many of the senior officers on both sides were totally new to warfare. It was a different scene from what John Moncure Daniel had lately witnessed in Europe, where larger armies, buttressed by conscription systems, were led by large cadres of experienced officers.

The Union forces took heavy casualties at Bull Run, three thousand men; they panicked and were routed. Beauregard wrote years later that the battle had borne the fate of the new Confederacy, adding bitterly that if Jefferson Davis had approved the plan he had submitted to the president some days before the battle, he might have turned McDowell's flank and captured Washington. When Beauregard said as much in his report just after the battle, Davis took offense, and lasting hostility ensued between the two, as it did for other reasons between Davis and Joseph E. Johnston.[57] The quarrel between Davis and Johnston broke out after the president's message to the Senate of the Confederacy on August 31, 1861, forwarding the names of the first five Confederate officers who were to be awarded the rank of full general. Joseph E. Johnston stood fourth on the list of five; Adj. Gen. Samuel Cooper was first, and Robert E. Lee was only third. Johnston was enraged by this ranking. He wrote a long and furious letter to Davis, saying that he was the most senior officer of the United States army to resign and join the Confederacy and that he should therefore rank first in the Confederate army. This letter did Johnston no good, and nothing Davis did could assuage him.[58] But Daniel admired Johnston and said so continually in his paper.

While bickering was increasing in the Confederacy, there was also elation at the Manassas victory. In the North, however, there was great gloom. Lincoln said, "It's damned bad" when he first heard that McDowell had been routed, and many Northerners blamed Lincoln for forcing McDowell to fight before his army was ready.[59] Horace Greeley of the *New York Tribune*, late a major war hawk who had launched the slogan "On to Richmond," now wrote Lincoln urging him not to shrink from the idea of making peace at once and on the South's own terms.

For his part, Daniel urged the Confederacy to exploit quickly its first significant victory, at Manassas on July 21. Three days later, the *Examiner* said that the strength of the Confederate army should be raised at once to 450,000 men and then to 500,000, and that it should immediately go on the offensive. Within four weeks, this army should strike north into Ohio and Pennsylvania, levying contributions in money and materials on Northern towns and villages.[60] The *Examiner* continued to press the idea of aggressive war for the next two months, arguing that attacks aimed at Northern cities were the best defense for the South rather than placing garrisons along the long Southern coast (as Davis was doing) to protect against possible invasion from the sea.

In retrospect, a more aggressive approach by the Confederacy early in the war might conceivably have won major gains, if not necessarily an early overall victory. It has been pointed out that Daniel's argument ignored the question of logistics and supplies.[61] It is also true that, later in the war, Jefferson Davis operated on the belief that the South could only win by seizing the military initiative.[62] The less industrialized South was short on weapons, however. From the beginning, Governor John Letcher, who had opposed secession, had nevertheless begun to call for increased spending on Virginia's military forces. In the crisis of early 1861, as Daniel well knew, the pace of mobilization in Virginia had quickened, but weapons and equipment did not suffice for the thousands of volunteers—partly because Letcher loaned weapons to other Confederate states in short supply—and many of these Virginia men had to be sent home.[63]

But if Daniel's call for an army of a half-million was not realistic in 1861, his demand for an aggressive Southern strategy was in line with the thinking of at least two Southern generals, Joseph E. Johnston and P. G. T. Beauregard, who petitioned Jefferson Davis for 20,000 men from the coastal garrisons to join with their forces then totaling 40,000. This, they thought, would make an army large enough to invade the North and bring pressure on the North to make peace. On August 1, 1861, Davis turned down the two generals, wanting to keep the coastal garrisons in place because he feared that Northern landings along the coast were a prelude to full-scale invasions. In fact, the landings were intended to help strengthen the Northern sea blockade of Southern ports, a blockade that could strangle the South only slowly and did not, in the first years of the war, cut off Southern commerce with Europe.[64] Daniel still did not abandon his call for an aggressive strategy. In late September, he argued that the reason for the Union landings was to compel the Confederates to pull back from the battlefield to defend their homes. The proper course for the Confederacy was therefore to thrust into the North and create "a thrill of terror at the heart of every Dutchman and Yankee in Ohio and Pennsylvania."[65] But Jefferson Davis was not moved by these arguments.

Thirteen

Fierce Editor, Wounded Warrior

In the first months of the Civil War, hopes ran high in the Confederacy for help from Europe. John Daniel shared those hopes. In August 1861, the *Examiner* predicted flatly that the war would end by the first of May 1862 for two reasons. One was that the Northern public would be unable to tolerate the suffering and ruin visited on it. The other reason was that the Europeans would soon intervene since their stocks of cotton and tobacco would have been exhausted by then.[1] The paper cautioned that it was not a question of European friendship. Daniel had never thought Europeans cared much for Americans in general.

In August 1861, he sounded a warning about European attitudes toward Southerners in particular: "the entire European public is animated by the most unfriendly sentiment towards the Southern community. . . . [O]ur character has been so successfully darkened by their representations of our Northern fellow-citizens that it is assumed to be the combination of everything that is villainous." As proof, Daniel recalled at length the *Bianchi e Negri* ballet he had seen in Genoa four years earlier and reported to his great-uncle in Washington. At the end of this loathsome spectacle, he wrote in 1861, when thirty young white women were shown dancing with the black slaves who had killed their masters, the "plebeians of the pit" had roared their approbation, while the Piedmontese aristocrats in the boxes above clapped their gloved hands. The particular contempt of Europeans for the American South was shown, Daniel added, by the fact that they never criticized either slaveholding Brazil or Spain, the latter of which was both a slave-holding and a slave-trading nation. And so, wrote the editor, "On our own swords we must lean, on our own arms we must alone rely for help, till we shall no longer need any other."[2]

As 1861 wore on, it began to look as if European recognition of the Confederacy, not to speak of European action to lift the Northern blockade, was a distant hope. The Confederacy sent three commissioners, among them A. Dudley Mann, former U.S. assistant secretary of state, to England and France, but they failed to win recognition. In October, two new commissioners were sent: James M. Mason and John Slidell, former U.S. senators from Virginia and Louisiana. En route to Europe they were taken off the British mail steamer *Trent* by Capt. Charles Wilkes

John B. Floyd, governor of Virginia, U.S. secretary of war, and Confederate general. National Archives.

of the Union Navy. This seizure caused a great stir in London; Mason and Slidell were soon released, and they continued to Europe. However, they failed to win European recognition for their new government. Indeed, Southerners must continue to lean on their own swords.

John Moncure Daniel was also thinking about a sword for himself. He had interested himself in warfare for some years, in Europe and now in America, and he decided that he should leave his Richmond desk and go to war. His major patron had done so; former Secretary of War John B. Floyd was now Brigadier General Floyd, C.S.A., commanding a brigade of what was styled the Army of the Kanawha, in western Virginia. Daniel decided to request a commission to join Floyd's staff. John was not the first of the Daniel brothers to enter the military; in April, Frederick had enlisted in the Richmond Howitzers as a private.[3] John Daniel may have turned to thoughts of military service only after failing to win a political seat. In May 1861, he had run for a seat in the state senate but placed third in a field of about ten candidates.[4]

On September 11, 1861, Daniel was appointed a first lieutenant and aide-de-camp to General Floyd. It seems that the former U.S. minister to Sardinia wanted something better; twelve days later, he was raised to the rank of major, still to report to Floyd.[5] Daniel quickly joined his general in the field.

By September 24, just after Daniel's lawyer had dissolved his *Examiner* partnership with William Lloyd, the new officer was writing reports (two of which are still extant) on behalf of Floyd from their headquarters at Meadow Bluff, near the Gauley River east of Charleston, to Maj. Gen. Robert E. Lee, who then commanded Confederate forces in western Virginia.[6] The Confederate campaign there was unsuccessful, in part due to the lack of cooperation with Floyd shown by his fellow brigadier general and (like Floyd) former governor of Virginia Henry A. Wise, who commanded a "legion" of three thousand men and was supposed to be subordinate to Floyd. Wise and Floyd had long been at odds as Virginia Democrats; and while the *Richmond Enquirer* had supported Wise, the *Examiner* had been for Floyd. Their differences continued in the field of war. Jacob D. Cox, Union major general in western Virginia, wrote years later that if Wise had been half as troublesome to Cox as Wise had been to his own comrade in arms, "I should, indeed, have had a hot time of it."[7]

By mid-October, a month after Daniel had been commissioned, the Confederate forces had been clearly outfought. There had been command problems in addition to the quarreling between Wise and Floyd. The gentlemanly Lee had not pressed hard enough on a subordinate general named William Wing Loring, who did not forget that he had more fighting experience than Lee. Beyond this, the Confederate supply system worked poorly, and, as Douglas Southall Freeman put it, Lee was pursued by a rain demon that turned roads to bogs. The Confederates withdrew eastward from the Gauley and Kanawha Valleys up to the Appalachian ridges. Lee's reputation had been damaged, and he was irritated by the criticisms in the newspapers. Lee was sent south to work on the fortifications of Charleston. As the general wrote with some bitterness to his wife, his subordinate, John Floyd, had three editors on his staff—John Daniel, of course, being one of them—and the armies had not kept pace with editors' expectations.[8]

Nor had the military reputation of either John Floyd and Henry Wise been enhanced by the disastrous campaign beyond the mountains; and the overall Confederate cause suffered.[9] In October 1861, representatives from thirty-nine counties of western Virginia met to begin organizing West Virginia as a free state in the Union. The Confederate army never returned. Daniel must have found that his short stay that autumn in western Virginia amounted to less than a fully satisfactory experience. Daniel stayed with Floyd when his brigade was transferred to Kentucky, but after a short period at Bowling Green, during which the brigade saw no action, Daniel left the army on a leave of absence and returned to his newspaper in Richmond.[10]

The editor of the *Examiner* had no brief for Robert E. Lee that autumn. With what Henry Wise's son later styled a cynical sneer, Daniel's paper expressed the hope that at Charleston the general would do better with the spade than he had with the sword.[11] For his part, Robert E. Lee remarked that it was too bad that all the worst generals were in command of the armies while the best generals were editing newspapers![12]

It was as well for Daniel's own reputation that he had taken off his uniform. In early 1862, Floyd and his brigade were ordered into Tennessee to help defend Nashville. At Fort Donelson, when Confederate forces were surrounded by Union troops led by Gen. Ulysses S. Grant, Floyd extricated himself and his Virginia troops, but most of the other Confederate units surrendered. There were suggestions that Floyd had run away. Floyd may have feared that if captured, he would be tried for the theft of Indian bonds while he was U.S. secretary of war—or for treason. Daniel tried to put the best face on Floyd's action, printing a letter, said to be from an officer in Floyd's command, which reported that Floyd had resolved to "cut his way through the enemy or die in the effort."[13] Nevertheless, Floyd was relieved of his command by Jefferson Davis and dropped out of public view. But if John Daniel would not serve under John B. Floyd, he still would serve.

In 1861, Richmond was being flooded with new residents: civilian employees of the Confederate government departments and their families; thousands of workers in munitions and ordnance plants, foundries, and uniform factories; military officers assigned to Richmond or in transit; refugees from elsewhere in Virginia and places farther afield; merchants, army purveyors, and profiteers. Eventually, the city's prewar population of almost 40,000 swelled to three times that number.

For some, there was money to be made. Daniel had not returned to Virginia in order to enrich himself, but he was the son of an impoverished country doctor and he had been determined since young manhood to make his way in the world. Mortality among Virginia newspapers was high during the Civil War; more than nine-tenths had closed their doors by January 1863.[14] Not so with the frank, if not sensational, *Richmond Examiner;* it flourished, and so did its editor. The price for the paper in 1861 was reasonable: the daily edition (there were also semi-weekly and weekly editions) cost two cents a copy, ten cents a week, or six dollars a year by mail. Advertisements cost fifty cents for a "square" of eight lines for the first day, and twenty-five cents for succeeding days. Cash was demanded; no credit was given.[15] The stated price for an issue of the *Examiner* increased steadily as the war went on. In March 1862, the price for a single copy went from two cents to three cents, and the cost of a year's subscription rose from $6 to $8. By 1863, the price for a six months' subscription had risen to $10. By 1864, a mail subscription to the daily edition cost $32 a year, over five times the price three years earlier.[16] The actual asking price increased still more steeply. In 1863, the three-cent price for a single copy disappeared from the masthead, and we do not know how much a copy of the paper actually sold for. There were also "extras," mere slips of paper that seldom contained more than one column and often gave the first news of a battle. By the autumn of 1862, these were being sold for ten cents to newsboys, who in turn might sell them for as much as twenty-five cents.[17] George Cary Eggleston recalled that at some point late in the war he had to pay a dollar for a single copy of the *Examiner*, twice the asking price of the *Whig* or the *Enquirer*.[18] How much of that dollar went into the proprietor's own pocket is not known. However, he was doing very well.

Accounts survive for receipts and expenditures at the *Examiner* for much of the period between 1862 and 1865. By March 1862, the paper was taking in $1,500 a week; during 1863, this sum increased to almost $4,000; in 1864 it rose to as much as $8,000; and by early 1865 weekly receipts were more than $15,000. These increases had much to do with inflation in the value of Confederate currency, but they still show financial success. The editor and proprietor paid himself increasingly large sums: from $215 to $520 weekly in 1863, and often more than $1,000 a week in 1864. For the week ending April 23, 1864, Daniel paid himself $4,293, conceivably in part to reimburse himself for some unspecified business expenditure.[19]

George Bagby later wrote that it could be safely assumed that after deducting personal expenses of every kind, on which Daniel never stinted himself, Daniel's paper cleared at least $50,000 during the third year of the war, and perhaps even double that amount.[20] This figure is impossible to prove, but unquestionably Daniel became very prosperous. One should note in contrast that early in the war members of the Confederate Congress received yearly salaries of only $2,750, and members of the president's cabinet got $6,000 annually. (Many of these officials admittedly had outside incomes, as well.) Outside government service, even some menial jobs paid relatively well in wartime. One free black man told a white Richmond resident in 1863 that he earned $3,000 a year as a cobbler.[21] However, a Confederate private made only $11 a month until June 1864, when pay was raised to $18.

Daniel was not generous with salaries for others on his staff. John Mitchel, the Irish patriot, had gone to work for the *Examiner* at the beginning of 1864 and was receiving $300 per week by early 1865. Edward A. Pollard seems never to have received more than $100 per week before he left for England in 1863. However, Daniel paid better than other Richmond newspapers. At the same time, while he shrewdly used his new gains to buy houses in Richmond, sheltering his capital from inflation, he also furnished them at his own expense and then rented them to his assistant editors on very reasonable terms. George Bagby did not forget that

Daniel even made a trip to Charlottesville once at Bagby's request to buy a Richmond house at an auction in order to rent it cheaply to Bagby.[22]

Daniel, as well as other Richmond editors, ran into labor trouble in 1862 from dissatisfied compositors who had formed the Richmond Typographical Society. At least four compositors involved in the dispute quit the *Examiner*. The paper then advertised for replacements, saying that the proprietor would pay fifty cents per thousand ems, which would permit good compositors to make from twenty to thirty dollars a week.[23] Daniel might not have paid his editorial staff well, but the rate he offered compositors was more than the protesters had asked.

The paper that the editor and his staff put together was modest in size because of the paper shortage. Not only was it reduced to a single two-page sheet, but it was also often printed on paper of poor quality. Given the paper shortage, the editor had to make every line count. He gave considerable space to reports of proceedings in the Confederate Congress. War news, from Northern as well as Southern sources, had to be covered. News from abroad was also featured. However, it was always the editorials, two or three for each issue, to which John Daniel gave highest priority. Some room was also found for human interest items and for advertisements about theatrical performances, furniture, farms, "blockade goods," runaway slaves sought by their masters, or positions available for teachers of music or a "good gardner [*sic*]." Reader interest was paramount. Daniel wanted to keep readers informed not only about news from the front or up north but about rumors and scandals in Richmond as well. His model, Daniel told Bagby, was the *Times* of London, and if the Confederate cause prevailed he aimed to make his paper fully equal to this model. Even without victory, perhaps he succeeded. An English visitor in 1862 thought that many editorials in "the clever, sparkling *Examiner*" compared favorably with the *Times* in force, point, wit, and directness.[24]

With the mails and telegraph lines cut, news from the North no longer flowed as easily as it had. However, the flow of information increased after Confederate and Union officers signed a cartel for the exchange of prisoners of war in July 1862, and thereafter flag-of-truce boats began to ply the James River carrying not only prisoners but some mail and newspapers.[25] Soon there was a Confederate Reading Room on the south side of Eleventh Street in downtown Richmond, where for an admission price of ten cents one could peruse the latest Northern papers as well as those from other Southern cities.[26]

After his return to Richmond in February 1861, Daniel had taken up lodgings in two rooms on the second floor of the *Examiner* building on the west side of Governor Street, south of Franklin Street. The front room was his bedroom; in the rear were his study and a kind of audience chamber where he received guests. The audience chamber contained a number of chairs, but the one that Daniel preferred resembled a barber chair, with a high seat covered with horsehair. Bagby

Wartime Richmond, *Harper's Weekly,* May 31, 1862. Valentine Museum.

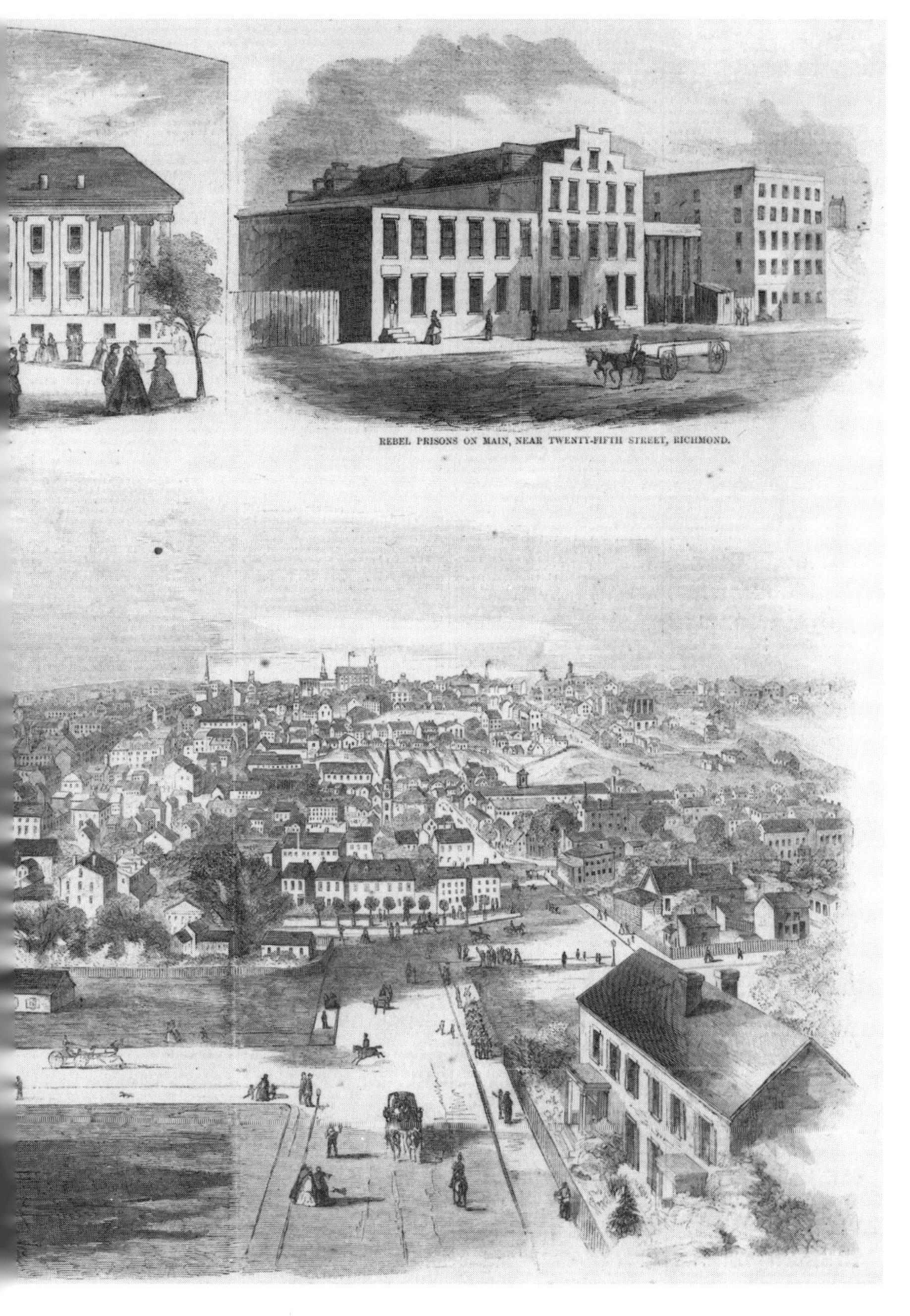

REBEL PRISONS ON MAIN, NEAR TWENTY-FIFTH STREET, RICHMOND.

later remembered Daniel sitting there in a somewhat pontifical style, wearing a pair of spotless white duck trousers but without either coat or vest, looking down on his visitors (and no doubt hoping he was creating the proper effect) while he conversed with them.

As he prospered, Daniel bought a three-story brick house on East Broad Street, near the corner of College Street and opposite the African Church. This house, near both Capitol Square and the offices of the *Examiner*, remained his home until his death, and there he offered hospitality to a number of friends. Daniel asked Arthur Peticolas to bring his family and stay with him there; Louis Wigfall spent much time there when his family was absent from Richmond, and so did Daniel's collaborator, Robert W. Hughes. Daniel had always loved books and, although his collection had been sold when he was in Italy to pay damages awarded to Shearjashub Spooner, he began to build a new collection after he returned to Richmond. It was a buyer's market. Refugees and other hard-up persons were selling their libraries, and eventually Daniel accumulated a large and fine collection that he kept on the third floor of the Broad Street house.[27] Daniel disliked the England of his time, but he admired English writing and collected the works of Swift, Addison, Sterne, Scott, Johnson, Hazlitt, Hobbes, and, not least, Thackeray, whom he had once met in Richmond.

George Bagby has left a detailed description of what he called John Daniel's commodious and comfortable house on Broad Street. On the first floor in the front was a parlor with two large oil paintings "of decided merit" (one wonders whether Daniel brought them back from Italy) plus an inlaid chess table and some mahogany chairs. Behind the parlor was the dining room, with two or more antique dining tables, a handsome sideboard, a writing table for the editor, and his iron safe. Daniel liked to tell visitors that he had bought the tables from "old Memminger," the Confederate secretary of the treasury—of whom more will be said later.

A large front room on the second floor was Daniel's bedroom. This contained an old-fashioned four-poster bed that, along with other pieces of furniture, he had bought from refugees who had fled Northern armies. Between the two front windows was a tall mirror, which stretched from floor almost to ceiling, and a smaller mirror opposite that allowed the editor to see his whole figure, front and rear. The only other bedroom furniture consisted of a few chairs. Over the mantle hung an exquisite miniature in ivory whose face was the most beautiful Bagby had ever seen. The picture had been presented to Daniel by the titled and accomplished lady who had painted it, and it was her own likeness. Daniel would not tell Bagby her name, but it was Marie de Solms. She had given it to Daniel after he had taken her to the court ball and enraged Napoleon III.

The top floor of Daniel's house in Richmond contained three rooms, including a library and a back room that faced south and enjoyed good light in the afternoon. There was a view over the James River toward the hills of Henrico County and the lower-lying fields and woods in Chesterfield. Here Daniel liked to sit in a leather-bottomed chair with a little table next to him, reading Voltaire, Latin poets, or the latest contributions or letters to the *Examiner*. In this room, too, he kept a collection of medals and seals he had acquired, mainly, if not entirely, in Italy.

Behind the house and across a yard was a building with four rooms, the kitchen and quarters for his three slaves: a cook, a hostler to care for his horses and carriage, and a valet who also served at table. Initially, all three were male. Bagby observed that Daniel liked the hostler but treated the young valet very roughly. Two of the slaves ran away. One was caught, punished, and sold. The other made good his escape, although Daniel had offered a reward of $2,000 for his capture. Daniel thereupon bought "a very likely woman, nearly white," who remained in his service until his death.

Bagby described Daniel as a man who indulged in clothing. During the war, he paid as much as a thousand dollars for a fine suit and did not stint on coal for heating or gas for lighting, although both became very expensive. Daniel was temperate in eating and drinking, which Bagby attributed in part to the editor's feeble digestion. Daniel drank wine but disliked whiskey, and when his doctor prescribed an evening glass of whiskey and water he said it left him with a headache the next day. He loved coffee, and taught Frank and Fanny, his two pet terriers, to drink it. The dogs, said Bagby, were devoted to their master, although he teased them to the point of cruelty.

Daniel was both an accomplished writer and a careful editor. According to Bagby, as the war went on, Daniel increasingly preferred to have others put his ideas into words first. He looked over some contributions at home. Then he went down to the *Examiner* offices at 10:00 o'clock in the evening, took up the articles proposed for the paper's next issue, and amended them until he had everything right. His editing included spelling, including one Daniel idiosyncrasy, the addition of an archaic "k" to words ending in "-ic." (One assumes the publick liked it.) By midnight or soon after, the editor's work was finished and he returned home. Daniel, of course, cared about the main issues that faced the Confederacy, but he was also bent on selling his paper; when Daniel sat down to write an article, his first question was not "What is the news?" but "What are people talking about?" Like modern American editors, he aimed to make his paper interesting by focusing on subjects uppermost in the popular mind.

Daniel knew the value of money and was careful with personal finances, but he had less than a full understanding of the economics and financial problems that faced the Confederacy. Daniel was creating wartime propaganda, so perhaps he actually knew better when he wrote, for example, on June 1, 1861, that war would not disturb the Southern industrial system: "We have read the lessons of history in vain if a population of twelve million, one-third of whom are slaves, be not, in time of war, more than equivalent to a population of twenty million without slaves."

The following week, the paper insisted that the Confederacy should avoid an increase in direct taxation to pay the costs of the war, and that loans could be piled mountain high for a just cause. While taxes, said the paper, made governments odious among their people, government loans could produce powerful support from capitalists.[28] For once, the line taken by Jefferson Davis and his administration resembled that of the fiery editor. The succeeding months and years saw the Davis administration shy away from raising taxes to a much greater extent than was the case in the North, and this was one factor that brought on worrisome inflation in the South. However, John Daniel eventually came to believe that taxes were badly needed.

Daniel preached a kind of economic autarky during the early months of the war. He insisted that a three years' war would be better than an early peace, since early peace would see the South flooded again with Northern manufactures, as well as "Yankee teachers, preachers, pedlers [*sic*] and drummers." In contrast, a long war would bring about self-reliance and economic independence.[29] Meanwhile, shortages became evident, including a shortage of good paper for printing. Daniel admitted wryly in early July 1861 that the *Examiner* seemed to have been "dipt in the river Styx" —one of the effects of the blockade. In a few days, he hoped, the defects would be remedied.[30] However, the quality of the paper worsened as the weeks and months went on, and even poor paper was in short supply. By the summer of 1862, most if not all Confederate newspapers were printed in single-sheet, two-page editions.

Shortages were also increasingly felt in every other sector of the economy, including intellectual life. Daniel himself was able to build up a fine collection of older books, but the South was cut off from new works published in the North, and it appears that no one thought of importing literature from England on blockade runners. George Eggleston looked through the issues of the *Examiner* for most of 1864 and found only one book advertised.[31] Bibles were perhaps in better supply than novels, at least in the army. Dr. Moses Hoge, of the Second Presbyterian Church in Richmond, sailed from Charleston on a blockade runner in 1862 and shipped home from England 10,000 Bibles, 50,000 New Testaments, and a quarter-million Scriptural tracts for military use.[32] A slaveholder, Hoge also spoke to British religious groups and met with a number of people who sympathized with the South, including Thomas Carlyle, who had written so forcefully about the need to compel black men's labor.[33]

The *Examiner* continued to have competition throughout the war. At the beginning of 1861, there were three other dailies in Richmond: the *Enquirer*, *Whig*, and *Dispatch*. The *Dispatch* was largely nonpartisan, and its circulation was greater than any of the others, at one point during the war reaching as high as thirty thousand.[34] The *Examiner*'s old Democratic rival, the *Enquirer*, became a loyal supporter of the Davis administration, while the *Whig* gradually became, like the *Examiner*, a critic.

But the hard-hitting *Examiner* remained the paper that everyone wanted to read—including the soldiers, who wondered why they should be plagued so by the mud from God's rain, by the fire of the enemy, and by the mistakes and shortcomings of their own commanders. They also wanted assurance that beyond their present difficulties lay victory. And while no editor was more critical than Daniel of faults in the Confederacy, he kept insisting that the Confederacy could win. A Confederate soldier named Robert Cowart recalled decades after the war how in the trenches in front of Richmond, during the bad days of 1864–65, his company had been reduced to a handful of men without an officer. Every day, they would join together and buy a copy of the *Examiner*, which was very costly by then. The paper would be passed around until the last man had read and pondered every editorial. The *Richmond Examiner*, Cowart recalled, was "the inspiration of Lee's Army."[35]

Jefferson Davis had entered the Confederate presidency on a provisional, unelected basis. In the autumn of 1861, a presidential election was held under the permanent constitution recently adopted. There was no other presidential candidate, but stories of Davis's micromanagement and incompetence were already widespread. Among Confederate troops there was initially a decided disposition to vote against him. However, officers told their men that a negative vote would do no good, and indeed would show a divided front to the enemy. Eventually the army, as well as the civilian vote, went to Davis. The *Examiner* supported Davis's election, but only reluctantly. Thereafter, its attacks on him mounted in number and intensity.

Davis was not a healthy man. He apparently had herpes simplex of the eye, which flared up when he was under stress, and he suffered pain in his foot from a wound received during the Mexican War. He also suffered at times from malaria and rheumatism.[36] The press attacks did not improve his health. Others have described how, as the war progressed, Davis's bouts of illness, frequent bad news from the front, and bitter criticisms from editors like Daniel caused the president to develop a defensive shell into which he withdrew.

The main target of the *Examiner*'s editorial attacks was not initially Davis and his administration, but the North—those bitter and unprincipled Yankees, all of whom hated every Southern white from the day of their birth. Alas, wrote Daniel late in the summer of 1861, all of the South's friends in the North save two—Franklin Pierce and antiwar Ohio congressman Clement Vallandigham—had vied with the fiercest men in the North in "fiendish screams for a bloody subjugation of the South."[37]

In later months, the *Examiner* found much to criticize in Davis's conduct of the war. Beginning in a not impolite tone, the paper expressed the hope on the occasion of the president's inauguration on February 22, 1862, that he would soon change his ways. Until then, it said, the cabinet secretaries had been mere clerks, and in fact the incumbents were fit to be nothing else. Daniel did not need to add that until recently, there had been at least one cabinet member of a different sort: R. M. T. Hunter. It was Hunter who, as U.S. senator from Virginia, had supported John Daniel for a diplomatic appointment in 1853 and who might have become president of the Confederacy early in 1861. Instead, he became secretary of state. He announced on accepting the appointment that he did not intend to become merely Davis's clerk. However, when Hunter expressed an opinion on the military situation during a cabinet meeting, Davis reminded him that he was secretary of state, "and when information is wished of that department it will be time for you to speak." In response, Hunter promptly resigned.[38]

Things were no better on the military side, wrote the *Examiner*, than in civilian affairs. "The most puerile partiality has been displayed in the treatment of individual officers; little lieutenants and colonels have been erected into major-generals without achievement or justice, and it would almost seem that the Government was afraid of genius and will, so sedulously has it kept at a distance individuals of lofty intellect, wide knowledge and enduring energy."[39]

The president's wife, Varina Davis, had been concerned that Davis's inaugural address might furnish the *Examiner* a new excuse to attack him, and before he spoke she left the speaker's platform and returned home. (It was also raining hard.)[40] Her fears were realized. Aside from the puerile partiality that President Davis had shown, said the paper, he had simply not given a good speech. The public had expected much more. The speech might better have been omitted from the ceremony, had it not been customary for presidents to say something on such occasions. But the paper's main point was that the president could not run the government by himself, although he was trying to do so. Even Napoleons had to share their administrative tasks with the best men they could find. The president of the Confederacy simply must bring in "real men, who can comprehend the state of affairs, [who] know the resources and character of this country and of the adversary, who have the vigor to call into full action the powers and resources of the Southern Republic!"[41]

At this point, early in 1862, Confederate fortunes seemed to be at a low point. Fort Donelson on the Cumberland River had surrendered, Nashville was lost, and the whole Confederate position in Kentucky and Tennessee had disintegrated. In February 1862, a Union brigadier general named Ambrose Burnside led 13,000 troops ashore on Roanoke Island, North Carolina, and won control of North Carolina's inland sea, leaving only the port of Wilmington open to the vitally important blockade runners. Norfolk, it seemed, was the next Union target. There was panic in Richmond, and for a time the city was placed under martial law. The *Examiner* warned that the war could be very long. However, people should not be discouraged, and they should be prepared for great trials and privations. After all, Jehovah had kept Moses and his people wandering for forty years before he gave them a country and independence.[42]

In early April 1862 came the greatest battle of the war so far, when a hundred thousand men met near a small log church called Shiloh in southern Tennessee. Losses totaled over 23,000 on both sides, a number greater than the total casualties in all three wars that the United States had fought so far.[43] In the end, the Confederates were driven from the field, yet on April 8 the *Richmond Examiner* claimed that Shiloh's results had been "more splendid than that which made the plains of Manassas forever famous." Shiloh would lift the South from dejection, wipe "hallucinations of arrogance" from Northern minds, and make European governments and publics realize that the Confederacy was an established fact that they must deal with.[44] Perhaps Daniel was right to see positive results on April 8, but on the last day of the month New Orleans fell to Union forces and Commodore David Farragut pointed his vessels farther up the Mississippi River, aiming to split the eastern part of the Confederacy from Texas, Arkansas, and western Louisiana. Much nearer to Richmond, Union general George McClellan began to move his massive army up the Virginia peninsula, aiming to capture the capital of the Confederacy. On April 19, the *Examiner* warned that a great battle on the Peninsula was inevitable. Either McClellan would be ruined or Richmond would be taken. The loss of Richmond would essentially mean the loss of Virginia, and that would cripple the South.

The editor of the *Examiner* acknowledged the danger, but he also wrote that the government had frittered away the power of the South.[45] Worse, an apparently desperate Jefferson Davis was calling for prayers and letting it be known that he had been confirmed in the Episcopal church. As John Daniel knew or surmised, the sickly president was distraught over the military situation. After Davis told his wife that he longed for someone to share his burden, she had called in the Rev. Charles Minnigerode, rector of St. Paul's Church, and the result was Davis's confirmation. But from Daniel's point of view, to see the president standing in a corner, "telling his beads" and counting on a miracle to save the country, was depressing in the extreme. When a ship sprang a leak, an efficient captain did not order all hands to prayers, but to the pumps.[46]

The paper emphasized that all was not lost. Everything would change in an hour if only the Confederate troops gained some great victory. The paper forecast on May 8, 1862, that if the Confederacy succeeded in holding Richmond there would be foreign intervention and peace before the end of June.

Meanwhile, McClellan's army was almost at the door of Richmond. Jefferson Davis sent his family to North Carolina, and some government archives were packed in crates to be shipped out if the capital was evacuated. Firing was sometimes audible in the city, and as the *Examiner* reported, people could even see a federal observation balloon floating high on its tether.[47]

Daniel decided in the summer of 1862 that the time had come for him to return to the army. The *Examiner* had insisted that ten men on each daily newspaper must be exempted from conscription if the free press were to survive.[48] However, that did not mean that a paper's editor must stay home. We cannot be sure of Daniel's reasons for going back to the front, but they probably involved pride, as well as patriotism. Before he had joined Floyd's staff the previous year, Daniel had told George Bagby that, although he could not bear pain, he wanted to be able to show an honorable scar. He had come home unscathed from western Virginia, but he wanted another chance. Reentering the army would also give him a chance to defend his city, which was being hard pressed by the enemy. Furthermore, Daniel could not forget that O. Jennings Wise, son of the former governor and editor of the rival *Enquirer,* had taken a captain's commission and gone to war in his late twenties and that he had been killed in February 1862 at the battle for Roanoke Island.

In June 1862, Major Daniel joined the staff of Gen. A. P. Hill, who commanded the Light Division just outside Richmond. The distance was short and Daniel took with him a tent of his own design, a chest of victuals and belongings, a complete set of cooking gear, and his own valet and cook.

Hill's division came under the overall command of Robert E. Lee, who had returned from Charleston to be entrusted with what had become the Army of Northern Virginia. Another of Lee's divisions was commanded by Gen. James Longstreet, who outranked Hill. Both units were considered crack divisions, and there was rivalry between them. The Richmond papers reached the field each day and were read widely in the army. It was clear that the *Examiner* was paying particular attention, and giving particular praise, to the doings of Hill's division and to Hill himself, who in only three months had risen from colonel to major general. The paper's praise led to a major rift in the army—but first came the Seven Days' battles outside Richmond.

Lee, although considerably outnumbered, decided to attack McClellan's right wing outside Richmond. As part of the attack, A. P. Hill and his Light Division crossed the Chickahominy River at a point about six miles north of the city and moved southeast down the river to strike at units commanded by Gen. Fitz John Porter. The Battle of Gaines' Mill, which came on the third day of the Seven Days' battles around Richmond, was fought on June 27. A participant later recalled seeing A. P. Hill before the battle, sitting on his horse and wearing simple dress, a gray flannel fatigue jacket, and felt hat. Near him was "a splendidly dressed officer who attracted my attention, and on inquiry I found that he was none other than the famous editor of the Richmond *Examiner*, John M. Daniel, who was destined to be wounded quite severely that day and have fresh gall added to his trenchant pen."[49]

In the height of the battle, at about 4:00 P.M., Daniel was discussing with Col. James G. Field an order from General Hill when Daniel's right arm was badly shattered by a minié ball. As Daniel fell, Hill and his men saw large units coming to reinforce them—Stonewall Jackson's men, it was thought at first, but they turned out to be Longstreet's division. The Battle of Gaines' Mill was huge, with more men on the field than in any previous battle of the war: about 75,000 Confederate troops, reported the *Examiner*, and perhaps even more on the Union side.[50]

The Union force withdrew after the battle and the Confederates claimed victory, although Lee had lost 8,700 men and McClellan 6,800. Richmond hospitals overflowed, and private citizens opened their homes to the wounded men. Daniel was fortunate to have his two slaves to help him back to Richmond and to have his own house and bed where he could begin to recover from what was perhaps a more severe wound than he had envisioned eventually receiving.[51] Minié balls were inch-long lead projectiles that could rip into a man hard; if they struck a bone, it usually shattered. Virginius Dabney wrote decades later that Daniel's wound was not seriously disabling, but military records indicate that he was in fact seriously hurt. Robert Hughes said that the wound completely disabled him. When John Mitchel, the Irishman, called on Daniel some two and a half months after the battle, "I found him confined to his bed with a broken arm, a wound received while he served with Floyd [Hill]."[52] Daniel seems never to have regained full use of his arm, but his general health improved to the point that he told George Bagby sometime in 1863 that he was sure he would live long. He came, he said, of a long-lived race, and he had an infallible sign of longevity: his sleep was invariably sound and refreshing and he never dreamed.[53] (The Daniels were in fact hardly a long-lived family. While his great-uncle the justice lived into his mid-seventies, both John Daniel's father and his grandfather had died in their mid-forties.)

The *Examiner* found itself in some embarrassment over its account of the situation on the field at the moment Daniel was wounded. The paper stressed two days after the event that Major Daniel had been on the field solely in his capacity as a staff officer, and although the *Examiner* had reported the day's events, Daniel himself had reported nothing about any army units or dispositions.[54] It seems not unlikely that rumblings had come from the War Department about a possible leak of information from the officer-editor. Richmond had been under martial law since March, and some weeks after the editor's return from battle, the *Examiner* said that "this newspaper has received numerous menaces from the parasites of power, and it is well known that the army of clerks and underlings employed in the numberless bureaux and departments of the government . . . have been clamorous for its suppression. When the weak, impressible and petulant character of the President is considered, it is really surprising that this last outrage upon public liberty has not been attempted."[55] Surprising or not, it is to the credit of Jefferson Davis that he did not crack down on the *Richmond Examiner.* Nor did he censor other papers. In the North, however, a number of newspapers were suppressed in the course of the war, for reporting too much and for saying what Lincoln's administration thought wrong. There were also arrests of Northern editors, and after Lincoln suspended the writ of habeas corpus at least four editors were tried by military tribunals.

Daniel's wound came at a good moment for the Confederacy. George McClellan, whose pickets had been within four miles of Richmond at one point, and whose forces had outnumbered Lee's by 30,000, withdrew down the Peninsula and sailed back north with his army. His campaign to take Richmond had been a failure. McClellan wrote Lincoln that the president needed a general-in-chief and indicated modestly that he was willing to serve. (McClellan wrote separately to his wife that Lincoln was a coward, an idiot, and a baboon.) What Lincoln in fact needed was a better general than McClellan, who exaggerated both his own worth and the size of Confederate forces that faced him. Several months later, Lincoln finally replaced him. After McClellan's departure, the *Examiner* characterized him briefly, and not incorrectly, as "an avaricious railroad President, of doubtful loyalty, who . . . adopted in war the sedate tactics of the mud-turtle."[56] For once, Abraham Lincoln would not have disagreed with John Moncure Daniel.

Before the present conflict, the only war that either Daniel or McClellan had seen was in Europe. McClellan had gone to Europe in 1855 and had been impressed by the Russians' defensive positions in the Crimean War; Daniel, in 1859, had observed the successful offensive of French and Piedmontese armies in Lombardy. Now, in America, McClellan had repeatedly hung back from taking the offensive, while Daniel had pushed as best he could for the Confederacy to go on the attack.

After Daniel returned to Richmond, the *Examiner* continued its high praise for A. P. Hill's division. On July 2, the *Examiner* reported that Hill had had to take over command of Longstreet's division two days earlier at the Battle of Frazier's Farm because Longstreet had absented himself. Learning about this report, Longstreet reached the end of his patience. He drafted a letter to the *Richmond Whig* that flatly contradicted the *Examiner* and criticized Hill for allowing such reports to reach the press. Statements like these, wrote Longstreet, did great injury to the army, both at home and abroad. At Longstreet's request, his assistant adjutant general, G. Moxley Sorrel, signed and sent the letter, which appeared in the *Whig* on July 9. A little later, when Sorrel wrote Hill to request some routine report, his request was returned with the endorsement that "General Hill declines to hold further communication with Major Sorrel." In response, Longstreet then fired off a bitter letter to Hill, to which Hill replied in kind. Furious, Longstreet told Sorrel to place Hill under arrest, and Hill wrote to Lee requesting a transfer from Longstreet's command. The affair ended only after Lee came in to resolve matters and moved Hill elsewhere.[57] The dispute had all started with John Moncure Daniel's paper, and it had done no good at all for the Confederate cause.

Soon Daniel's boyhood home, Stafford County, would become the major scene in the carnage. In early August, on Aquia Creek, not far from the old home of the Travers and Daniel families at Crow's Nest, Union steamboats began to unload troops coming up from North Carolina under the command of Ambrose Burnside. Their purpose was to defend the approaches to Washington from Lee's advance into northern Virginia. It was, however, not in Stafford County but again near Bull Run that, in late August, the next great clash occurred. At what the Confederacy called the Second Battle of Manassas, a Northern army commanded by John Pope was routed by Robert E. Lee; but Pope's army did not panic, and Lee did not succeed in destroying it. In early September, Lee crossed the Potomac, invaded Maryland, and was defeated at Antietam. But Lee saved his army. In November, Lincoln finally replaced McClellan as the commanding general of the Army of the Potomac, naming Ambrose Burnside in his stead. Burnside, a West Point graduate who had some experience in fighting Mexicans and Apaches, had no illusions about his own capabilities; nor should he have had any, despite his victory nine months earlier on the North Carolina coast.

In November 1862, Burnside moved his splendid army of almost 150,000 southward across Stafford County to the Rappahannock River. Before the river came a line of heights, on which Burnside massed over 140 cannon, the greatest artillery concentration yet seen in the war. Below, beyond the river, lay the pretty town of Fredericksburg, where young John Daniel had for a time read law. Beyond the town, a Confederate army of 80,000 manned the heights looking down on Fredericksburg and the river and across at the Union forces on the opposing heights. Burnside's intentions were not clear. The *Examiner* reported on November 21 that it seemed very improbable that he would attempt a flat-out advance across the river. On November 24, the paper wrote that if there was an attack, "Before Burnside gets very far he will find that there are lions in his patent path. . . . [T]he Federal Government and Generals . . . may find the plains around Fredericksburg, the highlands in front and the river in their back, the prettiest place to be drubbed in, that Yankees ever saw." Daniel was often wrong. This time, it turned out, he was right. But it did not take great military acumen to see what trouble Burnside was getting into. Gen. Joseph E. Johnston wrote almost ruefully to Senator Wigfall "What luck some people have. Nobody will ever come to attack me in such a place."[58]

No doubt there were many former friends, and indeed some blood relatives, who found themselves on opposite sides of the front at Fredericksburg. Two such friends were Irishmen Thomas Francis Meagher and John Mitchel, who had led the then-hopeless struggle for Irish independence and for their efforts been tried and transported to Tasmania. They escaped to America. When Mitchel arrived in New York in 1853, his comrade Meagher was on the dock to meet him. Meagher stayed in the North, and when the war began he raised an Irish brigade for the Union army. While Meagher and his brigade waited now on Burnside's orders to cross the Rappahannock, John Mitchel stood a mile away on Marye's Heights looking down at the river and the Union army beyond. Mitchel was not a soldier, but he had come South and had taken up the Confederate cause. Some thought that he did so because he equated the South with his oppressed homeland,[59] but it went beyond that. Even before the war he had written, "I consider negro slavery the best state of existence for the negro . . . the taking of negroes out of their brutal slavery in Africa and promoting them to a humane and reasonable slavery here."[60]

Mitchel had particularly fond memories of Virginia, dating from a visit in 1854 some months after his arrival in America, when he spoke at the University of Virginia and found a courteous and friendly people.[61] He had traveled to Fredericksburg in late 1862 from Richmond, where he had recently called on the ailing Daniel soon after arriving from the North. A year later he was to join Daniel on the *Examiner*, where still later he would carry on for the proprietor as Daniel lay slowly dying.[62] Mitchel had three sons, and all joined the Confederate army. He had come to Fredericksburg to see one of them, Willy, before the battle. Willy survived that battle, but he and another brother were killed later; the third son survived the war but lost an arm.

At Fredericksburg, Burnside had to wait longer than he liked to get pontoon bridges built across the Rappahannock. He then attacked straight on. The Union troops came across the river and on through Fredericksburg toward the foot of Marye's Heights. There, not visible from a distance, a sunken road ran along the bottom of the hill. It had a four-foot stone wall on the side that faced the federal advance. There, four—some later said six—ranks of Southern riflemen stood, well protected by the wall, and fired volley after volley into the attackers. It was a slaughter. Only one Northerner, perhaps an officer, got as near as a hundred feet from the wall before he fell. Nine thousand Union soldiers fell trying to storm Marye's Heights.

Burnside eventually left Fredericksburg and marched his army uselessly up the Rappahannock in cold rain and thick mud. Indeed, much of John Daniel's old green Stafford County became a treeless field of mud, and the fine white house that his ancestors had built at Crow's Nest was burned to the ground. It would be decades before the Stafford landscape recovered from its denuding by the Union army. But as Daniel's paper had made clear before the Battle of Fredericksburg, the way to take Richmond was not to come down the straight route from Washington through Stafford; the vulnerable side lay toward the Tidewater. McClellan had come from there, and he had come close. Eventually a general named Grant would come all the way. But John Moncure Daniel would no longer be there; would never see Richmond in defeat.

Fourteen

How to Attack a President

The Civil War created conditions in Richmond that are difficult to comprehend in the twenty-first century. For four years, the city was a prime target for Northern armies, and from Pawnee Sunday in 1861 until the city finally fell in 1865, Richmond was always near, or felt near, to the conflict. Daniel had written of the martial atmosphere in Washington in early 1861, but that was nothing like conditions in wartime Richmond. Within a few months of the war's beginning, the scene changed greatly. Men in uniform were everywhere. A young woman named Sallie Brock Putnam recalled, "We were awakened in the morning by the reveille of the drum . . . and the evening 'taps' reminded us of the hour for rest. At all hours of the day the sounds of martial music fell upon our ears, and the 'tramp, tramp' of the soldiers through the streets was the accompaniment. Nothing was seen, nothing talked of, nothing thought of, but the war."[1]

Shortages brought high prices for goods and food. Daniel could afford to buy what he liked, but most people could not. J. B. Jones, a mid-level official in the War Department with a family of six, wrote in his diary during the summer of 1863 that they were all in a half-starving condition and that he had lost twenty pounds. The family relied heavily on a vegetable garden for food, but Jones could get little meat—by mid-1864, no more than one ounce a day for each family member (including the parrot and the cat).[2] The well-to-do did not lose so much weight. But the white people of Richmond—rich and poor—by and large supported the Southern cause strongly, and the ladies of Richmond wanted badly to show their support for the soldiers. It was perhaps the ladies who thought up the idea of "starvation parties," soirées where no food or drink was served, except cold water. Gallantry and talk flowed undiminished—talk mainly of the war, which on occasion came close to the city and was never more than a hundred miles away.

Not all soirées were starvation parties. Mary Chesnut and her husband, who had represented South Carolina in the U.S. Senate and who was one of several senior military aides to Jefferson Davis, one evening during the winter of 1862–63 attended a dinner at Laburnum, the suburban home of their friends the Lyons. James Lyons was a prosperous lawyer, and Mrs. Chesnut later described the evening as a great affair. She found herself seated next to "a clever unknown" whose name she had not caught and whom she did not recognize, although he seemed to know her. Mrs. Chesnut was pleased to find that her table companion was an agreeable sort. Indeed, she recalled,

> My neighbor was bright and clever beyond my wildest hopes. He knew everybody and everything, and his paragraphs were as cool and ready, as incisive and as decisive as the Examiner's. Once when he was particularly epigrammatical, I said 'Don't try that style! That is like the Examiner.' Which remark caused him a moment's reflection. Someone had had the bad taste to arraign the President to his handsome secretary, Burton Harrison. I said: 'How rude! I know how angry Mr. Harrison feels. They do that to me, although I am the wife of one of Mr. Davis's A.D.C.'s.'
>
> 'And you!' said he, 'You hit harder and nearer than an aide-de-camp tonight.' 'What do you mean?' 'In all innocence, of course, for you do not know who I am, apparently; and we have had an altercation!' 'Conversation, you ought to say. But you have abused everybody, friend or foe, and you hit so hard I shiver even for my enemies.'
>
> He asked with unmoved face: 'Do you include the Examiner among those newspapers you denounce as giving aid and comfort to—or doing yeoman service for—the Yankees.' 'Yes, they are splitting us into a thousand pieces. I think of the editor of the Examiner in his cozy den, in warm dressing-gown and comfortable slippers, with a good fire and a good cigar; and the President for a tidbit to tear and crunch.' He looked grimmer than ever. 'Did you tell Mrs. Petigru you hoped to see Daniels [*sic*] hanged? 'I do not know. I say too much, as you may have noticed. But you must own that he deserves it. He is a standing vote of dissatisfaction with the Administration. I am for the gentlemen privates! If I were a shouting character, I should say: "Three cheers for the gentlemen privates! To the lantern for the dissenting editors!" As for Congress, I would blow them from the guns, as the English did the Sepoys—though the Sepoys only did what the English laud and magnify John Brown for trying to get the Negroes to do here.' Here I stopped to take breath. After we were once more in the drawing room, someone said: 'What a brilliant conversationalist Mr. Daniels is!' 'Is Mr. Daniels here?' 'He sat by you at table.'[3]

If Mrs. Chesnut found Mr. Daniel so interesting, did other ladies do so as well? It appears that John Daniel may have been squiring around some other lady two years earlier, before he had broken completely with Jefferson Davis. In August 1861, Mary Chesnut recorded in her diary that she had been at the Davis mansion, and that "Mr. & Mrs. Daniels were there—the Editor of the *Examiner*. Miles said he thought he would feel odd in going to see people he abused as the administration is abused in the *Examiner*."[4] It may seem odd that, having seen "Mr. Daniels" in 1861, Chesnut completely failed to remember his face when she sat next to him two years later. However, it appears that Chesnut's friend William Porcher Miles also identified the man at the Davis mansion as the editor of the *Examiner*. There is no evidence as to the identity of the lady who some thought was Mrs. Daniel.

Is it straining to show that John Moncure Daniel enjoyed heterosexual relationships? John Mitchel wrote that Daniel was a bachelor and a woman-hater, and "for good reasons." This seems to have been what Daniel himself told Mitchel, just as Daniel was clearly the source for Mitchel writing that "he is very familiar with life amongst the higher classes of Turin and Genoa, and intimately knew Cavour, who never once (as Daniel declares) told the truth where a lie would serve him as well."[5]

One wonders if Daniel's misogyny was a pose. Certainly he was not indifferent to women. He often told George Bagby that he could never love a girl who was not pretty, but he could not thing of marrying a girl who was a "pretty fool." Daniel could be courteous to women; he encouraged them to write and contribute to his paper and expressed in print his admiration for such a brave soul as Margaret Fuller. However, Daniel wanted Bagby to believe that he thought "There are but two ways to manage a woman—to club her or to freeze her."[6] If he ever married, he said, he and his wife would need to occupy separate houses; he could not stand either the noise of children or "the gabble of a woman with her lady friends."[7] Bagby thought that Daniel had never had a serious affair in all his years abroad. Whether he ever had any other sort of affair, one can only guess.

Although one might charge the editor of the *Richmond Examiner* with aiding and abetting the enemy, as Chesnut did, that was far from his aim. When one reads through the wartime issues of Daniel's paper, one sees increasingly sharp criticism of the Jefferson Davis administration. But at the same time there is firm insistence that the Confederacy could win, an insistence, even in dark hours, that things were brighter than they seemed. However, John Daniel did not believe in deceiving his readers. On New Year's Day 1863, the paper said that the Confederacy's means of resistance were greater than ever before but that the North had a million soldiers, "a real million, actually under arms." Daniel did not need to tell his readers that a million was twice as many men as were serving in the Confederate forces.

In early February 1863, the *Examiner* noted that prevailing sentiment in the South held that peace would be made within three months. However, it added, while the next three months might settle the conflict, this might not yet bring peace, just as peace with England had not come for two years after the Battle of Yorktown in 1781.

On March 27, 1863, the *Examiner* asserted that the fighting that spring would not only demonstrate the superiority of the Southern soldier but would determine the outcome of the war. The paper added that the enemy had never yet successfully fought Confederate forces in the open field; "their only triumphs have been achieved on the water or in its immediate vicinity." Was Daniel perhaps thinking about Vicksburg, the Southern strongpoint on the Mississippi River? A great contest was looming there.

Meanwhile, there was considerable disaffection, both North and South. Many in the North wanted peace. In July 1863, anticonscription mobs would rampage through New York City, killing and looting. On the morning of April 2, 1863, Richmond experienced what came to be called the Bread Riot. The incident began when hundreds of people, mainly women and boys, gathered on Capitol Square, ostensibly to protest food shortages and high prices. This was not a spontaneous demonstration; it followed a protest meeting held the previous evening at a church on Oregon Hill, a western, working-class suburb of Richmond. The women started off down the city streets from the Capitol and many men followed. The mob grew to more than a thousand, perhaps even several thousand, people. William Munford, head of the local Young Men's Christian Association, called out that he would issue food to people who went to the YMCA office. Some did, but the mass continued down Main Street and began to attack and loot stores. President Davis came out of his office and appealed to the crowd to go home. The rioting stopped after two hours, and order was restored. The next morning, crowds gathered again and many feared a repetition of the previous day, but the people dispersed after authorities took the extreme step of placing cannon on the streets to intimidate possible rioters.[8]

Jefferson Davis took the unusual step of personally requesting Richmond newspapers not to make any direct or indirect reference to the disturbance, which he said was liable to misconstruction and misinterpretation abroad.[9] All the papers agreed—except for the *Richmond Examiner*. Some writers have viewed this as one more example of John Moncure Daniel's heedless and inflammatory ways. However, the editor had quickly realized that there was no reason to keep quiet about the matter; the news was going to get out: "As three hundred Yankee prisoners went off by flag of truce yesterday, the whole story, with all the additions which malice and invention can supply, has already got as far as Old Point."[10] Daniel was right. A few days later, the *Examiner* reported that accounts had already appeared in the Northern press of a just-released Union colonel named Stewart who had seen from his prison window three thousand women rioting in a Richmond street.[11] It had been, better, then, to report the riot and to put the best face on it, as Daniel had done. He denied that the riot had been brought about by "starving people." The South had made large appropriations for the poor that had gone unused. Indeed, after the trouble began, a charitable institution (presumably, the YMCA) had offered to distribute rice and flour, but the recipients had dashed the food into the muddy street where it lay. Daniel claimed that the whole affair was the work of Union agents. Two weeks earlier, there had been a disturbance in Atlanta, then others in Mobile, Saulsbury, and Petersburg. Having done their work in one city, claimed Daniel, the instigators had taken the train to the next.[12] All in all, Daniel's coverage of the affair may have done the Confederate cause at least as much good as harm.

John Mitchel, who had gone to call on Daniel soon after his arrival in Richmond in 1862, had been looking at that time for a newspaper job. Mitchel had experience in journalism; he had founded a newspaper in New York soon after his escape from Tasmania. But he did not, then, agree with Daniel's negative view of Jefferson Davis. Mitchel was soon hired as editor of the rival *Enquirer,* which was close to the administration. But he was much taken with John Moncure Daniel, who he decided was the most singular and original—and the most accomplished—American he had yet known. Mitchel was apparently taken with Daniel's looks as well as his manners. Daniel, he wrote, was a man of middle height; he was straight, slender, and very swarthy; he had keen eyes and a somewhat ferocious mouth, which was partly hidden by a black mustache.[13] (Daniel had apparently shaved off the beard he wore on his return from Turin.)

During the summer and autumn of 1863, Mitchel began to view Jefferson Davis and his administration in a far less favorable light, however, and he began to think of joining Daniel on the *Examiner*. Daniel indicated that he would be pleased to have Mitchel with him.[14] There was a place for him on the paper, since Daniel's associate editor, Edward Pollard, had recently gone off to England. Sometime around the end of 1863, Mitchel joined the staff of the *Examiner*, where he apparently took over the main responsibility of drafting editorials. Mitchel quickly made a reputation for himself. Constance Cary Harrison, the wife of Jefferson Davis's private secretary, Burton Harrison, recalled years later that there were three "literary magnates" in Richmond during the Civil War. One was John R. Thompson, the poet who had edited the *Southern Literary Review* and become the Virginia state librarian. The others were John Moncure Daniel and John Mitchel, whom Harrison remembered as opposites. She remembered Daniel as being very unpopular, "a sort of a social sphinx," whereas Mitchel was regarded as the humanizing element of the partnership, "the one hope of sufferers who essayed through him to subdue the roar of that autocratic lion."[15] But that lion would not be subdued, not yet.

If there was one determining year in the war, it was 1863. At the end of April and the beginning of May, the latest top Union commander, Joseph Hooker, who liked to be known as "Fighting Joe," suffered major defeats at Chancellorsville and the Wilderness; and the most gifted and admired of Confederate commanders, Thomas ("Stonewall") Jackson, was mortally wounded. In July, Robert E. Lee was defeated at Gettysburg by George Meade's army, and Vicksburg fell to Union forces led by U. S. Grant. The editor of the *Examiner* paid deep homage to Jackson upon his death, as did all Southerners, and tried to put the best possible face on the Vicksburg disaster, which left the lower Mississippi in Union hands. The *Examiner* claimed that the Confederacy had ceded no military advantage in the loss of Vicksburg, which it had held for a year chiefly from pride. It was true that the Confederacy had a bloody nose and a black eye, but it had never been sounder in wind and limb.[16]

There was far more that the *Examiner* wanted to say about both Vicksburg and Gettysburg. On August 5, the paper published a long editorial entitled "Ohe! Jam Satis!" This was identified as a letter written by someone on the Mississippi, but George Bagby recalled that the original draft was the work of "a lady distinguished for her attainments and performances in literature"[17] who had sent it to Daniel. The editor had reworked it considerably, as he often did with contributions. It appeared as a ferocious attack on the incompetent general who had surrendered Vicksburg, Northern-born John Pemberton, and on his protector, Jefferson Davis, who had promoted the unworthy former captain to the rank of lieutenant general.

The editorial recalled that before the final days of the Vicksburg siege, people on every street corner had been heard to say that if Pemberton retained his command, the South would lose Vicksburg. Pemberton had been urged to provision Vicksburg for a twelve-month siege, but he had not done so. Meanwhile, said the editorial, Jefferson Davis sat serene, wrapped in sublime self-complacency upon the frigid heights of an infallible egotism, and had turned a deaf ear to all criticisms of his protegé. After the fall of Vicksburg, the editorial continued, the Southern people could see that it was not Pemberton, but Davis who was to blame.

> The people are weary of the flagrant mismanagement of the Government. . . . Had the people dreamed that Mr. Davis would carry all his chronic antipathies, his bitter prejudices, his puerile partialities, and his doting favoritisms into the Presidential chair, they would never have allowed him to fill it. . . . He has alienated the hearts of the people, by his stubborn follies. . . . [O]ur people lift their eyes toward Richmond, and cry, with Tennyson:
>
> "Ah God! for a man with heart, head, hand,
> Like some of the simple great ones gone
> Forever, and ever by!"
>
> The country is not discouraged by Federal advances, but we know that, unless the errors of the past are promptly corrected, the future holds no promise. . . .

In contrast to Pemberton, the *Examiner* praised Pemberton's nominal commander and Daniel's hero, Joseph E. Johnston, whom Davis had expected to work miracles and accomplish impossibilities with a brave but small army. The people, said the paper, wanted to see conduct of the war entrusted to such generals as Johnston and Beauregard. They did not share Jefferson Davis's chronic hallucination that he was a great military genius who could conduct campaigns in distant states with unerring skill.

A few days later, on August 10, the *Examiner* delivered its judgment on Gettysburg and on Lee's conduct of the campaign. It had not been wrong, the paper stressed, for Lee to launch a campaign that struck far into the North. In fact, the greatest mischief that the defeat might do to the South would be to make the Southern public oppose any similar campaign in the future. But the fact was, Lee had made a serious mistake. He could, said the *Examiner,* have done either of two things that he did not: he could have carried out a campaign to destroy Northern towns and farms in retaliation for the havoc that Northern troops had wreaked on the South, which would have caused the North to change its ways; or he could have carried out a campaign to capture Maryland and Washington, which would have caused a crisis in the North that would have quickly ended the war. Lee had refused to do the first and had failed to do the second. He had permitted the enemy to choose his own position, by all accounts one of the strongest on the continent. After the enemy was well entrenched, Lee had blindly "rushed on him like a bull," persisted in the attack for three days, and only then made the campaign a confessed failure by retreating. To be sure, it was an orderly retreat and the general had brought with him herds of fat cattle and many loaded wagons. But it was still a retreat, and the campaign had been a failure. The editor was perhaps even more distressed over the defeat than he admitted in print. Edward A. Pollard recalled in *The Lost Cause* how Daniel often said that Pickett's charge at Gettysburg had brought the Confederacy within a stone's throw of peace.

Soon after Gettysburg, John Daniel took a personal loss when John B. Floyd died on August 26, 1863. Floyd had been his major political patron and, briefly, his commanding general. Daniel once told George Bagby that he admired Floyd's strength, calling him "a man of bronze." But he also told Bagby that while people said Floyd had made Daniel, "The truth is, I made Floyd."[18] What Daniel apparently did not say to Bagby, and perhaps had done his best to forget, was that Floyd had done less than his utmost—less than he had promised—to help Daniel retain his post at Turin in the Buchanan administration.

Without mentioning Jefferson Davis, the *Examiner* made Floyd a weapon in its anti-Davis campaign.[19] Floyd had not been successful as a general or, for that matter, as U.S. secretary of war; but the paper insisted that no one who knew

Floyd doubted he could have managed the overall forces of the Confederacy in a way, and for a purpose, very different from what Southerners had seen to their sorrow. Of all the public men in or out of Washington thirty months earlier, it had been John Floyd, said the paper, who had foreseen that the war would be long and that the South would not benefit from foreign intervention. If John Floyd had led the South, he would have undertaken the military and financial preparation that such a war required. If this account of Floyd's 1861 views is true, one can surmise that Floyd played a significant role in leading Daniel to see, and say, that the coming war would be no trifling thing but a bloodbath—although Daniel did believe, for a long time, that foreign intervention was likely and would shorten the war.

Among the members of Jefferson Davis's cabinet whom Daniel greatly disliked was Judah P. Benjamin, attorney general, secretary of war, and later secretary of state. Before the war, Benjamin had been a U.S. senator from Louisiana. He might have become a diplomatic colleague of Daniel at one point during the Buchanan administration when Benjamin hoped to become minister to France and was offered instead (but did not accept) the legation in Madrid.[20] Benjamin was Jewish, and that was not lost in that anti-Semitic age. Mary Chesnut wrote that "The mob calls him 'Mr. Davis's pet Jew,' a King Street Jew, cheap, very cheap, &c&c."[21] Chesnut's diary was private, but Daniel's paper told the public, when Benjamin was appointed secretary of war, that "the representation of the synagogue is not diminished; it remains full."[22]

One biographer of Judah Benjamin, Eli N. Evans, who has made clear the often anti-Semitic atmosphere of Richmond society during the Civil War, wrote that John Moncure Daniel was particularly vicious. Evans has written that "Daniel was the pen of anti-Semitism"[23] and that as "the author of a pro-slavery tract called 'The Nigger Question,' he was unyielding in his extremism."[24] It was not, however, Daniel but the Scottish philosopher Thomas Carlyle who wrote that infamous tract that seems to have led young Daniel toward racism and his long defense of the South's peculiar institution. As for anti-Semitism, a review of the *Examiner* during the years Daniel was its editor and proprietor (as well as a review of other contemporary newspapers and publications) leads to the conclusion that Daniel and his paper were not unusual in their anti-Semitism. In December 1862, senior Union commander U.S. Grant issued a general order that all Jews "as a class" should be expelled within twenty-four hours from the Department of Tennessee. In the Confederate Congress, Henry Foote spoke of Jews trading with the enemy and of "Jewish Shylocks" buying up property.[25] Evans counted forty derogatory references to Jews in the wartime diary that J. B. Jones of the War Department kept in Richmond.

Daniel did not initially find bad things to say about Judah P. Benjamin. As another biographer of Benjamin has brought out, the *Examiner* at first called Benjamin a man with a wonderful capacity for work who had never failed in any business he had undertaken.[26] However, the paper's opinion soon turned negative. And certainly Daniel was at least as anti-Semitic as his compatriots.

A decidedly outrageous treatment of Jews and blacks in the *Richmond Examiner,* not mentioned in Evans's biography of Benjamin, came in a long piece that the paper published on October 1, 1863. The author is unknown, but John Moncure Daniel edited and published it. The article was meant to be a latter-day version of Jonathan Swift's satirical "modest proposal" of 1729 to alleviate the situation of the Irish poor by using their children for food. The *Examiner* proposed a similar solution to deal with shortages caused by the continuing influx of people into Richmond, whose population, said the article, would soon number three million.

The paper said that the blacks could go naked; they would be kept warm in daytime by hard work, including the digging of catacombs in which they could be confined at night. Gamblers and courtesans, the most numerous class, could be confined to the coal pits. Jews, Yankee tradesmen, and restaurant and hotel proprietors, who altogether numbered half a million, would have their "honest gains" taken from them and would be lodged in mills and warehouses. Mechanics and artisans, whom the Confederate government had cleverly accustomed to live on very little, could be accommodated in empty tobacco hogsheads, each of which could shelter a family of six. These measures would leave Richmond's better class, from the president on down, to be accommodated in proper style.

However, noted the paper, this proposal still left the problem of food shortages. That, too, could be dealt with. The gamblers and harlots could feed on one another; Jews could eat restaurant keepers, who would then be thrown to the poor; and the poor would, in turn, be eaten by the blacks, "so that the dangerous classes will be destroyed at a blow, and nobody be left but Government and negroes, and the Sociology of the South be established on the only firm basis possible."

One suspects that few Richmond readers found this a useful kind of satire. Frederick Daniel did not include it in his later compendium of wartime *Examiner* articles. It not only goes beyond the satirical to the outrageous, but it is anti-Semitic and antiblack. However, all this was typical of the editor and his time.

The *Examiner* did not single out Judah Benjamin for criticism from among members of the Davis cabinet or his officers and other top officials. The incompetent generals and the president who appointed them remained Daniel's main targets, but not his only ones. Nor was it only Benjamin personally whom Daniel criticized in the bureaucracy of the Confederate State Department. At the end of 1863, after the Confederacy had failed to gain diplomatic recognition from any other government, the *Examiner* exploded after learning that the government was still paying a salary of twelve thousand dollars in gold "to each of a numerous and distinguished diplomatic corps, which holds no communication with any Minister of Foreign Affairs, other than his excellency, Mr. Judah P. Benjamin, at Richmond."[27]

Even John Reagan, the Texan who served as postmaster general, came under attack. The *Examiner* could not forgive delays in the delivery of the mails, and it hammered the postmaster general over shortages of postage stamps. In August 1863, the *Examiner* called Reagan a fool and a coward for negotiating with striking postal workers instead of having them thrown into the army.[28] Daniel may not have fully appreciated—or perhaps he preferred to ignore—the problems Reagan faced and the efforts he made to solve them. Reagan had known something about running the mails before the war: he had served on the committee on postal affairs of the U.S. House of Representatives. Soon after he was named postmaster general of the Confederacy, he had recruited five senior officials from the U.S. Post Office Department in Washington, and they had brought to Richmond all the information they could about the postal system in the South. Reagan had also left in place all the Southern postmasters willing to remain in their posts.[29] However, even the prewar United States postal system had functioned poorly, and Reagan and his colleagues in the Confederacy could not fully meet the new challenges posed not only by the overburdened railroads and the lack of materials (there were no postage stamps at all for the first few months, and it was necessary to order stamps, dies, and so forth, from Europe), but by the Union army's inroads into the Confederate states.

Reagan ignored Daniel's attacks, even the charge of cowardice, as Daniel himself had done two years earlier when called a coward. Outside the Davis administration, Daniel had long criticized Virginia governor John Letcher, who, as mentioned earlier, Daniel did not think had properly prepared the state for war. The *Examiner* had called Letcher "an imbecile Governor" in November 1861, and did not change its opinion later. When Daniel continued his attacks even after Letcher's three-year-old daughter died of diphtheria, the governor's brother, Sam Houston Letcher, published a note in the *Richmond Whig* calling John Daniel a mendacious slanderer and a coward. Daniel remained under the peace bond that Mayor Joseph Mayo had imposed on him after his encounter with Marmaduke Johnson, and no challenge or duel ensued.[30]

Another member of the Davis cabinet whom Daniel despised was the Confederate secretary of the treasury, Christopher Memminger, a native of Germany who had settled in South Carolina. Daniel had no experience in financial matters before the war, but Memminger had long chaired the finance committee in South Carolina's house of representatives. However, Memminger had never had to finance a war. Initially, the *Examiner* expressed the belief that the South's wartime finances could be kept healthy by bonds. The Confederacy did manage to float some bond issues in Europe and at home, but these were not enough and the irresponsible printing of paper currency meant that by early 1863 more than $400 million in treasury notes—four times the normal currency of the country—were outstanding.[31] By then, Daniel was urging that an effective system of taxation be established. The people, asserted the *Examiner*, stood ready to pay any taxes needed.[32] But Memminger was still not prepared to launch a comprehensive tax system.

On April 3, 1863, the paper elaborated its own tax proposal. The *Examiner* called for what it described as a "tax in kind," really an income tax. Citizens would be required to pay the government a portion of all that their labor or property produced. Farmers and other direct producers would pay their tax in kind, "without its previous conversion into money," but doctors, mechanics, and the like would pay their tax—perhaps a fifth of their earnings—in cash. Clearly, it would be better to have a regularized tax in kind than to continue to rely, as the Confederacy was doing, on the government's system of "impressment" of farmers' crops to feed the army.

Daniel did not invent income tax. William Pitt had first introduced such a tax in England in 1799 to help finance the war with France. In North America, after the Civil War broke out, the federal government had introduced an income tax in 1862 at the flat rate of 3 percent. Even before the *Examiner* article of April 3, 1863, the Confederate Senate had been working on an income tax law. Shortly after the article was published, Treasury Secretary Memminger proposed, and the Confederate Congress approved, in the Act of April 24, 1863, a system including a graduated income tax and a 10 percent tax in kind on agricultural products. At best, the taxes would cover only a small part of expenditures. In any case, revenue collection lagged, the printing of Confederate treasury notes continued at a quick pace, and the paper money fueled inflation.[33]

From the beginning of the conflict, the question of cotton loomed large. The *Examiner* reflected general Southern sentiment when it initially expressed confidence that Britain's need for cotton to supply its mills would lead to intervene in America's war. What Daniel did not consider was the possibility that the Confederate government might buy up the South's entire cotton crop and ship it—before the North could begin to blockade Southern ports—to Europe, where it would be safe. In 1861, there was no shortage of cotton in Europe, but Southern cotton could have been warehoused there and sold whenever market conditions became favorable. In 1863, the *Examiner* lamented that this course had not been taken.[34] After the war, Jefferson Davis and Joseph E. Johnston criticized Memminger for not shipping the cotton abroad. But there had been clamor in the South for an embargo on shipping cotton—the idea being that holding back cotton would help force the Europeans to recognize the Confederacy—and Davis had at one point disapproved a proposal by Treasury Secretary Memminger for acquisition of a shipping line to carry cotton abroad.[35] This should, however, not disguise the fact that, as Daniel kept reiterating in his paper (and as modern historians generally agree), Christopher Memminger was all in all an incompetent secretary of the treasury. The *Examiner* kept hammering on the need to control inflation, to deal with "the waxing plethora of paper money,"[36] but the problem was never solved.

Memminger resigned in June 1864. George A. Trenholm, a Charleston businessman, replaced him. Trenholm had certainly already done all he could to get Confederate cotton abroad; at one point his company is said to have had sixty vessels running the Union blockade, taking cotton to Europe and bringing home war materials as well, no doubt, as the brocades and brandies advertised in the Richmond newspapers.[37] Trenholm could not solve the cotton export problem after he took over the treasury, but he understood it. He noted in his November 1864 report to the Confederate Congress that the two million bales of cotton then in the Confederacy would, if landed in England, be worth four hundred million dollars in gold, or ten times that amount in Confederate dollars—a sum far greater than the Confederacy's entire official debt.[38]

Long before, the military situation had become appalling. In September 1863, a Confederate army under Gen. Braxton Bragg defeated a Union army in a large and exceptionally bloody battle near Chickamauga Creek in northern Georgia. Bragg was slow to exploit his victory but finally moved his forces north to the heights that overlooked the key city of Chattanooga on the Tennessee River. There was dissension among the Confederate commanders, and Jefferson Davis himself traveled out to Bragg's headquarters and decided to leave Bragg in command. On November 25, Bragg, who had held a strong position on Missionary Ridge near Chattanooga, was defeated in an audacious advance by the Union troops under U. S. Grant. The Confederate position collapsed into what Edward Pollard later called a disgraceful panic and an unmitigated rout. The *Examiner* called for Davis to replace Bragg with Joseph E. Johnston, and the president reluctantly did so.[39] But it was very late in the day. The *Examiner* tried to find something positive in such Southern defeats, but its mood on the last day of 1863 was somber:

> To-day closes the gloomiest year of our struggle. . . . The Confederacy has been cut in twain along the line of the Mississippi, and our enemies are steadily pushing forward their plans for bisecting the eastern moiety. . . . Meanwhile the financial chaos is becoming wilder and wilder . . . [B]ut our enemies need not be jubilant over our depression. . . . Whatever number of men, or whatever amount of money shall be really wanting, will be forthcoming. . . . Wise, cool, decided, prompt action would put us in good condition for the spring campaign of 1864,

and the close of next year would furnish a more agreeable retrospect than the *annus mirabilis* of blunders which we now consign to the dead past.

Coming months proved it was right to sound tentative. In May 1864, Grant sought a showdown with Lee in Virginia that could produce a Northern victory to end the war. He failed in the effort, in the bloody Battles of the Wilderness and Spotsylvania Court House. Then in June, Grant began the siege of Petersburg, slightly more than twenty miles south of Richmond. Another Union army under W. T. Sherman began moving on Atlanta. And the Republican party nominated Abraham Lincoln for another term.

Perhaps, the *Examiner* suggested on June 12, by the time of its November elections, the North would be so at odds politically, with George McClellan challenging Lincoln for the presidency, that the North would be "writhing in intestine convulsion" while the South would be standing "erect redeemed, radiant, triumphant." All this, the paper said, would depend on the Confederate army. However, the paper and its editor no longer had advice to offer on just how the army could bring about victory. Nor was there much other good news. Memminger's resignation from the Treasury was not necessarily a harbinger of better policy, but "At all events we have got rid of this dreadful Secretary."[40] In July 1864, there was an attempt at peace talks involving, among others, newspaperman Horace Greeley and George Sanders, Daniel's former comrade in Young America. No one in the Confederacy, said an editorial in the *Examiner,* longed more for peace than the writer, but the more anxious the South showed itself for peace, the further off peace would be.[41]

Meanwhile, the *Examiner* turned its attention to matters relating not to the competence of Jefferson Davis but to his ethics. On February 13, 1864, the paper reprinted a report from the *Sun* newspaper in Columbus, Georgia, that a large distillery was under construction at Hamburg, South Carolina. The owner was said to have a Confederate government contract for 500,000 gallons of whiskey and he was the brother-in-law of Jefferson Davis. Davis's father-in-law had once been the collector of the Port of New Orleans, and it appeared that the son had been nominated to replace the father in that capacity and might be collecting a salary as such.

The Davis administration may not have noticed the report in the *Columbus Sun,* but its replay in the *Richmond Examiner* drew a rejoinder the same day in a letter to Daniel from Burton Harrison, Davis's private secretary. Harrison asserted that "the gentleman evidently referred to," William F. Howell, was not a port collector and had not drawn a salary as such. Nor did he have a government contract to make whiskey. He was, however, a navy agent, and it was under Confederate navy orders that he had erected a distillery for the manufacture of whiskey "to be used by the Medical Purveyor and as rations." It was true that physicians at that time often prescribed whiskey for medicinal purposes. But half a million gallons was a lot of medicine, or rations, for a navy that in 1864 numbered around four thousand officers and enlisted men. Daniel hardly needed to point out the profits that could be derived if the whiskey were diverted to the public. As early as 1861, George Bagby had reported in the *Southern Literary Messenger* that one distiller was making a profit of four thousand dollars a day. By 1864, people in Richmond paid well over one hundred dollars for one gallon of whiskey.[42]

Harrison included with his letter to Daniel a second letter, also addressed to the editor, which requested that his first letter, refuting (or attempting to refute) the "slanderous" charge against Howell that "someone" in Daniel's office had inserted in the paper, be published in the *Examiner* on February 15. Harrison added that the *Examiner* had also printed an article "relative to the burning of the President's cotton" sometime earlier. Although Col. John Taylor Wood of the president's staff had immediately written to the newspaper to correct errors in that article, a correction never appeared. Harrison hoped that his letter would not share the same fate. If it did, he would be forced to conclude that it was not some subordinate but Daniel himself who "indulges the petty personal malignity which inspires the articles which assail the private character and personal concerns of the President and the members of his family."

One imagines Jefferson Davis standing behind Harrison, not just figuratively but in the flesh, when the secretary wrote these letters to Daniel. The editor quickly saw that they were more grist for his mill.

In reply, Daniel first took up the question of the cotton. What the *Examiner* had initially said, in an article that warned of the danger that Southern cotton crop might fall into enemy hands, was simply that very few planters—not even the president—burned their cotton to prevent enemy capture. A letter had thereupon been sent to the paper over the signature of John Taylor Wood and enclosed was a copy of a telegram sent by the president about his cotton, as well as other "morsels of hard language." According to Daniel, this evidence amounted to an abusive but unsatisfactory contradiction of the charge: Wood's letter and its enclosures had not "corrected" anything in the *Examiner*. The president's own telegram said that he did not know what had been done with his cotton; it therefore appeared that he had neither burned it nor ordered others to do so; it was legitimate to infer that if the president neglected to burn his cotton, few others would burn theirs. Furthermore, said Daniel with editorial tongue firmly in cheek, the paper's decision not to publish Wood's letter had been based on patriotic motives. Indeed, it had not thought that such exhibitions of temper and manners by the president could be pleasing or beneficial to the country. After hearing such angry denials, people might begin to think there really was substance to the charges.

The *Examiner* also addressed the question of the distillery. It was a question of public functionaries and public business and not, as Burton Harrison had written, simply of the president's personal concerns. Or were certain subjects taboo for the public? Harrison's letter, said the paper, permitted one to conclude that it was indeed the brother-in-law of the president who, as naval agent, was called upon to distill 500,000 gallons of whiskey for the Confederate government.[43]

There is no indication that the president's office sent further letters to the *Examiner.* Nor did either Jefferson Davis or Varina Howell Davis mention this exchange in anything they published after the war. And although by 1864 neither Jefferson Davis nor his wealthy brother, Joseph, had any cotton, the fact was that the president's brother-in-law, William F. Howell, had succeeded his father as a navy agent after the father's death in March 1863 and moved the agency to Augusta. The city of Augusta was far up the Savannah River from the sea, but it was just across the river from Hamburg, site of the distillery that Howell had built on navy orders for a very small navy. Howell's enterprise perhaps represented a case of a man mixing public and private interest. If so, it was not the only such case, North or South, then or now.

Although neither Jefferson nor Varina Davis later referred to these matters in their writings, what each did take up—he in *The Rise and Fall of the Confederate Government* and she in her later memoir of her husband—were Daniel's attacks on the president for failing to institute a policy of retaliation for Union army attacks on Southern civilians and inhumane Union treatment of captured Southern soldiers. As early as May 12, 1862, the *Examiner* insisted that "We must pay the enemy back in savage coin of vengeance, and settle our accounts in blood." Reports continued of Southern manor houses being burned and of Confederate officers being shot as spies. (At some later point, perhaps in the summer of 1864, the editor presumably learned that the Daniels' old family home, at Crow's Nest in Stafford County, had been shelled by a Union vessel and had burned to the ground.) The reports of Union general Benjamin Butler's acts in occupied New Orleans particularly outraged Daniel and the entire South. The *Examiner* continued to demand that the Confederacy retaliate for the "diabolical" way the Union waged war. But, said the paper, the Confederate government made no promise to retaliate; every statement of the president indicated that his main aim was for Southerners to be reckoned chivalrous knights, in contrast to the bloody barbarians of the North. To the *Examiner,* this suggested "self-conscious vanity."[44]

This was not a theme that Daniel tired of. In contrast, when reports appeared that the Confederate side, too, was guilty of unlawful acts if not atrocities—for example, at the Andersonville prison camp—the editor dismissed them as insignificant. It was in part, as he saw it, a question of keeping the South properly warlike. If the South did not wage all-out war, Northern atrocities would continue and the South would lose. As Grant began to besiege Petersburg (just down the road from Richmond) in the early summer of 1864, the *Examiner* claimed that even though citizens of the capital were continuing to go about their business calmly, the Union generals planned on "crushing, sacking and burning the place, drenching these leafy shades with blood, and strewing them with mangled bones and splattered brains."

Perhaps most historians will agree that an announced Southern policy of retaliation would not have helped the Confederacy militarily, but would have damaged its image, particularly in Europe, at a time when it still hoped to gain foreign recognition. And there were also reports of atrocities in the Confederacy, like the horrors in the prison camp at Andersonville and the killing at Fort Pillow of several hundred Union soldiers, most of them black, who had already surrendered. Besides, Jefferson Davis had in fact initially agreed to some retaliatory action. In November 1861, after a court in Philadelphia had sentenced a Confederate privateer captain to death, Secretary of State Benjamin had ordered the execution of a Union officer if the sentence was carried out, with more such executions if the North continued to issue such death sentences. And the North had backed down.[45]

But it was not only retaliation for unjust executions that Daniel sought. He had urged the Confederacy as early as February 1862 to undertake a scorched earth policy: "If Virginia would escape impending ruin, she must make the war *a l'outrance*! When we cannot beat back the enemy, we may make him know the work he has in hand, by rendering the ground over which he marches a desert."[46]

Years later, Varina Davis wrote of her husband that the attacks of the *Examiner* on the issue of retaliation "annoyed and galled him greatly. . . . The *Examiner* was ably edited, and ingenious in ways and means to make the President odious—but was unable at least to engraft an ignoble policy upon that of the Administration."[47] In this instance, her defense of the president seems justified, and Daniel's attacks on him were not only unproductive but wrong. However, retaliation is not the same as scorching the enemy's, or one's own, earth. Davis and Lee never agreed to that policy, but a Union general named Sherman, who had taken reprisals as early as 1862, did, and he later scorched the earth as he marched through Georgia.

One vignette of the tragic times in wartime Richmond bears on Daniel's old comrade in Young America and former diplomatic colleague in Europe, George N. Sanders. Sanders spent much of the war as a Confederate agent in England and Canada, leaving his wife, Anna, in Virginia. Their son, Reid, became a Confederate major and was captured late in 1863. One morning in the spring of 1864, Jefferson Davis kindly sent his secretary, Burton Harrison, to see the military paymaster, who agreed to pay Reid's salary to Anna Sanders.[48] Six months later, she learned that Reid had died in a federal prison.[49]

Davis was less kind to George Sanders after the war. In 1869, both men were in London, seeking ways to make money; neither enjoyed much success. Sanders planned to approach the Marquis of Salisbury about a project in Nova Scotia and asked Davis if he might at least mention Davis's name. But Davis preferred that Sanders not do so, on grounds he knew nothing of the project (and presumably did not want to learn).[50] Daniel was already in his grave. Had he ever heard of this exchange, it could only have confirmed his judgment of Jefferson Davis. Which is not to say that Daniel ended with much admiration for his old colleague Sanders, who, as mentioned earlier, had been involved in an effort for peace. When the effort backfired and the affair was publicized, the *Examiner* was straightforward: Peace might conceivably be nearer than people thought, but it would not come through "amateur negotiators" or any possible correspondence between George Sanders and Horace Greeley.[51]

On July 22, 1864, just as Christopher Memminger was resigning from the Treasury, the *Examiner* carried another satire in the style of its earlier pieces mimicking Casti and Swift. This one was a long report to the Emperor of Japan from his commissioner in Richmond, "the Capital of the Powerful Republic of the Southern Barbarians." It mocked Benjamin and Memminger, but it concentrated on the Tycoon, President Davis:

> As a military leader he has no superiors . . . and the remarkable skill and genius with which he directed the events that culminated at two localities entitled "Vicksburg" and "Missionary Ridge," have placed him high in the affections of his countrymen. . . .
>
> There are many persons among the Barbarians who violently oppose the conduct of the Tycoon; but they are bad and unpatriotic men, who are unwilling to lose their all that the Tycoon may have an opportunity of exhibiting his wonderful humanity. . . . Nevertheless he has his reward. The people love him devotedly. . . .

One imagines the visage of the already sickly and melancholy president turning yet grimmer when he read this piece, as he unquestionably did.

Although the Davis administration did not prevent Daniel and his *Examiner*, or other Southern papers, from printing what they would—at a time when Lincoln's administration in the North not infrequently closed down newspapers for alleged military leaks or seditious sentiment—a number of Union sympathizers were arrested and imprisoned in the South. One of these was John Minor Botts, the Unionist who as a Whig congressman had been the butt of Daniel's prewar satire. Botts was arrested by the Confederate authorities in March 1862 and held for two months. Later, paroled to his farm in Culpeper County, his livestock and crops were taken by Confederate units without compensation, and he was again arrested and held, for a briefer time, on the orders of Gen. J. E. B. Stuart.

In October 1863, Botts wrote a long letter to John Moncure Daniel, detailing his sufferings. Although Daniel had in the past mocked Botts, Botts wrote Daniel that the *Examiner* was the only Richmond paper that he thought might publish his account. Daniel would not do so. Botts was told that his letter took too many "hard hits" at the Confederacy.[52] Perhaps the real reason was that Daniel, himself the author of many hard hits at the Confederate government, had a continuing dislike for Botts the Unionist—a dislike that outweighed the possibility of a gentlemanly act toward a man who had lost much.

“Too Late Now . . .”

In the late summer of 1864, the focus of John Moncure Daniel’s attention changed abruptly, from the issues of the Confederate president and the future course of the war to the question of his own ethics and honor.[1] This had to do with the treasurer of the Confederacy.

The resignation of Christopher Memminger from the post of secretary of the treasury had left in place the treasury’s other senior officials, including the treasurer, Edward C. Elmore. Like Memminger, Elmore was a South Carolinian, although he had moved to Alabama shortly before the war and then joined the treasury sometime after Memminger did.[2] By the autumn of 1863, both the attorney general and the postmaster peneral were suggesting to Davis in private that it would be well to remove Elmore from office.[3]

As Daniel’s paper had indicated in its Swiftian satire of the previous year, there was a lot of gambling in wartime Richmond. Officials tried to crack down, but faro parlors flourished in which the house provided wine, food, and cigars gratis for those who could afford to gamble. On August 1, 1864, the *Examiner* reported that an unnamed high official of the Treasury had been using official funds to play at a Richmond faro table, had lost immense sums to professional gamblers, and had paid someone a bribe of ten thousand dollars to keep the story from leaking out. On August 3, Elmore wrote Daniel that the story inferred that he and his office were involved and that as a consequence there was gossip to that effect. Elmore asked if the expression “high official” referred to him. His accounts were being audited, and he was confident that he could leave office with untarnished honor and without the loss of even a dollar due either to carelessness or criminal conduct by any subordinate.

Daniel responded the following day. He had seen the article in question before publication; but since it did not contain the name of any person in particular, he had not given it his attention. The article had been written by the paper’s police reporter, who had received the information from a government detective. The detective had refused to name names but had said that the story was, in part, already publicly known and that the rest would soon come out through court examination of a prisoner already under arrest. Nothing in the article pointed to Elmore, continued Daniel, and if rumor pointed to him,

> I cannot oppose any effectual bar to the words of people who say what my newspaper has in no wise said, nor do I consider myself as obligated to attempt so doing. Nevertheless, I am sincerely desirous to prevent injustice or prejudice from arising out of any words, however vague, which may have been published by me; and this is what I propose to do for that end: You inform me that your accounts are about to be closed, and that their settlement will be satisfactory. When that is concluded I shall make it a special duty to publish the fact, as proving that the rumours, which you tell me are circulated to your prejudice, were evidently unfounded. This I think the most proper course. But, if you prefer it, I will cause a paragraph to be printed at once, stating that you have written to say that there has been no defalcation in the Treasury; that no one in your department has been authorized to bribe or silence the detectives; that the accounts of your department are under examination, and their settlement will prove them correct.

Either of these steps, Daniel wrote, would fulfill the requirements of justice and propriety. Elmore wrote back to Daniel on August 5 that the *Examiner* article was "scurrilous" and "gossiping," and the editor's proposal was unsatisfactory. If there had been reason to suspect an imminent criminal investigation, it would have been better to await a court's decision rather than create prejudice or suspicion or wound a gentleman's honor. Elmore trusted that "[Y]ou will not hesitate to confess regret in your paper that this article should have appeared under the circumstances; and that you know of no fact to justify the truth of such a charge, so far as my name and publick character are involved."

Elmore's response may have surprised Daniel. He had published—as another editor might have done then, and would certainly do today—a report based on what seemed to be a credible official source that, without naming names, pointed to criminal activity in high places. In 1864, a war was going on, but that did not lessen the possibility of a duel in Virginia. Was it possible that Elmore, knowing the editor had suffered a serious wound to his right arm, thought Daniel would never dare to fight him? Daniel responded to Elmore that he had offered a fair solution, and would never agree to make the statement of regret Elmore wanted.

After a week, Elmore wrote to Daniel on August 13 "to demand personal satisfaction for an unretracted insult." Lt. Thomas Taylor, who delivered the letter, would make the necessary arrangements for Elmore. Evidence suggests that the challenge did not come entirely as a surprise to Daniel; he had written out his last will and testament the day before. He apparently did not tell anyone that he was writing a will, perhaps because he did not want anyone to think he was concerned about what Elmore might do.[4]

Daniel knew what he needed to do after receiving Elmore's latest letter. He wrote Elmore on August 14 that the only scurrility in the matter was in Elmore's own letters. He had answered the first letter from Elmore, a stranger, in conciliatory style, making a fair offer. He could never have gone as far as Elmore had asked and written that he knew nothing that might justify a charge against Elmore,

> because I should have had to utter a falsehood to do so. I do know most distinctly, from gentlemen of unimpeached veracity, who saw you with their eyes, that you, the Confederate Treasurer, entrusted with the custody of vast sums, have been a frequenter of faro banks; that you played high and lost much, while your salary was only four or five thousand dollars. I do also know from the highest sources that the late Secretary, Mr. Memminger, hearing of this conduct, sent for you and questioned you; that you admitted the truth of the charge, and promised not to go any more. But statements that you continued to play having been sent him, he had with you a second communication, which resulted in your resignation. . . . I know, further, that you remain nominally in place only till the first of October, for the purpose of settling your accounts.
>
> Statements that there is a deficit of ten million in your accounts have lately been made to me.—But that information does not partake of the exact and authoritative character like the rest. I *do* know, however, that $75,000 worth of bonds have disappeared from the office of the Confederate Registry, whose Register is Robert Tyler: for he has advertised the fact. . . .
>
> [N]o merchant, no banker . . . could fail to feel the most painful suspicion if he *knew* that his cashier or bookkeeper, with a small salary, was a frequenter of gambling houses, especially if he heard of his betting $10,000 on a card, or losing $40,000 in a night. . . .
>
> I have the strongest moral conviction that you and other men in a like position, who are deliberately seeking and forcing this quarrel and duel on me, do it in the simple hope of drawing off the publick attention from criminal facts. . . . I feel certain that this is not an ordinary or legitimate affair of honour; but a violent abuse and perversion of the custom, by you and other culpable persons who put you forward.
>
> Nevertheless, I have determined to give you what you want. . . . [Y]ou and your class labour under the hallucination, because I was sincerely and openly desirous to avoid an issue, that my conduct was due to intimidation. Heaven permitting, I will teach you this lesson, that when gentlemen exhibit a disposition to peace, it does not necessarily follow that you may safely bully them. For these and other reasons you shall have the duel which you and your "class"

> have so pertinaciously sought to fix on me; and the rest of the matter is now in the hands of Mr. Pollard.

We do not know who the "other culpable persons" were. Nor can we be sure of the identity of Daniel's "highest sources," but his old friend, W. W. Crump, had been the assistant secretary of the treasury since 1861.[5]

John Moncure Daniel and Edward C. Elmore met with pistols at 5:30 A.M. on Tuesday, August 16, 1864, on a field several miles from Richmond, at Dill's farm along the Central Railroad in Henrico County. George Bagby reported that Daniel had a calm bearing that morning in the presence of death, for it was known that Elmore was no trifler. Because of the injury to his right arm from the minié ball, Daniel fired with his left hand. Perhaps because of this, he missed Elmore. (But we do not know whether Daniel in fact ever aimed at any opponent whom he faced in a duel.) Elmore did not miss. He fired and wounded Daniel in the right leg. For the second time in two years, the editor had to take to his bed to heal.

The following day, the *Examiner* (which had not yet published the letters between Daniel and Elmore, and had not reported the duel which was of course illegal) carried an editorial noting that the treasurer of the Confederacy had been charged with habitual gambling at faro tables. The public, said the paper, would be gratified if the treasurer ended up being acquitted, since the public's money had been passing through his hands. If he were found guilty, the public would be gratified to know that it was not the public's money with which he had gambled, but his own. In the latter case, the paper added, Elmore might be congratulated for possessing an ample fortune.

News of the duel began to circulate on Richmond streets within hours after it took place. After reports began to appear in other papers, the *Examiner* published on August 18 the texts of the letters between Daniel and Elmore. Mayor Joseph Mayo, who presided over the Mayor's Court, decided to look into the matter and called Elmore and Daniel's second, H. Rives Pollard, into court.[6] But it was Daniel's friend Edward A. Peticolas, whose mishandling of the "garlic letter" had caused Daniel trouble more than a decade earlier, who suffered for their friendship. Peticolas was arrested by the magistrates in Henrico County for refusing to answer questions about the duel on grounds that it might incriminate him. Another friend of Daniel, Patrick Henry Aylett, acted as counsel for Peticolas, whose silence was eventually found to fall within his constitutional rights.

There can be little doubt that most informed people in Richmond thought Daniel had acted ethically and honorably in this affair. One imagines that his reputation was, if anything, improved by it. But his health, never robust, had again suffered. For some time—we do not know how long—Daniel kept to his bed, and his newspaper was edited and managed by others, mainly John Mitchel. Unlike the earlier wound to his arm, Elmore's bullet broke no bone in Daniel's leg. Robert Hughes later wrote that it had struck Daniel some distance above the right ankle, and although it had broken neither tibia nor fibula, it had scraped both bones, causing him constant pain and intense suffering. Indeed, Hughes thought that the wound affected Daniel's whole nervous system and was the remote cause of his death.

Daniel must have taken some comfort a month after the duel when news came out that Edward Elmore had been indicted for betting at faro. Elmore sent a message to the commonwealth attorney—John Daniel's uncle, Raleigh T. Daniel—that he would plead guilty, and he was fined five hundred dollars.[7] However, treasury auditors apparently failed to find that he had lost any official funds.[8]

Sometime before the winter of 1864, Daniel was back at work and feeling well enough to tell George Bagby that he regretted that he was not still in the army. By then, Daniel said, he might have been a brigadier, perhaps even a major general. Bagby replied that Daniel had more influence as editor of the *Examiner* than he would as a general officer. "'True,' he answered; 'but what good is the *Examiner*, or any other paper, or all the papers in the Confederacy combined, doing? Besides, I like to command men. I love power.'"[9]

Daniel also commented to Bagby, perhaps around this time, that he was still young, although he would soon be forty, and that he knew no other young man who had better prospects and few who had done so well. He was, he said, worth almost $100,000 "in good money" (which could not have meant Confederate currency). He was not rich yet, but he expected to live a long life, and the *Examiner* would make him rich. And then, he said, "When I am rich I shall buy the old family estate in Stafford County, and shall add to it all the land for miles around. I shall build a house to my fancy, and, with my possessions walled in, I shall teach these people what they never knew—how to live like a gentleman."[10] These dreams were not destined to be fulfilled, and it seems that Daniel knew it. Bagby thought it was the only time he knew of Daniel indulging his fancy.

Daniel's scorn for Jefferson Davis continued unabated in what he said and wrote. For his part, Davis ignored the *Richmond Examiner* and its editor. But each morning before daylight the president's body servant went to the *Examiner* office for a copy of the paper; the servant indiscreetly told Daniel's staff that Davis did not get out of bed or eat his breakfast until he had read the paper through.[11] Indeed, almost everyone read the *Examiner* if they could get their hands on a copy. That included everyone from Abraham Lincoln to Confederate soldiers at the front to the aristocratic Elizabeth Van Lew, who lived in a Richmond mansion and was a Union spy. Daniel would have denied that he ever published military secrets, but one assumes that the *Examiner* (and other Richmond papers) provided Van Lew good leads.[12]

Beyond that, there can be no question that the newspapers both North and South were useful sources of military information. There are frequent references in Lee's dispatches to information gleaned from New York and Philadelphia papers, and in the North Lincoln and his generals looked carefully at the reports of the *Examiner* and other Richmond papers. However, Douglas Southall Freeman thought it was not the *Examiner* but its nonpartisan competitor the *Richmond Dispatch* that federal commanders drew on most frequently for information on Confederate troop movements.[13]

Sometimes it may have been a case not of *Examiner* reports providing intelligence to the North but of *Examiner* editorials putting a damper on Northern readers' confidence. On February 3, 1864, for example, the *New York Times* reprinted an editorial from the *Examiner* of January 21 that discussed the question of Southern military strength. Daniel's paper calculated that the Confederacy had at least a million men who could serve the war effort either at home or in the field. Of that million, half were fit for military service and four-fifths, or 400,000, could take the field. That was fifty thousand more men, said the paper, than the North had ever brought into actual service on the field. Moreover, one must add to the calculation of Southern manpower the many Southern blacks employed behind the lines building earthworks and maintaining railroads and thus freeing white men for fighting. The *Examiner* concluded that Southern reverses had come not from lack of manpower but from "want of valor in the people, or of capacity in the Government." That could well change, if responsible Southern people would carry out their duty with wisdom, honesty, and ability. One can imagine Northern readers worrying that just such a change might occur in the South.

Yet Daniel had good reason for his bitter comment to Bagby in late 1864 about the uselessness of the Confederate press. What good in the end was anything he wrote? Grant continued to besiege Petersburg, and all too often cannon fire could be heard in the capital. In September, Sherman took Atlanta, cut telegraph links to the North, and disappeared with his army into central Georgia. The *Examiner* wanted its readers to believe that the loss of Atlanta, although mortifying, did not matter militarily: "Atlanta was never a strategick point, so much as a point of honour. It was once, to be sure, called the 'Gate City'; but that gate has long been off its hinges; and is one of those passages that lead to nothing."[14]

It is strange to read in notices that appeared in the *Examiner* during the summer of 1864 and on into the autumn how people in Richmond strained to maintain normality. In August, a British journalist commented on how peaceful the city was, with ladies laughing and song drifting from open windows while two great armies confronted each another only a few miles away.[15] In September, the press noted that the mayor had returned from his usual sojourn at springs in the western mountains; no doubt some other residents of the capital had been with him. Exciting theatrical performances were advertised by Richmond theaters. Runaway slaves were sought, with much higher rewards than before. Blockade runners still brought in goods. Hebener and Company on Main Street advertised "920 yards English Gray Shirting Flannel," and Yerby's on Twelfth Street offered good sherry, Martel brandy, Scotch herring, Colman's Mustard, and fresh sardines—all at a price.[16] But for most people, goods and food were becoming ever more scarce; inflation was unchecked, and the *Examiner* no longer bothered to state its price on its masthead. Sally Brock Putnam recalled how in 1864 the city was growing rusty and dilapidated, with few houses getting painted and broken hinges and locks unrepaired because the painters and repairmen were in the field.

When Lincoln was reelected in November 1864, the *Examiner* did not try to deceive its readers. The United States government was going to remain in the hands of those who had vowed to destroy the Confederacy. The South must be victorious or be annihilated. Furthermore, asserted the paper with a brave tone, it was better that way.

But what did the South stand for in 1864? Its peculiar institution of slavery and the belief that black people were inferior? Daniel insisted that the South fought not for slavery, but for independence. At the same time, the *Examiner* mocked and castigated the North in early 1863 for its decision to enlist black soldiers, calling it "the insane malignity of fanaticism . . . driven to desperation."[17] But in 1864, there were Confederate generals and politicians who thought that the South, too, must help meet its manpower shortage by enlisting black soldiers. The Confederacy had long drafted blacks for service as manual laborers. In fact, as early as July 1861 the Virginia secession convention had passed an ordinance that allowed local governments to impress free black men for up to sixty days to work on fortifications and similar projects.

Arming blacks was far different, and the proposal involved arming slaves as well as free men. The *Examiner* was utterly frank with its readers that November. The South would surrender its position if it introduced black men to arms. If a black was fit to be a soldier, he was not fit to be a slave. To use black men as soldiers would be the first step to universal abolition.[18] Other papers, notably the *Dispatch*, agreed. Meanwhile, some Southerners were beginning to rethink the whole slavery question. Robert Kean of the Confederate War Department wrote in his diary on Christmas Day 1864, that perhaps it was best for slavery to be abolished if it would ensure the Confederacy's independence. On March 13, 1865, the Confederate Congress approved an act to authorize enlistment of slaves and free blacks for armed service in the Confederacy. Nine days later, two black companies could be seen drilling at Capitol Square in Richmond.

Throughout the autumn of 1864 the Richmond press wondered about the whereabouts of Gen. William Tecumseh Sherman. Jefferson Davis himself went to Georgia and told people that Sherman's army would be destroyed, just as Napoleon's army had been destroyed on its retreat from Moscow in 1812. However, in Georgia there was no fierce winter to freeze the ranks of the invader. In mid-October, the *Examiner* could still suggest that Sherman had fallen into an abyss in Georgia from which there was no escape.[19] In mid-November, however, there were reports that Sherman might be thirty miles south of Atlanta and headed for Macon, a good seventy miles beyond.[20] Then, in late December, came the awful news that Sherman had marched far beyond Macon to the sea and taken Savannah, and was turning northward to the Carolinas—and Virginia.

Even at this point, dueling was not finished in Richmond. In late November 1864, John Mitchel, now editing the *Examiner* on behalf of John Daniel, for some reason sent a challenge to Henry Foote, who was, like Daniel's paper, a fierce opponent of Jefferson Davis. The challenge was carried to Foote's house by a fellow congressman named Swan; Foote would not accept it. Swan, taking offense, assaulted Foote in his own house, until Foote's wife interposed and forced Swan to stop.[21] A senseless scuffle, it was perhaps a reflection of the desperate times.

The end was nearing for the Confederacy, and for John Moncure Daniel. At the end of December 1864, the *Examiner* could still claim that it hoped for a favorable outcome to the war, if only Robert E. Lee was made supreme commander in chief. With some delay, this was finally done. Meanwhile, late in January 1865, Daniel came down with pneumonia. He had had pneumonia at least once before, around the time of his departure for Italy in 1853. This time, again, the pneumonia abated, and he returned to work at the *Examiner*. However, he also had tuberculosis, and the disease began to affect both his lungs and his intestinal tract. Again, he took to his bed. Besides tuberculosis, he may have suffered to some degree from mercury poisoning. He liked to dose himself with the infamous "blue mass," a compound of mercury and chalk that was a favorite remedy for constipation.[22]

Daniel had already written out his last will before the duel with Elmore. The newspaper would go not to Mitchel or Hughes or Bagby or one of the Pollards but to his faithful business manager, R. F. Walker. We do not know whether Daniel said anything about this arrangement either to Walker or to his other colleagues. In any event, as Daniel's condition worsened, it was Walker who kept the *Examiner*'s operations and finances in order and Walker who spent long hours looking after his chief, sometimes returning home long after midnight or even, at Daniel's request, sleeping in an adjoining room. As for the rest of Daniel's possessions, he decided that his brother, Frederick, would receive two thousand dollars in gold. Three other brothers would receive a thousand dollars each, also in gold. Henry Rives Pollard, his second at the duel with Elmore, was to have his dueling pistols, and John Mitchel would get his set of the *Dictionnaire de la Conversation*, almost a library in itself. Everything else, including his residence and other properties, would go to Elizabeth R. Daniel, the eldest daughter of a man who had meant so much to him, his great-uncle, "the late Judge Peter V. Daniel who was my friend. This I give to her, not because of any personal regard of she to me, or I to her; but because she is poor, helpless, and the daughter of my friend."[23]

The sick man was now seeing few people aside from his doctor, female servant, and Walker. Daniel had already given George Bagby the key to his house, but he did not want to see him. Once he invited in a small group of prominent politicians headed by R. M. T. Hunter. It was Hunter to whom, as a U.S. senator, Daniel had turned long ago to seek a post abroad. Hunter was a Confederate senator, and the editor wanted to impress on him that the Confederate cause was hopeless, that the only course left was reconstruction on the best terms that the South could make.[24]

Hunter and his friends must have gone to see Daniel after (and to some extent as a consequence of) two visits that Francis P. Blair made to Richmond in January 1865. This was the same "Old Blair" who had once driven out to see Daniel fight a duel in Maryland and who was an influential adviser to Abraham Lincoln. Old Blair had come to Richmond to talk to Jefferson Davis about peace, and the result was the trip down the James River made by Senator Hunter together with Vice President Alexander Stephens and Assistant Secretary of War John Campbell (once a colleague of Peter Daniel on the U.S. Supreme Court) at the end of January 1865. On a ship anchored in Hampton Roads, the three met for some hours on February 3 with Abraham Lincoln and Secretary of State Seward. Lincoln made clear that he would not deal with the Confederacy as a separate entity; there could be no terms. The Confederate leaders returned to Richmond and reported to Jefferson Davis. The Confederate President went to a rally at the African church and gave a long and inspired—or was it feverish?—speech, insisting that the Confederate army could still bring Lincoln to sue for peace. Davis returned to speak at another rally three days later and insisted again that the South could win. Vice President Stephens was present when Davis spoke, but he did not speak. Stephens had just seen Lincoln and heard what Lincoln had to say, and he thought what Davis was saying was demented.[25] In February, too, Davis sent a special message to the Confederate Congress, assuring them that if Richmond should have to be abandoned, it would not mean the end of the Confederacy; rather, this could give rise to a renewed, and successful, effort by the South.

Lincoln's hard position, and Davis's apparent flight from reality, cannot have been a surprise to John Moncure Daniel as he lay in his house on Broad Street. In March, at Daniel's request, Robert Hughes wrote an article on the question of giving up Richmond. Daniel inserted a few lines in the proof-sheet; they were the last he ever wrote for his paper. The *Examiner* told its readers that Davis had been wrong in what he told the Congress; if Richmond were abandoned, the Confederate government would lose all its authority and the army would disintegrate. As

The ruins of Richmond, April 1865. Library of Congress.

the winter ended, news circulated in Richmond that Daniel's days were numbered. He had already lived longer than most people of that era who suffered from tuberculosis.[26] Rawlings, the physician, told Walker that his chief was going to die and suggested that Walker ask Daniel if he wanted to see a minister of the Gospel. One morning when Daniel seemed stronger and free of pain, Walker asked Daniel if he would like to see the Reverend Dr. Hoge, whom Daniel had spoken of as a sincere, good man. Daniel looked up, smiled, and said "Walker, *I am no woman!* I don't want anyone but yourself to come into this room except the doctor."[27]

Perhaps knowing that Daniel was nearing his end in mid-March, the commonwealth attorney dropped a libel suit against him that stemmed from what he had written about the Confederate treasurer.[28] It was also time for Daniel to make peace with alienated friends. He had experienced differences with Thomas Wynne, but the two were reconciled, and Daniel entrusted his diaries to Wynne, telling him that he also wanted him to have the little picture of Marie de Solms. One day, Wynne's young daughter brought Daniel a bouquet of the earliest spring flowers. Daniel took it in an emaciated hand and then laid it aside, murmuring, in a final gesture, "Too late now; too late!"[29]

It was, indeed, too late—for Daniel and for the Confederacy. John Moncure Daniel died at the age of thirty-nine on the thirtieth day of March 1865. Five days later, Abraham Lincoln entered fallen Richmond. Shortly afterward, Jefferson Davis and his generals gave up their struggle. But in Virginia, more flowers bloomed as the spring came on.

Postlude

After the fighting ended, life continued. Basil Gildersleeve, the professor of Greek who had enlisted as a private and been seriously wounded, tried later to speak for everyone in a sonnet on the loss of their editor:

We miss your pen of fire, whose cloven tongue
  Illum'd the good and blasted what was base.
  We miss you, fearless fighter for our race,
Your arrows words, your bow a will highstrung.
We miss you, for you tower'd from among
  The herd of writers with that careless grace
  That springs from undisputed strength. Your place
Is vacant still. Your bow is still uphung.
'Tis well. This were no time for you. The strings
  Of your proud heart forefelt the blow and broke;
    And when you died, 'twas better thus to die
Than live to see this swarm of crawling things,
  And burn with words that must remain unspoke
    Where 'art is tongue-tied by authority.'[1]

We can only guess whether John Daniel would have found the postwar scene quite so squalid as Professor Gildersleeve described it. There can be no doubt that Daniel would have smiled and declared himself unsurprised to see the masthead of his old enemy the *Richmond Whig* report on April 4, 1865, while Richmond's ruins still smoldered, that "the *Whig* will . . . be issued hereafter as a *Union paper*." John Campbell, the former Supreme Court justice who had met with President Lincoln in February to talk peace, met him again in occupied Richmond to discuss the full restoration of Virginia to the Union, but Lincoln was assassinated, and Reconstruction took a different course. That April, John Daniel's death went unnoticed by most Northern papers, but the *New York Times*, after castigating him for outdoing the most virulent of that traitorous Southern crew, concluded that "much of the good that he had aimed at and achieved in his better days will doubtless be remembered, when the terrible errors of his later years are forgotten."[2]

As enmity and hatred lessened, some Southerners went North to make their fortunes. John Mitchel, who soon began writing for the *New York Daily News*, was briefly imprisoned at Fortress Monroe for the positive account he gave of the Confederacy. Eventually, Mitchel returned to Ireland and was elected a member of the British Parliament, despite Prime Minister Benjamin Disraeli's attempt to bar him as a felon. Edward Pollard moved to New York and wrote copiously about the war. His works included a book about his brother, Henry Rives Pollard, who had been Daniel's second in the duel with Elmore and who, for a time, revived the *Richmond Examiner*, and who was killed in a postwar duel in Virginia.[3] Later, Edward Pollard sharply changed his views about the war, arguing that secession had been wrong and rejoicing that the North had won.[4]

Among others moving north was Roger Pryor, sometime Virginia editor and brigadier general, C.S.A., who ended his years as a justice of the New York State Supreme Court. Burton Harrison, Jefferson Davis's faithful private secretary, married young Constance Cary, whose writing John Daniel had once encouraged, and developed a successful law practice in New York City. John Pemberton, the general who had lost Vicksburg for the South, went back to Pennsylvania, whence he had come, and started farming for his living.

Some other former military leaders of the Confederacy enjoyed careers they could never have foreseen, including some, like Gen. William Loring, who went abroad to take top posts in the Egyptian army. A few of those who stayed home eventually won federal posts, at home and abroad. Fifteen years after Appomattox, in 1880, Gen. James Longstreet was appointed American minister to Turkey, and five years later Henry Jackson of Georgia, who had also been a Confederate general, became minister to Mexico. Gen. Joseph E. Johnston, whom Daniel had so admired, was elected to the U.S. Congress and then served as U.S. commissioner of railroads. That great guerrilla raider John Singleton Mosby, who had not surrendered even when Lee did, became the American consul at Hong Kong in 1878 and did admirable service uncovering a nest of official corruption. A number of Southern writers, although not moving to the North, found Northern publishers receptive to their works. Between 1866 and 1885, leading Northern publishers brought out almost two dozen works by John Esten Cooke, including his novel *Mohun*, with its portrait of John Moncure Daniel.

Only a couple of years after the war, George Bagby's sketch "John M. Daniel's Latch-Key" appeared, giving Daniel's faithful friend Thomas Wynne an idea: Why not attempt a full biography of the short, full life of that most interesting Virginian who had died so early? Wynne, who had become president of what remained

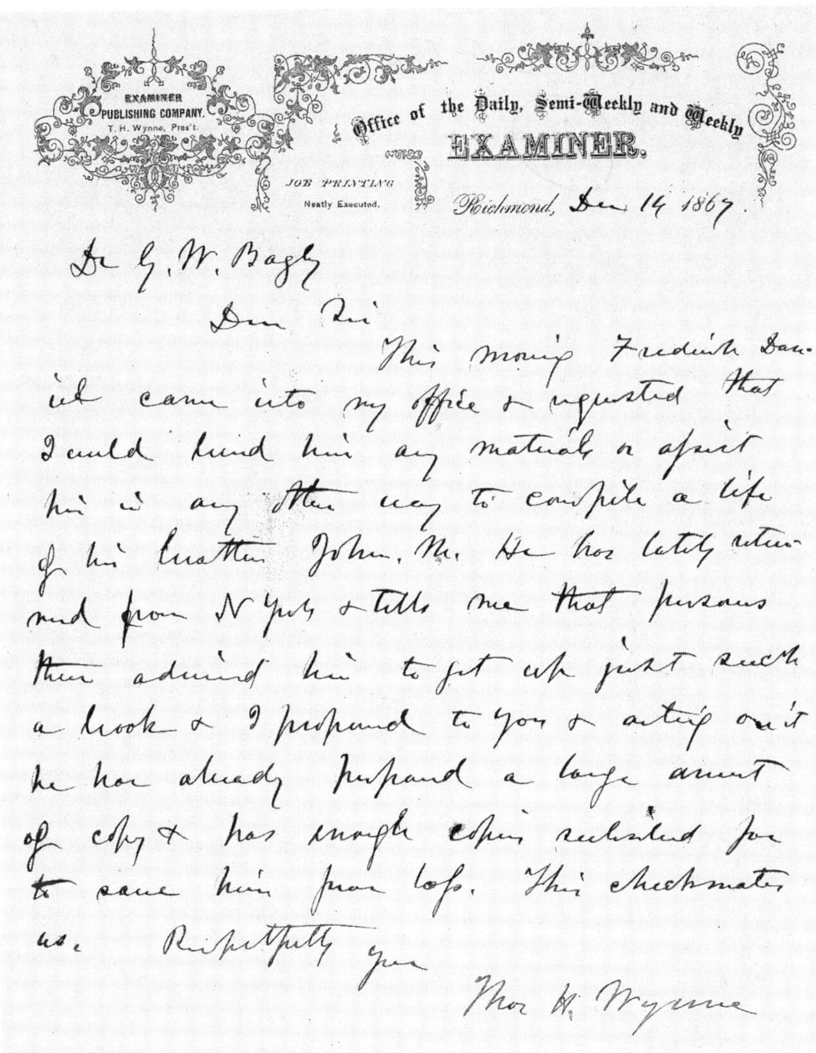

EXAMINER PUBLISHING COMPANY.
T. H. Wynne, Pres't.

Office of the Daily, Semi-Weekly and Weekly
EXAMINER.

JOB PRINTING
Neatly Executed.

Richmond, Dec 14 1867.

Dr G. W. Bagby

Dear Sir

This morning Frederick Daniel came into my office & requested that I would lend him any material or assist him in any other way to compile a life of his brother John M. He has lately returned from N York & tells me that persons there advised him to get up just such a book & I proposed to you & acting on it he has already prepared a large amount of copy & has enough copies subscribed for to save him from loss. This checkmates us.

Respectfully yours

Thos H. Wynne

The December 14, 1867, letter to George W. Bagby from Thomas H. Wynne, saying the planned book by Daniel's brother Frederick "checkmates us." Virginia Historical Society.

of the *Richmond Examiner*, wrote Bagby that he had in his hands almost a full set of the paper from Daniel's time there, as well as Daniel's journals beginning with the year 1844. Wynne also had in his possession the miniature on ivory that had hung in John's room, and he knew the full history of the lady's relationship with John. Frederick Daniel could help with the biography, Wynne thought, by adding his recollections from the years in Turin. All this would complement what Bagby had written of Daniel since they had met in 1861. Bagby could do the overall biography, and it might amount to one of the most curious and readable books published in years.[5]

When Thomas Wynne met with John Daniel's younger brother, Frederick, he learned that Frederick had decided to write his own book about his brother. Frederick Daniel had already met in New York with a number of people who had urged him to proceed, and he had begun to write what became *The Richmond Examiner During the War*. It was published privately in 1868 by the author, who had obtained enough orders to make some profit. It was not a fine work, just an incomplete compendium of *Examiner* articles that appeared during the Civil War, plus a brief and not entirely accurate fifteen-page memoir of John Daniel. But, said Wynne, "This checkmates us," and he and Bagby dropped their own idea for what might have been a better book.[6] Thomas Wynne, who had not enjoyed continuing prosperity, died seven years later, and his books and papers, which included the journals of John Moncure Daniel, were dispersed.

Ten years after the war ended, John's cousin Moncure Daniel Conway returned from England and made his first visit to Stafford County since the 1850s. He found that his relatives still lived in their respectable old houses, but they were now very poor. They had just one or two cows and horses, and they raised much of their own food in vegetable gardens. There was a labor shortage, since most blacks had moved out of the countryside to Fredericksburg and Richmond. Still, Conway wrote, his relations "all seem serene & cheerful in their poverty, and all glad to be rid of Slavery."[7] It was hardly a scene that Daniel would have imagined when he had dreamed of someday rebuilding the family home at Crow's Nest.

Meanwhile, James Mitchell Daniel, who had gone out to Texas before the war as a civil engineer, became a leading citizen of Paris, Texas, and an owner of silver mines in Colorado and Mexico. Frederick Daniel, who also ended his days in Paris, Texas, continued to write, no longer as his brother John's amanuensis but on his own. One of several pieces on Virginia that he contributed to *Harper's New Monthly Magazine* two decades after the war, describes his visit to White House and Romancoke, neighboring Virginia estates owned by the youngest son of Robert E. Lee, where prosperity had returned and "the silver, porcelain, and glass in ordinary use . . . antedate the republic."[8] Although he did not say so, Frederick Daniel must have lamented the destruction of his own ancestors' once prosperous estate at Crow's Nest. However, the Civil War did not end success in the Daniel family, and there are successful and prosperous Daniels today, including some in Washington and Virginia, as well as a number of equally successful and prosperous Moncures.

In the course of the next century and a half, the United States sent one other Virginian as its chief diplomatic representative to Italy: Thomas Nelson Page, who served creditably as ambassador in Rome from 1913 to 1919. Page was born in 1853, shortly before John Daniel was appointed chargé d'affaires at Turin. At nine, he had watched Stonewall Jackson's army pass the Page family plantation, en route to the Battle of Gaines' Mill where Daniel fell wounded.[9] Page became a Richmond lawyer, contributed pieces to a Richmond newspaper, edited the stories of Daniel's friend George W. Bagby, and eventually became known for his own black dialect stories.

The lovely lady in Daniel's miniature, Marie de Solms, lived for many years after marrying Urbano Rattazzi in Turin in 1863. In 1867, when the new Kingdom of Italy had moved its capital from Turin to Florence and Rattazzi was prime minister, the news reached Florence that Marie Rattazzi had published in France a novel called *Le Chemin du Paradis*. The novel described in detail a city that she called "Bicheville," a place full of every sort of vice, which was clearly meant to be Florence. Scandal erupted. Marie's friend John Daniel had scandalized the Italians with a frank letter not meant to be made public, but her novel was deliberately published. A Florentine nobleman, the Marchese di Pepoli, recognized himself as one of the characters in Bicheville and demanded satisfaction from the prime minister. A duel might have ensued if a jury of honor had not decided that it was impossible while Rattazzi remained in office.[10]

What of John Moncure Daniel's immediate successor at Turin, George Perkins Marsh, the Vermonter whom Lincoln had appointed in early 1861 to the newly upgraded position of minister to Italy? Marsh, who sailed to Europe just after the attack on Fort Sumter, never came back to America. He died as minister to Italy during a visit to Tuscany in 1882, after twenty-one years at his post, still a record for a chief of an American diplomatic mission. Marsh was decidedly more fortunate than Daniel as regarded leaks from private letters. In August 1865, Minister Marsh wrote home to Spencer Baird, his friend at the Smithsonian Institution (and earlier a supporter of Agassiz's racist polygenesis theory), that Florence, which had recently replaced Turin as the capital of Italy, was a place of "Vile climate, detestably corrupt society, infinite frivolity."[11] Fortunately for Marsh, Baird kept the letter to himself. Marsh was less fortunate five years later, when the State Department published in its series *Foreign Relations of the United States* a secret dispatch from Marsh commenting that Italy's government followed the dictation of Napoleon III. However, Marsh weathered that storm, just as Daniel had done in the furor after the garlic letter.

Daniel never published a book. Marsh published a number of books, both before he went to Italy and during his long years there. The best known of them, a pioneering work on the environment titled *Man and Nature*, is still in print. In contrast, the existing copies of the *Richmond Examiner*, the work of a fiery editor who died before he was forty, are increasingly brittle, torn, and unread.

Daniel's friends have long since gone to their graves. As long as they lived, they remembered him. Over three decades after Daniel died, Basil Gildersleeve, the

Hellenist, wrote an account of the 1897 Olympic games for the *Atlantic Monthly*. He suddenly veered from his subject to add a reminiscence of John M. Daniel—"the foremost editor in the Confederate States"—talking to him in Richmond about the power of the press.[12]

There still stands a tall stone shaft in Hollywood Cemetery in Richmond erected long ago over the grave of John Moncure Daniel, who was "Of Stafford Co. Virginia and for many years Editor of THE RICHMOND EXAMINER."[13] He lies by his great-uncle, the Justice, whom he loved. Nearby rest two presidents of the United States, James Monroe and John Tyler, as well as Daniel's old colleague from his diplomatic days in Europe, John Y. Mason. At the western end of the cemetery, some distance from John Moncure Daniel—but would either he or Jefferson Davis have thought that distance great enough?—lies the only president of the Confederate States of America.

Acknowledgments

I have had help and encouragement from many people and institutions while writing this book, and I can name at least some of them here. Staige Blackford, editor of the *The Virginia Quarterly Review,* kindly accepted an article I had written about John Moncure Daniel—after he had published an article I wrote on Daniel's diplomatic successor, George Perkins Marsh—and I began to envisage a possible book on Daniel. John Hubbell, director of the Kent State University Press and himself a historian of the Civil War, agreed to my proposal for a Daniel biography, although my previous book for Kent State in no way proved my worth as a biographer or historian.

The Virginia Historical Society awarded me an Andrew W. Mellon Fellowship, which greatly facilitated my research in the rich and well-cataloged holdings of the Society. The Society's professional staff did all they could to help me. I must express my thanks to Frances Pollard, assistant director for Library Services, and her staff; to E. Lee Shepard, assistant director for Manuscripts and Archives; and particularly to Nelson D. Lankford, assistant director for Publications and Education and editor of the *Virginia Magazine of History and Biography*, who took time to read my manuscript and offered a number of useful suggestions. Sara Bearss, the editor of the *Dictionary of Virginia Biography*, also agreed to read the manuscript. She has herself done considerable research into Daniel's years in Italy, and I was relieved when she found no serious lacunae in my own work. Brent Tarter, assistant director for Publications and Educational Affairs of the Library of Virginia, kindly introduced me to the rich collections of the Library that, in his day, John Moncure Daniel valued highly. Elsewhere in Virginia, the staffs of the Anderman Library at the University of Virginia in Charlottesville and of the Swem Library at the College of William and Mary in Williamsburg helped me locate valuable materials in their collections on John Daniel and his family, friends, and other contemporaries.

One day on a visit to Houston, I called on Lynda Crist, editor of *The Papers of Jefferson Davis,* who then and subsequently provided me key materials relating to Daniel and his relationship to Davis. Milton Gustafson of the National Archives at College Park, Maryland, pointed me to many useful sources, above all the old letterbooks of the American Legation in Turin with their wealth of Daniel's personal as well as official correspondence. (George Bagby indicates that Daniel took home with him from Turin still another set of "handsomely bound volumes" of his dispatches, but these have vanished, as have his diaries.) The professional staff members of the Library of Congress in Washington—especially in the Manuscript Division, the Main Reading Room, and the Newspaper and Current Periodical Room—have always been helpful in answering my many requests. At a time when I feared I had found all of John Daniel's correspondence that still existed, Olga Tsapina of the Huntington Library in California turned up a number of valuable items. In Italy, the staff of the Archivio Storico Diplomatico at the Ministry of Foreign Affairs in Rome gave me full access to and guided me through their priceless records. This also gave me the valuable opportunity to meet Pietro Pastorelli, professor of the history of international relations at the University of Rome, who oversees the Ministry's archives and heads the Ministry's commission for the publication of Italian diplomatic documents. Isabella Massabo Ricci, director of the Archivio di Stato in Turin, kindly provided several key documents. I am equally grateful to Daniela Masci of the American embassy in Rome, who provided the introductions and documentation required to gain me access to Italian records. The staff of the Virginia Room in the Arlington Public Library kindly made available several works from their special collection. And I owe very much to Jo Laird and her colleagues at the Crested Butte Library, who made it possible for me to receive, through interlibrary loans, a steady stream of scarce books in a small mountain town in Colorado.

It is no exaggeration to say that every archivist and librarian I have turned to, from California to Scotland, has been more helpful than I could have expected. Such people form, I am convinced, one of the best classes of human beings.

When I began to interest myself in John Moncure Daniel I knew next to nothing about Stafford County, where he was born and raised, even though my own family had come from another Tidewater county. Daniel's distant kinsman Thomas M. Moncure Jr., the longtime clerk of court in Stafford County, was generous with his time in introducing me to the county, to a number of its people, and, not least, to the court house records. Skipper Steely of Paris, Texas, a distant relation of James Mitchell Daniel, provided me a considerable amount of information on the Daniels. Jerrilynn Eby, well-known historian of Stafford County, took time to answer my questions and introduced me to George Gordon, whose service as commissioner of the revenue in Stafford began in 1940. D. P. Newton of the White Oak Museum in Stafford, which has an impressive collection of arms and artifacts from local encampments and battlefields, brought to my attention a number of Union wartime records. Harold Wiggins of the U.S. Army Corps of Engineers provided canoes for a Saturday paddle to the old Daniel home at Crow's Nest, as well as good company and much information on local archaeology, wildlife, vegetation, and history. As this is written, Crow's Nest has been proposed for a national fish and wildlife refuge. I have made clear to the U.S. Fish and Wildlife Service that although I cannot speak to ecological considerations, I see strong historical reasons to preserve this site for the nation.

Whatever errors of fact exist in this book are of course entirely my own responsibility, and my judgment of John Moncure Daniel is also entirely my own.

While I am grateful to the staff of the Library of Congress for much help, I want to make clear my concern over the condition of one group of Library holdings. The Library has devoted much effort to duplicating on microfilm its holdings of old periodicals and newspapers like the *Richmond Examiner*. At the same time, it continues to hold what I understand to be about thirty thousand bound volumes of the original old newspapers. Of these volumes, fully one-third, I have been told by Library staff, are in poor condition. I have seen many of them in deteriorating bindings. Surely the Library management can seek, and Congress should provide, adequate funding to preserve these volumes properly. Microfilms are valuable and useful, but the original newspapers are a part of our national heritage and need to be protected.

My wife, Mary Jane, not only tolerated my tiresome concentration on John Daniel over many months but did not cease to remind me that I needed to produce a readable book as well as one that was well documented. I am glad that she did, and I hope that I have.

Notes

PROEM

1. The text for the Reverend Dr. Hoge's sermon was reported in the *Richmond Whig* for April 1, 1865. Richmond weather for each day of March 1865 was recorded by J. B. Jones in *A Rebel War Clerk's Diary at the Confederate States Capital* (1866; reprint, Alexandria, Va.: Time-Life Books, 1982), 2:436–63. The *Examiner* reported how "Celia was accommodated with twenty-five lashes." Hoge was not only a minister but a slaveholder, as described in the memorial to him by Robert P. Kerr in *Southern Historical Society Papers* 30 (1902): 262–64. The account of Daniel's death is based on George W. Bagby, "John M. Daniel's Latch-Key," in *The Old Virginia Gentleman, and Other Sketches* (Richmond: Dietz Press, 1948), 141–42.

2. Christopher Andrew and Vasili Mitrokhin, *The Sword and the Shield: The Mitrokhin Archive and the Secret History of the KGB* (New York: Basic Books, 1999), 475–83.

3. Harrison A. Trexler, "The Davis Administration and the Richmond Press, 1861–1865," *Journal of Southern History* 16.2 (May 1950): 185. Trexler was professor of history at Southern Methodist University.

4. Douglas Southall Freeman, *The South to Posterity* (New York: Charles Scribner's Sons, 1939), 26–27.

5. This is the judgment of *The Cambridge History of English and American Literature*, v. XVI, Chapter 21 ("Newspapers, 1775-1860"), quoted on the Internet at <www.bartleby.com/226/1210.html>.

6. John Moncure, "John M. Daniel, the Editor of the Examiner," *The Sewanee Review* 15.3 (July 1907): 257.

CHAPTER 1

1. I am indebted to Thomas M. Moncure Jr., longtime clerk of court in Stafford County and a distant relative of John Moncure Daniel (hereafter in notes JMD), for helping me to discover Stafford and its history and for providing me a wealth of information, not least his own brief history of the county. See also *Jamestown Narratives*, ed. Edward Wright Haile (Champlain, Va.: RoundHouse, 1998); Richard H. Dillon, *North American Indian Wars* (New York: Facts on File, Inc., 1983); Bernard W. Sheehan, *Savagism and Civility: Indians and Englishmen in Colonial Virginia* (New York: Cambridge Univ. Press, 1980); and *Virginia: A Guide to the Old Dominion* (Richmond: Virginia State Library and Archives, 1992), 346–47.

2. Horace Edwin Hayden, *Virginia Genealogies* (1891; reprint, Washington, D.C.: Rare Book Shop, 1931), 301.

3. Nell Marion Nugent, ed., *Cavaliers and Pioneers: Abstracts of Virginia Land Patents and Grants 1623–1666* (Baltimore, Md.: Genealogical Publishing, 1963), 241.

4. Hayden, *Virginia Genealogies,* 297-301. The marriage is listed on page 24 of the copy of the Overwharton Parish Register, section 2, George Harrison Sanford King Papers, Virginia Historical Society (hereafter VHS), Richmond, Va.

5. Hayden, *Virginia Genealogies,* 292. In more recent years the leading Stafford County genealo-

gist, George H. S. King, looked carefully into the Travers and Daniel family history without, it seems, proving a line back to ancestors in England. King's extensive files are in the Virginia Historical Society.

6. See W. W. Abbot and Dorothy Twohig, eds., *The Papers of George Washington*, Colonial Series (Charlottesville: Univ. Press of Virginia, 1983–98), 7 (1996): 219–25; 8 (1998): 62–65.

7. Peter Daniel and Travers Daniel to Francis Fauquier, Oct. 5, 1765, quoted in Hayden, *Virginia Genealogies*, 296.

8. Customs records from the little port of Dumfries, Virginia, between 1795 and 1800, show the *Crow*, twenty-four tons burden, belonging to Travers Daniel of Stafford County, William Simmons, master. Stack 10E3, row 17, cap. 6, shelf 6, RG 36, National Archives and Records Administration (hereafter NARA). If the vessel's tonnage was calculated under the system introduced in 1773, it might have been about eighty-five feet in length, with a beam of twenty-five feet. Peter Kemp, ed., *The Oxford Companion to Ships and the Sea* (New York: Oxford Univ. Press, 1976), 876. See also Howard I. Chapelle, *History of American Sailing Ships* (New York: Bonanza Books, 1982), 219–72.

9. For a plan of the house taken from an 1805 insurance policy, see Jerrilynn Eby, *They Called Stafford Home* (Fredericksburg, Va.: Heritage Books, 1997), 192. Bricks found at the site with glass fused to them suggest that the house burned. The remains of the *Crow* may still lie nearby, offshore. George Gordon, Stafford County's commissioner of revenue from 1940 to 1997, told the author on March 17, 2000, that in 1940 an old man named Dobson told him of having seen the hulk of a great black schooner that went down off Crow's Nest with all sails set. Supposedly the master decided to drive it aground to keep the Union forces from seizing it.

10. Selwood was an ancient forest in the west of England, still recalled in current place names. Conceivably it was the name of a family farm in Somerset or Devon that was still remembered after the family had emigrated to Virginia. Information from Mr. David Craig and his Web site <www.strum.co.uk/twilight/selwood.htm>.

11. Netti Schreiner-Yantis and Florence Speaman Love, *The 1787 Census of Virginia* (Springfield, Va.: Genealogical Books in Print), 2:998.

12. Moncure Daniel Conway, *Autobiography, Memories and Experiences* (Boston and New York: Houghton, Mifflin, 1904), 1:8. A biographic sketch of Sharp may be found in the Spartacus Internet Encyclopedia at <www.spartacus.schoolnet.co.uk/REsharp.htm>.

13. Ibid., 7. See also, William Meade, *Old Churches, Ministers and Families of Virginia* (Philadelphia: J. B. Lippincott, 1857), 2:197–205.

14. Sermon dated July 28, 1756, George Harrison Sanford King Papers, Section 2, folder "Moncure," VHS.

15. *A Guidebook to Virginia's Historical Markers*, compiled by John S. Salmon (Charlottesville: Univ. Press of Virginia, 1996), 28.

16. As late as 1940 there were only 9,548 residents of the county. See "On the Edge - A Short History of Stafford County," by Thomas M. Moncure, Jr., in the booklet for the dedication of Stafford County's new judicial center on June 12, 1993. By 2000, however, the population had multiplied ten times, to over 95,000. See "Applying the Brakes in Stafford County," *Washington Post*, Mar. 6, 2000.

17. Simon Bennett, assistant archivist of the University of Glasgow, has informed the author that the graduation of John Moncoeur Daniel in 1791 is confirmed in a Roll of Graduates 1727–1897, published in 1898. There is a letter dated to about 1790 addressed to "Moncoeur Daniel Esqr., Tontine, Glasgow," Section 1, Daniel Family Papers 1790–1854, VHS. (The Tontine was a Glasgow hotel; the building still stands.) Conceivably the young man found relatives in Scotland who preferred Moncoeur over Moncure. He did not use the Moncoeur spelling in America.

18. In 1919, the Reverend Dr. A. Hord reported that the 1806–9 Order Book of Stafford County included a list of men who had served as county justices; eighteenth on the list was "John M. Daniel (Removed from the State)." *Virginia Magazine of History and Biography* (hereinafter *VMHB*) 19 (1911): 199.

19. Hayden, *Virginia Genealogies,* 308.

20. *National Cyclopaedia of American Biography* (New York: James T. White, 1924), 8:169. See also Harry Wright Newman, *The Stones of Poynton Manor* (Washington: DAR Library, 1996).

21. Hayden, *Virginia Genealogies,* 315. Anne Turkos and Richard Behles, university archivists of the University of Maryland, kindly verified the fact of Daniel's graduation in 1822.

22. George Harrison Stanford King, "Copies of Extant Wills from Counties Whose Records Have Been Destroyed," *Tyler's Quarterly Historical and Genealogical Magazine* 31.4 (Apr. 1950): 268.

23. The 1827 transactions are recorded in Stafford County deed book GG, pp. 421–22, 431–33; the 1838 transactions are in deed book LL, pp. 245–46, 283.

24. Hayden, *Virginia Genealogies,* 313. The license is in Section 9, Daniel Family Papers, VHS.

25. Personal memoirs of James Mitchell Daniel (1833–1916), younger brother of JMD, kindly provided to the author by James Mitchell Daniel's cousin Skipper Steely of Paris, Texas.

26. Robert W. Hughes, "John Moncure Daniel: His Times and Career," *Baltimorean,* Jan. 10, 1885, 1.

27. Peter V. Daniel to John M. Daniel, Apr. 13, 1858, Turin Legation letterbooks, 166:107–31, RG 84, NARA.

28. Raleigh T. Daniel to Dr. John M. Daniel, May 21, 1833, Section 4, Daniel Family Papers, VHS.

29. Raleigh T. Daniel to Dr. John M. Daniel, Jan. 25, 1837, Section 4, Daniel Family Papers, VHS.

30. "I have accepted your draft at 30 days. I hope you will be able to meet it." Raleigh T. Daniel to Dr. John M. Daniel, Jan. 24, 1842, Section 4, Daniel Family Papers, VHS.

31. Frederick S. Daniel, *The Richmond Examiner During the War* (1868; reprint, New York: Arno and The New York Times, 1970), 218.

32. John A. Garraty and Mark C. Carnes, eds., *American National Biography* (New York: Oxford Univ. Press, 1999), 6:86.

33. Raleigh T. Daniel to Dr. John M. Daniel, July 29, 1832, Section 4, Daniel Family Papers, VHS.

34. JMD to Henry A. Washington, undated, folder 4, Henry A. Washington Papers, VHS.

35. Moncure Daniel Conway, *Testimonies Concerning Slavery* (London: Chapman and Hall, 1864), 28.

36. Personal memoirs of James Mitchell Daniel.

37. Jean N. [Daniel] Crane to Dr. John M. Daniel, July 11, 1840, Section 5, Daniel Family Papers.

38. Raleigh T. Daniel to Dr. John M. Daniel, July 20, 1845, Section 4, Daniel Family Papers, VHS. Young John was presumably "coming in" to Richmond from Justice Daniel's suburban home, Spring Farm. Later the Justice built a house at 612 East Grace Street in Richmond, which was his residence until he died. Frank Burnette Jr., "Peter V. Daniel: Agrarian Justice," *VMHB* 62.3 (July 1954): 289.

39. Raymond K. Cooley, "John Moncure Daniel, Editor of the Richmond Examiner and Gadfly of the Confederacy" (Master's thesis, Old Dominion University, 1973), 23.

40. Frank Burnette Jr., "Peter V. Daniel: Agrarian Justice," *VMHB* 62.3 (July 1954): 298–300.

41. John P. Frank, *Justice Daniel Dissenting* (Cambridge: Harvard Univ. Press, 1964), vii–ix.

42. Ibid., 89–90.

43. Thomas H. Wynne wrote to John Daniel on April 30, 1854 that the Miss Seddon who had just died at the age of 85 was "the lady who urged her brother to a fatal duel." Daniel Papers, Huntington Library, San Marino, Calif.

44. Robert Reid Howison, "Twice Forty Years of American Life," pp. 102–4, Manuscripts and Rare Books Department, Swem Library, College of William and Mary (hereafter W&M), Williamsburg, Va. Seddon was the uncle of James Alexander Seddon who became the Confederate secretary of war. Howison could not recall what year the duel was fought, but Stafford County genealogist George H. S. King established the date as November 5, 1808, from Seddon's tombstone and a report in the *Fredericksburg Virginia Herald.* "Duels" folder, section 2, King Papers, VHS.

45. W. J. Cash, *The Mind of the South* (New York: Alfred A. Knopf, 1941), ix, 3.

46. When Travers Daniel died in 1824, his obituary said that he "descended from an ancestor who was a captain in the Royal Army in the Civil Wars." Hayden, *Virginia Genealogies,* 304.

47. John M. Daniel, Turin, to Peter V. Daniel, Sept. 12, 1857, Turin letterbook, 166:210; and Jan. 1, 1860, 168:85. For Mason's career, see *National Cyclopaedia of American Biography,* 6:7.

48. As noted later, when John Daniel arrived at the American legation in Turin in 1853 he found that his British counterpart was James Hudson, whom he had known as secretary of the British legation in Washington. Hudson's tour of duty in Washington ended in 1843, when Daniel was at most eighteen. Sir Leslie Stephen and Sir Sidney Lee, eds., *The Dictionary of National Biography* (London: Oxford Univ. Press, 1950), 10:149.

49. Information from genealogical files of Mary Vivian Daniel (1874–1960), granddaughter of Dr. JMD, provided to the author by Skipper Steely of Paris, Texas.

50. Stafford County deed book MM, 395–97.

51. *National Cyclopaedia of American Biography,* 5:531.

52. John T. Kneebone et al., eds., *Dictionary of Virginia Biography* (Richmond: Library of Virginia, 1998), 1:331–32.

53. Dr. John M. Daniel to Raleigh T. Daniel, January 28, 1844, Section 4, Daniel Family Papers, VHA.

54. Raleigh T. Daniel to Dr. John M. Daniel, July 20, 1845, Section 4, Daniel Family Papers, VHS.

55. Hayden, *Virginia Geneologies,* 315, gives the year of the doctor's death as around 1845. The doctor's son, James Mitchell Daniel, recalled in his memoirs that his father had died in 1844. It seems clear that he died in mid-1845.

56. Conway, *Autobiography,* 1:60; Frederick S. Daniel, *Richmond Examiner,* 218.

CHAPTER 2

1. Virginius Dabney, *Richmond: The Story of a City* (Garden City, NY: Doubleday, 1976), 133.

2. W. Asbury Christian, *Richmond: Her Past and Present* (1913; reprint, Spartanburg, SC: The Reprint Company, 1973), 20–21.

3. 1840 census figures from <www.census.gov/population/documentation/twps0027/tab07.txt>.

4. J. Malcolm Bridges, "Industry & Trade," *Richmond: Capital of Virginia* (Richmond: Whittet & Shepperson, 1938), 72.

5. John Brook Mordecai, "Travel and Communications," *Richmond: Capital of Virginia,* 277.

6. Emeline Lee Stearns, "John M. Daniel and the Confederacy" (Master's thesis, Univ. of Chicago, 1928), 3. The society did not have its own quarters but used the premises of the library. A report of the 1850 meeting of the Richmond Library Company (*Richmond Whig,* May 13, 1850) states that "a small additional sum may be expected from the 'Patrick Henry Society,' who hold their meetings in our Library room."

7. George F. Mellen, "Famous Southern Editors: John Moncure Daniel," *Methodist Review* (July–Aug. 1897): 381.

8. This was the figure given for the library several years later, in *Montague's Richmond Directory and Business Advertiser for 1850–1851* (Richmond: J. W. Randolph, 1851), 19, which added that "for want of encouragement, it is not in a very flourishing condition."

9. Robert W. Hughes, "John Moncure Daniel: His Times and Career," *Baltimorean,* Jan. 10, 1885, 1.

10. Conway, *Autobiography,* 1:60.

11. Personal memoirs of James Mitchell Daniel.

12. Hughes, "John Moncure Daniel," 1.

13. Box 5, folder 42, Charles Campbell Papers, W&M.

14. Letter of August 28, 1846, box 6, folder 8, Campbell Papers, W&M.

15. Letter of October 1, 1846, box 6, folder 19, Campbell Papers, W&M.

16. Imaged text available on Internet at <http://moa.umdl.umich.edu/browse.author/d.6.html>. In the review, Daniel gave particular praise to his putative forebear Sir Walter Raleigh as "the Father of Virginia."

17. Howison, "Twice Forty Years," 124.

18. *Biographical Directory of the American Congress 1774–1996* (Alexandria, Va.: CQ Staff Directories, 1997), 37. Census figures are available on the Internet at <http://fisher.lib.virginia.edu/census>.

19. Thos. H. Wynne to G. W. Bagby, Dec. 5, 1867, in Bagby Family Papers, VHS.

20. Frederick S. Daniel, *Richmond Examiner,* 218–19.

21. A. N. Wilkinson, "John Moncure Daniel," *Richmond College Historical Papers* 1.1 (June 1915): 74.

22. Contributions to Richmond newspapers were often not signed but readers often knew, or thought they knew, who wrote them.

23. *Southern Planter* 1.1 (Jan. 1841): 1.

24. Daniel W. Crofts, "Late Antebellum Virginia Reconsidered," *VMHB* 107.3 (Summer 1999): 253–86; William G. Shade, *Democratizing the Old Dominion* (Charlottesville: Univ. Press of Virginia, 1996).

25. Edgar Allan Poe to Peter D. Bernard, Mar. 24, 1843, and to Thomas Gilliat Mackenzie, Apr. 22, 1843, <www.eapoe.org/works/letters>.

26. J. H. Whitty, ed., *The Complete Poems of Edgar Allan Poe* (Boston: Houghton Mifflin, 1917), xlviii–l.

27. A. N. Wilkinson, "John Moncure Daniel," 74.

28. *Southern Literary Messenger,* Jan. 1847, 14.

29. *Southern Planter,* Jan. 1848, 7.

30. Virginius Dabney, *Richmond: The Story of a City,* 41, quoting from the *Examiner.*

31. Stanley Harrold, *The Abolitionists and the South, 1831–1861* (Lexington: Univ. Press of Kentucky, 1995), 3, 154.

32. John M. Daniel to Charles Campbell, Sept. 24, 1847, box 6, folder 81, Campbell Papers, W&M.

33. Charles Campbell to John M. Daniel, Sept. 27, 1847, box 6, folder 83, Campbell Papers, W&M.

CHAPTER 3

1. Emeline Lee Stearns, "John M. Daniel," 5; Robert W. Hughes, *Editors of the Past* (Richmond: W. E. Jones, 1897); Virginius Dabney, *Pistols and Pointed Pens* (Chapel Hill, N.C.: Algonquin Books, 1987), 23.

2. Lester J. Cappon, *Virginia Newspapers 1821–1935* (New York: D. Appleton-Century, 1936), 7–8.

3. *Richmond Examiner,* Nov. 4, 1847.

4. Cooley, "John Moncure Daniel," 21.

5. Quoted in Dabney, *Pistols and Pointed Pens,* xvii.

6. W. Asbury Christian, *Richmond,* 23, 49–50.

7. Carl R. Osthaus, *Partisans of the Southern Press* (Lexington: Univ. Press of Kentucky, 1994), 21.

8. Letter from William Scott in the *Enquirer,* Apr. 14, 1846.

9. W. Asbury Christian, *Richmond,* 154; Dabney, *Pistols and Pointed Pens,* ch. 2.

10. Bettina F. McKinnell, "A Check-List of Richmond, Virginia Imprints from 1841 through 1852 with a Historical Introduction" (Master's thesis, Catholic University of America, 1956), 6.

11. David Hackett Fischer, *Bound Away: Virginia and the Westward Movement* (Charlottesville: Univ. Press of Virginia, 2000), 137.

12. David M. Potter, *The Impending Crisis 1848–1861* (New York: Harper & Row, 1976), 6.

13. *Examiner,* July 3, 1849.

14. Edwin DeLeon, *Thirty Years of My Life on Three Continents* (London: Ward and Downey, 1890), 1:38–60.

15. Robert W. Johannsen, *Stephen A. Douglas* (New York: Oxford Univ. Press, 1973), 344–45.

16. The famous boxer, it will be recalled, was John L. Sullivan.

17. Edward L. Widmer, *Young America: The Flowering of Democracy in New York City* (New York: Oxford Univ. Press, 1999), 12ff.

18. Robert E. May, "A 'Southern Strategy' for the 1850s: Northern Democrats, the Tropics, and Expansion of the National Domain," *Louisiana Studies* 14.4 (1975): 333–59.

19. *Richmond Daily Whig*, Mar. 20, 1850.

20. John Esten Cooke, *Mohun, or the Last Days of Lee and His Paladins* (1869; reprint, Charlottesville, Va.: Historical Publishing, 1936), 165–66. Perhaps there is also something of JMD in Lynn Holmes, a character in the 1854 Richmond novel *Alone,* by Marion Harland (pseudonym of Mary Virginia Terhune). Holmes is an artist and poet lately returned from Italy, a man of medium height whose hair is "purplish in its blackness" and who dies of "lung fever."

21. George W. Bagby, "The Old Virginia Gentleman," *The Old Virginia Gentleman and Other Sketches,* 19.

22. Frederick S. Daniel, *Richmond Examiner,* 219–20.

23. *Examiner,* Nov. 10, 1849.

24. Ibid., June 22, 1849.

25. *Enquirer,* Jan. 7, 1832, quoted in William Edwin Hemphill et al., *Cavalier Commonwealth* (New York: McGraw-Hill, 1957), 227.

26. William Sumner Jenkins, *Pro-Slavery Thought in the Old South* (Gloucester, Mass.: Peter Smith, 1960), 87–88.

27. Henry Nash Smith, *Virgin Land: The American West as Symbol and Myth* (Cambridge: Harvard Univ. Press, 1971), ch. 12; summarized at <http://xroads.virginia.edu/~hyper/HNS2/c12.html>.

28. Conway, *Testimonies Concerning Slavery,* 29.

29. Frank Otto Gatell, "Peter V. Daniel," in *The Justices of the United States Supreme Court 1789–1969,* eds. Leon Friedman and Fred L. Israel (New York: Chelsea House Publishers, 1969), 1:795–805.

30. Edward Lurie, *Louis Agassiz: A Life in Science* (Baltimore: The Johns Hopkins Univ. Press, 1988), 257.

31. William Sumner Jenkins, *Pro-Slavery Thought in the Old South,* 242–53; Conway, *Autobiography,* 1:73.

32. Conway, *Autobiography,* 1:73.

33. In "Characteristics," *The Harvard Classics* (New York: F. Collier and Son, 1909), 25:365–66.

34. Thomas Carlyle, *The Nigger Question,* ed. Eugene R. August (New York: Appleton-Century, Crofts, 1971), 6, 10.

35. *Examiner,* Oct. 27, 1848.

36. Conway, *Autobiography,* 1:28.

37. Moncure D. Conway, "Fredericksburg First and Last," *Magazine of American History* 17.6 (June 1887): 450. See also Conway, *Autobiography,* 1:61.

38. Carl Sandburg, *Abraham Lincoln: Volume II, The War Years, 1861–1864* (New York: Dell Books, 1968), 200. Conway went with Rev. William Ellery Channing to see Lincoln.

39. Conway, *Testimonies,* 12–13.

40. Skipper Steely, "James Mitchell Daniel: A Small Scrapbook of the Man, His Home and Family" (Paris, Tex.: Privately printed, March 2002).

41. George Cary Eggleston, *A Rebel's Recollections* (1874; reprint, Baton Rouge: Louisiana State Univ. Press, 1996), 29.

CHAPTER 4

1. Hughes, *Editors of the Past.*

2. *Encyclopedia of Virginia Biography,* ed. Lyon Gardiner Tyler (New York: Lewis Historical Publishing Company, 1915), 3:154.

3. Oscar Penn Fitzgerald, "John M. Daniel and Some of His Contemporaries," *South Atlantic Quarterly* 4 (Jan.–Oct. 1905): 15.

4. L. Moody Simms Jr., "Talented Virginians: The Peticolas Family," *VMHB* 85.1 (Jan. 1977): 55–64.

5. Bagby, *Old Virginia Gentleman,* 109, 36.

6. Letter of July 6, 1850 in Clement Read Vaughan Correspondence, Presbyterian Historical Society, Montreat, NC. Vaughan was born in 1827, two years after Daniel.

7. *Examiner*, Sept. 29, 1848.

8. K. Jack Bauer, *Zachary Taylor* (Baton Rouge: Louisiana State Univ. Press, 1985), 214, 222.

9. *Examiner*, Apr. 14, 1848.

10. On June 23, 1848.

11. *Examiner*, June 30, 1848.

12. Ibid., Sept. 26, 1848.

13. Ibid., Oct. 20, 1848.

14. Ibid., Dec. 19, 1848.

15. Ibid., Dec. 26, 1848.

16. Ibid., Mar. 16, 1849.

17. The reporter may have been accurate in his description of the speech's delivery, but the printed text is brief, logical, and free of contradiction.

18. There were in fact three inaugural balls.

19. *Examiner*, Apr. 3, 1849.

20. *The Collected Works of Abraham Lincoln*, ed. Roy Basler (New Brunswick: Rutgers Univ. Press, 1953), 4:95.

21. *Richmond Portraits,* intro. Louise F. Catterall (Richmond: The Valentine Museum, 1949), 20–21.

22. Dabney, *Pistols and Pointed Pens,* 15.

23. Robert L. Scribner, "The Code Duello in Virginia," *Virginia Cavalcade* 3.2 (Autumn 1953): 28–31.

24. William Harlan Hale, *Horace Greeley: Voice of the People* (New York: Harper & Brothers, 1950), 20–21.

25. *Examiner,* Jan. 19, 1849.

26. Hustings Court Minutes, no. 19, 1850–52, 339, City of Richmond records, microfilm reel 92, Library of Virginia.

27. *Richmond Whig,* Aug. 23, 1851.

28. Robert M. Hughes and Joseph A. Turner, "Roanoke Female Seminary," *William and Mary College Quarterly* ser. 2, 9.4 (Oct. 1929): 325–29.

29. Undated letter in Swem Library, folder 6, Henry A. Washington Papers, Special Collections, W&M.

30. Dr. Garnett was married to a daughter of Henry A. Wise, former duelist and future governor.

31. Myra K. Spaulding, "Duelling in the District of Columbia," *Records of the Columbia Historical Society* 29–30 (1928): 117–210. Spaulding is the source for the fact that the Daniel-Johnston duel took place at Bladensburg.

32. *New York Daily Times*, Jan. 29, 1852. For details of the Scott affair, see *Baltimore Sun,* Apr. 1, 3, 4, 7, 8, 1851.

33. Hustings Court Minutes no. 19, 1850–52, 541; no. 20, 1852–53, 232, City of Richmond records, microfilm reel 92, Library of Virginia.

34. Edgar A. Poe to Thomas Gilliat Mackenzie, Apr. 22, 1843, <www.eapoe.org/works/letters/p4304220.htm>.

35. Mary E. Phillips, *Edgar Allan Poe the Man* (Chicago: John C. Winston, 1926): 2:1305–7, reporting information from the poet's friend James H. Whitty.

36. The source of the quarrel is related by J. H. Whitty in his memoir in *The Complete Poems of Edgar Allan Poe* (Boston: Houghton Mifflin, 1917), lxix. Dabney, *Pistols and Pointed Pens,* 40, describes the keyhole incident and also quotes from an account by Whitty in the Richmond *Evening Journal* for January 19, 1909.

CHAPTER 5

1. *Examiner,* Nov. 13, 1849.
2. Ibid., Feb. 1, 1850.
3. Ibid., Apr. 12, 1850.
5. Ibid., Apr. 23, 30, 1850.
6. Ibid., Sept. 17, 1850.
7. Ibid., Oct. 8, 1850.
8. Ibid., Nov. 12, 1850.
9. Ibid., Dec. 24, 1850.
10. Ibid., Aug. 21, 1849.
11. Poe to Clemm, Aug. 28, 1849 <www.eapoe.org/works/letters/p4908280.htm>.
12. Phillips, *Edgar Allan Poe,* 2:1445–46.
13. Whitty, *Complete Poems,* lxxxiii.
14. *Examiner*, Oct. 9, 1849.
15. Ibid., Oct. 12, 19, 1849. The Hazlitt to whom Daniel compared Poe was William Hazlitt, the English essayist who died in 1830.
16. Julian Symons, *The Tell-Tale Heart* (New York: Harper and Row, 1978), 166–67.
17. E. Lee Shepard, "Two Early Libraries of Richmond," *The Richmond Quarterly* 4.1 (Summer 1981): 50–51.
18. *Examiner*, June 22, 1849.
19. Quoted in Dabney, *Pistols and Pointed Pens*, 41.
20. Thackeray to Albany Fonblanque, Richmond, Mar. 4, 1853, in *The Letters and Private Papers of William Makepeace Thackeray*, ed. Gordon N. Ray (New York: Octagon Books, 1980), 4:228–29.
21. Charles Dickens, *American Notes* (London: Chapman and Hall, 1842), 2:199.
22. Eyre Crowe, *With Thackeray in America* (London: Cassell and Co., 1893), 35, 130.
23. As noted earlier, John Daniel's great-great-great-grandmother Hannah Ball had a half-sister named Mary, who became the mother of George Washington and of his brother Augustine who was Henry Washington's great-grandfather.
24. *Examiner*, Nov. 10, 1848, Jan. 9, 1849.
25. "Professors at William and Mary College," *Tyler's Quarterly* 4 (1923): 135.
26. Folder 4, Henry A. Washington Papers, VHS.
27. Robert W. Hughes, "John Moncure Daniel: His Times and Career," *Baltimorean*, Jan. 10, 1885, 1.
28. Conway, *Autobiography*, 1:61.
29. *Examiner*, Sept. 15, 1848.
30. Conway, *Autobiography*, 1:61.
31. Philip Slaughter and Raleigh Travers Green, *Genealogical and Historical Notes on Culpeper County, Virginia* (1900; reprint, Baltimore: Regional Publishing, 1971), 2:140.
32. Wynne to JMD, Aug. 13, 1854, Daniel Papers, Huntington Library.
33. Mary Boykin Chesnut, *A Diary from Dixie*, ed. Ben Ames Williams (Cambridge, Mass.: Harvard Univ. Press, 1980), 286. Curiously, she recorded earlier, in August 1861, that she had been at Jefferson Davis's house and "Mr. & Mrs. Daniels [*sic*] were there—the Editor of the *Examiner*." See Mary Boykin Chesnut, *The Private Mary Chesnut: The Unpublished Civil War Diaries*, ed. C. Vann Woodward and Elisabeth Muhlenfeld (New York: Oxford Univ. Press, 1984), 136.
34. Mrs. Burton Harrison [Constance Cary Harrison], *Recollections Grave and Gay* (New York: Charles Scribner's Sons, 1912), 119.
35. *Examiner*, July 30, 1850.
36. A. E. Howard, *Commentaries on the Constitution of Virginia* (Charlottesville: Univ. Press of Virginia, 1974), 2:649–50.

37. Hughes, "John Moncure Daniel."

38. F. N. Boney, *John Letcher of Virginia* (Tuscaloosa: Univ. of Alabama Press, 1966), 45.

39. JMD to R. M. T. Hunter, letter dated November 27, year not given but certainly 1852 since it refers to the incoming Pierce administration. R. M. T. Hunter Papers (Microfilm M-1814, Roll 4), Special Collections, Alderman Library, University of Virginia (also available in VHS).

40. The agreements are in Daniel Family Papers, VHS.

41. The name was singular but not unique; there had been Shearjashub Spooners in New England since before the Revolution. <www.gendex.com/users/hhadaway/harry/nti07291.htm>. Other early New England Spooners enjoyed such given names as Peleg, Zepheniah, Amazia, Experience, and Ruggles. This Spooner's life is summarized in *Dictionary of American Biography* (1936), 9:467.

42. Jane Turner, ed., *The Dictionary of Art* (New York: Grove's Dictionaries, 1996), 4:607.

43. This and other details of the Spooner affair are discussed in a paper by Sexson E. Humphreys, "Spooner vs. Daniel: A 'Sectional' Libel Case of the 1850s" (Ann Arbor: Assoc. for Education in Journalism, Aug. 1961), copy of which is in the Daniel Family Papers, VHS.

44. Shearjashub Spooner, *Prospectus for Publishing an American Edition of Boydell's Illustrations of Shakespeare* (New York: S. Spooner, 1849), inside cover, 13–15, 20. See also Shearjashub Spooner, *An Appeal to the People of the United States, in Behalf of Art, Artists, and the Public Weal* (New York: J. J. Reed, 1854), 22–23.

45. Spooner, *An Appeal*, 17, 26.

46. Robert Wyness Millar, *Civil Procedure of the Trial Court in Historical Perspective* (New York: Law Center of New York Univ., 1952), 79–81, noted in Humphreys, "Spooner vs. Daniel," 2.

47. David H. Fenimore, "Horace Greeley (1811–1872), Editor of the *New York Tribune*," <www.honors.unr.edu/~fenimore/greeley.html>.

48. As noted in Humphreys, "Spooner vs. Daniel," this was reprinted in the *Examiner*, July 22, 1851.

49. *Examiner*, July 1, 1851.

50. *Richmond Whig*, Aug. 23, 1851.

51. Spooner, *An Appeal*, 5–6.

52. "Daniel—'76, '98, '44, '48, and a Fast Man!" *Democratic Review*, May 1852, 385–96.

53. William Hincks and F. H. Smith, *Proceedings of the Democratic National Convention Held at Baltimore, June, 1852* (Washington, D.C.: Buell & Blanchard, 1852), 3–5.

54. Ibid., 32–33.

55. *New-York Daily Tribune*, June 3, 1852.

CHAPTER 6

1. JMD to "My very dear Friend," n.d., box 59, Tucker-Coleman Collection, Special Collections, Swem Library, W&M.

2. Larry Gara, *The Presidency of Franklin Pierce* (Lawrence: Univ. Press of Kansas, 1991), 44.

3. *Examiner*, May 13, 1853.

4. Daniel wrote to Davis from Richmond, recommending his friend Judge W. W. Crump for the position of U.S. District Attorney for the Eastern District of Virginia and saying that Davis was "the only member of the Cabinet whom I have the honour to know"—not quite true, but when he had met Marcy he was only a boy. Undated letter, presumably written after Davis arrived in Washington on March 5, 1853; copy kindly furnished to author by Lynda L. Crist, ed., *The Papers of Jefferson Davis*, Rice University.

5. Copy of Marcy letter to James Buchanan, Mar. 5, 1853, container 29, William L. Marcy Papers, Manuscript Division, Library of Congress (hereafter LC).

6. Almost none of the men Douglas recommended for diplomatic posts received an appointment. Compare Robert W. Johannsen, ed., *The Letters of Stephen A. Douglas* (Urbana: Univ. of Illinois

Press, 1961), 260–66, with *Principal Officers of the Department of State and United States Chiefs of Mission 1778–1988* (Washington, D.C.: Office of the Historian, U.S. Department of State, 1988).

7. The letters are in Recommendations for Appointment 1852–54, microfilm publication M967, reel 11, NARA.

8. J. G. Mason to Marcy, Mar. 10, 1853, containter 29, Marcy Papers, LC.

9. Letter of June 5, 1853, in microfilm publication M90, roll 7, NARA.

10. Letter from R. K. Meade to R. M. T. Hunter, May 30, 1853, in R.M.T. Hunter Papers, University of Virginia. As noted in chapter 10, four years later Meade finally got his post, when President James Buchanan named him minister to Brazil.

11. *New-York Daily Times*, July 23, 1853.

12. Letter of July 29, 1853, microfilm publication M90, roll 7, NARA.

13. In his so-called "garlic letter" to Arthur Peticolas, quoted in Frederick S. Daniel, *Richmond Examiner*, 225.

14. John W. Forney to Howell Cobb, July 29, 1853, in Ulrich Bonnell Phillips, ed., *Annual Report of the American Historical Association, 1911* (Washington, D.C.: American Historical Association, 1913), 2:330.

15. Letter of Aug. 19, 1853, box 26, Hunter-Garnett Collection, Special Collections, Alderman Library, University of Virginia.

16. JMD, at Clarendon House, New York City, July 27, 1853, to W. W. Crump, Daniel Family Papers, VHS. Ms. Mary Schnabel of the Niagara Falls Public Library, Niagara Falls, N.Y., informed the author that from a review of the local press, the only notable event of the summer of 1853 at Niagara was the start of work on the Hydraulic Canal that bypassed the Falls. Niagara was already becoming a notable summer resort; it seems not improbable that John Daniel went there simply for a short vacation.

17. Parker to Mr. C. Ellis, Aiken, S.C., Mar. 28, 1853, microfilm reel 2, v. 5, 78, Manuscript Division, Theodore Parker Papers, LC.

18. *Richmond Enquirer*, Aug. 19, 1853.

19. Two decades later, President U.S. Grant would offer Greeley the post of minister to the United Kingdom, to get him out of the way when the *Tribune* was attacking official corruption; Greeley refused the offer. William Harlan Hale, *Horace Greeley* (New York: Harper & Brothers, 1950), 324–25.

20. *New York Tribune*, quoted in *Examiner*, July 29, 1853.

21. *Times*, Aug. 18, 1853.

22. *Examiner*, Jan. 14, 1853. Daniel's paper also published statements by Virginia politicians that the state's jails were filled mainly with persons of color. However, the superintendent of the Virginia Penitentiary at Richmond reported that in the institution's first half-century, from 1800 to 1850, a total of 2,036 whites and 655 blacks had been incarcerated there. *The Richmond Directory and Business Advertiser, for 1852* (Baltimore: T. W. Woods, 1852), 15.

23. *Frederick Douglass' Paper*, Rochester, N.Y., Aug. 5, 1853.

24. Terry Coleman, *The Liners* (New York: G. Putnam's Sons, 1977), 24–25. The following year, the *Arctic* sank off Cape Race, with the loss of more than two hundred persons, including Edward Collins's wife and two children.

25. "Our Foreign Ministers," *Democratic Review*, Nov.–Dec. 1852, 420–32.

26. Merle E. Curti, "George N. Sanders—American Patriot of the Fifties," *South Atlantic Quarterly* 27.1 (Jan. 1928): 85–86.

27. Widmer, *Young America*, 198.

CHAPTER 7

1. Castigation of the British was not uncommon in the American South. See, for example, the *Enquirer* editorial for March 24, 1846, which commented that while the British press attacked America's

"peaceful" annexation of Texas, the British had recently slaughtered 30,000 Sikhs who were defending their country's soil.

2. JMD to Marcy, Turin, Oct. 10, 1853, microfilm publication M90, roll 7, NARA.

3. Secretary Marcy wrote to Mason on May 6, 1853, "I do not think the President had any definite object in view when he made the remark to which you refer in your two last letters." Marcy had nonetheless mentioned the possible need for a new chief justice to one of his associates, when reports were circulating that the chief justice was seriously ill. The associate thought that Maryland's politicians would insist on a replacement from their state. Folder "Addition," container 88, Marcy Papers, LC.

4. James Buchanan wrote to Marcy from London on January 19, 1854, "I have just received authentic information that our friend Mason is greatly better. He has recovered his speech and his thoughts to a considerable degree and fair hopes are entertained of his final recovery." Letterbook 1853–55, container 79, Marcy Papers, LC. Mason apparently suffered a second stroke a year later. Daniel wrote his Richmond friend W. W. Crump on January 24, 1855, that a visitor from Paris said that "Judge Mason nearly went off a short time since with an apploplectic [*sic*] attack." Daniel Family Papers, VHS.

5. *American National Biography*, ed. John A. Garraty and Mark C. Carnes (New York: Oxford Univ. Press, 1999), 14:654–56.

6. Joseph J. Ellis, *American Sphinx: The Character of Thomas Jefferson* (New York: Vintage Books, 1998), 82.

7. Belmont, The Hague, to Daniel at Turin, Feb. 5, 1854, Daniel Papers, Huntington Library.

8. Third-person note from Daniel at Hotel d'Europe, Turin to Minister, Oct. 8, 1853; copy kindly furnished to author by Dr. Isabella Massabo Ricci, director, Archivio di Stato, Turin.

9. Information kindly furnished the author by Massabo Ricci in a letter of Oct. 17, 2000. In 1854, the legation's offices moved to Contrada Borgo Nuovo, 19B. It has not been possible to ascertain where John Daniel resided in Turin.

10. *Examiner*, Sept. 13, 1850.

11. JMD to John Magoun, William's brother, Oct. 19, 1857, Turin letterbooks, 166:311.

12. For a sketch of Kinney, see *National Cyclopaedia of American Biography* (New York: James T. White & Company, 1906), 13:156; for De Forest, see James A. Hijiya, *J. W. De Forest and the Rise of American Gentility* (Hanover, N.H.: Univ. Press of New England, 1988), 21.

13. William L. Vance, *America's Rome* (New Haven: Yale Univ. Press, 1989), 2:110.

14. Lester's doings are documented in *L'Unificazione italiana vista dai diplomatici statunitensi*, ed. Howard R. Marraro (Roma: Istituto per la Storia del Risorgimento Italiano, 1963), 1:213–86.

15. Tinto's report, dated Jan. 17, 1855, is in the *New York Daily Times*, Mar. 1, 1855.

16. An interesting summary of early Italian-American contacts is A. A. Bernardi, "Contributi italiani alla formazione degli Stati Uniti d'America" (reprint from *Il Giornale di Politica e di Letteratura*, Roma, 1942; rare copy in Centro di Studi Americani, Rome).

17. Jefferson to Major L'Enfant, Philadelphia, Apr. 10, 1791; <http://odur.let.rug.nl/~usa/P/tj3/writings/brf/jefl90.htm>.

18. Ben L. Bassham, *Conrad Wise Chapman* (Kent, Ohio: Kent State Univ. Press, 1998). This does not exhaust the list of Americans in Italy during those years. The first American Mormon missionaries, for example, landed in Genoa in June 1850. See the 1998 lecture by Michael W. Homer at <www.cesnur.org/testi/Homer.htm>.

19. Giovanni Schiavo, *The Italians in America Before the Civil War* (New York: Vigo Press, 1934), 257.

20. Giorgio Spini, "Le relazioni politiche fra l'Italia e gli Stati Uniti durante il Risorgimento e la Guerra Civile," in *Italia e Stati Uniti nell'eta del Risorgimento e della Guerra Civile* (Florence: "La Nuova Italia" Editrice, 1969), 121–86.

21. A good summary of the early years of American relations with the Kingdom of Sardinia is in Cinzia Maria Aicardi and Alessandra Cavaterra, eds., *I fondi archivistici della Legazione Sarda e delle*

rappresentanze diplomatiche italiane negli U.S.A. (1848–1901) (Rome: Istituto Poligrafico e Zecca dello Stato, 1988).

22. The author has drawn on a useful paper entitled "Highlights in the History of the United States Diplomatic and Consular Posts at Turin, Italy," Research Project No. 432, Historical Office, Department of State (Washington, D.C., January 1961).

23. Foreign Ministry dispatch to Count Augusto Avogadro de Colobian [di Collobiano], unnumbered, Sept. 29, 1838, Busta 292, Moscati I, Archivio Storico Diplomatico, Ministero degli Affari Esteri, Rome (hereafter ASMAE). ("Moscati" refers to the ASMAE indexes prepared by the late Professor Ruggero Moscati; "Busta" is folder.)

24. Foreign Ministry dispatch, unnumbered, Sept. 28, 1840, Busta 292, Moscati I, ASMAE.

25. Walter B. Smith II, *America's Diplomats and Consuls of 1776–1865*, Foreign Service Institute, Department of State, Occasional Paper No. 2 (Washington, D.C.: 1986), 12.

26. Texts of the relevant correspondence are in Marraro, *L'Unificazione italiana*, 1:149–68.

27. Foreign ministry dispatch to Chargé d'Affaires Luigi Mossi, unnumbered, May 11, 1849, Busta 292, Moscati I, ASMAE.

28. Dispatch no. 25 to Mossi, Aug. 26, 1850, Busta 292, Moscati I, ASMAE.

29. Unnumbered dispatch from Foreign Minister to Taliacarne, Nov. 13, 1853, Busta 292, Moscati I, ASMAE.

30. JMD to Marcy, Oct. 10, 1853, roll 7, M90, NARA.

31. Department of State dispatch no. 3 to Chargé at Turin, Nov. 7, 1853, roll 7, M90, NARA.

32. Turin dispatch no. 16 to Department, October 21, 1854, roll 7, M90, NARA.

33. Buchanan to Marcy, Nov. 1, 1853, container 79, letterbook, Marcy Papers, LC.

34. JMD to Marcy, Feb. 1, 1854, container 47, Marcy Papers, LC.

35. Wynne to JMD, Oct. 2, Dec. 17, 27, 1853, Daniel Papers, Huntington Library.

36. The text of the letter—except the request to keep it out of the papers—is in Frederick S. Daniel, *Richmond Examiner*, 225. An extended but incomplete account of what became known as the affair of the "garlic letter" is Sexon E. Humphreys, "John Moncure Daniel: 'The Garlic Letter,'" in *Il Risorgimento e l'Europa* (Catania: Bonanno Editore, 1969), 187–206.

37. John George Keysler, *Travels* (London: G. Keith, 1760), 1:330.

38. Joseph J. Ellis, *American Sphinx: The Character of Thomas Jefferson* (New York: Vintage Books, 1998), 99–100.

39. Shelley, *Letters*, in *The Complete Works*, 10:12, quoted in John Varriano, *A Literary Companion to Rome* (New York: St. Martin's Griffin, 1991), 17.

40. Copy of letter of May 10, 1854, from A. E. Peticolas to JMD, enclosing undated letter to JMD from Ro.W. Hughes, Turin letterbooks, 162:163–4.

41. J. W. De Forest, *European Acquaintance* (New York: Harper and Brothers, 1858), 194. John De Forest is better known today as the author of the 1867 novel *Miss Ravenel's Conversion from Secession to Loyalty* (New York: Penguin Books, 2000).

42. Marcy to JMD, "Private," Dec. 15, 1853, Turin letterbooks, 162:401–4.

43. Marcy papers, container 47, LC.

44. Department of State dispatch no. 6 to Turin, Feb. 27, 1854, roll 101, M77, NARA.

45. *Journal of the Executive Proceedings of the Senate of the United States of America* (Washington, D.C.: GPO, 1887), 9:223, 228, 237.

46. JMD to Marcy, Apr. 4, 1854, container 49, Marcy Papers, LC.

47. JMD to Peter V. Daniel, Sept. 12, 1857, Turin letterbooks, 166:210.

48. Keysler, *Travels*, 1:312–13.

49. Daniel Papers, Huntington Library.

50. B. de Saint Marsan to JMD, Mar. 6, 1854, Turin letterbooks, 162:53–54.

51. JMD to Saint Marsan, Mar. 14, 1854, Turin letterbooks,162:53–54.

52. Saint Marsan to JMD, Mar. 21, 1854, Turin letterbooks, 162:53–54.

53. Confidential unnumbered dispatch, Foreign Minister to Taliacarne, Mar. 22, 1854, Busta 292, Moscati I, ASMAE.

54. Humphreys, "John Moncure Daniel," 198, quoting Taliacarne dispatch to Foreign Minister, Mar. 16, 1854.

55. JMD to Marcy, Apr. 4, 1854, Turin letterbooks, 162:54.

56. Private letter, Marcy to JMD, Apr. 30, 1854, Turin letterbooks, 162:63–64.

57. Humphreys, "John Moncure Daniel," 205–6, quoting Taliacarne dispatch to Foreign Minister, June 1, 1854.

58. Dispatch 96, Foreign Minister to Taliacarne, June 10, 1854, Busta 292, Moscati I, ASMAE. Dispatch 26, Hudson to Foreign Office, London, Mar. 17, 1854; text in Federico Curato, ed., *Le Relazioni diplomatiche tra la Gran Bretagna ed il Regno di Sardegna dal 1852 al 1856* (Turin: ILTE, 1956), 2:44.

59. Wynne to JMD, Feb. 6, Mar. 9, 22, 1854, Daniel Papers, Huntington Library.

60. Wynne to JMD, Apr. 30, 1854, Daniel Papers, Huntington Library.

61. *Harper's New Monthly Magazine,* May 1854, 841–44.

62. Samuel Flagg Bemis and others, *The American Secretaries of State and Their Diplomacy* (New York: Pageant Book, 1958), 170–71.

63. Anna Reid had been a pioneering woman editor in New York.

64. Alexander Herzen, *My Past and Thoughts*, ed. Dwight Macdonald (Berkeley: Univ. of California Press, 1982), 479.

65. Ibid., 481.

66. Buchanan to Marcy, Feb. 24, 1854, container 79, Marcy Papers, LC.

67. Confidential note, Foreign Minister to Kinney, Sept. 19, 1851, Busta 396, Moscati VI, ASMAE.

68. James A. Field, *America and the Mediterranean World 1776–1882* (Princeton: Princeton Univ. Press, 1969), 232.

69. Donn Piatt, "Cuba and the Ostend Manifesto," *Harper's New Monthly Magazine* 40.240 (May 1870).

70. *New-York Daily Times*, Feb. 15, 1854.

71. The *New-York Daily Times* printed the full text on Oct. 27, 1854.

72. JMD to W. W. Crump, May 21, 1854, Daniel Family Papers, VHS.

73. Taliacarne to Foreign Minister Dabormida, Apr. 7, 1854; not found by author but quoted in Humphreys, "John Moncure Daniel."

74. There are biographical sketches of Marie de Solms, later Marie Rattazzi, in Jean Tulard, ed., *Dictionnaire du Second Empire* (Paris: Librairie Artheme Fayard, 1995), 1205; and *Grand Dictionnaire Universel du XIXe Siecle (Larousse)* (Paris: Slatkine, 1982), 13:730.

75. Ubaldo Rogari, *Due regine dei salotti nella Firenze capitale* (Florence: Edizioni Remo Sandron, 1992), 89–91.

76. Ibid., 97.

77. Pierfelice Borelli, *Urbano e Maria Rattazzi* (Cavallermaggiore, Italy: Gribaudo Editore, 1993), 26.

78. JMD to John B. Floyd, July 31, 1859, Turin letterbooks, 167:309. One might speculate whether Alexandre Dumas *fils* borrowed from John Daniel and Marie de Solms the theme for his 1855 play *Le Demi-Monde,* in which Raymond de Nanjac, an officer just arrived from Africa, becomes infatuated with the Baroness d'Ange, a lady with a dubious reputation who plans to buy a chateau on Lake Como.

79. Jean-Louis Bory, *Eugene Sue* (Paris: Hachette Littérature, 1962), 392.

CHAPTER 8

1. JMD to Crump, May 21, 1854, Daniel Family Papers, VHS.

2. JMD to Crump, Apr. 2, 1854, Daniel Family Papers, VHS.

3. Dispatch 96, Foreign Minister to Taliacarne, June 10, 1854, Busta 292, Moscati I, ASMAE.

4. 22 Fed. Cases 935–936 (case no. 13, 244a, *Spooner vs. Daniel*), quoted in Humphreys, "Spooner vs. Daniel," 5.

5. JMD to W. W. Crump, May 6, 1855, Daniel Family Papers, VHS.

6. JMD to Crump, Aug. 18, 1854, Daniel Family Papers, VHS.

7. Breckenridge to Daniel, May 17, 1854, Daniel Papers, Huntington Library.

8. Humphreys, "Spooner vs. Daniel," 6–7.

9. JMD to Crump, Jan. 24, 1855, Daniel Family Papers, VHS.

10. Turin dispatch 17 to Department, Dec. 24, 1854, Turin letterbooks, 162:165–76.

11. "Highlights in the History of . . . Posts at Turin, Italy," 25, 28.

12. Ibid., 30.

13. Turin dispatch 18, Dec. 27, 1854, Turin letterbook, 162:177–84.

14. JMD to Crump, Jan. 24, 1855, Daniel Family Papers, VHS.

15. Turin dispatch 19 to Department, Jan. 12, 1855, Turin letterbooks, 162:232–35.

16. Turin dispatch 20, Jan. 24, 1855, Turin letterbooks, 162:243–46.

17. Denis Mack Smith, *Cavour* (New York: Alfred A. Knopf, 1985), 84.

18. A decade later, Isabella, no longer on the throne, took as a paramour Daniel Sickles, the American minister at Madrid who, as a congressman, had killed his wife's paramour in Washington, D.C., and later lost a leg as a Union general at Gettysburg.

19. JMD to Crump, Jan. 24, 1855, Daniel Family Papers, VHS.

20. JMD to Buchanan, July 20, 1854, Turin letterbooks, 162:448–50. Although the mysterious Albinola said he had never been in the United States and seemed to speak no English, it is interesting that Julia Ward Howe had, sometime before this, known two Italian patriots in New York whom the Austrians had imprisoned at Spielberg. One was Foresti, who hoped to become American consul at Genoa. The other was named Albinola. See Laura E. Richard and Maud Howe Elliott, *Julia Ward Howe, 1819–1910* (Boston: Houghton Mifflin, 1916), 1:5. An Albinola is also listed among Italian political refugees in America during the 1850s. Schiavo, *Italians in America*, 213; and at <www.digital.library.upenn.edu/women/richards/howe-I-V.html>. A stirring picture of nineteenth-century Italian freedom fighters is found in the 1897 novel *The Gadfly*, by Ethel Boole Voynich. Her novel, little known in the West, was later celebrated in the Soviet Union, and a film was made from it, featuring music by Dmitri Shostakovich. Further research might ascertain whether Daniel's visitor was in fact Giovanni Albinola, no simple soldier in Italy's fight for freedom but the former secretary of Young Italy. <www.viggiu-in-rete.org/emigrazione/baker08.htm> and <www.viggiu-in-rete.org/emigrazione/baker13a/htm>.

21. Buchanan to Marcy, Oct. 25, 1854, letterbook, container 79, Marcy Papers, LC.

22. Buchanan to Marcy, Dec. 27, 1854; *The Works of James Buchanan*, ed. John Bassett Moore (1911; reprint, New York: Antiquarian Press Ltd., 1960), 9:293.

23. Buchanan to Marcy, Nov. 10, Dec. 8, 22, 1854, *The Works of James Buchanan*, 9:292–93.

24. *New-York Daily Times*, Oct. 27, 1854.

25. Turin letterbooks, 162:226–29.

26. Henry R. Jackson, who had been colonel of a Georgia regiment in the Mexican War, was minister to Austria. In the Civil War, he served as a Confederate brigadier general. Two decades later, he again became an American diplomat, as minister to Mexico.

27. Ruth J. Bartlett, ed., *The Record of American Diplomacy* (New York: Alfred A. Knopf, 1950), 241.

28. Amos Aschbach Ettinger, *The Mission to Spain of Pierre Soulé 1853–1855* (New Haven: Yale Univ. Press, 1932), 348.

29. Marcy to Mason, Oct. 19, 1854, container 80, Marcy Papers, LC.

30. Signed by "Dick Tinto" who had reported earlier on how cheap life was for Americans in Florence.

31. Piatt, "Cuba and the Ostend Manifesto."

32. JMD to Piatt, Oct. 13, 1855, Turin letterbooks, 162:336–40.

33. Turin dispatch 31 to Department, Oct. 14, 1855, Turin letterbooks, 162:341–43.

34. Piatt to JMD, Oct. 17, 1855, Turin letterbooks, 162:388–90.

35. Mason to JMD, Nov. 12, 1855, Turin letterbooks, 162:390–92; original is in Daniel Papers, Huntington Library.

36. Dr. St. George Peachey to JMD, Nov. 13, 1855, Turin letterbooks, 162:393–94. It is not clear whether Daniel consulted Dr. Peachey as well as Dr. Rawlings in Paris about his medical problems. The *Dictionary of American Biography* (1934) said briefly that Donn Piatt "served with distinction" at the Paris legation. Piatt was a county judge in Ohio before going to Paris as secretary of legation. He served as a Union colonel in the Civil War and later was a journalist and author who criticized Lincoln for shaming Gettysburg by having a ribald song sung on the battlefield (a story without foundation), and who was indicted by President Grant for allegedly inciting insurrection. Piatt began the construction of a castle at West Liberty, Ohio, which stands today.

37. Marcy to Mason, Oct. 8, 1855, container 64, Marcy Papers, LC.

38. Piatt to JMD, May 11, 1855, Daniel Papers, Huntington Library.

39. Mason to JMD, Turin letterbooks, 162:311–12.

40. Department dispatch 14 to Turin, Oct. 30, 1855, Turin letterbooks, 162:11–12.

41. JMD to Commodore S. L. Breese, Feb. 25, 1856, Turin letterbooks, 162:85–87.

42. Cushing himself served abroad two decades later, as minister to Spain in 1874–77.

43. Bemis, *American Secretaries of State,* 170–72.

44. JMD to Marcy, Private, Oct. 22, 1855, container 64, Marcy Papers, LC.

45. Cass to JMD, Dec. 18, 1855, and JMD to Cass, Dec. 25, 1855, Turin letterbooks, 162:425–32.

46. JMD to Crump, Jan. 22, 1856, Turin letterbooks, 162:153–63.

47. JMD to Crump, Nov. 26, 1855, Turin letterbooks, 162:140–47. The volumes of legation letterbooks now in the National Archives contain some of "these things," but much of his correspondence seems to be lost. As noted elsewhere, so far as known John Daniel never found time to begin writing a book.

48. Turin dispatches 39, 40, and 41, Jan. 1, 1856, Turin letterbooks, 164:1–49.

49. Turin dispatch 42, Feb. 1, 1856, Turin letterbooks, 162:51–57.

CHAPTER 9

1. James G. Bennett, Florence, to JMD, Feb. 15, 1856; JMD to Bennett, Feb. 26, 1856, Turin letterbook, 162:69–72. Original of Bennett's letter is in Daniel Papers, Huntington Library.

2. John J. Farrell, ed., *Zachary Taylor 1784–1850 and Millard Fillmore 1800–1874: Chronology, Documents, Bibliographic Aids* (Dobbs Ferry, N.Y.: Oceana Publications, 1971), 65.

3. JMD to Crump, Jan. 22, 1856. Quoted in Sara B. Bearss, "Not a Humbug," *History Notes, The Newsletter of the Virginia Historical Society* 39 (Summer 2000): 4–5. John Daniel repeated his paragraphs on Fillmore in a letter to his great-uncle Peter V. Daniel.

4. Turin letterbooks, 164:205–8. The Turin Legation letterbook contains many pages of correspondence regarding Mrs. Ward.

5. JMD to Mason, Dec. 12, 1856, Turin letterbooks, 164:49–58.

6. Owen to JMD, "Strictly Confidential," Apr. 26, 1856, Turin letterbooks, 164:168.

7. JMD to Cavour, May 16, 1856, Turin letterbooks, 164:183–84.

8. JMD to "Mr. Wynne, Richmond," May 30, 1856, Turin letterbooks, 164:256–69.

9. Turin dispatches 2 [misnumbered], May 20, 1856, and 51, June 7, 1856, Turin letterbooks, 164:189–95, 275–85.

10. Mack Smith, *Cavour,* 85.

11. Ibid., 93.

12. Bemis, *American Secretaries of State,* 283–85.

13. Department dispatch 18 to Turin, July 29, 1856, Turin letterbook, 164:293–99.

14. Turin dispatch 64, Feb. 3, 1857, roll 7, M90, NARA.

15. Turin dispatch 66, Mar. 7, 1857, Turin letterbooks, 165:253–59.

16. Mack Smith, *Cavour,* 146.

17. Howard R. Marraro, *American Opinion on the Unification of Italy 1846–1861* (1932; reprint, New York: AMS Press, 1969),174; Turin dispatch 21, Mar. 10, 1855, roll 7, M90, NARA.

18. JMD to Commodore Breese, Jan. 3, 1857, Turin letterbooks, 164:79–80; Turin dispatch 65 to Department, Mar. 1, 1857, Turin letterbooks, 165:225–28. See also Field, *America and the Mediterranean World,* 219–20, 238.

19. Wynne to JMD, June 22, 1856, Daniel Papers, Huntington Library.

20. Department unnumbered dispatch to Turin, Sept. 15, 1856, Turin letterbooks, 165:335–37.

21. Turin dispatch 58, Nov. 27, 1856, Turin letterbooks, 165:25–31.

22. JMD to Mason, Dec. 12, 1856, Turin letterbooks, 165:49–58.

23. Wynne to JMD, May 18, 1856, Daniel Papers, Huntington Library.

CHAPTER 10

1. JMD to PVD, Jan. 22, 1857, Turin letterbooks, 165:167–68.

2. JMD to Mason, Feb. 3, 1857, Turin letterbooks, 165:182–87.

3. Diary entry, Mar. 17, 1857, container 81, Marcy Papers, LC.

4. Diary entry, Mar. 27, 1857, container 81, Marcy Papers, LC.

5. JMD to Crump, Jan. 30, 1857, Turin letterbooks, 165:188–97. Walter B. Smith II has calculated that an American minister abroad in the 1850s could expect to save around 15 percent of his salary after paying all expenses for office and residence, including wages of employees. Smith, *America's Diplomats and Consuls of 1776–1865,* Foreign Service Institute, Occasional Paper No. 2 (Washington, D.C.: U.S. Department of State, 1986), 13. John Daniel saved much more.

6. JMD to "Honorable John B. Floyd, Washington City, D.C.," Mar. 3, 1857, Turin letterbooks, 165:229–34.

7. JMD to PVD, Mar. 3, 1857, Turin letterbooks, 165:234–38.

8. Turin dispatch 68 to Department, Mar. 31, 1857, Turin letterbooks,165:300–301.

9. William Carl Klunder, *Lewis Cass and the Politics of Moderation* (Kent, Ohio: Kent State Univ. Press, 1996), 97–99.

10. Turin dispatch 67, Mar. 26, 1857, Turin letterbooks, 165:207.

11. A. J. Whyte, *The Evolution of Modern Italy* (New York: W. W. Norton, 1965), 101–2.

12. PVD to JMD, Apr. 6, 1857, Turin letterbooks, 165:305–22.

13. JMD to PVD, Apr. 30, 1857, Turin letterbooks, 165:305–22.

14. JMD to Wynne, May 5, 1857, Turin letterbooks, 165:333–44.

15. PVD to JMD, June 6, 1857, Turin letterbooks, 165:414–29.

16. JMD to PVD, June 28, 1857, Turin letterbooks, 165:430–40.

17. Turin unnumbered dispatch to Department, July 1, 1857, Turin letterbooks, 165:446–51.

18. Turin dispatch 73 to Department, July 25, 1857, Turin letterbooks, 165:461–65.

19. Floyd to JMD, June 1, 1857, Turin letterbooks, 166:16–23.

20. Wynne to JMD, May 31, 1857, Turin letterbooks, 166:1–15.

21. Hughes to JMD, June 17, 1857, Turin letterbooks, 166:23–33.

22. Lloyd to JMD, July 3, 1857, Turin letterbooks, 166:55–65.

23. JMD to Lloyd, undated, Turin letterbooks, 166:66–72.

24. Crump to JMD, July 16, 1857, Turin letterbooks, 166:73–86.

25. JMD to PVD, Aug. 2, 1857, Turin letterbooks, 166:102–15.

26. JMD to Floyd, Aug. 4, 1857, Turin letterbooks, 166:116–31.

27. PVD to JMD, July 30, 1857, Turin letterbooks, 166:157–79.

28. Dodge's name was actually Augustus Caesar Dodge.

29. Wheaton had been chargé d'affaires in Denmark for eight years, 1827–35, when Daniel was a boy.

30. JMD to W. W. Crump, Sept. 1, 1857, Turin letterbooks, 166:254.

31. JMD to W. W. Crump, Sept. 1, 1857, Turin letterbooks, 166:254; also JMD to PVD, Sept. 12, 1857, 166:210–38.

32. Turin letterbooks, 166:210–38.

33. See, for example, Christopher Hibbert, *The Great Mutiny: India 1857* (London: Penguin Books, 1986), 31, 37–39, 45, 49–50, 56.

34. Marraro, *American Opinion*, 192.

35. JMD to Mr. Herbemont, Consul at Genoa, Nov. 26, 1856, Turin letterbooks, 165:21–22.

36. JMD to Samuel L. [*sic*] Morse, Jan. 1, 1858, Turin letterbooks, 166:383–83.

37. Turin dispatch 79, Nov. 21, 1857, Turin letterbooks, 166:326–28.

38. Mack Smith, *Cavour*, 125, says there were only 200 priests in the group, not 260.

39. JMD to PVD, Sept. 12, 1857, Turin letterbooks, 166:84.

40. PVD to JMD, July 30, 1857, Turin letterbooks, 166:47.

41. Lloyd to JMD, Sept. 2, 1857, Turin letterbooks, 166:59–76.

42. Lloyd to JMD, Oct. 17, Nov. 27, 1857, Turin letterbooks, 166:305–10, 167:92–98.

43. PVD to JMD, Apr. 13, 1858, Daniel Papers, Huntington Library. This is the same letter in which, as noted earlier in this book, the associate justice wrote of seeing John's father in a long and vivid dream.

44. W. W. Crump to JMD, June 2, 1858, Turin letterbooks, 167:143–50.

45. JMD to Floyd, Jan. 12, 1859, Turin letterbooks, 167:323–29, and R. W. Hughes to JMD, Dec. 22, 1858, Turin letterbooks, 167:333–39. It appears that no message was sent to Daniel directly requesting his resignation.

46. Crump to JMD, June 2, 1858, Turin letterbooks, 167:143–50.

47. JMD to Lloyd, July 10, 1858, Turin letterbooks, 167:183–95.

48. Lloyd to JMD, Aug. 9, 1858, Turin letterbooks, 167:283–89.

49. Turin dispatches 90 and 91 to Department, Aug. 5, 6, 1858, roll 7, M90, NARA.

50. "Highlights in the History of . . . Posts at Turin, Italy," 33–34.

51. Franklin Pierce to JMD, Sept. 7, 1858, Turin letterbooks, 167:281–82. It is not clear whether Pierce and Daniel got together, but it would seem probable that they did.

52. Turin dispatch 92 to Department, Sept. 17, 1858, roll 7 M90, NARA.

53. Foresti had, as described earlier, been imprisoned by the Austrians as a fighter for Italian unification, and he later enjoyed an honorable career as an American professor before being named consul. What was, and is, less known is that after his arrest by the Austrians, he reportedly offered to inform on his imprisoned comrades to try to save himself. Silvio Pellico, *Le mie prigioni*, ed. Egidio Bellorini (Milan: Casa Editrice Dottor Francesco Vallardi, 1924), 83, editorial note.

54. PVD to JMD, Dec. 31, 1858, Turin letterbooks, 167:365–73.

55. W. Medill, Comptroller of the Treasury, to JMD, Jan. 11, 1859, Turin letterbooks, 167:350–51.

CHAPTER 11

1. Whyte, *Evolution of Modern Italy,* 105.

2. Daniel's translation, in Turin dispatch 95 to Department, Jan. 11, 1859, Turin letterbooks, 167:312–22.

3. JMD to Floyd, Jan. 12, 1859, Turin letterbooks, 167:323–29.

4. Turin dispatch 96 to Department, Jan. 28, 1859, Turin letterbooks, 167:346–49.

5. JMD to Floyd, July 31, 1859, Turin letterbooks, 168:309–20.

6. Paul Ginisty, *Eugene Sue* (Paris: Editions Berger-Levrault, 1929), 208.

7. Bory, *Eugene Sue,* 376.

8. Turin dispatch 121 to Department, July 31, 1859, Turin letterbooks, 168:294–99.

9. Virginia Clay-Copton, *A Belle of the Fifties: Memoirs of Mrs. Clay, of Alabama* (New York: Doubleday, Page, 1905), 70–71. The daughter of Bertinatti and Mrs. Bass married a Marchese Incisa di Camerana, and from them descends a present-day Italian ambassador.

10. PVD to JMD, June 24, 1859, Turin letterbooks, 169:111–23.

11. JMD to Floyd, July 31, Turin letterbooks, 169:111–23.

12. JMD to Floyd, July 31, Turin letterbooks, 169:111–23.

13. Borelli, *Eugene Sue,* 19–20.

14. Turin dispatch 98 to Department, Mar. 18, 1859, Turin letterbooks, 167:393–403.

15. Turin dispatch 101 to Department, Apr. 16, 1859, Turin letterbooks, 167:418–24.

16. Turin dispatch 102 to Department, Apr. 21, 1859, Turin letterbooks, 167:437–40.

17. This is one of several indications that John Daniel had learned French and Italian well enough that they occasionally affected his English. In Italian, the word *sempre* can mean both "always" and "still." With *sempre* probably in the back of his mind, Daniel wrote "always" instead of "still."

18. Turin dispatch 103 to Department, Apr. 25, 1859, Turin letterbooks, 167:441–48.

19. Turin dispatch 104 to Department, Apr. 27, 1859, Turin letterbooks, 167:457–64.

20. Mack Smith, *Cavour,* 144, 150.

21. Turin dispatch 106 to Department, May 15, 1859, Turin letterbooks, 168:1–13.

22. Turin dispatch 108 to Department, May 31, 1859, Turin letterbooks, 168:29–36.

23. Turin dispatch 109 to Department, June 8, 1859, Turin letterbooks, 168:37–43.

24. Daniel learned later that Lt. Carr was a great-nephew of Thomas Jefferson. Daniel was to recommend Carr for a Confederate commission in 1861, saying that he had gained much from Carr's observations in Italy. Two years later Carr was a colonel commanding the 57th Virginia Infantry.

25. Turin dispatch 115 to Department, July 13, 1859, Turin letterbooks, 168:139–51.

26. Turin dispatch 116 to Department, July 14, 1859, Turin letterbooks, 168:152–58.

27. Turin dispatch 118 to Department, July 16, 1859, Turin letterbooks, 168:166–78.

28. Department dispatch 31 to Turin, July 14, 1859, Turin letterbooks, 168:308–9.

29. Hughes, "John Moncure Daniel."

30. *The Dictionary of National Biography,* ed. Sir Leslie Stephen and Sir Sidney Lee (London: Oxford Univ. Press, 1950), 10:149. It was rumored that Hudson was the illegitimate son of King George IV (Curato, 1:xii).

31. Henry T. Shanks, *The Secession Movement in Virginia 1847–1861* (1934; reprint, New York: AMS Press, 1971),184.

32. Wynne to JMD, July 18, 1859, Daniel Papers, Huntington Library; PVD to JMD, Dec. 19, 1858, Turin letterbooks, 167:352–64.

33. PVD to JMD, Dec. 19, 1858, Turin letterbooks, 167:352–64.

34. Wynne to JMD, Dec. 13, 1859, Turin letterbooks, 169:35–40.

35. JMD to PVD, Jan. 1, 1860, Turin letterbooks, 169:85–95.

36. The Virginia Historical Society holds a passport issued by the American legation in Paris on December 26, 1859, to JMD, "Ministre des Etats-Unis en Sardaigne. Allant a Turin," Palmer Family Papers, section 13, VHS.

37. Wynne to JMD, Dec. 13, 1859, Daniel Papers, Huntington Library.

38. JMD to Wynne, Apr. 25, 1860, Turin letterbooks, 168:348–53.

39. JMD to Crump, Apr. 25, 1860, Turin letterbooks, 168:354–64.

40. Parker to Sumner, Mar. 11, 1859, Theodore Parker Papers, LC.

41. Travers Daniel to JMD, June 1, 1860, Turin letterbooks, 170:42–47.

42. Wynne to JMD, May 22, 1860, Turin letterbooks, 169:429–39.

43. Turin dispatch 132 to Department, Jan. 24, 1860, Turin letterbooks, 168:62–84.

44. Turin dispatch 133, Jan. 31, 1860, Turin letterbooks, 168:75–84.

45. Turin dispatch 134, Feb. 7, 1860, Turin letterbooks, 168:96–110.

46. Turin dispatch 138, Feb. 29, 1860, Turin letterbooks, 168:157–80.

47. JMD to Minister of War, Mar. 8, 1860, Turin letterbooks, 168:265–66.

48. Turin dispatch 139, Mar. 4, 1860, Turin letterbooks, 168:181–96.

49. Turin dispatch 135, Feb. 14, 1860, Turin letterbooks, 168:131–46.

50. Department dispatches to Turin 36, Feb. 7, 1860, and 37, Mar. 1, 1860, Turin letterbooks, 168:256–57.

51. JMD to Secretary of State, Mar. 20, 1860, Turin letterbooks, 168:258–59.

52. W. L. G. Smith, *The Life and Times of Lewis Cass* (New York: Derby and Jackson, 1856), 337–40, 371. During his Italian travels, Cass visited Genoa but not Turin.

53. Cass to Garibaldi, printed in *New York Herald,* Aug. 27, 1850, and quoted in Marraro, *American Opinion on the Unification of Italy 1846–1861* (1932; reprint, New York: AMS, 1969), 168.

54. Christopher Hibbert, *Garibaldi and His Enemies* (Boston: Little, Brown, 1966), 187–88.

55. Turin dispatch 143 to Department, Apr. 10, 1860, Turin letterbooks, 168:272–80. Some writers have suggested, incorrectly, that Garibaldi went so far as to raise the question of American annexation of Nice. See, for example, Marraro, *American Opinion,* 267n.189, perhaps based on Frederick S. Daniel, *Richmond Examiner,* 229.

56. Turin dispatch 147, May 10, 1860, Turin letterbooks, 168:373–89.

57. Turin dispatch 153, June 19, 1860, Turin letterbooks, 170:9–18.

58. Turin dispatch 156, July 3, 1860, Turin letterbooks, 170:106–11.

59. Turin dispatch 154, June 26, 1860, Turin letterbooks, 170:87–91.

60. Turin dispatch 173, Oct. 16, 1860, roll 8, M90, NARA.

61. *Congressional Globe* (1860), 3056, 3063.

62. Quoted in Marraro, *American Opinion,* 300–303.

63. *New York Times*, Apr. 24, 1860.

64. JMD to "My dear Friend," n.d., Turin letterbooks, 170:192–95.

65. W. Medill, Comptroller, to JMD, Sept. 21, 1860, Turin letterbooks, 170:303–4.

66. Lloyd to JMD, Sept. 29, 1859; JMD to Lloyd, n.d., Turin letterbooks, 168:376–81. Lloyd to JMD, Dec. 15, 1859, and JMD to Lloyd, Jan. 20, 1860, Turin letterbooks, 169:41–46.

67. Lloyd to JMD, Mar. 10, 1860, Turin letterbooks, 169:263–64; Lloyd to JMD, Mar. 19, 1860, and JMD to Lloyd, Apr. 10, 1860, Turin letterbooks, 169:300–313.

68. Floyd to JMD, May 25, 1860, Turin letterbooks, 169:440–46.

69. JMD to Floyd, June 13, 1860, Turin letterbooks, 169:447–61.

70. Avery O. Craven, *The Growth of Southern Nationalism 1848–1861,* vol. 6, *A History of the South,* ed. Wendell Holmes Stephenson and E. Merton Coulter (Baton Rouge: Louisiana State Univ. Press, 1953), 314–15.

71. Turin dispatch 176, Nov. 13, 1860, Turin letterbooks, 170:327–35.

72. Turin dispatch 177, Nov. 20, 1860, Turin letterbooks, 170:338–40.

73. Microfilm roll 8, M90, NARA.

74. Turin dispatch 179, Dec. 11, 1860, Turin letterbook, 170:355–56.

75. Frederick S. Daniel, *Richmond Examiner,* 230.

76. Department dispatch 47 to Turin, Jan. 30, 1861, roll 101, M77, NARA. (Daniel cannot have received this commendation by the date of his final dispatch.)

77. Turin unnumbered dispatch to Department, Feb. 5, 1861, roll 8, M90, NARA.

78. Conway, *Autobiography,* 2:259.

79. Stearns, "John M. Daniel," 12.

80. Frederick S. Daniel, *Richmond Examiner,* 232.

81. Field, *America and the Mediterranean World,* 305.

82. Frederick S. Daniel, *Richmond Examiner,* 226–27.

83. Wynne to "Morris," Jan. 15, 1861, Section 27, Bagby Family Papers, VHS.

CHAPTER 12

1. Virginia Clay-Clopton, *A Belle of the Fifties: Memoirs of Mrs. Clay, of Alabama* (New York: Doubleday, Page, 1905), 42.

2. Russell to John Thadeus Delane, Mar. 26, 1861, in Martin Crawford, ed., *William Howard Russell's Civil War* (Athens: Univ. of Georgia Press, 1992), 23.

3. Edward A. Pollard, *Life of Jefferson Davis* (1869; reprint, Freeport, N.Y.: Books for Libraries, 1969), 63–66.

4. The warrant was offered at auction on the Internet in January 2001 as Document 4284 by the Gallery of History <www.galleryofhistory.com>.

5. *Examiner*, Aug. 2, 1864. This seems to be the only case in which John Daniel quoted in print from his diaries, which vanished after his death.

6. William Norwood Brigance, *Jeremiah Sullivan Black* (Philadelphia: Univ. of Pennsylvania Press, 1934), 77, 86–88, 90.

7. Black to A.V. Parsons, Jan. 17, 1861, reel 18, Jeremiah S. Black Papers, LC.

8. Dispatch 65, Bertinatti to Foreign Minister, Turin, Jan. 15, 1861, Busta 264, Moscati I, ASMAE.

9. George W. Bagby, "John M. Daniel's Latch-Key," *The Old Virginia Gentleman, and Other Sketches,* 110–11. Bagby's memoir is a main source for personal details about Daniel after he returned to Richmond in 1861.

10. JMD to W. W. Crump, Apr. 2, 1854. Daniel Family Papers, VHS.

11. Floyd wrote on February 6, 1861, from his home at Abingdon, Virginia, to Senator Louis T. Wigfall, to introduce Hughes, who "goes to Washington to ascertain the exact condition of things there in respect to my affairs—and to consult with you & other friends as to what it is proper for me to do now." Container 1, Wigfall Family Papers, LC.

12. Hughes, *Editors of the Past,* 22.

13. Frederick S. Daniel, *Richmond Examiner,* 230.

14. Black's account of Floyd is in pages 17–18, 57–64, and 112 of his "Historical Notes" on the last four months of the Buchanan administration, in Container 77, Jeremiah S. Black Papers, LC. This account is consistent with what the well-informed John A. Campbell told R. G. H. Kean in Richmond in 1863. *Inside the Confederate Government: The Diary of Robert Garlick Hill Kean*, ed. Edward Younger (Baton Rouge: Louisiana State Univ. Press, 1985), 36–37.

15. Bagby, *Old Virginia Gentleman.*

16. Thomas Cooper DeLeon, *Four Years in Rebel Capitals* (New York: Collier Books, 1962), 104–9.

17. Sarah Woolfolk Wiggins, ed., *The Journals of Josiah Gorgas 1857–1878* (Tuscaloosa: Univ. of Alabama Press, 1995), 98.

18. Daniel Papers, University of Virginia.

19. Unsigned letter to William Lloyd, June 1, 1861 in JMD's handwriting; E. D. (Mrs. William) Lloyd

to JMD, Aug. 22, 1861; undated request by William Lloyd to Hon. Wm. Henry Lyons, Judge of the Hustings Court, City of Richmond, asking that the sale on September 19, 1861, be set aside. Daniel Papers, University of Virginia.

20. *Examiner*, Mar. 4, 1861, quoted in Frederick S. Daniel, *Richmond Examiner*, 5.

21. John G. Nicolay and John Hay, eds., *Complete Works of Abraham Lincoln* (New York: Tandy-Thomas, 1905), 6:131.

22. Harriet Lane had acted as hostess for her unmarried uncle, President Buchanan.

23. Charles Stone, "Washington on the Eve of the War," in *Battles and Leaders of the Civil War*, eds. Robert Underwood Johnson and Clarence Clough Buel (1887; reprint, Edison, N.J.: Castle, n.d.), 1:7–25. William Howard Russell of the *London Times* recorded in his diary on April 4 that most of the volunteers he saw in Washington were "starved, washed-out creatures" (*My Diary North and South* [New York: Harper and Brothers, 1954], 37).

24. Crofts, "Late Antebellum Virginia," 281–82.

25. Robert L. Scribner, "Submission, Coercion, or Secession?" *Virginia Cavalcade* 3.2 (Autumn 1953): 43–47.

26. *Charleston Mercury*, Mar. 12, 1861.

27. *Examiner*, Nov. 27, Dec. 27, 1860, quoted in Cooley, "John Moncure Daniel," 88.

28. George L. Christian, "Reminiscences of Some of the Dead of the Bench and Bar of Richmond," *Virginia Law Register* 14.9 (Jan. 1909): 668–69.

29. *Confederate Scrap-Book* (Richmond: J. L. Hall, 1893), 137.

30. *Examiner* and *Charleston Mercury*, Apr. 13, 1861; see also Bagby, *Old Virginia Gentleman*, 133. A later, apocryphal version reported by Dabney and others was that Johnson pulled out a pistol and fired at Daniel, who fired back, but that neither hit the other.

31. Dabney, *Richmond: The Story of a City*, 160–61.

32. Cooley, "John Moncure Daniel," 94–95.

33. Bagby, "Editor's Table," *Southern Literary Messenger*, Apr. 1861, 319.

34. John Minor Botts, *The Great Rebellion: Its Secret History, Rise, Progress, and Disastrous Failure* (New York: Harper, 1866), 194–202.

35. Ernest B. Furgurson, *Ashes of Glory: Richmond at War* (New York: Alfred A. Knopf, 1996), 32–33.

36. Those who voted in favor of secession included Marmaduke Johnson, although he had been elected as a Union man. George H. Reese, ed., *Proceedings of the Virginia State Convention of 1861* (Richmond: Virginia State Library, 1965), 4:98–100, 144.

37. *Examiner*, May 8, 1861, quoted in Frederick S. Daniel, *Richmond Examiner*, 15.

38. Text kindly provided to author by Dr. Lynda Lasswell Crist, ed., *The Papers of Jefferson Davis.*

39. Lynda Lasswell Crist, ed., *The Papers of Jefferson Davis* (Baton Rouge: Louisiana State Univ. Press, 1992), 7:114–15.

40. Index to Bills and Resolutions of the Confederate Congress, RG 109, NARA.

41. *Examiner*, Aug. 28, 1862.

42. "Highlights in the History of . . . Posts at Turin, Italy," 39.

43. See Peter Bridges, "The Polymath from Vermont," *The Virginia Quarterly Review* (Winter 1999): 82–94.

44. Hudson Strode, *Jefferson Davis: Confederate President* (New York: Harcourt, Brace, 1959), 158.

45. Soon after the war, in 1867, Pollard published what became known in some quarters as the standard Southern history of the conflict, *The Lost Cause*. Pollard listed himself on the book's title page as having been "Editor of the Richmond 'Examiner' during the War." This implies that he ran the paper, but it was Daniel who did so when he was not away in the army. Toward the end, when Daniel took to his death-bed, it was John Mitchel rather than Pollard—who had gone to England in 1863—who was in charge. There is no extant list of just who was what at the *Examiner*, but an advertisement in the paper on

March 10, 1862, for Pollard's book *The First Year of the War* described him as the newspaper's associate editor. For a critical account of Pollard see Jack P. Maddex, *The Reconstruction of Edward A. Pollard: A Rebel's Conversion to Postbellum Unionism* (Chapel Hill: Univ. of North Carolina Press, 1974).

46. Hughes, "John Moncure Daniel," Jan. 10, 1885.

47. *Examiner*, Nov. 29, 1861.

48. Edward A. Pollard, *The Second Year of the War* (New York: Charles B. Richardson, 1863), 22.

49. Edward A. Pollard, *The Lost Cause* (1867; reprint, New York: Bonanza Books, n.d.), 656.

50. Rembert W. Patrick, *Jefferson Davis and His Cabinet* (Baton Rouge: Louisiana State Univ. Press, 1944), 41.

51. Mrs. D. Giraud Wright [Louise Wigfall], *A Southern Girl in '61: The War-Time Memories of a Confederate Senator's Daughter* (New York: Doubleday, Page, 1905), 91–92.

52. *The War of the Rebellion: A Compilation of the Official Records of the Union and Confederate Armies* (Washington, D.C.: GPO, 1880), ser. 1, 2:55.

53. DeLeon, *Four Years in Rebel Capitals*, 137.

54. *SLM*, Aug. 1861, 157.

55. DeLeon, *Four Years in Rebel Capitals*, 135.

56. *Examiner*, July 2, 8, 1861.

57. [P.] G. T. Beauregard, "The First Battle of Bull Run," *Battles and Leaders of the Civil War*, eds. Robert Underwood Johnson and Clarence Clough Buel (1887; reprint, Edison, N.J.: Castle, n.d.) 1:196–227.

58. Douglas Southall Freeman, *Lee's Lieutenants* (New York: Charles Scribner's Sons, 1944), 1:112–16.

59. William C. Davis et al., *First Blood: Fort Sumter to Bull Run* (Alexandria, Va.: Time-Life Books, 1983), 152, 155.

60. *Examiner*, July 24, 1861.

61. For example, by Alfred Hoyt Bill in *The Beleaguered City: Richmond, 1861–1865* (New York: Alfred A. Knopf, 1946).

62. Joseph L. Harsh, *Confederate Tide Rising* (Kent, Ohio: Kent State Univ. Press, 1998), 17–19.

63. F. N. Boney, "Virginia," in *The Confederate Governors*, ed. W. Buck Yearns (Athens: Univ. of Georgia Press, 1985), 218–20.

64. Bevin Alexander, *Robert E. Lee's Civil War* (Holbrook, Mass: Adams Media, 1998), 9–10.

65. *Examiner*, Sept. 27, 1861.

CHAPTER 13

1. *Examiner*, Aug. 5, 1861.

2. Ibid., Aug. 7, 1861.

3. Frederick Daniel served in the Howitzers for three years until sent to the hospital with "remittent fever." Years after the war, he became an occasional contributor (as noted hereafter) to *Harper's New Monthly Magazine* and published a memoir entitled *Richmond Howitzers in the War*. See also <www.richmondhowitzers.com/Danielintro.htm>

4. *Examiner*, May 26, 1861, quoted in Wilkinson, "John Moncure Daniel."

5. Compiled Service Records of Confederate General and Staff Officers, and Non-Regimental Enlisted Men, roll 70, M331, NARA. See also Consolidated Index to Compiled Service Records of Confederate Soldiers, roll 114, M253, NARA.

6. Two of Daniel's reports still exist in the Virginia Historical Society.

7. Jacob D. Cox, "McClellan in West Virginia," in *Battles and Leaders*, 1:145.

8. Lee wrote to his wife on October 7, 1861. Clifford Dowdey, ed., *The Wartime Papers of Robert E. Lee* (New York: Da Capo Press, 1987), 80. Albert Z. Conner, president of the Stafford County Historical

Society and author of the forthcoming *Not for Fame or Reward: VMI's Civil War Soldiers,* kindly identified the two other editor-soldiers as Wyatt Mosely Elliot of the *Richmond Whig* and Nathaniel Tyler of the *Richmond Enquirer.*

9. John S. Wise, *The End of an Era* (Boston: Houghton Mifflin, 1899), 177.

10. Hughes, "John Moncure Daniel." Existing records indicate neither when Daniel was granted leave nor what period it covered but only that on December 10, 1861, he requested an extension. Roll 70, M331, NARA.

11. Wise, *End of an Era,* 171.

12. Dabney, *Pistols and Pointed Pens,* 46.

13. *Examiner,* Mar. 10, 1862.

14. *Virginia: A Guide to the Old Dominion* (Richmond: Virginia State Library, 1992); <http://xroads.virginia.edu/~HYPER/VAGuide/newspaper.html>.

15. *Examiner,* Aug. 3, 1861.

16. Lizzy Cary Daniel, *Confederate Scrap-Book* (1893; reprint, Nashville, Tenn.: Dixie Press, 1996), 135.

17. Cooley, "John Moncure Daniel," 124.

18. Eggleston, "A Rebel's Recollections," 97.

19. The accounts of receipts and expenditures are in the Daniel Papers, University of Virginia.

20. Bagby, *Old Virginia Gentleman,* 125. This is not the same as saying (Osthaus, *Partisans of the Southern Press,* 106) that Daniel himself made $50,000 a year.

21. J. B. Jones. *A Rebel War Clerk's Diary* (Philadelphia: J. B. Lippincott, 1866), 1:291.

22. Bagby, *Old Virginia Gentleman,* 136.

23. *Examiner,* Aug. 14, 18, 1862.

24. W. C. Corsan, *Two Months in the Confederate States,* ed. Benjamin H. Trask (Baton Rouge: Univ. of Louisiana Press, 1996), 83.

25. The text of the cartel, which deals only with prisoners and not with newspapers or other items, can be found in Pollard, *The Lost Cause,* 618–20.

26. *Examiner,* Jan. 23, 1863.

27. Hughes, *Editors of the Past,* 27–28.

28. *Examiner,* June 7, 1861.

29. Ibid., July 4, 1861.

30. Ibid., July 8, 1861.

31. Eggleston, "A Rebel's Recollections," 107.

32. "A Memorial—Moses Drury Hoge, D.D. LL.D," *Southern Historical Society Papers* 30 (1902): 262.

33. Furgurson, *Ashes of Glory,* 217.

34. Cooley, "John Moncure Daniel," 109, 116–17. In addition to the papers listed, the *Sentinel,* previously published in Alexandria, began to appear in Richmond in March 1863.

35. Robert E. Cowart, "The Thunderer of the Confederacy," 4, Special Collections Department, Robert W. Woodruff Library, Emory University, Atlanta.

36. Bruce Chadwick, *The Two American Presidents* (Secaucus, N.J.: Birch Lane Press, 1999), 18–19, 190–91, 193.

37. *Examiner,* Aug. 14, 1861.

38. Shelby Foote, *The Civil War: A Narrative* (New York: Random House, 1958), 1:221–22.

39. *Examiner,* Feb. 24, 1862.

40. Eron O. Rowland, *Varina Howell, Wife of Jefferson Davis* (New York: Macmillan, 1931), 2:242–50.

41. *Examiner,* Feb. 24, 1862.

42. Ibid., Mar. 6, 1862.

43. Foote, *Civil War,* 350–51.

44. *Examiner,* Apr. 8, 1862.

45. Ibid., May 1, 16, 1862.

46. Ibid., May 19, 1862.

47. Ibid., June 9, 1862. This was the balloon of the intrepid T. S. C. Lowe, who had made an experimental flight from Ohio that landed him in South Carolina just as the war was beginning.

48. *Examiner,* Mar. 13, 1862.

49. J. William Jones, "Seven Days around Richmond," Reminiscences of the Army of Northern Virginia, Paper No. 8, *Southern Historical Society Papers* (Jan.–Dec. 1881).

50. *Examiner,* June 28, 1862.

51. Since Daniel's name does not appear on published lists of wounded admitted to hospitals (*Examiner,* July 10, 11, 1862), it appears that he went home to mend. DeLeon, *Four Years in Rebel Capitals,* 234, describes how other citizens opened their homes to wounded men.

52. This quotation is taken from an addendum to Mitchel's "Jail Journal," quoted in William Dillon, *Life of John Mitchel* (London: Kegan Paul, Trench, 1888), 2:174. The military record that describes Daniel as "severely wounded" is on microfilm roll 70, M331, NARA.

53. Bagby, *Old Virginia Gentleman,* 128.

54. *Examiner,* June 30, 1862.

55. Ibid., Aug. 28, 1862.

56. Ibid., Feb. 4, 1863.

57. G. Moxley Sorrel, *Recollections of a Confederate Staff Officer* (New York: Neale Publishing, 1905), 85–87. See also William Hassler, *A. Hill: Lee's Forgotten General* (Richmond: Garrett and Massie, 1957), 2, 66–68.

58. Johnston to Wigfall, Dec. 15, 1862, container 2, Wigfall Family Papers, LC; also quoted in Bruce Catton, *Never Call Retreat* (Garden City, NY: Doubleday, 1965),12.

59. Corsan, *Two Months in the Confederate States,* 115.

60. Letter of 1858 quoted in Dillon, *Life of John Mitchel,* 2:107.

61. John Mitchel, *Jail Journal* (Dublin: M. H. Gill & Son, 1913), 391–93.

62. For a modern account of Meagher and Mitchel, see Thomas Keneally, *The Great Shame and the Triumph of the Irish in the English-Speaking World* (New York: Nan A. Talese/Doubleday, 1999). The author would like to point out one minor error in Keneally's book, relating to the author's great-great-uncle Daniel Joseph Devlin. Keneally says Meagher was at Devlin's house in New York when, in August 1865, Meagher was offered the post of military secretary of Montana. In fact, the offer was telegraphed to Meagher in Minnesota, as documented by Robert G. Athearn in *Thomas Francis Meagher* (New York: Dover Press, 1976), 145.

CHAPTER 14

1. Sallie Brock Putnam, *Richmond during the War* (1867; reprint, Lincoln: Univ. of Nebraska Press, 1996), 41.

2. J. B. Jones, *A Rebel War Clerk's Diary* (Philadelphia: J. B. Lippincott, 1866), 1:381, 2:185.

3. Mary Boykin Chesnut, *A Diary from Dixie,* ed. Ben Ames Williams (Cambridge, Mass.: Harvard Univ. Press, 1980), 286.

4. Entry for Aug. 24, 1861, in Mary Boykin Chesnut, *The Private Mary Chesnut: The Unpublished Civil War Diaries,* ed. C. Vann Woodward and Elisabeth Muhlenfeld (New York: Oxford Univ. Press, 1984), 136.

5. Dillon, *Life of John Mitchel,* 199.

6. Bagby, *Old Virginia Gentleman,* 121.

7. Ibid.

8. A considered account of the riot is given by Michael B. Chesson in "Harlots or Heroines? A New Look at the Richmond Bread Riot," *VMHB* 92.2 (Apr. 1984): 131–75.

9. Davis's letter is quoted in Burke Davis, *They Called Him Stonewall* (New York: Holt, Rinehart and Winston, 1961), 188.

10. *Examiner*, Apr. 4, 1863.

11. Ibid., Apr. 13, 1863.

12. Ibid., Apr. 4, 1863.

13. Dillon, *Life of John Mitchel*, 174.

14. Ibid., 187.

15. Note from Mrs. Harrison quoted in ibid., 197.

16. *Examiner*, July 16, 1863.

17. Bagby, "John M. Daniel's Latch-Key," 116.

18. Ibid., 131–32.

19. On Aug. 27, 1863.

20. Eli N. Evans, *Judah P. Benjamin: The Jewish Confederate* (New York: Free Press, 1988), 96.

21. Quoted from *Mary Chesnut's Civil War*, 1981, in Evans, *Judah P. Benjamin*, 154.

22. Quoted in Evans, *Judah P. Benjamin*, 156.

23. Evans, *Judah P. Benjamin*, 203.

24. Evans, *Judah P. Benjamin*, 178, 203.

25. Quoted in Furgurson, *Ashes of Glory*, 191.

26. Robert Douthat Meade, *Judah P. Benjamin, Confederate Statesman* (New York: Oxford Univ. Press, 1943), 180.

27. *Examiner*, Dec. 10, 1863.

28. Ibid., Aug. 21,1863, quoted in Cooley, "John Moncure Daniel," 191.

29. John H. Reagan, *Memoirs, with Special Reference to Secession and the Civil War* (1906; reprint, Austin, Tex.: Pemberton Press, 1968), 124–25, 158.

30. Furgurson, *Ashes of Glory*, 98–99.

31. Douglas B. Ball, *Financial Failure and Confederate Defeat* (Urbana: Univ. of Illinois Press, 1991), 230.

32. *Examiner*, Feb. 28, 1863.

33. Confederate tax revenues were 1 percent of income, a significant contrast to the Union's 23 percent. See Richard E. Beringer et al., *Why the South Lost the Civil War* (Athens: Univ. of Georgia Press, 1986), 11.

34. See, for example, *Examiner*, Apr. 11, 1863.

35. Ball, *Financial Failure*, 249–50.

36. *Examiner*, Nov. 12, 1863.

37. *Who Was Who in America 1607–1896* (Chicago: A. N. Marquis, n.d.), 608.

38. *Report of the Secretary of the Treasury*, Richmond, Nov. 7, 1864. Copies of identical reports to the president of the Senate and the speaker of the House of Representatives are in the Rare Book Collection, LC.

39. *Examiner*, Dec. 1, 1863.

40. Ibid., June 18, 1864.

41. Ibid., July 28, 1863.

42. Furgurson, *Ashes of Glory*, 283.

43. *Examiner*, Feb. 15, 1864. The article, which included the texts of the letters from Harrison, is reprinted in Frederick S. Daniel, *Richmond Examiner*, 168–71.

44. *Examiner*, Sept. 2, 1862.

45. Furgurson, *Ashes of Glory*, 94–95.

46. *Examiner*, Feb. 20, 1862.

47. Varina H. Davis, *Jefferson Davis* (New York: Belford, 1890), 2:550–51.

48. Burton N. Harrison to Mrs. Sanders, Mar. 30, 1864. Folder "George N. Sanders Personal Correspondence 1864–65," container 2, George N. Sanders Papers, LC.

49. Anna Sanders diary, Sept. 13, 1864, folder "Anna J. Sanders 1863–64/George N. Sanders, Jr. 1864–65," container 1, George N. Sanders Papers, LC.

50. Jefferson Davis to "Saunders," June 30, 1869, folder "George N. Sanders Personal Correspondence 1866–1904," container 2, George N. Sanders Papers, LC.

51. *Examiner,* July 26, 1864.

52. Botts, *Great Rebellion,* 297–307.

CHAPTER 15

1. The letters exchanged between Edward C. Elmore and JMD before their duel were printed in the *Examiner* on August 18, 1864. The subsequent court proceedings involving Elmore, H. Rives Pollard, and Arthur E. Peticolas were reported in the *Examiner* on August 18, 19, 22, 24, 30, and 31, and September 1 and 3, 1864. Virginius Dabney wrote in *Pistols and Pointed Pens* (52) that the duel was on August 17, but it is clear from the newspaper accounts that it took place on Tuesday morning, August 16.

2. There is some question as to when Elmore joined the treasury. Confederate treasury records include a letter dated November 3, 1862, to "Dear Tom" from E. C. Elmore at the Farmers Bank of Alabama in Montgomery. Treasury Department—Letters Received 1861–65, box 3, RG 109, NARA

3. Crist, *Papers of Jefferson Davis,* 10:5.

4. The will is in Book 23, pp. 520–21, Hustings Wills, Richmond City, reel 75, Library of Virginia. It was signed but not witnessed, presumably because Daniel did not want anyone to know he felt the need to make a will before his duel with Elmore. The record includes a statement on oath by Robert W. Hughes and Thomas H. Wynne on April 1, 1865, attesting that the will was written in Daniel's hand.

5. Lyon G. Tyler, ed., *Men of Mark in Virginia* (Washington, D.C.: Men of Mark, 1909), 5:78.

6. As noted earlier, H. Rives Pollard was the brother of Edward A. Pollard, and he had worked at the *Richmond Examiner* since at least 1862.

7. Notice in *Richmond Sentinel,* September 16, 1864, kindly brought to the author's attention by Lynda L. Crist. Elmore presumably resigned his position that autumn; he was replaced as treasurer by John N. Hendren on January 7, 1865. As Crist has also noted to the author, it seems possible that Edward Elmore was the son of Franklin Harper Elmore (1799–1850), a South Carolina senator who was elected president of the Bank of South Carolina in 1839, who was briefly a colleague of Jefferson Davis in 1850, and who must have been well acquainted with Christopher Memminger.

8. Robert Garlick Hill Kean, a division chief in the Confederate War Department, wrote in the margin of his diary at some point subsequent to July 14, 1864, that an investigation of Elmore showed he had not lost treasury funds. Edward Younger, ed., *Inside the Confederate Government: The Diary of Robert Garlick Hill Kean* (Baton Rouge: Louisiana State Univ. Press, 1985), 165. The author has not found any evidence of an audit in the apparently incomplete Confederate treasury records in RG 109, NARA .

9. Bagby, *Old Virginia Gentleman,* 114.

10. Ibid., 138.

11. Ibid., 128.

12. Most of the reports by the astute Van Lew, who was never caught, were later destroyed at her request. After the war, she wrote into her diary two quotations from the wartime *Examiner,* one of which described the execution of a Union spy in Richmond. David D. Ryan, ed., *A Yankee Spy in Richmond: The Civil War Diary of "Crazy Bet" Van Lew* (Mechanicsburg, Pa.: Stackpole Books, 1996), 64–67, 78–80.

13. Douglas Southall Freeman, ed., *Lee's Dispatches* (New York: G.Putnam's Sons, 1957), 241.

14. *Examiner,* Sept. 7, 1864.

15. *London Times,* Aug. 4, 1864, quoted in Furgurson, *Ashes of Glory,* 275.

16. *Examiner,* Sept. 16, 1864.

17. Ibid., Feb. 9, 1863.

18. Ibid., Nov. 8, 1864.

19. Ibid., Oct. 10, 1864.

20. Ibid., Nov. 18, 1864.

21. J. B. Jones, *Rebel War Clerk's Diary*, 2:337.

22. Bagby, *Old Virginia Gentleman*, 129.

23. Will of August 12, 1864, which as noted earlier is in the microfilm collection of the Library of Virginia.

24. Bagby, *Old Virginia Gentleman*, 140.

25. Furgurson, *Ashes of Glory*, 293–94.

26. Thomas Dormandy notes in *The White Death: A History of Tuberculosis* (New York: New York Univ. Press, 1999), 22, that until the 1950s standard textbooks reckoned that tuberculosis was fatal in 80 percent of cases within five to fifteen years. If Daniel contracted the disease from his mother, as seems likely, he lived with it for a quarter-century. Some afflicted people lived longer; Ralph Waldo Emerson died at age seventy-nine. Daniel was reported to have died of "phthisis." This was then the usual medical term for tuberculosis; the layman's equivalent was "consumption." Ibid., 2, 9.

27. Bagby, *Old Virginia Gentleman*, 138. Physicians were not licensed in Virginia until well after the Civil War, and it has not been possible to identify the Dr. Rawlings who saw Daniel in Paris and attended him in his final days.

28. Book 29, pp. 290 (Aug. 12, 1864), 294 (Aug. 13, 1864), and 484 (Mar. 17, 1865), Hustings Court Minutes, Richmond City records, reel 97, Library of Virginia.

29. Bagby, *Old Virginia Gentleman*, 141.

POSTLUDE

1. The text of the poem is in Ward W. Briggs Jr., *Soldier and Scholar: Basil Lanneau Gildersleeve and the Civil War* (Charlottesville: Univ. Press of Virginia, 1998), 387.

2. *New York Times*, Apr. 7, 1865.

3. This was not the only duel that involved a Richmond editor after the Civil War. In 1869, Daniel's former colleague Robert W. Hughes, who later spent almost a quarter-century as a federal judge, shot and wounded William E. Cameron of the *Richmond Index*. *Dictionary of American Biography* (New York: Charles Scribner's Sons, 1934), 7:551. The last such duel was apparently one in 1881 between William C. Elam of the *Richmond Whig* and Richard C. Beirne of the *Richmond State*, in which Elam was severely wounded. Scribner, "The Code Duello in Virginia," 30.

4. Jack Maddex, *The Reconstruction of Edward A. Pollard: A Rebel's Conversion to Postbellum Unionism* (Chapel Hill: Univ. of North Carolina Press, 1974), 64–70.

5. Wynne to Bagby, Dec. 5, 1867, Bagby Family Papers, VHS.

6. Wynne to Bagby, Dec. 14, 1867, Bagby Family Papers, VHS.

7. Conway letter from Fredericksburg to his wife, Sept. 19, 1875, folder 6, box 1, Moncure D. Conway Papers, Waidner and Spahr Library, Dickinson College, Carlisle, Pa.

8. Frederick Daniel, "A Visit to a Colonial Estate," *Harper's New Monthly Magazine* 76.454 (Mar. 1888): 517–24. Other articles by Frederick Daniel are in the issues for March 1885 and July 1890. He also contributed at least one article to *Harper's Weekly* (Nov. 19, 1904).

9. Rosewell Page, *Thomas Nelson Page: A Memoir of a Virginia Gentleman*. (New York: Charles Scribner's Sons, 1923), 32.

10. Rogari, *Due regine dei salotti nella Firenze capitale*, 132–33.

11. David Lowenthal, *George Perkins Marsh, Prophet of Conservation* (Seattle: Univ. of Washington Press, 2000), 313. David Lowenthal, author of a 1958 biography of George Perkins Marsh, four decades later produced a magnificent new work on his subject.

12. Basil L. Gildersleeve, "My Sixty Days in Greece: The Olympic Games, Old and New." *Atlantic Monthly,* Feb. 1897; <www.theatlantic.com/issues/1897feb/greece.htm>.

13. The author is grateful to Woody Harper, assistant general manager of Hollywood Cemetery, for locating JMD's grave in section L, lot 21 and providing photographs of the monument above the grave. Because he was buried in a family lot and not in the Soldiers' Section, Daniel is not listed in the *Register of the Confederate Dead, Interred in Hollywood Cemetery, Richmond, Va.* (Richmond: Gary, Clemmitt and Jones, 1869).

Bibliography

UNPUBLISHED PERSONAL PAPERS

Bagby Family Papers. Virginia Historical Society, Richmond.

Black, Jeremiah S. Manuscript Division, Library of Congress, Washington, D.C.

Campbell, Charles. Manuscripts and Rare Books Department, Swem Library, College of William and Mary, Williamsburg, Va.

Conway, Moncure D. Archives and Special Collections, Waidner and Spahr Library, Dickinson College, Carlisle, Pa.

Cowart, Robert E. Special Collections Department, Robert W. Woodruff Library, Emory University, Atlanta, Ga.

Daniel Family Papers, 1790–-1854. Virginia Historical Society, Richmond.

Daniel, James Mitchell. Skipper Steely, Paris, Tex.

Daniel, Mary Vivian. Skipper Steely, Paris, Tex.

Daniel Papers. Huntington Library, San Marino, Calif.

Daniel Papers. Special Collections, Alderman Library, University of Virginia, Charlottesville.

Davis, Jefferson. Rice University, Houston, Tex.

Howison, Robert Reid. Manuscripts and Rare Books Department, Swem Library, College of William and Mary, Williamsburg, Va.

Hunter, R. M. T. Special Collections, Alderman Library, University of Virginia, Charlottesville.

King, George Harrison Sanford. Virginia Historical Society, Richmond.

Marcy, William L. Manuscript Division, Library of Congress, Washington, D.C.

Palmer Family Papers. Virginia Historical Society, Richmond.

Parker, Theodore. Manuscript Division, Library of Congress, Washington, D.C.

Sanders, George N. Manuscript Division, Library of Congress, Washington, D.C.

Tucker-Coleman Collection. Manuscripts and Rare Books Department, Swem Library, College of William and Mary, Williamsburg, Va.

Vaughan, Clement Read. Presbyterian Historical Society, Montreat, N.C.

Washington, Henry A. Virginia Historical Society, Richmond.

Wigfall Family Papers. Manuscript Division, Library of Congress, Washington , D.C.

UNPUBLISHED GOVERNMENT DOCUMENTS AND RECORDS

Confederate States of America. Consolidated Index to Compiled Service Records of Confederate Soldiers. Microfilm publication M253. National Archives, Washington, D.C.

———. Compiled Service Records of Confederate General and Staff Officers, and Non-Regimental Enlisted Men. Microfilm publication M331, National Archives, Washington, D.C.

Kingdom of Sardinia. Records of the Ministry of Foreign Affairs. Archivio di Stato, Turin, Italy.

———. Records of the Ministry of Foreign Affairs. Moscati 1 and 6. Archivio Storico Diplomatico, Ministero degli Affari Esteri, Rome, Italy.

Richmond City. Hustings Court Minutes, Book 29. Microfilm reel 97. Library of Virginia, Richmond, Va.

———. Hustings Wills, Book 23. Microfilm reel 75. Library of Virginia, Richmond, Va.

Stafford County. Deed Books. Stafford Court House, Va.

U.S. Department of State. Recommendations for Appointment 1852–53. Microfilm publication 967, National Archives, College Park, Md.

———. Records of Foreign Service Posts. Italy. Letterbooks, Turin. Records Group 84, National Archives, College Park, Md.

———. Records of Foreign Service Posts. Italy. Microfilm publication M77, National Archives, College Park, Md.

———. Records of Foreign Service Posts. Italy. Microfilm publication M90, National Archives, College Park, Md.

U.S. Department of the Treasury. Records of the Customs Bureau. Record Group 36, National Archives, Washington, D.C.

NEWSPAPERS AND PERIODICALS

Baltimorean (Md.)

Charleston (S.C.) Mercury

Democratic Review

Frederick Douglass' Paper (Rochester, N.Y.)

New-York Daily Times

New York Tribune

Richmond Examiner

Richmond Enquirer

Richmond Whig

Southern Literary Messenger (Richmond, Va.)

Southern Planter (Richmond, Va.)

Stafford County (Va.) Sun

Washington Post

PUBLISHED SOURCES

Abbot, W. W., and Dorothy Twohig, eds. *The Papers of George Washington*. Colonial Series. Vols. 7 and 8. Charlottesville: Univ. Press of Virginia, 1983–95.

Aicardi, Cinzia Maria, and Alessandra Cavaterra., eds. *I fondi archivistici della Legazione Sarda e delle rappresentanze diplomatiche italiane negli U.S.A. (1848–1901)*. Rome: Istituto Poligrafico e Zecca dello Stato, 1988.

Alexander, Bevin. *Robert E. Lee's Civil War*. Holbrook, Mass.: Adams Media, 1998.

Andrew, Christopher, and Vasili Mitrokhin. *The Sword and the Shield: The Mitrokhin Archive and the Secret History of the KGB*. New York: Basic Books, 1999.

Athearn, Robert G. *Thomas Francis Meagher*. New York: Dover Press, 1976.

Bagby, George W. *The Old Virginia Gentleman and Other Sketches*. Edited by Ellen M. Bagby. Richmond: Dietz Press, 1948.

Bagby, Ben. "Saving Crow's Nest." *Stafford County Sun*, May 28, 1999.

Ball, Douglas B. *Financial Failure and Confederate Defeat*. Urbana: Univ. of Illinois Press, 1991.

Bartlett, Ruhl J., ed. *The Record of American Diplomacy*. New York: Alfred A. Knopf, 1950.

Basler, Roy P. *The Collected Works of Abraham Lincoln.* Vol. 4. New Brunswick, N.J.: Rutgers Univ. Press, 1953.

Bassham, Ben L. *Conrad Wise Chapman.* Kent, Ohio: Kent State Univ. Press, 1998.

Bauer, K. Jack. *Zachary Taylor.* Baton Rouge: Louisiana State Univ. Press, 1985.

Bearss, Sara B., ed. "Not a Humbug." *History Notes: The Newsletter of the Virginia Historical Society* 39 (Summer 2000):4–5.

Beauregard, [P.] G. T. "The First Battle of Bull Run." In *Battles and Leaders of the Civil War,* edited by Robert Underwood Johnson and Clarence Clough Buel, 1: 112–16. 1887. Reprint, Edison, N.J.: Castle, n.d.

Bemis, Samuel Flagg et al. *The American Secretaries of State and Their Diplomacy.* New York: Pageant Book, 1958.

Benson, Lee. *Toward the Scientific Study of History.* Philadelphia: Lippincott, 1972.

Beringer, Richard E. et al. *Why the South Lost the Civil War.* Athens, Ga.: Univ. of Georgia Press, 1986.

Bernardi, A. A. "Contributi italiani alla formazione degli Stati Uniti d'America." *Giornale di Politica e di Letteratura,* Rome, 1942. (Copy available in Centro di Studi Americani, Rome.)

Bill, Alfred Hoyt. *The Beleaguered City: Richmond, 1861–1865.* New York: Alfred A. Knopf, 1946.

Biographical Directory of the American Congress 1774–1996. Alexandria, Va.: CQ Staff Directories, 1997.

Boney, F. N. *John Letcher of Virginia.* Tuscaloosa: Univ. of Alabama Press, 1966.

———. "Virginia." *The Confederate Governors.* Edited by W. Buck Yearns. Athens: University of Georgia Press, 1985.

Borelli, Pierfelice. *Urbano e Maria Rattazzi.* Cavallermaggiore, Italy: Gribaudo Editore, 1993.

Bory, Jean-Louis. *Eugene Sue.* Paris: Hachette Littérature, 1962.

Botts, John Minor. *The Great Rebellion: Its Secret History, Rise, Progress, and Disastrous Failure.* New York: Harper, 1866.

Bridges, J. Malcolm. "Industry & Trade." *Richmond: Capital of Virginia.* Richmond: Whittet and Shepperson, 1938.

Bridges, Peter. "A Pen of Fire." *The Virginia Quarterly Review* 78.1 (Winter 2002): 41–53.

———. "The Polymath from Vermont." *The Virginia Quarterly Review* 75.1 (Winter 1999), 82–94.

Brigance, William Norwood. *Jeremiah Sullivan Black.* Philadelphia: Univ. of Pennsylvania Press, 1934.

Briggs, Ward W., Jr. *Soldier and Scholar: Basil Lanneau Gildersleeve and the Civil War.* Charlottesville: Univ. Press of Virginia, 1998.

Burnette, Frank, Jr. "Peter V. Daniel: Agrarian Justice." *VMHB* 62.3 (July 1954): 289–305.

The Cambridge History of English and American Literature. <www.bartleby.com>

Cappon, Lester J. *Virginia Newspapers 1821–1935.* New York: D. Appleton-Century, 1936.

Carlyle, Thomas. "Characteristics." *The Harvard Classics.* New York: P. F. Collier and Son, 1909. 25: 365–66.

———. *The Nigger Question.* Edited by Eugene R. August. New York: Appleton-Century, Crofts, 1971.

Cash, W. J. *The Mind of the South.* New York: Alfred A. Knopf, 1941.

Catterall, Louise F. Introduction to *Richmond Portraits.* Richmond: Valentine Museum, 1949.

Catton, Bruce. *Never Call Retreat.* Garden City, N.Y.: Doubleday, 1965.

Chadwick, Bruce. *The Two American Presidents.* Secaucus, N.J.: Birch Lane Press, 1999.

Chapelle, Howard I. *History of American Sailing Ships.* New York: Bonanza Books, 1982.

Chesnut, Mary Boykin. *A Diary from Dixie.* Edited by Ben Ames Williams. Cambridge, Mass.: Harvard Univ. Press, 1980.

———. *The Private Mary Chesnut: The Unpublished Civil War Diaries.* Edited by C. Vann Woodward and Elisabeth Muhlenfeld. New York: Oxford Univ. Press, 1984.

Chesson, Michael B. "Harlots or Heroines? A New Look at the Richmond Bread Riot." *Virginia Magazine of History and Biography* 92.2 (Apr. 1984): 131–75.

Chesson, Michael B., and Leslie Jean Roberts, eds. *Exile in Richmond: The Confederate Journal of Henri Garidel.* Charlottesville: Univ. Press of Virginia, 2001.

Christian, George L. "Reminiscences of Some of the Dead of the Bench and Bar of Richmond." *Virginia Law Register* 14.9 (Jan. 1909): 668–69.

Christian, W. Asbury. *Richmond: Her Past and Present.* 1912. Reprint, Spartanburg, S.C.: Reprint Company, 1973.

Clay-Copton, Virginia. *A Belle of the Fifties: Memoirs of Mrs. Clay, of Alabama.* New York: Doubleday, Page, 1905.

Coleman, Terry. *The Liners.* New York: G. P. Putnam's Sons, 1977.

Confederate Scrap-Book. Richmond: J. L. Hall, 1893.

Congressional Globe. 46 vols. Washington, D.C., 1834–73.

Conway, Moncure Daniel. *Autobiography, Memories and Experiences.* 2 vols. Boston: Houghton, Mifflin, 1904.

———. "Fredericksburg First and Last." *Magazine of American History* 17.6 (June 1887): 450.

———. *Testimonies Concerning Slavery.* London: Chapman and Hall, 1864.

Cooke, John Esten. *Mohun, or the Last Days of Lee and His Paladins.* 1869. Reprint, Charlottesville, Va.: Historical Publishing, 1936.

Cooley, Raymond K. "John Moncure Daniel, Editor of the Richmond Examiner and Gadfly of the Confederacy." Master's thesis, Old Dominion University, 1973.

Corsan, W. C. *Two Months in the Confederate States.* Edited by Benjamin H. Trask. Baton Rouge: Louisiana State Univ. Press, 1996.

Cox, Jacob D. "McClellan in West Virginia." In *Battles and Leaders of the Civil War,* edited by Robert Underwood Johnson and Clarence Clough Buel, 1:145. 1887. Reprint, Edison, N.J.: Castle, n.d.

Craven, Avery O. *The Growth of Southern Nationalism 1848–1861.* Vol. 6 of *A History of the South,* edited by Wendell Holmes Stephenson and E. Merton Coulter. Baton Rouge: Louisiana State Univ. Press, 1953.

Crawford, Martin, ed. *William Howard Russell's Civil War.* Athens: Univ. of Georgia Press, 1992.

Crist, Lynda Lasswell, ed. *The Papers of Jefferson Davis.* Vol. 7. Baton Rouge: Louisiana State Univ. Press, 1992.

Crofts, Daniel W. "Late Antebellum Virginia Reconsidered." *Virginia Magazine of History and Biography* 107.3 (Summer 1999): 253–86.

Crowe, Eyre. *With Thackeray in America.* London: Cassell and Company, 1893.

Curato, Federico, ed. *Le Relazioni diplomatiche tra la Gran Bretagna ed il Regno di Sardegna dal 1852 al 1856.* Vol. 2. Turin, Italy: ILTE, 1956.

Curti, Merle E. "George N. Sanders—American Patriot of the Fifties." *South Atlantic Quarterly* 27.1 (Jan. 1928): 85–86.

Dabney, Virginius. *Pistols and Pointed Pens.* Chapel Hill, N.C.: Algonquin Books, 1987.

———. *Richmond: The Story of a City.* Garden City, N.Y.: Doubleday, 1976.

Daniel, Frederick S. *The Richmond Examiner During the War.* 1868. Reprint, New York: Arno and The New York Times, 1970.

———. "A Visit to a Colonial Estate." *Harper's New Monthly Magazine* 76.454 (Mar. 1888): 517–24.

Daniel, Lizzie Cary. *Confederate Scrap-Book.* 1893. Reprint, Nashville: Dixie Press, 1996.

Davis, Burke. *They Called Him Stonewall.* New York: Holt, Rinehart and Winston, 1961.

Davis, Jefferson. *The Rise and Fall of the Confederate Government.* 1881. 2 vols. Reprint, New York: Da Capo Press, 1990.

Davis, Robert Ralph, Jr. "Republican Simplicity: The Diplomatic Costume Question, 1789–1867." *Civil War History* 15.1(Mar. 1969): 19–29.

Davis, Varina H. *Jefferson Davis.* 2 vols. New York: Belford, 1890.

Davis, William C. et al. *First Blood: Fort Sumter to Bull Run.* Alexandria, Va.: Time-Life Books, 1983.

De Forest, J. W. *European Acquaintance.* New York: Harper and Brothers, 1858.
DeLeon, Edwin. *Thirty Years of My Life on Three Continents.* 2 vols. London: Ward and Downey, 1890.
DeLeon, Thomas Cooper. *Four Years in Rebel Capitals.* New York: Collier Books, 1962.
Dickens, Charles. *American Notes.* Vol. 2. London: Chapman and Hall, 1842.
Dictionary of American Biography. Vols. 7 and 9. New York: Charles Scribner's Sons, 1934 and 1936.
Dillon, Richard H. *North American Indian Wars.* New York: Facts on File, 1983.
Dillon, William. *Life of John Mitchel.* 2 vols. London: Kegan Paul, Trench, 1888.
Dormandy, Thomas. *The White Death: A History of Tuberculosis.* New York: New York Univ. Press, 1999.
Dowdey, Clifford, ed. *The Wartime Papers of Robert E. Lee.* 1961. Reprint, New York: Da Capo Press, 1987.
Eby, Jerrilyn. *They Called Stafford Home.* Fredericksburg, Va.: Heritage Books, 1997.
Eggleston, George Cary. *A Rebel's Recollections.* 1874. Reprint, Baton Rouge: Louisiana State Univ. Press, 1996.
Ellis, Joseph J. *American Sphinx: The Character of Thomas Jefferson.* New York: Vintage Books, 1998.
Ettinger, Amos Aschbach. *The Mission to Spain of Pierre Soulé, 1853–1855.* New Haven: Yale Univ. Press, 1932.
Evans, Eli N. *Judah P. Benjamin: The Jewish Confederate.* New York: Free Press, 1988.
Farrell, John J., ed., *Zachary Taylor 1784–1850 and Millard Fillmore 1800–1874: Chronology, Documents, Bibliographic Aids.* Dobbs Ferry, N.Y.: Oceana Publications, 1971.
Fenimore, David H. "Horace Greeley (1811–1872), Editor of the *New York Tribune.*" <www.honors.unr.edu/~fenimore/greeley.html>
Field, James A. *America and the Mediterranean World 1776–1882.* Princeton: Princeton Univ. Press, 1969.
Fischer, David Hackett. *Bound Away: Virginia and the Westward Movement.* Charlottesville: Univ. Press of Virginia, 2000.
Fitzgerald, Oscar Penn. "John M. Daniel and Some of His Contemporaries." *South Atlantic Quarterly* 4 (Jan.–Oct. 1905): 15.
Foote, Shelby. *The Civil War: A Narrative.* Vol. 1. New York: Random House, 1958.
Frank, John P. *Justice Daniel Dissenting.* Cambridge: Harvard Univ. Press, 1964.
Freeman, Douglas Southall. *Lee's Lieutenants.* Vol. 1. New York: Charles Scribner's Sons, 1944.
———. *The South to Posterity.* New York: Charles Scribner's Sons, 1939.
———, ed. *Lee's Dispatches.* New York: G. P. Putnam's Sons, 1957.
Furgurson, Ernest B. *Ashes of Glory: Richmond at War.* New York: Alfred A. Knopf, 1996.
Gara, Larry. *The Presidency of Franklin Pierce.* Lawrence: Univ. Press of Kansas, 1991.
Garraty, John A., and Mark C. Carnes, eds. *American National Biography.* Vols. 6, 14. New York: Oxford Univ. Press, 1999.
Gatell, Frank Otto. "Peter V. Daniel." In *The Justices of the United States Supreme Court 1789–1969,* edited by Leon Friedman and Fred L. Israel, 1:795–805. New York: Chelsea House, 1969.
Gay, H. Nelson. "Garibaldi's Sicilian Campaign as Reported by an American Diplomat." *American Historical Review* 27.2 (Jan. 1922): 245–70.
Ginisty, Paul. *Eugene Sue.* Paris: Editions Berger-Levrault, 1929.
Grand Dictionnaire du XIXe Siecle (Larousse). Vol. 13. Paris and Geneva: Slatkine, 1982.
Haile, Edward Wright, ed. *Jamestown Narratives.* Champlain, Va.: RoundHouse, 1998.
Hale, William Harlan. *Horace Greeley: Voice of the People.* New York: Harper, 1950.
Harland, Marion [Mary Virginia Terhune]. *Alone.* New York: J. C. Derby, 1856.
Harrison, Mrs. Burton [Constance Cary Harrison]. *Recollections Grave and Gay.* New York: Charles Scribner's Sons, 1912.
Harrold, Stanley. *The Abolitionists and the South, 1831–1861.* Lexington: Univ. Press of Kentucky, 1995.
Harsh, Joseph L. *Confederate Tide Rising.* Kent, Ohio: Kent State Univ. Press, 1998.

Hassler, William Woods. *A. P. Hill: Lee's Forgotten General.* Richmond: Garrett and Massie, 1957.

Hayden, Horace Edwin. *Virginia Genealogies.* 1891. Reprint, Washington, D.C.: Rare Book Shop, 1931.

Hemphill, William Edwin et al. *Cavalier Commonwealth.* New York: McGraw-Hill, 1957.

Herzen, Alexander. *My Past and Thoughts,* edited by Dwight Macdonald. Berkeley: Univ. of California Press, 1982.

Hibbert, Christopher. *Garibaldi and His Enemies.* Boston: Little, Brown, 1966.

———. *The Great Mutiny: India 1857.* London: Penguin Books, 1986.

"Highlights in the History of the United States Diplomatic and Consular Posts at Turin, Italy." Research Project No. 432, Historical Office, Department of State. Washington, D.C.: U.S. Department of State, Jan. 1961.

Hijiya, James A. *J. W. De Forest and the Rise of American Gentility.* Hanover, N.H.: Univ. Press of New England, 1988.

Hincks, William, and F.H. Smith. *Proceedings of the Democratic National Convention Held at Baltimore, June, 1852.* Washington, D.C.: Buell and Blanchard, 1852.

Hord, A. Untitled list of Stafford County, Va., justices. *Virginia Magazine of History and Biography* 19 (1911): 199.

Howard, A. E. Dick. *Commentaries on the Constitution of Virginia.* Vol. 2. Charlottesville: Univ. Press of Virginia, 1974.

Hubbell, John T. "Jeremiah Sullivan Black and the Great Secession Winter." *Western Pennsylvania Historical Magazine* 57.3 (July 1974): 255–74.

———, ed. *Battles Lost and Won: Essays from Civil War History.* Westport, Conn.: Greenwood Press, 1975.

Hughes, Robert W. *Editors of the Past.* Richmond, Va.: W. E. Jones, 1897.

———. "John Moncure Daniel: His Times and Career." *The Baltimorean,* Jan. 10, 1885, 1.

———, and Joseph A. Turner. "Roanoke Female Seminary." *William and Mary College Quarterly* ser. 2, 9.4 (Oct. 1929): 325–29.

Humphreys, Sexson E. "John Moncure Daniel: 'The Garlic Letter.'" In *Il Risorgimento e l'Europa.* Catania, Italy: Bonanno Editore, 1969.

———. "Spooner vs. Daniel: A 'Sectional' Libel Case of the 1850s." Ann Arbor, Mich.: Association for Education in Journalism, Aug. 1961.

Jenkins, William Sumner. *Pro-Slavery Thought in the Old South.* Gloucester, Mass.: Peter Smith, 1960.

Johannsen, Robert W., ed. *The Letters of Stephen A. Douglas.* Urbana: Univ. of Illinois Press, 1961.

———. *Stephen A. Douglas.* New York: Oxford Univ. Press, 1973.

Jones, J. B. *A Rebel War Clerk's Diary at the Confederate States Capital.* 2 vols. 1866. Reprint, Alexandria, Va.: Time-Life Books, 1982.

Jones, J. William. "Seven Days Around Richmond." Reminiscences of the Army of Northern Virginia, Paper No. 8. *Southern Historical Society Papers.* Vol. 9 (Jan.–Dec. 1881).

Jordan, Ervin L., Jr. *Black Confederates and Afro-Yankees in Civil War Virginia.* Charlottesville: Univ. Press of Virginia, 1995.

Journal of the Executive Proceedings of the Senate of the United States of America. Vol. 9. Washington, D.C.: GPO, 1887.

Kemp, Peter, ed. *The Oxford Companion to Ships and the Sea.* New York: Oxford Univ. Press, 1976.

Keneally, Thomas. *The Great Shame and the Triumph of the Irish in the English-Speaking World.* New York: Nan A. Talese/Doubleday, 1999.

Kerr, Robert P. "A Memorial—Moses Drury Hoge, D.D. LL.D." *Southern Historical Society Papers* 30 (1902): 262–64.

Keysler, John George. *Travels.* Vol. 1. London: G. Keith, 1760.

King, George Harrison Sanford. "Copies of Extant Wills from Counties Whose Records Have Been Destroyed." *Tyler's Quarterly Historical and Genealogical Magazine* 31.4 (Apr. 1950): 268.

Klunder, William Carl. *Lewis Cass and the Politics of Moderation*. Kent, Ohio: Kent State Univ. Press, 1996.

Kneebone, John T., et al. *Dictionary of Virginia Biography*. Vol. 1. Richmond: Library of Virginia, 1998.

Lowenthal, David. *George Perkins Marsh, Prophet of Conservation*. Seattle: Univ. of Washington Press, 2000.

Lurie, Edward. *Louis Agassiz: A Life in Science*. Baltimore: The Johns Hopkins Univ. Press, 1988.

Mack Smith, Denis. *Cavour*. New York: Alfred A. Knopf, 1985.

McKinnell, Bettina F. *A Check-List of Richmond, Virginia Imprints from 1841 through 1852 with a Historical Introduction*. Master's thesis, Catholic University of America, 1956.

Maddex, Jack P. *The Reconstruction of Edward A. Pollard: A Rebel's Conversion to Postbellum Unionism*. Chapel Hill: Univ. of North Carolina Press, 1974.

Marraro, Howard R. *American Opinion on the Unification of Italy 1846–1861*. 1932. Reprint, New York: AMS, 1969.

———. *L'Unificazione italiana vista dai diplomatici statunitensi*. Rome: Istituto per la Storia del Risorgimento Italiano, 1963.

———, ed. *Diplomatic Relations between the United States and the Kingdom of the Two Sicilies*. 2 vols. New York: S. F. Vanni, 1951.

May, Robert E. "A 'Southern Strategy' for the 1850s: Northern Democrats, the Tropics, and Expansion of the National Domain." *Louisiana Studies* 14.4 (1975): 333–59.

Meade, Robert Douthat. *Judah P. Benjamin, Confederate Statesman*. New York: Oxford Univ. Press, 1943.

Meade, William. *Old Churches, Ministers and Families of Virginia*. Vol. 2. Philadelphia: J. P. Lippincott, 1857.

Mellen, George F. "Famous Southern Editors: John Moncure Daniel." *Methodist Review* (July–Aug. 1897): 378–95.

Millar, Robert Wyness. *Civil Procedure of the Trial Court in Historical Perspective*. New York: Law Center of New York Univ., 1952.

Mitchel, John. *Jail Journal*. Dublin: M. H. Gill and Son; London: T. Fisher Unwin, 1913.

Moncure, John. "John M. Daniel, the Editor of the Examiner." *Sewanee Review* 15.3 (July 1907): 257–70.

Montague's Richmond Directory and Business Advertiser for 1850–1851. Richmond: J. W. Randolph, 1851.

Montanelli, Indro. *L'Italia del Risorgimento*. Milan: Rizzoli, 2001.

Moore, John Bassett, ed. *The Works of James Buchanan*. Vol. 9. 1911. Reprint, New York: Antiquarian Press, 1960.

Mordecai, John Brook. "Travel and Communications." *Richmond: Capital of Virginia*. Richmond: Whittet and Shepperson, 1938.

Mordecai, Samuel. *Richmond in By-Gone Days*. 1856. Reprint, New York: Arno Press, 1975.

National Cyclopaedia of American Biography. Vols. 5, 6, 8, 13. New York: James T. White, 1906, 1907, 1924, 1929.

Newman, Harry Wright. *The Stones of Poynton Manor*. Washington, D.C.: DAR Library, 1996.

Nicolay, John G., and John Hay, eds. *Complete Works of Abraham Lincoln*. Vol. 6. New York: Tandy-Thomas, 1905.

Nugent, Nell Marion, ed. *Cavaliers and Pioneers: Abstracts of Virginia Land Patents 1623– 1666*. Baltimore: Genealogical Publishing, 1963.

Osthaus, Carl R. *Partisans of the Southern Press*. Lexington: Univ. Press of Kentucky, 1994.

Page, Rosewell. *Thomas Nelson Page: A Memoir of a Virginia Gentleman*. New York: Charles Scribner's Sons, 1923.

Patrick, Rembert W. *Jefferson Davis and His Cabinet*. Baton Rouge: Louisiana State Univ. Press, 1944.

Pellico, Silvio. *Le mie prigioni*. Edited by Egidio Bellorini. Milan: Casa Editrice Dottor Francesco Vallardi, 1924.

Phillips, Mary E. *Edgar Allan Poe the Man*. Vol. 2. Chicago: John C. Winston, 1926.

Phillips, Ulrich Bonnell, ed. *Annual Report of the American Historical Association, 1911*. Vol. 2. Washington, D.C.: American Historical Association, 1913.

Piatt, Donn. "Cuba and the Ostend Manifesto." *Harper's New Monthly Magazine*. 40.240 (May 1870).

Pinto, Paolo. *Vittorio Emanuele II*. Milan: A. Mondadori, 1995.

Pollard, Edward A. *Life of Jefferson Davis*. 1869. Reprint, Freeport, N.Y.: Books for Libraries, 1969.

———. *The Lost Cause*. 1867. Reprint, New York: Bonanza Books. n.d.

———. *The Second Year of the War*. New York: Charles B. Richardson, 1863.

Potter, David M. *The Impending Crisis 1848–1861*. New York: Harper and Row, 1976.

Principal Officers of the Department of State and United States Chiefs of Mission 1778–1988. Washington, D.C.: Office of the Historian, U.S. Department of State, 1988.

Putnam, Sallie Brook. *Richmond During the War*. 1867. Reprint, Lincoln: Univ. of Nebraska Press, 1996.

Ray, Gordon N. *The Letters and Private Papers of William Makepeace Thackeray*. Vol. 4. New York: Octagon Books, 1980.

Reagan, John H. *Memoirs, with Special Reference to Secession and the Civil War*. 1906. Reprint, Austin, Tex.: Pemberton Press, 1968.

Reese, George H., ed. *Proceedings of the Virginia State Convention of 1861*. Vol. 4. Richmond: Virginia State Library, 1965.

Register of the Confederate Dead, Interred in Hollywood Cemetery, Richmond, Va. Richmond: Gary, Clemmitt and Jones, 1869.

Reniers, Perceval. *The Springs of Virginia*. Chapel Hill: Univ. of North Carolina Press, 1941.

Report of the Secretary of the Treasury. Richmond, 1864.

Richard, Laura E., and Maud Howe Elliott. *Julia Ward Howe, 1819–1910*. Vol. 1. Boston: Houghton Mifflin, 1916.

The Richmond Directory and Business Advertiser, For 1852. Baltimore: T. W. Woods, 1852.

Rogari, Ubaldo. *Due regine dei salotti nella Firenze capitale*. Florence: Edizioni Remo Sandron, 1992.

Rowland, Eron O. *Varina Howell, Wife of Jefferson Davis*. New York: Macmillan, 1931.

Russell, William Howard. *My Diary North and South*. New York: Harper and Brothers, 1954.

Ryan, David D., ed. *A Yankee Spy in Richmond: The Civil War Diary of "Crazy Bet" Van Lew*. Mechanicsburg, Pa.: Stackpole Books, 1996.

Salmon, John S., comp. *Guidebook to Virginia's Historical Markers*. Charlottesville: Univ. Press of Virginia, 1996.

Sandburg, Carl. *Abraham Lincoln: Volume II, The War Years, 1861–1864*. New York: Dell Books, 1968.

Sanders, George N. "Daniel—'76, '98, '44, '48, and a Fast Man!" *Democratic Review* 30.167 (May 1852): 385–96.

———. "Our Foreign Ministers." *Democratic Review* 30.173–74 (Nov.–Dec. 1852): 420–32.

Schiavo, Giovanni. *The Italians in America Before the Civil War*. New York: Vigo Press, 1934.

Schreiner-Yantis, Netti, and Florence Speakman Love, comps. *The 1787 Census of Virginia*. Vol. 1. Springfield, Va.: Genealogical Books in Print, 1987.

Scribner, Robert L. "The Code Duello in Virginia." *Virginia Cavalcade*. 3.2 (Autumn 1953): 28–31.

———. "Submission, Coercion, or Secession?" *Virginia Cavalcade* 3.2 (Autumn 1953): 43–47.

Sears, Stephen W., ed. *The Civil War Papers of George B. McClellan*. New York: Ticknor and Fields, 1989.

Shade, William G. *Democratizing the Old Dominion*. Charlottesville: Univ. Press of Virginia, 1996.

Shanks, Henry T. *The Secession Movement in Virginia 1847–1861*. 1934. Reprint, New York: AMS Press, 1971

Sheehan, Bernard W. *Savagism and Civility: Indians and Englishmen in Colonial Virginia*. New York: Cambridge Univ. Press, 1980.

Shepard, E. Lee. "Two Early Libraries of Richmond." *Richmond Quarterly* 4.1 (Summer 1981): 50–51.

Simms, L. Moody, Jr. "Talented Virginians: The Peticolas Family." *Virginia Magazine of History and Biography* 85.1 (Jan. 1977): 55–64.

Slaughter, Philip, and Raleigh Travers Green. *Genealogical and Historical Notes on Culpeper County, Virginia.* 1900. Reprint, Baltimore, Md.: Regional Publishing, 1971.

Smith, Henry Nash. *Virgin Land: The American West as Symbol and Myth.* Cambridge, Mass.: Harvard Univ. Press, 1971.

Smith, Walter B., II. *America's Diplomats and Consuls of 1776–1865.* Foreign Service Institute, Occasional Paper No. 2. Washington, D.C.: U.S. Department of State, 1986.

Smith, W. L. G. *The Life and Times of Lewis Cass.* New York: Derby and Jackson, 1856.

Sorrel, G. Moxley. *Recollections of a Confederate Staff Officer.* New York: Neale, 1905.

Spaulding, Myra K. "Duelling in the District of Columbia." *Records of the Columbia Historical Society* 29.20 (1928): 117–210.

Spini, Giorgio. "Le relazioni politiche fra l'Italia e gli Stati Uniti durante il Risorgimento e la Guerra Civile." In *Italia e Stati Uniti nell'eta del Risorgimento e della Guerra Civile.* Florence: "La Nuova Italia" Editrice, 1969.

Spooner, Shearjashub. *An Appeal to the People of the United States, in Behalf of Art, Artists, and the Public Weal.* New York: J. J. Reed, 1854.

———. *Prospectus for Publishing an American Edition of Boydell's Illustrations of Shakespeare.* New York: S. Spooner, 1849.

Stearns, Emeline Lee. "John M. Daniel and the Confederacy." Master's thesis, Univ. of Chicago, 1928.

Steely, Skipper. "James Mitchell Daniel: A Small Scrapbook of the Man, His Home and Family." Paris, Tex.: Privately published, March 2000.

Stephen, Sir Leslie, and Sir Sidney Lee, eds. *The Dictionary of National Biography.* Vol. 10. London: Oxford Univ. Press, 1950.

Stock, Leo Francis, ed. *United States Ministers to the Papal States.* Washington, D.C.: Catholic Univ. Press, 1933.

Stone, Charles P. "Washington on the Eve of the War." *Battles and Leaders of the Civil War,* edited by Robert Underwood Johnson and Clarence Clough Buel. Vol. 1. 1887. Reprint, Edison, N.J.: Castle, n.d.

Strode, Hudson. *Jefferson Davis: Confederate President.* New York: Harcourt, Brace, 1959.

Symonds, Craig L. *Joseph E. Johnston.* New York: W. W. Norton, 1992.

Symons, Julian. *The Tell-Tale Heart.* New York: Harper and Row, 1978.

Trexler, Harrison A. "The Davis Administration and the Richmond Press, 1861–1865." *Journal of Southern History* 16.2 (May 1950): 177–95.

Tulard, Jean, ed. *Dictionnaire du Second Empire.* Paris: Librairie Artheme Fayard, 1995.

Turner, Jane, ed. *The Dictionary of Art.* Vol. 4. New York: Grove's Dictionaries, 1996..

Tyler, Lyon Gardiner, ed. *Encyclopedia of Virginia Biography.* Vol. 3. New York: Lewis Historical Publishing Co., 1915.

———. *Men of Mark in Virginia.* Vol. 5. Washington, D.C.: Men of Mark, 1909.

———. "Professors at William and Mary College." *Tyler's Quarterly* 4 (1923): 135.

Vance, William L. *America's Rome.* 2 vols. New Haven, Conn.: Yale Univ. Press, 1989.

Varriano, John. *A Literary Companion to Rome.* New York: St. Martin's Griffin, 1991.

Virginia: A Guide to the Old Dominion. Richmond: Virginia State Library and Archives, 1992.

Walsh, Louis J. *John Mitchel.* Dublin: Talbot Press, 1934.

The War of the Rebellion: A Compilation of the Official Records of the Union and Confederate Armies. Ser. 1, vol. 2. Washington, D.C: GPO, 1880.

Whitty, J. H., ed. *The Complete Poems of Edgar Allan Poe.* Boston: Houghton Mifflin, 1917.

Who Was Who in America 1607–1896. Chicago: A. N. Marquis, n.d.

Whyte, A. J. *The Evolution of Modern Italy.* New York: W. W. Norton, 1965.

Widmer, Edward L. *Young America: The Flowering of Democracy in New York City.* New York: Oxford Univ. Press, 1999.

Wiggins, Sarah Woolfolk, ed. *The Journals of Josiah Gorgas 1857–1878*. Tuscaloosa: Univ. of Alabama Press, 1995.

Wilkinson, A. N. "John Moncure Daniel." *Richmond College Historical Papers* 1.1 (June 1915).

Wise, John S. *The End of an Era*. Boston: Houghton Mifflin, 1899.

Wright, Mrs. D. Giraud [Louise Wigfall Wright]. *A Southern Girl in '61: The War-Time Memories of a Confederate Senator's Daughter*. New York: Doubleday, Page, 1905.

Wyly-Jones, Susan. "John Moncure Daniel." *American National Biography*. Vol. 6. New York: Oxford Univ. Press, 1999.

Younger, Edward, ed. *Inside the Confederate Government: The Diary of Robert Garlick Hill Kean*. Baton Rouge: Louisiana State Univ. Press, 1985.

Index

Pen of Fire: John Moncure Daniel

was designed and composed by Will Underwood and Christine Brooks

in 10/13.5 Minion with display type in Poppl-Residenz Regular;

printed on 55# Supple Opaque stock

by Thomson-Shore, Inc., of Dexter, Michigan,

and published by

THE KENT STATE UNIVERSITY PRESS

Kent, Ohio 44242